The Friday Mosque in the City

The Friday Mosque in the City
Liminality, Ritual, and Politics

A. Hilâl Uğurlu and Suzan Yalman

 intellect

Bristol, UK / Chicago, USA

The Friday Mosque in the City: Liminality, Ritual, and Politics is the sixth book in the Critical Studies in Architecture of the Middle East series. The series is edited by Mohammad Gharipour (Morgan State University, Baltimore) and Christiane Gruber (University of Michigan, Ann Arbor). Critical Studies in Architecture of the Middle East is devoted to the most recent scholarship concerning historic and contemporary architecture, landscape and urban design of the Middle East and of regions shaped by diasporic communities more globally. We invite interdisciplinary studies from diverse perspectives that address the visual characteristics of the built environment, ranging from architectural case studies to urban analysis.

First published in the UK in 2020 by
Intellect, The Mill, Parnall Road, Fishponds, Bristol, BS16 3JG, UK

First published in the USA in 2020 by
Intellect, The University of Chicago Press, 1427 E. 60th Street,
Chicago, IL 60637, USA

A catalogue record for this book is available from the British Library.

Copy editor: MPS Technologies
Cover designer: Aleksandra Szumlas
Cover image: View of the Süleymaniye Mosque and the
  Golden Horn, Istanbul, 1962. Detail of photograph by
  Ara Güler, ©Ara Güler Doğuş Sanat ve Müzecilik A.Ş.
Production editor: Laura Christopher
Series: Critical Studies in Architecture of the Middle East
Series editors: Mohammad Gharipour and Christiane Gruber
Typesetting: Contentra Technologies

Series ISSN: 2059-3562
Print ISBN: 978-178938-302-7
ePDF ISBN: 978-178938-303-4
ePUB ISBN: 978-178938-304-1

Printed and bound by Page Bros, UK.

This is a peer-reviewed publication.

Contents

Acknowledgements

Beginning from its inception by two architectural historians to the final publication as a volume of collected papers, this volume owes much to numerous individuals. First and foremost, this book would not be possible without the varied and invaluable contributions of our colleagues: Nebahat Avcıoğlu, Susanna Calvo-Capilla, Mehreen Chida-Razvi, Farshid Emami, May Farhat, Fadi Ragheb, and Abbey Stockstill. We are sincerely thankful for their cooperative spirit and collaboration throughout the extended production period.

In our early formulation of the project, we had the ambitious goal to incorporate vast regions and diverse time periods from the whole Islamic world. With this in mind, we sent out a call-for-papers and also reached out to different researchers. We received many interesting abstracts and recommendations, however, ultimately, we were restricted by conflicting schedules, overlapping ideas, as well as the need to move forward with our timeline. Many scholars provided us with their suggestions during this preliminary stage. We would like to express our special thanks to Gülru Necipoğlu for her initial encouragement and foresight. We are also grateful to Doris Behrens-Abouseif, Grigor Boykov, Sibel Bozdoğan, Mattia Guidetti, Hani Hamza, Ruba Kanaan, Ebba Koch, Elizabeth Lambourn, Zeynep Oğuz Kursar, Bernard O'Kane, Kristian Petersen, Nasser Rabbat, Kishwar Rizwi, Aila Santi, and Zeynep Yürekli, who provided comments and support in various ways.

In November 2016, we held a panel entitled 'Liminal Spaces from Sacred to Urban' at the annual meeting of MESA in Boston. Thanks to the insightful suggestions that we received from the audience, in particular from Jennifer Pruitt and David Roxburgh, this proved to be a formative stage for the project. We are also thankful to Chanchal Dadlani, Emine Fetvacı, Hakan Karateke, D. Fairchild Ruggles, and İklil Selçuk who shared their constructive feedback and support. For further discussions on liminality and the anthropological perspective, we are indebted to Nur Yalman.

In the publication process, we were very fortunate to receive a generous publication grant from The Barakat Trust and support for images from the Koç University College of Social Sciences and Humanities, thanks to Dean Aylin Küntay. The striking black-and-white photograph used on the cover of this book is a detail from a work of the late renowned photographer and photojournalist Ara Güler (1928–2018). We extend our gratitude to Doğuş Sanat ve Müzecilik A.Ş. for allowing us to use this image. Obtaining this permission would not have been possible without the kind support of Alper Önder, Çağla Saraç, as well as Görkem Ergün and Zeynep Özkaya.

At Intellect Books, we are extremely grateful to a number of people who played decisive roles. As the series editors for the Critical Studies in Architecture of the Middle East, Christiane Gruber and Mohammad Gharipour provided us with their guidance and critical advice. While Tim Mitchell and Faith Newcombe oversaw the initial stages of the book proposal, later on, our assigned production editor Laura Christopher saw us through the publication of the volume. The meticulous copy-editing of Janet Raucher and Henry Johnson was instrumental in this book taking its final shape. In the last stages of production, we were assisted by a number of students who were involved in different tasks, including preparing the index: Bihter Esener, Pelin Kalafatoğlu İslamoğlu, and Deniz Kocabağlı. We express our sincere thanks to all of them.

Finally, we would like to express our deepest and most heartfelt thanks to our families (parents, partners, and all five children) who showed their unconditional love and unwavering support throughout this long journey.

A Note on Transliteration

For transliteration of words in foreign languages, the Critical Studies in Architecture of the Middle East follows the *International Journal of Islamic Architecture* guidelines which discourages the use of special characters in order to reach a broad and interdisciplinary readership. To achieve this purpose, the transliteration systems in this volume have been simplified. Thus, while the general guidelines for Arabic and Persian follow the *International Journal of Middle East Studies* transliteration guidelines, all special characters, such as lines over vowels and dots under consonants have been removed. In the case of Ottoman Turkish, modern Turkish orthography has been preferred.

Introduction

A. Hilâl Uğurlu and Suzan Yalman

Liminal entities are neither here nor there; they are betwixt and between the positions assigned and arrayed by law, custom, convention, and ceremonial.[1]

–Victor Turner

*T*he *Friday Mosque in the City: Liminality, Ritual, and Politics* explores the relationship between two important entities in the Islamic context: the Friday mosque and the city. Earlier scholarship has examined these concepts separately and, to some degree, in relation to each other.[2] This volume seeks to understand the relationship between them. In order to begin this discussion, defining the terminology is necessary. The English term 'mosque' derives from the Arabic *masjid*, a term designating a place of prostration, whereas the term *jami'*, which is translated variously as Friday mosque, great mosque or congregational mosque, originates from the Arabic term *jama'*, meaning to gather. The religious obligation for Muslims to congregate on Fridays eventually created an Islamic social code.[3] Similarly, the migration from Mecca to Medina was instrumental in transforming a society based on tribal kinship into a community (*umma*).[4] The Prophet himself played a vital role in establishing the first congregational space in Medina. Whatever the original terminology that defined it, this space is usually accepted as the prototype of the 'mosque' by architectural historians.[5] The distinctions in terminology are important because, according to Islamic legal tradition, the presence of a Friday mosque was an important parameter in defining a city (*madina*).[6]

As the dominion of Islam (*dar al-Islam*) spread across continents, it gradually embraced both local sociocultural traditions and the architectural heritage of earlier cultures of the lands it inhabited. The problems of succession after the death of the Prophet would ultimately lead to a major rift in Islam, the Sunni–Shi'i division. By the tenth century, contestation of power and rival claims to the universal Islamic caliphate created new bases within and between these branches. As embodiments of political rivalry, Friday mosques were instrumental in the urban development and the identity of new Islamic caliphal capital cities. When we consider their impact diachronically and synchronically, the Friday Mosques of Umayyad Damascus, Abbasid Baghdad, Spanish Umayyad Cordoba, and Fatimid Cairo played a crucial role as prototypes whose designs were disseminated across the Islamic geography and over the course of centuries.[7] The weakening and demise of the caliphates eventually led to the rise of new states that established their own power centres – and, hence, to a proliferation of Friday mosques.

Thanks to the symbolic importance of the Friday sermon (*khutba*), these mosques also became loci for the displays of power and declarations of independence that became increasingly important with the proliferation of Islamic states. Being closely associated with political authority – especially with the name of the ruler declared in the *khutba* delivered from the pulpit (minbar) – Hanafite jurists favoured a single political and religious centre: a single Friday mosque in a city, as Baber Johansen has discussed.[8] In the medieval period, Hanafite legal opinion supported the hierarchical classification of places of worship as an important feature of the city that distinguished it from the countryside. Extant medieval Anatolian mosques of the Hanafite Seljuks indeed demonstrate a preference for a centralized and hierarchical system, with one Friday mosque (*jami'*) and numerous neighbourhood mosques (*masjid*) per city.[9]

While legal opinion preferred one Friday mosque, need dictated more: the medieval traveller Ibn Jubayr (*d.*1217) reported that 'the full number of congregational mosques in Baghdad, where Friday prayers are said, is eleven'.[10] Thus, although Baghdad was established with the idealized round plan that featured a single Friday mosque, over the course of centuries the number of mosques in the city multiplied.[11] The successive establishment of Friday mosques in Fatimid Cairo demonstrates that similar developments occurred in a Shi'i context.[12] Later on, in Safavid Isfahan, debates concerning 'permissibility of Friday prayer in the absence of the awaited Twelfth Imam' initially impacted the patronage of Friday mosques; however, once these issues were resolved at the turn of the sixteenth century, the number immediately multiplied.[13] Following the conquest of Constantinople, the Hanefite Ottomans also studded their capital in Istanbul with numerous monumental Friday mosques, departing from the earlier tradition that preferred one Friday mosque per city.[14]

As the chief signifier of the religion, the Friday mosque was given an important role in urban development throughout Islamic history. This fact placed Friday mosques in the centre of 'Islamic City' debates, the problematic nature of which has been addressed at length in scholarship and is not the focus here.[15] Instead, this volume is particularly interested in the ambiguous and dynamic relationship between the Friday mosque and its surrounding urban context.

In the sixteenth century, the renowned traveller/explorer André Thévet (*d.*1590), who accompanied the French ambassador to the Ottoman Empire in 1546, described how the Ottoman sultan, Süleyman the Magnificent (*r.*1520–66), ceremoniously rode on horseback, with great pomp and circumstance, to the Friday mosque that he patronized; 7000 janissary soldiers accompanied him. This procession, with its visual grandeur and awe-inspiring silence, made a great impact on the viewer.[16] The approach to the mosque was likely through the neighbourhoods leading to the rationally planned paths that passed between the geometrically organized dependencies of the complex. Eventually, one would reach the walls of the outer courtyard. This expansive green space surrounded the mosque as well as the royal mausolea, which were also closed-off behind the qibla wall of the mosque. This kind of 'complex' (which had at its heart a mosque with an arcaded forecourt), enclosed in an outer courtyard and then surrounded by various socio-religious dependencies, was a particular Ottoman phenomenon.

Let us return to Süleyman's Friday procession. These ceremonials acted as an interface between the state/office of the sultan and the public; therefore, an extraordinary crowd attended these important weekly events. In addition to pious Muslim citizens, subjects and travellers curious to see the sultan and the magnificent procession, people from disparate parts of the empire hoping to submit their petitions, opportunity seekers, and beggars would fill those spaces. While Süleyman, his retinue, and some of the above-mentioned people performed their Friday prayers, the remaining crowd would have waited for the sultan to emerge from the mosque. Where did these functions take place? Where did people perform their prayers: in the mosque proper or spread out to the inner and maybe even the outer courtyards? If the latter, where did those who were not performing the Friday prayer – for instance, the 7000 janissaries and the non-Muslims – wait?

Without further textual evidence, these questions are difficult to answer. What can be said, however, is that, similar to the sixteenth-century example, religious holiday (*eid*) prayers today spill beyond the walls of the outer courtyard, toward the dependencies. The delineation of space aside, actual usage points to the porous nature and frequent transgression of physical boundaries. Most notably, for instance, historical sources demonstrate that the interior of the mosque was used for non-religious activities. Many nineteenth-century sources describe how the Süleymaniye Mosque was used for safekeeping: the 'galleries are full of boxes, bags, bales of merchandise, and all sorts of valuables which have been left there for security, and no man can guess to what extent'.[17] As these instances reveal, not only the 'in between' spaces, such as the inner and outer courtyards, but even the most straightforward and well-defined spaces, such as the mosque proper, could be transformed in function from time to time. The articles in this volume provide further evidence that there was (and continues to be) a tremendous variety in the way architectural borders became more fluid in and around Friday mosques across the Islamic geography, from Cordoba to Jerusalem and from London to Lahore.

The 'Great Mosque' of Cordoba and the Badshahi Masjid in Lahore present two distinct examples of the relationship between the Friday mosque and the urban context. While in the former case the doors on the eastern and western facades act as the primary interface between the city and the mosque, in the latter this relationship is established through an architecturally demarcated liminal space. In her chapter 'Liminal Spaces in the Great Mosque of Cordoba: Urban Meaning and Politico-Liturgical Practices', Susana Calvo Capilla examines how the mosque interacted with urban life. While it was situated in the heart of a dense urban setting, near the administrative centre, the mosque was surrounded by an empty zone that affected visitors' spatial perception and allowed for both daily and religious practices to take place. Along with these areas, the entrances that were employed for various religious practices were visually emphasized through ornamental and epigraphic programmes. Their political, ideological, and religious significance transformed these architectural thresholds into liminal spaces and 'ultimately made them suitable urban public spaces for displaying official propaganda'. Lahore presents a different case study. In her chapter 'Lahore's Badshahi Masjid: Spatial Interactions of the Sacred and the Secular', Mehreen Chida-Razvi examines the relationship between Lahore Fort (Shahi Qila) and the Mughal-era Friday mosque built across from it, known as the Badshahi Masjid (completed 1674), through the lens of the enclosed space that separated the two. This transitional zone, initially a walled-in courtyard but later turned into a garden, the 'Garden of Reception' (Hazuri Bagh), mediated between the political and religious centres of the Mughal city. Apart from how these areas were initially conceptualized and utilized under the Mughals, the capture of the city by the Afghans (1748), Sikhs (1758), and British (1848) meant that they were variously employed (or abandoned) and interpreted by their new rulers.

In the range of case studies discussed in this volume, what contributed to the penetration of spatial zones – whether they were tangible or intangible – was the human factor. Individual and collective human experiences, activities, memories, and perceptions made physical boundaries more porous, and the 'in between' or 'liminal' spaces more dynamic. The concept of 'liminality' was introduced at the turn of the twentieth century by the ethnographer Arnold van Gennep (1873–1975) through his tripartite *les rites de passage*, which describe the changeover from one state to another (separation, margin or *limen*, and aggregation).[18] In the 1960s, the cultural anthropologist Victor Turner (1920–83) further developed van Gennep's framework and discussed the intervening 'liminal' period as necessarily ambiguous.[19] Turner's elaboration and reconceptualization of the 'liminal' has provided a useful theoretical model across different disciplines. For the Islamic world, recent publications by anthropologists address social factors through this lens.[20] For architectural and urban history, however, the scholarly conversation continues.

The anthropological definition of 'liminal' brings the social force to a spatial conceptualization of 'liminal' and broadens our understanding and perception of the transitional zones between a Friday mosque and a city. As cited at the beginning of this introduction, in *The Ritual Process*, Turner situates the liminal entity as 'neither here nor there; they are betwixt and between the positions assigned and arrayed by law, custom, convention, and ceremonial'.[21] These four factors also play a vital role in the formation of cities in the Islamic context. While Islamic law arranges the daily life of a Muslim society, enforcing the need for a gathering space for Friday prayers, customs, and conventions across different time periods and geographies not only impacted the architectural preferences determined for mosques, but also were decisive in determining the number of Friday mosques that were built within a city. The presence of inhabitants transforms the city from architectural masses and voids into a living urban landscape. As noted in the case of Süleyman the Magnificent's Friday procession in Istanbul, ceremonials and rituals help establish networks among these individuals and create urban nodes.

In the Islamic context, the obligatory pilgrimage (hajj), one of the five pillars of Islam, is the embodiment of the Turneresque liminal mode of state. This ultimate experience consists of visiting sacred destinations – buildings, places, landscapes – within the city, Ka'ba being primary.[22] The rituals intertwined with these sacred destinations created a network that spread the sacredness throughout the whole city. Medina and Jerusalem shared a similar status. Both the former, housing the burial place of the Prophet Muhammad (*d.*632), and the latter, being the first qibla (from 610–23) and the locus of the Prophet's Ascension (*al-mi'raj*), were considered holy cities alongside Mecca. In his chapter 'City as Liminal Space: Islamic Pilgrimage and Muslim Holy Sites in Jerusalem During the Mamluk Period', Fadi Ragheb demonstrates how Jerusalem lived up to its 'holy' name (*al-Quds*). This perception of the city was shared by all three Abrahamic religions, creating a multi-layered understanding and practice of sanctity. This was a reason for contested claims over the city, which led to 'holy' wars and crusades in the medieval period. As Ragheb discusses, following the Crusades, during the time of the Mamluk Sultanate, pilgrimage guides to Jerusalem, known as *Fada'il al-Quds*, promoted 'the great reward of stopping in Jerusalem en route to the hajj' and thereby revived pilgrimage to the city. As the *fada'il* demonstrate, a network of holy sites around the Haram were incorporated into the pilgrimage route; thus, individual pious acts and collective rituals multiplied, spreading all over the city. Moreover, these guide books encouraged pilgrims to enter the ritual 'state of *ihram* at the gates of the city'. The reference to '*ihram*' – understood both as a spiritual state and as the ritual donning of the white garment – was and still is closely associated with the hajj, which puts Jerusalem on par with Mecca, further enhancing the sanctity of the city and extending it beyond the city gates. Ragheb also compares the nature of liminality in Jerusalem with that in medieval Mecca, similarly demonstrating how the sacred in Mecca was not limited to the boundaries of the Ka'ba and al-Masjid al-Haram, but, rather, it permeated the entire city of Mecca and its neighbouring regions through holy sites connected with the hajj along with the multiplication of many secondary sacred sites in and outside the city during the medieval period.

Not every city contained palimpsestous accumulations of sacredness as the holy cities of Mecca, Medina, and Jerusalem did. Nevertheless, after the Prophet Muhammad's death, his successors, first the caliphs and later the sultans, attempted to create their own 'sacred' capitals by creating and recreating urban nuclei and establishing novel rituals connected to them. Jonathan Z. Smith defines 'ritual' as a 'mode of paying attention'.[23] Considering this definition, the construction of these 'built ritual environments' helped construct new 'sacred' places and provided grounds for rulers seeking legitimacy and public attention, both locally and in the broader Islamic lands.[24]

The reestablishment of a capital city with 'sacred' pretensions is a subject examined by Suzan Yalman in her chapter 'Sanctifying Konya: The Thirteenth-Century Transformation of the Seljuk Friday Mosque into a "House of God"'. The Anatolian city of Konya (ancient Iconium) became the capital of the Seljuk Sultanate in the twelfth century and had a Friday mosque in the citadel near the Seljuk palace. The building was expanded considerably by sultans Kayka'us (*r.*1211–19) and Kayqubad (*r.*1220–37) in the thirteenth century, when the enclosure of a large courtyard that housed two dynastic tomb towers created a liminal space and provided the first recognizable case of a multifunctional 'mosque complex' in Anatolia. Regarding the death of the two sultans' father, Yalman argues that 'the saintly status given to Kaykhusraw with his martyrdom, the return of his body in the manner of a saint's relic, the celebration of his burial, and the rituals developed around his commemoration, such as weekly Friday visitations, seem to indicate a desire to create a dynastic cult'. Alexei Lidov refers to such conscious efforts to create a new sacred space through relics and rituals as 'hierotopy',[25] a term composed of two Greek roots – *hieros* (sacred) and *topos* (place, space, notion) – that refers to a special form of creativity.[26]

In the case of Konya, the name of the 'hierotopic project' is evident by the unprecedented term that was employed in Kayqubad's completion of the rebuilt ritual space: 'house of God' (*bayt Allah*). This term, also found in the Qur'an, is usually associated with the Ka'ba in Mecca but may possibly refer to Jerusalem as well. Concurrent with the Friday mosque project, Kayqubad was also busy refortifying Konya with additional city walls. Yalman argues that this event was part of a greater transformation and amplification of the status of the city in the aftermath of the Fourth Crusade of 1204,[27] when the Seljuks began to have greater 'geostrategic' aspirations. The refashioning of the city as a 'house of God' created a pilgrimage destination and served to transform Konya into a 'city of God'.

Seventeenth-century Isfahan presents another case of a capital city being refashioned, in this case reflecting the Shi'i ideology of the Safavid Empire (1501–1722). While the Friday mosque in Konya was expanded for new imperial claims, in Isfahan the Old Mosque, which had long been associated with Sunni Islam, was left and two new mosques were commissioned. In his chapter 'Inviolable Thresholds, Blessed Palaces, and Holy Friday Mosques: The Sacred Topography of Safavid Isfahan', Farshid Emami examines how a new religious – particularly Shi'i – core was created as part of the urban transformation, rivalling the old centre of the city. Consecutively, Shah Abbas built two mosques, the Shaykh Lutfallah Mosque (c.1595–1618) and the Shah Mosque (c.1611–38), which were significant components of this core. This was a time when performing the Friday prayer in the absence of the awaited Twelfth Imam was a controversial and debated subject among Shi'i jurists – one that had prevented earlier Safavid shahs from commissioning Friday mosques. However, the fact that this dispute was settled in favour of Friday mosques is evident from the fact that the first – and relatively smaller – Friday mosque was built in the name of Shaykh Lutfallah, a jurist who believed in the obligatory nature of the Friday prayer. As for the second mosque, Emami discusses the conceptualization of its design within the new royal urban plaza and highlights the significance of the adoption of the Old Mosque's name (*al-masjid al-jami'*), demonstrating the competitive nature of the project. As he underscores, 'what differentiated the new congregational mosque perhaps was its sectarian ethos'. Ultimately, he demonstrates how Shah Abbas justified his patronage of not only one but two Friday mosques and argues that these projects 'provided a stage for royal ceremonies and projected a state-sanctioned orthodox narrative of Shi'ism'.

As these examples demonstrate, Konya and Isfahan were not among the 'holy' cities of Islam. In order to live up to their status as imperial capitals, they required more grandeur. In the absence of long-established Islamic 'holy' sites, they attempted to reconceptualise and sanctify spaces – whether Sunni or Shi'i – through their Friday mosques. However, unlike the Christian tradition, in which the church is perceived as an embodiment of Christ, the Friday mosque does not have sanctity in and of itself but requires further layers of religious associations, such as the placement of relics, the declaration of an epigraphic programme, the creation of a soundscape or the incorporation of incense.[28] In Konya, the body of Kaykhusraw was brought back to the city and interred in the tomb in the Friday mosque like a relic, and a new inscription declared the building as *bayt Allah* in reference to Mecca or Jerusalem. In Isfahan, as Emami states, the epigraphic programme was utilized both for 'proclaiming specifically Shi'i tenets of faith' and 'to convince the Sunnis of the validity of the Safavids' Shi'i creed through the former's own canonical sources'. The 'hierotopic projects' that attempted to create a 'sacred' mosque also made use of rituals in the form of state-sponsored religious ceremonies. In the same way that the *ihram* ritual extends sanctity beyond the boundaries of the Haram for Jerusalem, rituals for other cities too bring an aura of sanctity to the greater built environment. Even in cases where there are physical boundaries or barriers, ritual temporarily redefines them.

Chapters by Abbey Stockstill and A. Hilâl Uğurlu in this volume provide different case studies of rituals, such as court ceremonials, that blended religious rites with political aspirations – and breathed life into the architectural spaces of the urban landscape. In her chapter 'From the Kutubiyya to Tinmal: The Sacred Direction in Mu'minid Performance', Stockstill examines patronage under the first Almohad caliph, 'Abd al-Mu'min (*r.*1147–63), in Marrakesh and its vicinity, with a particular emphasis on the Kutubiyya Mosque, the pilgrimage site at Tinmal, and the public garden complex known as the Agdal. This period marked a key transition from the early Almohad religious movement (*al-muwahhidun*), led by Ibn Tumart (*d.*1130), to a political establishment based on dynastic succession (the Mu'minids, *r.*1147–1269). In seeking to legitimize his political power, 'Abd al-Mu'min was keenly aware that 'Almohadism revolved around the character of the Mahdi [Ibn Tumart]', and he literally built his claims around him. He reinforced his connection to the *mahdi* by building a mosque in his memory that eventually became a dynastic necropolis. Moreover, in his reestablishment of Marrakesh, he emphasized the directionality toward the Atlas Mountains and Tinmal, especially the site where Ibn Tumart was buried. By focusing on their 'ethnic, geographic and spiritual origins' in the manipulation of the local landscape, the mentioned sites were connected through processional routes. Ultimately, as Stockstill underscores, the 'space was then activated through the regular and repeated acts of ceremonial performance'.

In her chapter entitled '*Perform Your Prayers in Mosques!*: Changing Spatial and Political Relations in Nineteenth-Century Ottoman Istanbul', A. Hilâl Uğurlu offers another case study of ceremonies that utilized the urban landscape of the city as their background and a Friday mosque as their centre. The modern imperial mosques of Ottoman Istanbul underwent spatial, semantic, and social transformations in the nineteenth century. Moreover, in the second half of the Hamidian era (1876–1909), Friday processions were significantly altered. As soon as the Hamidiye Mosque was completed in 1885, it became the primary choice for all stately and religious processions. Furthermore, the number of participants increased dramatically. High officials were obliged to be present at these weekly events, as were an immense number of soldiers. Various mounted troops and foot soldiers marched through the narrow streets from their barracks – situated in different, and mostly distant, parts of the city – to the Hamidiye Mosque and back. These Friday processions created a weekly opportunity for the sultan to superintend administrative and military institutions in the presence of many other audiences, such as Istanbulites, visitors from other parts of the empire, and international guests. Furthermore, by making the mosque – and its environs – the ultimate destination for thousands of people every week, these ceremonies temporarily recast the mosque's physical boundaries. These repeated visual spectacles not only introduced novel sensual experiences and made the spectators active participants in the ceremony, but they also reinforced the sultan's message of the vigorous state of the empire, as well as his own claims to the universal caliphate.

For 'Abd al-Mu'min and Abdülhamid II, both of whom had caliphal claims, political legitimacy and a concern with permanence were intertwined with religious authority. Thus, the way they planned their state-staged rituals, utilizing the relationship between Friday mosques and the nearby landscape (rural and urban topography), present similarities. In both cases, the apparently political nature of the ceremony was infused with religious/caliphal overtones. However, once the Almohads and Ottomans ceased to exist, and, thus, the caliphal claims and rituals vanished, the hierotopic projects of Mu'minid Marrakesh and Ottoman Istanbul fell apart.

Unlike these politically constructed 'sacred' cities, Islamic 'holy' cities – from Mecca, Medina, and Jerusalem to Najaf, Karbala, and Mashhad – present a contrasting case. No matter who controls these cities, and whatever conflicts take place, throughout history and even up to the present day, they always remain 'sacred'. In her chapter entitled 'Urban Morphology and Sacred Space: The Mashhad Shrine during the Late Qajar and Pahlavi Periods', May Farhat examines how politically-motivated systematic physical interventions that aimed to deconstruct the 'sacredness' of Mashhad in the mid-twentieth century ultimately failed. With the shrine of the eighth Shi'i imam, Ali al-Rida (Imam Reza, *d.*818), at its heart, Mashhad, was, and still is, considered a 'sacred city', one which grew organically around the saint's tomb over the course of centuries, creating a dense urban landscape. As early as the tenth century, this nucleus transformed the entire city into a pilgrimage destination like Jerusalem. The shrine, being a protected territory, had its own administration and rules that no governmental forces could control; thus, it spread its sacredness to its dependencies, including the Timurid-era Gawharshad Mosque (1418).

When the Pahlavi dynasty (1925–79), in parallel with its modernization project, aspired to diminish the political power of the clergy, and thus establish a certain authority in the sacred quarter of the city (which had been beyond reach earlier), abolishing the system that had been shaped over centuries or demolishing the sacred shrine were out of question. However, redefining the borders of the sacred precinct, thereby physically preventing its connection with the city, was possible. First by isolating the shrine complex, by encircling it with a '30 m wide peripheral avenue', and then by demolishing and reconstructing (what in a modern sense were considered) 'secular' buildings, the socio-religious life around the shrine, which had been an integral part of the sacred precinct, was eliminated. Farhat argues that these interventions demonstrated the Pahlavi rulers' 'decision to refashion the shrine into a cultural institution and to minimize the religious visitation ritual centred on the imam's tomb'.

The case of Mashhad is particularly reflective of how the post-Enlightenment Western binary of 'sacred' and 'secular' was adopted and utilized in the name of 'modernization' by non-Western cultures (in this case a Muslim-dominant country), without any questioning of these concepts in the context of their cultural, social, and religious backgrounds. As Shahab Ahmed states in *What Is Islam?*, 'to conceptualize Islam in terms of the religious/sacred versus secular binary is both an anachronism and an epistemological error the effect of which is to *remake* the historical object-phenomenon in the terms of Western modernity'.[29] Ahmed's problematization of this 'error' comes to life with Farhat's case study of the Western-styled 'modern' Pahlavi interventions in Mashhad. In particular, the Gawharshad Mosque incident (1935) is a striking example of the transgression of boundaries. Unlike the hierotopic projects discussed above, the Gawharshad Mosque gained sanctity by its proximity to the 'holy' Imam Reza Shrine. When the troops of Reza Shah were ordered to confront the demonstrators seeking refuge in the sanctuary, killing a massive number of people, the lines between the mosque and the shrine were blurred. Thus, despite the severely invasive nature of the 'secular' intervention against the mosque and the shrine, neither the shrine complex nor the city of Mashhad lost any of its 'sacred' identity.

The violent nature of the clash in Mashhad had its roots in the tangible tension created with the assertion of Western secular ideas within a traditional Muslim society. When Reza Shah imposed new social codes and intervened in 'sacred' places, using Western concepts of 'sacred' and 'secular', he created an inevitable conflict with the people. While in Iran the implementation of imported concepts led to the abovementioned clashes, in Europe, where these notions were homebred, the situation was different. Nebahat Avcıoğlu explores the various motives behind the construction of mosques in the colonial empires of Europe as well as in modern states such as Turkey in her chapter 'Towards a New Typology of Modern and Contemporary Mosque in Europe, Including Russia and Turkey'. Her survey classifies these mosques into four categories – 'orientalist', 'nationalist', 'diasporic', and 'emancipated' – and dwells on the concept of 'otherness' as a form of liminality. The newly built mosques tended to stand out in the urban context of modern European cities; similarly, Muslims were perceived to be 'others'. Avcıoğlu identifies 'orientalist' mosques built by the French, British, and Russian Empires in their capital cities as a manifestation of 'imperialist tolerance' as well as their colonial aspirations over the East. While she identifies 'nationalist' mosques as a 'secularist doctrine of modernism', in which the architecture is modern and includes no references to religious symbolism, the 'diasporic' mosque embodies a postmodern reaction to the 'homogenizing tendencies of the modern movement'. In this case, the 'otherness' of Muslim immigrants to Europe in the last decades of the twentieth century played a significant role in shaping the spatial organization of mosques. Additionally, the postmodern 'partial return to traditional forms' helped to create new memory spaces for these 'others'. Avcıoğlu concludes by discussing 'emancipated' mosques as a 'discourse of multiculturalism and globalization', in which aesthetic concerns and a search for novel designs become ways of expressing creativity for secularist or ecumenical patrons.

In an age where nation-states began to proliferate around the world, replacing empires, the way in which modernity presented 'sacred and profane' or 'religion and state' as binary opposites affected how newly shaped political systems adopted, interpreted, and negotiated these concepts. It also triggered a scholarly debate that continues to this day. While scholars such as Mircea Eliade and Jonathan Z. Smith discussed these concepts in a Western Christian framework,[30] Talal Asad and Shahab Ahmad have questioned their suitability for an Islamic context.[31] As Asad states, the 'supposedly universal opposition between "sacred" and "profane" finds no place in premodern writing'.[32] However, in the modern world these concepts started to permeate beyond the realm of their origin. Roughly 50 Muslim states – with different sects or legal doctrines – encountered these concepts and responded in numerous ways. How each dealt with 'modernity' affected a wide range of issues, from the regimes they adopted to the ways they regarded Friday mosques and conceptualized their relationship to the urban landscape. Yet, regardless of the nature of these individual dynamics, Friday mosques appear to remain among the key signifiers of local and political intentions in the modern world for both monarchic and democratic countries. Aside from building new mosques, the acts of rebuilding, restoring, or even demolishing existing mosques are utilized as tools for claiming authority and, more importantly, for reshaping an existing community by impacting its cultural memory.

As an example, in post-1995 Bosnia,[33] mosques were restored by various states that claimed to be the new protectors of the war-torn country.[34] While Turkish governmental and civil institutions attempted to revive Ottoman architectural and cultural heritage through their funding of rebuilding activities, in reaction, various Gulf countries, notably Saudi Arabia, endeavoured to spread their own interpretation of Islam, namely Wahhabism, by literally whitewashing walls and thereby symbolically obliterating the memory of their historical Ottoman rivals.[35] The consequence of this rivalry manifested itself in the daily lives of modern-day Bosniaks, who are polarized between the Wahhabi and Ottoman versions of Islam.[36]

Another example in Bosnia reveals a different facet of financially supporting social, educational, and religious institutions. The King Fahd bin Abdul Aziz al-Saud Mosque was built in 2000 with the claim of being the biggest mosque in Sarajevo, following the trend of building mega mosques. The attempt to build the 'largest' mosques in the world particularly attests to a competitive political discourse.[37] Although such mega mosques were built for various purposes and claimed to address social 'needs', their proportions and capacities are so vast (from tens of thousands to up to 4 million in the case of Mecca during the hajj) that they no longer provide an intimate space or sense of community. However, creating a community is at the heart of the conceptualization of Islam and is inherent in the idea of gathering for the Friday prayer.

As in the case of Bosnia, where war tore the country and its communities apart, the current ongoing wars in the Middle East present similar tragic consequences.[38] The destruction of symbolic mosques, whether deliberate or accidental, instantly becomes a political statement in multiple ways. For example, various actors such as governmental forces, rebels, or militants of terrorist groups blame each other for destroying such symbolic mosques as the eleventh-century Seljuk minaret of Aleppo's Umayyad Mosque (2013)[39] and Mosul's Great Mosque of al-Nuri (2017).[40] These mosques, which constitute the ancient cores of modern cities, stood as memory spaces, protecting the cultural heritage of these societies. With the destruction of these edifices, the shared memories of these communities were also targeted, which caused an emotional reaction and an international outcry. Local residents and scholars state that during the rebuilding processes for both cities and their symbolic mosques, public engagement is essential and a top-down approach in reconstruction should be avoided.[41]

All of this brings us back to the people who populate and bring meaning to the Friday mosques and their vicinities, and to the term 'liminality', which assumes at least two defined states. This volume examines these defined entities as the Friday mosque and the city. Furthermore, it explores 'liminality' in spatial terms, according to which walls and boundaries define and delineate the mosque, separating it from the city. However, as may be seen in many of the papers, form does not always provide the full picture for understanding function. Spatial demarcations are porous, and with the human factor infusing life through ritual and ceremony, they may be transgressed.

Notes

1   Victor Turner, 'Liminality and Communitas', in *The Ritual Process: Structure and Anti-Structure* (Chicago: Aldine Publishing, 1969), 95.
2   For a collection of papers concerning the city, see, for example, Salma Khadra Jayyusi, Renata Holod, Attilio Petruccioli, et al., eds, *The City in the Islamic World*, 2 vols. (Leiden and Boston: Brill, 2008). As for the mosque, see Martin Frishman and Hasan-Uddin Khan, eds, *The Mosque: History, Architectural Development and Regional Diversity* (London and New York: Thames and Hudson, 1994). For a discussion of the mosque in the urban context, see Oleg Grabar, 'The Architecture of the Middle Eastern City from Past to Present: The Case of the Mosque', in *Middle Eastern Cities*, ed. Ira M. Lapidus (Berkeley: University of California Press, 1969), 26–46.
3   See 'Djuma', *Encyclopaedia of Islam*, 1st ed., by Theodor Willem Juynboll; 'Djuma', *Encyclopaedia of Islam*, 2nd ed. (hereafter, '*EI2* '), by Shelomo Dov Goitein; and 'Masdjid', *EI2* by Johannes Pedersen; Robert Hillenbrand; John Burton-Page et al.
4   John L. Esposito, *The Islamic Threat: Myth or Reality?* (New York: Oxford University Press, 1999). See also 'Community and Society in the Qur'an', *Encyclopaedia of the Qur'an*, by Frederick M. Denny.
5   See Jacob Lassner, *The Topography of Baghdad in the Early Middle Ages: Text and Studies* (Detroit: Wayne State University Press, 1970); Jeremy Johns, 'The "House of the Prophet" and the Concept of the Mosque', in *Bayt al-Maqdis: Jerusalem and Early Islam*, ed. Jeremy

Johns (Oxford: Oxford University Press, 1999), 59–112; Nasser Rabbat, 'In The Beginning was the House: On the Image of the Two Noble Sanctuaries of Islam', *Thresholds* 25 (2002): 56–59; Essam S. Ayyad, 'The "House of the Prophet" or the "Mosque of the Prophet"?', *Journal of Islamic Studies* 24 (2013): 273–34; and Aila Santi, 'Masjidu-hu wa masākinu-hu: "His Mosque and His Dwellings": New Perspectives on the Study of "the House of the Prophet" in Madīna', in *Mantua Humanistic Studies*, ed. Riccardo Roni, vol. 2 (Mantova: Universitas Studiorum, 2018), 97–116.

6   Hugh Kennedy, 'From *Polis* to *Madina*: Urban Change in Late Antique and Early Islamic Syria', *Past & Present* 106 (1985): 3–27.

7   See Nezar al-Sayyad, *Cities and Caliphs: On the Genesis of Arab Muslim Urbanism* (New York and London: Greenwood Press, 1991).

8   See Baber Johansen, 'The All-Embracing Town and Its Mosques: *al-miṣr al-ğāmī'*, *Revue de l'Occident Musulman et de la Méditerranée* 32 (1981–82): 99–100.

9   Medieval Anatolian Friday mosques were (and still are) known as 'Great Mosques' (Tur. *Ulu Cami*). See Suzan Yalman, 'Building the Sultanate of Rum: Memory, Urbanism and Mysticism in the Architectural Patronage of Sultan 'Ala al-Din Kayqubad (*r.* 1220–1237)' (PhD diss.: Harvard University, 2011), 244.

10   *The Travels of Ibn Jubayr*, trans. R. J. C. Broadhurst (London: Camelot Press, 1952), 238.

11   For the idealized round plan of Baghdad, see Jacob Lassner, *The Topography of Baghdad in the Early Middle Ages* (Detroit: Wayne State University Press, 1970), 95–99; al-Sayyad, 'Planned Capital Cities', in *Cities and Caliphs*, 117–39; and Françoise Micheau, 'Baghdad in the Abbasid Era: A Cosmopolitan and Multi-Confessional Capital', in *The City in the Islamic World*, ed. Salma Khadra Jayyusi, Renata Holod, Attilio Petruccioli, et al., 2 vols. (Leiden: Brill, 2008), 1:221–46.

12   Doris Behrens Abouseif, *Islamic Architecture in Cairo: An Introduction* (Leiden: Brill, 1989), 58–62, 63–65; and al-Sayyad, 'Planned Capital Cities', in *Cities and Caliphs*, 141–44.

13   See Farshid Emami's chapter in the present volume.

14   Although they were also Hanafite, Ottoman practice in sixteenth-century Istanbul reveals that they did not adhere to this stipulation. See Gülru Necipoğlu, *The Age of Sinan: Architectural Culture in the Ottoman Empire* (Princeton: Princeton University Press, 2005), 55–57; and Çiğdem Kafescioğlu, *Constantinopolis/Istanbul: Cultural Encounter, Imperial Vision and the Construction of the Ottoman Capital* (University Park: Pennsylvania State University Press, 2007).

15   For an in-depth overview of the scholarship on the 'Islamic City', including the early Orientalist approach and its later critique, see Giulia Annalinda Neglia, 'Some Historiographical Notes on the Islamic City with Particular Reference to the Visual Representation of the Built City', in *The City in the Islamic World*, eds Salma Khadra Jayyusi, Renata Holod, Attilio Petruccioli, et al., 2 vols. (Leiden: Brill, 2008), 1:3–46.

16   F. André Thevet, *Cosmographie de Levant* (Lyons, 1554), 59, as cited in Gülru Necipoğlu Kafadar, 'The Süleymaniye Complex in Istanbul: An Interpretation', *Muqarnas* 3 (1985): 98n22.

17   Henry Christmas, *The Sultan of Turkey: Abdul Medjid Khan* (London: John Farquhr Shaw, 1854), 42; Georgina Adelaide Müller, *Ondokuzuncu Asır Biterken İstanbul'un Saltanatlı*

Günleri (Istanbul: Dergâh, 2010), 62–63; Charles Pertusier, *Picturesque Promenades in and Near Constantinople, and on the Waters of the Bosphorus* (London: Sir Richard Phillips and Co., 1820), 68; and Miss Pardoe, *The City of the Sultan and Domestic Manners of the Turks in 1836*, 2nd ed., 3 vols. (London: Henry Colburn Publisher, 1838), 2:64.

18   Arnold van Gennep, *Les rites de passage: étude systématique des rites* (Paris: Éditions A. & J. Picard, 1909).

19   Turner, 'Liminality and Communitas', 95.

20   Patrick A. Desplat and Dorothea E. Schulz, eds, *Prayer in the City: The Making of Muslim Sacred Places and Urban Life* (Bielefeld: Transcript Verlag, 2012).

21   Turner, 'Liminality and Communitas', 95.

22   Uri Rubin, 'The Ka'ba: Aspects of Its Ritual Functions and Position in Pre-Islamic and Early Islamic Times', *Jerusalem Studies in Arabic and Islam* 8 (1986): 97–131; Oleg Grabar, *The Shape of the Holy: Early Islamic Jerusalem* (Princeton: Princeton University Press, 1996); Amikam Elad, *Medieval Jerusalem and Islamic Worship: Holy Places, Ceremonies, Pilgrimage* (Leiden: Brill, 1999); and David Roxburgh, 'Pilgrimage City', in *The City in the Islamic World*, eds Salma Khadra Jayyusi, Renata Holod, Attilio Petruccioli, et al., 2 vols. (Leiden: Brill, 2008), 2:753–74.

23   Jonathan Z. Smith, *To Take Place: Toward Theory in Ritual* (Chicago: University of Chicago Press, 1987), 103.

24   Smith, *To Take Place*, 104.

25   For 'hierotopy', see Alexei Lidov, 'Hierotopy: The Creation of Sacred Spaces as a Form of Creativity and Subject of Cultural History', in *Hierotopy: Creation of Sacred Spaces in Byzantium and Medieval Russia*, ed. Alexei Lidov (Moscow: Progress-tradition, 2006), 32–58; and Alexei Lidov, 'Creating the Sacred Space: Hierotopy as a New Field of Cultural History', in *Spazi e Percorsi Sacri*, eds Laura Carnevale and Chiara Cremonesi (Padua: Libreriauniversitaria.it, 2015), 61–90.

26   Lidov, 'Hierotopy', 32.

27   In the Byzantine context, references to 'Heavenly Jerusalem' in Constantinople are well known. See, for instance, Robert Ousterhout, 'Sacred Geographies and Holy Cities: Constantinople as Jerusalem', in *Hierotopy: The Creation of Sacred Space in Byzantium and Medieval Russia*, ed. Alexei Lidov (Moscow: Progress-tradition, 2006), 98–116.

28   For the Christian context, see Setha M. Low, 'Embodied Space(s): Anthropological Theories of Body, Space, and Culture', *Space and Culture* 6/1 (2003): 9–18; and Jelena Bogdanović, ed., *Perceptions of the Body and Sacred Space in Late Antiquity and Byzantium* (Abingdon, Oxon: Routledge, 2018). For studies on sensory layers that added sacredness to Friday mosques, see Nina Ergin, 'A Multi-Sensorial Message of the Divine and the Personal: Qur'anic Inscriptions and Recitation in Sixteenth-Century Ottoman Mosques', in *Calligraphy in Islamic Architecture: Space, Form, and Function*, eds Mohammad Gharipour and Irvin C. Schick (Edinburgh: Edinburgh University Press, 2013), 105–18; Nina Ergin, 'The Fragrance of the Divine: Ottoman Incense Burners and Their Context', *Art Bulletin* 96.1 (2014): 70–97; and Michael Frishkopf and Federico Spinetti, eds, *Music, Sound, and Architecture in Islam* (Austin: University of Texas Press, 2018).

29. Shahab Ahmed, *What Is Islam?: The Importance of Being Islamic* (Princeton: Princeton University Press, 2016), 210.

30   See Mircea Eliade, *The Sacred and the Profane* (New York: Harcourt Brace Jovanovich,1959); and Smith, *To Take Place.*

31   See Talal Asad, *Formations of the Secular: Christianity, Islam, Modernity* (Stanford: Stanford University Press, 2003); and Ahmed, *What Is Islam?.*

32   Asad, *Formations of the Secular*, 31–32.

33   Helen Walasek, ed., *Bosnia and the Destruction of Cultural Heritage* (Surrey, UK: Ashgate, 2015); and Tina Wik, 'Restoring war damaged built cultural heritage in Bosnia-Herzegovina' in *Bhopal 2011: Landscapes of Memory*, eds Amritha Balla and Jan af Geijerstam (New Delhi, India: Space Matters with Norwegian University of Science and Technology, 2011), 150–54.

34   András Riedlmayer, 'Erasing the Past: The Destruction of Libraries and Archives in Bosnia-Herzegovina', *Middle East Studies Association Bulletin* 29.1 (1995): 7–11; and James Noyes, *The Politics of Iconoclasm: Religion, Violence and the Culture of Image-Breaking in Christianity and Islam* (London: I. B. Tauris, 2013), 160.

35   'From 1992 to 1995, 614 of the 1144 mosques were destroyed and 307 were damaged; 218 of the 557 *masjids* were destroyed and 41 were damaged; out of the 1425 *waqf* holdings, 405 were destroyed and 149 were damaged. However according to the Islamic Community's Center for Islamic Architecture, by 2010 an estimated 95 per cent of all mosques destroyed during the war have been reconstructed (Karčić, 2011). Many of them were rebuilt following the Wahhabi criteria.' See European Parliament, Directorate-General for External Policies, Policy Department, 'Salafist/Wahhabite Financial Support to Educational, Social and Religious Institutions' (Belgium: AFET, 2013), http://www.europarl.europa.eu/RegData/etudes/etudes/join/2013/457136/EXPO-AFET_ET(2013) 457136_EN.pdf.

36   Daria Sito-Sucic, 'Bosnia's Muslims divided over inroads of Wahhabism', accessed December 1, 2018, https://www.reuters.com/article/us-bosnia-wahhabi/bosnias-muslims-divided-over-inroads-of-wahhabism-idUSL2972174820061229. See also Christopher Deliso, *The Coming Balkan Caliphate: The Threat of Radical Islam to Europe and the West* (Westport, CT: Praeger, 2007).

37   Some notable examples include the continuous expansion of the Great Mosque of Mecca in the twentieth century by the Kingdom of Saudi Arabia; the establishment of the Istiqlal Mosque in Jakarta, Indonesia, in 1978 to commemorate 33 years of independence; the Hasan II Mosque in Casablanca, commissioned by the king of Morocco in 1993; and, most recently, the Çamlıca Mosque in Istanbul, personally supervised by the Turkish president and completed in 2019.

38   See Ömür Harmanşah, 'ISIS, Heritage, and the Spectacles of Destruction in the Global Media', in 'The Cultural Heritage Crisis in the Middle East', special issue, *Near Eastern Archaeology* 78.3 (2015): 170–77; and Stephanie Mulder, 'Evliyaların ve Sultanların Türbeleri', *Aktüel Arkeoloji* (June 2016): 94–99. For an English version, entitled 'Shrines for Saints and Sultans: On the Destruction of Local Heritage Sites by ISIS', accessed December 1, 2018, see https://www.academia.edu/34200898/Shrines_for_Saints_and_Sultans_On_the_destruction_of_local_heritage_sites_by_ISIS_English. See also the special issue 'Imagining Localities of Antiquity in Islamic Societies', *International Journal of Islamic Architecture* 6, no. 2 (2017).

39 The Great Mosque of Aleppo had survived many tumultuous eras, including the Mongol invasions, and included a shrine dedicated to Zechariah. Thus, in addition to the historical nature of the mosque, the fact that the building also imbued sanctity contributed to the reactions. For the symbolic importance of the minaret, see also Johnathan Bloom, *Minaret: Symbol of Islam* (Oxford: Oxford University Press, 1989).

40 As for Mosul, the Great Mosque of al-Nuri had been the locus of self-fashioning for the militant group known as the Islamic State of Iraq and Syria (ISIS), whose leader, Abu Bakr al-Baghdadi, declared a 'caliphate' from its minbar in 2014. Although ISIS never claimed the mosque's destruction three years later, others perceived it as a final performative act by a waning terrorist organization. See Karel Nováček, Miroslav Melčák, Lenka Starková, et al., *Monuments of Mosul in Danger* (Prague: Czech Academy of Sciences, 2017); and 'Destroying Great Mosque of al-Nuri "is Isis declaring defeat"', accessed December 1, 2018, https://www.theguardian. com/world/2017/jun/21/mosuls-grand-al-nouri-mosque-blown-up-by-isis-fighters.

41 Robert Fisk, 'Syrians aren't just rebuilding an ancient mosque in Aleppo–they are rebuilding their community', *Independent*, accessed December 1, 2018, https://www.independent.co.uk/voices/syria-great-mosque-of-aleppo-ummayad-rebuild-the-city-a7858846.html; Jenny Morber, 'Expert Views: Beyond a Top-down Approach to Aleppo's Reconstruction', April 11, 2018, https://www.newsdeeply.com/syria/community/2018/04/11/expert-views-beyond-a-top-down-approach-to-aleppos-reconstruction; and Nour A. Munawar, 'Rebuilding Aleppo: Public Engagement in Post-Conflict Reconstruction', *ICOMOS University Forum* (ICOMOS International, 2018), 1–18.

Section I

Spatial Liminalities: Walls, Enclosures, and Beyond

Liminal Spaces in the Great Mosque of Cordoba: Urban Meaning and Politico-Liturgical Practices

Susana Calvo Capilla

To understand the formal and emblematic meanings of the Friday mosques in Andalusi cities, as well as their interactions with urban life, it is necessary to analyse not only the buildings themselves but also the Arab sources and the Christian documents. The case of the Great Mosque of Cordoba is paradigmatic because of its exceptionally good state of preservation and because of the volume of surviving textual information about it and the city of Islamic Cordoba.[1] The preservation of the mosque throughout the Middle Ages was probably due to the great admiration of Christian kings for the building: 'This is the largest and most excellent and noblest mosque of the Moors in Spain', exclaimed Don Juan Manuel, brother of King Alfonso X (1221–84).

Textual information enables us to surmise what the atmosphere around the mosque in medieval Cordoba, the bustling capital of al-Andalus, would have been like. Juridical texts (*fatwas* and legal opinions), biographical literature, *hisbah* treatises (books describing the official supervision of the markets and moral behaviour), and historical chronicles mention the diverse activities, of both religious and profane character, that took place around and in front of the Great Mosque (*jami'*) of Cordoba. The large amount of writings on Cordoba under the Umayyads is an exceptional case. In these texts, as well as in the inscriptions preserved, it is possible to notice the connections – the dialogues, we could say – that the building had with its urban surroundings from religious, political, and social points of view. These spaces and the activities that took place in them also left an important mark in the Christian documentation, which allows us to observe and understand the transformations that have occurred in the mosque to the present day.

Excavations carried out in Spain in the twentieth and twenty-first centuries, as well as conservation work begun in the nineteenth century, have corroborated much of the data found in the historical sources, deepening the extant knowledge concerning the religious architecture of al-Andalus. As far as the liminal spaces of the Cordoba Mosque are concerned, work by archaeologists and architects since 1882 – when the building was declared a National Historic-Artistic Monument – has been instrumental in substantiating the words of chroniclers and jurists. Archaeological work at the twelfth-century Great Mosque of Seville and at ninth- and tenth-century local mosques in Cordoba complements the study. This chapter will review the material concerning the area around the Great Mosque of Cordoba, and how it has changed over the centuries.

The Friday mosque of Cordoba was a freestanding monumental building with a fortified appearance and a high tower that was visible from any point in the city, characteristics that explain its great visual and symbolic impact on the city, even today. Furthermore, as it was located next to the seat of power (*al-qasr*) and other governmental institutions and surrounded by main souks, the Friday mosque became the centre of urban life in medieval Cordoba. As the dynastic and main Friday mosque in al-Andalus, *al-masjid al-jami'* of Cordoba was also a site for political ceremonies: it was here where official statements were made, where emirs and later caliphs were proclaimed (*bay'a*), and rulers appeared to the people, and where standards were tied before the troops set off on a campaign. Additionally, public edicts of every sort were read aloud at its gates. Other important activities related to justice (the supreme qadi of Cordoba had his seat in the mosque) and education were carried out in its interior.

Consequently, the mosque's facade and its impressive entrances also became the most suitable urban public spaces for displaying political, ideological, and religious messages – ultimately, official propaganda. Especially during the first centuries of Islam, the capital *jami'* became the setting for the main social and political events of a given territory: religious controversies, dynastic relays, political or military official announcements, legal enforcement, theological propaganda, and pious exhortations – everything took place in the great mosque and its immediate surroundings. In the case of Cordoba, the decoration and epigraphic programme of the caliphal expansion of the *jami'*, and especially of its gates, were conceived for several politico-religious purposes and in dialogue with the urban context.

We should first review the various phases of the edifice's construction in order to establish a better understanding of how its liminal spaces were developed. The Cordoba Mosque was built on the order of the first Umayyad emir of al-Andalus, 'Abd al-Rahman I (*d.*788), around 785. This first Friday mosque had a prayer hall divided into eleven naves and a patio with galleries. San Sebastian gate, also called the Viziers' door, is the oldest gate to the mosque and preserves an inscription documenting its restoration in 855–56, on the orders of the emir Muhammad I. The second emir, Hisham I (*r.*788–96), added the minaret and an ablutions hall adjoining the eastern side of the building. The mosque was first extended by emir 'Abd al-Rahman II (*r.*822–52), who ordered the qibla wall to be pulled down and the naves lengthened to the south. His successors, emirs Muhammad I (*r.*852–86), al-Mundhir (*r.*886–88), and 'Abd Allah (*r.*888–912), added several features, such as the first *maqsura* (royal enclosure) in 873 and the first *sabat*, a bridge joining the palace and the mosque by spanning the street below. In 929, 'Abd al-Rahman III (912–61) was proclaimed caliph, and, in the early 950s, he began work that would transform the old mosque into the showcase and symbol of a renewed Umayyad Caliphate. The chroniclers state that the first tasks included building a new monumental minaret and enlarging the courtyard so that it would be proportionate to the prayer hall. A few years later, 'Abd al-Rahman's son al-Hakam II (*r.*961–76) ordered the qibla wall to be pulled down again and several sections to be added to the naves. A huge ornate *maqsura* was built in the new oratory, featuring three covered sections with ribbed domes and decorated with splendid glazed and gilded mosaics. The last large project in the Friday mosque of Cordoba was completed during the time of caliph Hisham II, around 987–88, on the order of his minister Ibn 'Abi 'Amir, al-Mansur. This time, fortunately, the qibla wall and al-Hakam II's magnificent *maqsura* were preserved; eight naves were added to the east side of the prayer hall and the proportional part of the courtyard [Figure 1].

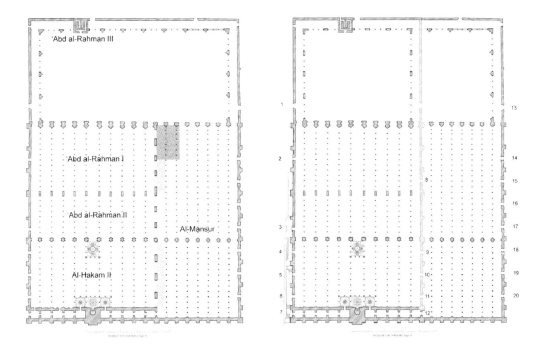

1. Gate of the Deans (no inscriptions)
2. St. Sebastian or Viziers door (foundational inscription from Muhammad I period)
3. St. Michael door (no inscriptions)
4. Door of the Holy Spirit (Q. 40:3)
5. Palace or Bishop door (Q. 40:12–14, 40:16–17)
6. St. Ildefonso door (no inscriptions)
7. The *sabat* doors
8. Door of the 'Abd al-Rahman II phase, found in the excavations (no inscriptions)
9. Door of the Saint Martha Altar (Q. 3:19)
10. Door of the St. Sebastian Altar (no inscriptions)
11. Door of the St. John the Baptist Altar (Q. 16:90)
12. The 'Punto' door or Treasure Gate (Q. 19:35)
13. Saint Catherine door (no inscriptions)
14. San Juan door (Q. 3:191–92)
15. Baptistery door (Q. 59:21–23)
16. St. Nicholas door (Q. 14:52 and 39:53)
17. Door of The Conception (Q. 36:78–79 and 43:68–71)
18. St. Joseph gate (Q. 3:1–4)
19. Magdalena gate (Q. 33:56 + Q.112)

Figure 1: Great Mosque of Cordoba. Left: Ground plan after al-Mansur expansion (987–88). The shaded areas represent the excavations. Right: Same plan with the disappeared facade of Caliph al-Hakam II (961–76), discovered inside the mosque, and main doors numbered. Based on A. Almagro's plan, 2014.

The Doors of the Great Mosque of Cordoba: Written Sources, Qur'anic inscriptions, and Architectural Remains

The great mosque was Cordoba's focal point during the medieval period. Everyone would have attended the great mosque at midday for congregational prayers every Friday and to hear the sermon, or *khutba*. In addition to the ritual prayers, other religious activities, many linked to popular piety and official protocol, were carried out in the mosques or next to them. Several liturgical and secular ceremonies took place before the doors and facades of the Great Mosque of Cordoba, so that the surrounding area became an extension of the prayer hall. When the prayer hall was full, the faithful prayed by the entrances and walkways outside the walls of the building. The *hisbah* treatises of al-Andalus refer to the custom of placing secondary muezzins at the outside doors and courtyard, who not only repeated the call to prayer, announcing that the *salat* was about to start, but also repeated the imam's words and gestures during the prayer, so that those outside could pray in unison with those inside.[2] According to Ibn 'Idhari (*d. c.*1325), in the tenth century, on Fridays, some muezzins lined up in the courtyard of the Great Mosque of Cordoba, at the entrances to the naves, to make the second call (*iqama*) [Figures 2–3].[3]

Figure 2: Great Mosque of Cordoba. View of the west facade, al-Hakam II phase (961–76). Doors (nos. 3 to 7) and platform.

Figure 3: Great Mosque of Cordoba. View of the al-Mansur extension east facade (987–88). Doors (no. 16 in the foreground), stone platform, and street.

Similarly, certain rituals that could not be performed inside the mosque – such as the funeral prayers, calls to burials, public readings from the Qur'an, and litanies (*du'a'* and *dhikr*) – took place at the entrances. The Maliki school considered the funeral bier (*al-jana'iz*) that held the corpse to be unclean, so this was left outside. Religious authorities also disapproved of excessive displays of piety by individuals inside the mosques.[4] These practices were often reflected in the names of the gates or spaces near the great mosque such as the *Bab al-yana'iz* in Ceuta.[5] All mosques also had one or more entrances through which women could access the area reserved for them inside the prayer hall, called *Bab al-nisa'*.[6] Ultimately, the great gatherings on Fridays proved useful for making calls from the doors for people to adhere to their moral and charitable duties, such as giving alms, and for publicly condemning heterodoxy by burning heretical books.

Inscriptions from the Qur'an preserved on the facades of the Great Mosque of Cordoba clearly depict many of these acts and reveal the dialogue between the mosque and its urban and social environment. It must be remembered that these inscriptions were part of a complex epigraphic programme developed with the enlargement of the oratory in the tenth century, which included the naves and *maqsura* as well as the outside portals. Far from being a random, repetitive selection of verses, the programme contained a message with strong symbolic and political implications for tenth-century Cordoba. The ideologues composed a rhetorical text from verses and fragments of verses – not always consecutive – which precisely and effectively conveyed the ideological discourse of the Cordoba caliphate.[7]

At the entrances to the great mosque in Cordoba, as in other cities in the Islamic world, one found inscriptions of doxologies, eulogies, and praises to God as well invocations (*tasliya*) asking the Prophet to intercede on Judgement Day.[8] This type of prayer made up the repertory of the daily doxologies and prayers (*du'a*) of the faithful. Ibn Bashkuwal (*d.*1183) cites a hadith according to which every Muslim who enters or leaves the mosque must offer the following prayer, dedicated to the Prophet:

> When the Prophet entered the mosque, he prayed silently, saying: 'Oh! God, forgive my sins and open the doors to your pity.' When he left, the Prophet also prayed for God to bless and save him, saying: 'Forgive my sins and open the doors to your favour.'[9]

The inscriptions also mention some of the duties of all good Muslims, such as giving alms. The chronicles relate that, in times of need and poverty, the authorities called upon the faithful from the doors of the great mosque, asking them to help the poorest of Cordoba. On other occasions, the ruler ordered money to be distributed in the street between the palace and the great mosque.[10] On the eastern facade of al-Hakam II's extension (nowadays in the interior of the oratory), the Qur'anic verse 16:90 was inscribed, urging the faithful to 'benevolence and liberality towards relations'. Similarly, verse 40:12–13, on a western entrance, reads: 'Therefore, the decision is Allah's, the Highest, the Great. / It is He who shows you His signs, who sends down sustenance to you from Heaven. But He does not punish anyone who repents and returns to Him' [See Figure 1, gates 11 and 5, respectively; Figure 4].

However, the most interesting aspect of the epigraphic programme on the great mosque is the presence of apologetic – and controversial – verses that insist on the dogma of Maliki religious orthodoxy and warn Muslims of the dangers of straying from the 'straight path', as doing so would have consequences in the next world as well as in this realm. At the doors on the western facade of al-Hakam II's extension from the mid-tenth century, a series of verses from *sura* 40 (*al-Ghafir*, 'the Forgiver') is inscribed; this *sura*, alluding to eternal punishment and reward, is unusual in epigraphy. These entrances were positioned exactly opposite the Justice gate (*Bab al-'Adl*) and the 'Azuda' gate (*Bab al-Sudda*) of the caliph's palace, the *mazalim* (court of appeals) judge's seat, and the scaffold where capital punishment took place, respectively[11] [See Figure 2].

On the eastern facade, as ordered by the Grand Vizier (*hajib*) al-Mansur toward the end of the tenth century, eschatological and reprimanding verses warn Muslims about the terrible punishments that could come on Judgement Day.[12] The texts focus on divine justice,

Figure 4: Great Mosque of Cordoba. Remains of doors 11 and 12 in the east facade of the al-Hakam II phase, disappeared after the al-Mansur extension.

pity, and salvation – or condemnation – on the Day of Reckoning,[13] and on the reward of resurrection.[14] It must be remembered that notices of funerals were announced on the doors, as were prayers for the dead as they were carried on the bier to the cemetery, and therefore these eschatological messages were well suited to this location.[15] Admonitory messages also could be related to the important role of al-Mansur in promoting the *jihad*[16] [See Figure 3].

The set of Qur'anic inscriptions carved or painted on the mosque's walls was also conceived as a response to the challenges and concerns raised about caliphal power in the tenth century. The threat of various deviations from orthodoxy, such as the sect of Ibn Masarra (*d.*931) – a topic of concern in Cordoba throughout the tenth century – and the suspicion that Fatimid agents had infiltrated the peninsula and were spreading Shiʻism, mobilised the Maliki jurists (*faqihs*) in defence of unity under Sunni orthodoxy. ʻAbd al-Rahman III and al-Hakam II sided with the defence of Malikism and trusted in the *faqihs* as the primary supporters of their infallible authority emanating from God, which was questioned by the followers of

Ibn Masarra and by the Mutazilites via the notion of 'free will'.[17] The *maqsura* has many epigraphs calling on the *umma* to remain united and to follow the straight path, guided by the caliph. Al-Mansur confirmed and legalised his power, usurped from the legitimate caliph, Hisham II, with the help of the most rigid Maliki jurists, and by persecuting science, Ibn Masarra's school, and all rational thought.[18] The sources state that edicts condemning the Masarri heresy were read at the doors of all mosques in al-Andalus, and its heretical books were burned at the eastern entrances and in the courtyard of the Great Mosque of Cordoba in 961.[19]

The third challenge faced by Cordoba in the tenth century – and appearing on the portals of the great mosque – was Christianity. Christians were present in al-Andalus society in a variety of ways: as the outside enemy (*kafirun*), as an internal threat, as protected people (*dhimmies*), as converts (*islami*), and as apostates (*murtaddun*).[20] In the early years of the tenth century, Umayyads rulers faced a serious rebellion by Ibn Hafsun, who was accused of apostasy and Fatimid sympathies. Even within the Umayyad family there were cases of converts to Christianity in the tenth century.[21] Consequently, we can assume that the Qur'anic verses against the trinity, inscribed on the walls of the caliphal extension to the Cordoba Mosque (6:101, 19:35, and Sura 112, with the addition of verse 33:56, extolling the role of the Prophet Muhammad), have an evident apologetic bias [See Figure 1, gates 12 and 20, respectively]. The epigraphy on the mosque is one of the earliest testimonies of anti-Christian theological polemics in al-Andalus, and finds its best-known parallel in the Dome of the Rock in Jerusalem (seventh century).[22] These texts, which include the essential elements of the Islamic dogma of oneness, provided Muslims with arguments for rejecting apostasy and the Christian creed, as well as reaffirming their faith in the Prophet.[23]

To make the inscriptions intelligible, and fully effective in conveying their message, they had to be easily visible and legible, and so great care was taken in both making and positioning them.[24] The inscriptions on the east and west facades were inserted into the ornate frames of the portals, together with vegetal and geometric motifs, and highlighted in colour. The bands of calligraphy were on the arches and lintels of the doors and in the rectangular frames (*alfiz*). Most of the inscriptions preserved are on the arches, as the frames suffered damage in the eighteenth century, when they were hidden by a layer of brick and plaster.[25] When architect Velázquez Bosco restored them between 1900 and 1918,[26] hidden inscriptions appeared that were scarcely touched, incomplete but in their original state [Figures 5–6].

We know about the original polychrome on the portals and their inscriptions due to the discovery of the remains of four doors from the time of al-Hakam II (*r.*961–76), which were covered a few years after their construction, when al-Mansur enlarged the building with eight new naves in the east side in 987. The remains, found by Velázquez Bosco, served not only as a model for restoring the external doors but also as a valuable record through which the strong visual impact of the city's great mosque could be appreciated. The words stood out against a background of lapis lazuli blue and were framed by red bands. The calligraphy was probably painted, too, and perhaps gilded, as in the interior of the prayer

Figure 5: Great Mosque of Cordoba. View of the Triumph square and the western facade in the nineteenth century, before restorations (notice the modern rooms built against the mosque west wall). Photo by Jean Laurent (1816–86), Ruiz Vernacci File, Fototeca del Patrimonio Historico VN-00252. (IPCE: Institute of Cultural Heritage of Spain, Madrid.)

Figure 6: Great Mosque of Cordoba. View of the eastern facade in the nineteenth century, before restorations. Photo by Jean Laurent (1816–86), Ruiz Vernacci File, Fototeca del Patrimonio Historico VN-00254. (IPCE: Institute of Cultural Heritage of Spain, Madrid.)

Figure 7: Great Mosque of Cordoba. Remains of the east doors of al-Hakam II Mosque. Notice that the inscriptions were polychromed.

hall.[27] Legibility was improved by wide walkways surrounding the mosque, onto which the doors opened, placing the viewer at the correct height and distance to read the inscriptions [Figure 7].

We can assume that the *faqihs* and *ulama* closest to power were behind this elaborate ideological and theological statement reaffirming orthodoxy and support for the caliph's power. To make the message more effective, a text was created with several Qur'anic excerpts, employing rhetorical resources that recall the dialectic strategies used in contemporaneous *khutbas*.[28] In this sense, one of the most prominent preachers in the Cordoban court, the qadi Mundhir b. Sa'id al-Balluti, a person very close to the caliph, could have played an important role in the composition of the Cordoban epigraphic programme. We should also emphasize the interrelationships between the internal and external inscriptions, as well as the inscriptions' interaction with the immediate urban setting and with the activities that took place in front of them.[29]

The Mosque Surroundings: Squares, Walkways, and Stone Benches

In the same manner in which the mosque doors were used in rituals and various pious actions, the immediate surroundings of the building became an extension of the prayer hall. These areas are particularly well known in the Great Mosque of Cordoba in the Umayyad era, and in the mosques of Seville under the Almoravids and Almohads. Arab sources use various terms to describe the areas surrounding the mosques: squares, esplanades, or parvises (*fina'*, pl. *afniya*; *rahba*, pl. *rihab*).[30] They also refer to an area with no buildings (*fada'*): it was an extension of the mosque as well as a transition point between the mosque and the urban environment. If there was no room inside the mosque, the faithful could pray here, especially on Fridays and during large festivals. The prayers offered on the esplanades had the same value as those inside the great mosque.[31]

The legal treatise by Ibn Habib (*d.*852) defines the open, clear space (*fina'* and *rahba*) in front of buildings (including houses and mosques) as 'a stopping place for horses and loads, an entrance for the people… a busy place' 'they reach the doors, so nobody can reduce their size or change the condition in which they are found'.[32] Polluting the *afniyat al-masajid* or the mosque's facades was prohibited; the qadi was charged with preventing people from unloading grain and oil as well as from trading livestock, especially behind the qibla wall, because these activities would have polluted the mosque.[33]

The historical chronicles mention that the Umayyad emirs and caliphs were involved in the urban planning of Cordoba in order to preserve the public streets.[34] 'Abd al-Rahman III and his son al-Hakam II were keen to keep the wide streets around the mosque clear for safety and for comfort, given their proximity to the Umayyad palace facing the western side. The *mahajja al-'uzma*, or main street separating the two buildings, which were connected by a bridge over the street, the *sabat*, was a place of transit for the ruler and his entourage, for troops leaving for campaigns, and for ambassadors and foreign visitors with their retinues, as well as the place from which the ruler regularly distributed alms [Figure 8].[35]

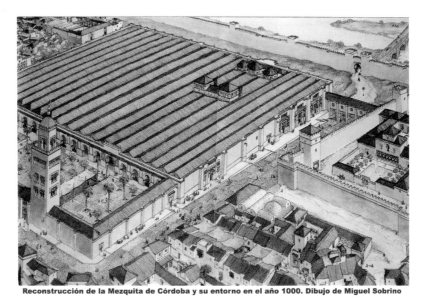

Reconstrucción de la Mezquita de Córdoba y su entorno en el año 1000. Dibujo de Miguel Sobrino

Figure 8: Great Mosque of Cordoba and urban surroundings. Drawing by Miguel Sobrino for the Instituto Cervantes (http://cvc.cervantes.es/actcult/mezquita_cordoba/indice.htm).

In many cases, these open spaces were used in the enlargement of the oratory. Several al-Andalus authors state that 'Abd al-Rahman II took the *fada'* to the south of the qibla to extend the Cordoba Mosque naves,[36] and Hisham I built a room for ablutions on its *fina'*.[37]

Near the facades of the mosque were stone benches or walkways that protected the bases of the walls and marked the transition from holy place to public space.[38] Prohibitions and constant warnings regarding street vendors in public spaces near the mosque, issued by market inspectors (*muhtasib*) and jurists in al-Andalus, demonstrate the popularity of these places, and that such rules were disregarded regularly[39].

The *dakakin* (sing. *dukkan*) and *masatib* (sing. *mastaba*) are, in general, stone benches, platforms, or walkways of varying widths running along the base of the facades of the mosque, which sometimes were shaded if they were used for a specific purpose.[40] They had various functions, serving as an extension of the prayer hall for the call to prayer or for prayers themselves. In the case of the *masatib* surrounding the great mosque, the ruler was responsible for their construction and upkeep, as he was for the mosque itself, as described in a fatwa by Ibn Rushd (*d.*1126).[41]

The reciters of the Qur'an were installed in the *masatib* of the Great Mosque of Cordoba. In his bio-bibliographic dictionary, Ibn al-Abbar (*d.*1260) mentions a Cordoban teacher, probably from the twelfth century, who recited the Qur'an in the *mastaba* of Ibn Rida in the *masjid al-jami'* of Cordoba.[42] This account shows that these places sometimes were given their own names, a phenomenon documented in other cities of the Islamic world.[43]

As with the *rihab* and *afniya*, there were also attempts to privatize the *dakakin* and *masatib* of the great mosque. A fatwa collected by al-Wansharisi deals severely with an imam who took over part of the *mastaba* and eventually converted it into a shop (*hanut*) with a roof, door, and lock, unequivocal signs of privatization. Not content with that, he later set up other stalls, where he charged money for teaching the children of the poor. The jurisprudence experts decided that the man had illegally appropriated public space under the false pretence that teaching was for the common good.[44] These same fatwas show that it was prohibited to erect buildings (even for godly purposes) against the facades of the great mosque by inserting beams into the walls.[45]

There is evidence that these places (*dakakin*, *masatib*, *rihab*, and *afniya*) were also found in neighbourhood mosques. The sources have provided critical information for interpreting items found outside religious buildings excavated in Cordoba, Toledo, and other cities in al-Andalus. In the areas now known as El Fontanar and Ronda de Poniente, districts that arose in the west of Cordoba during the Umayyad era, mosques were surrounded by streets that were wider than those elsewhere in the neighbourhood and featured a walkway or platform one-and-a-half metres wide running along its southwest and qibla facades.[46]

We must remember that these spaces were not exclusive to the mosques of al-Andalus. Al-Turtushi (*d.*1126) offers some interesting information on the mosque in Medina, where a *batha'* or *rahba*, an esplanade, was built 'at the side of the mosque'.[47] The Abbasids included a new element around their great mosques, the *ziyada*; see, for example, the partially preserved examples in the two great mosques in Samarra (Iraq) and in the Ibn Tulun Mosque in Cairo, built in the mid ninth century. In both cases, the *ziyada* consists of an open strip of land surrounding the building on four sides, closed off by a high wall.[48]

Written sources from al-Andalus mention the existence of a *ziyada* in some mosques, with the customary use of the areas surrounding the building. To dispense justice, a qadi from Malaga sat in 'the *ziyada* of the mosque', the place where he was buried upon his death in 500/1106 and which was given his name.[49] However, we do not know what shape it took, nor whether it was a space bounded by a high or a low wall or simply by the surrounding streets and buildings, like a public square. Thus far, very few such remains have been identified in al-Andalus.[50]

The immediate surroundings of mosques also contained ablutions areas, or *mida'a,* and baths (*hammam*), places where the faithful carried out their ritual obligation to purify themselves before praying to God. In the eighth century, Hisham I built the first ablutions room in the Great Mosque of Cordoba, adjoining the courtyard wall; some of its remains have been found under the current floor. Ibn 'Idhari said that the caliph, al-Hakam II, ordered two new ablutions rooms to be built once the extension had been completed, one on the east side and one on the west side. In this case, there were buildings on the other side of the wide street, so that impurities were kept well away from the mosque.[51] Around 987–91, the Great Mosque of Cordoba was extended again on the orders of al-Mansur, Hisham II's minister. When work was completed, he built a large ablutions room on the east side of the mosque, on the other side of the street.[52]

Excavations carried throughout the twentieth century in and around the mosque have brought many fragments of the facade and its medieval surroundings to light, and these can be used to physically document some of the elements mentioned previously. Early digs were carried out by the first architect to restore the mosque, Ricardo Velázquez Bosco, at the beginning of the twentieth century. His work was continued by Felix Hernández in the 1930s and later resumed by Pedro Marfil in the 1990s. The most important remains were found under the naves extended by al-Mansur [see Figure 1, left side].

Excavations by Hernández in 1932 found that the first mosque, built by 'Abd al-Rahman I, was surrounded on the east side by a very wide paved street that sloped toward the south. There was a three metres difference in height between the street and the floor of the prayer hall. This facade had buttresses jutting out about one and a half metres, as did the west facade, but it did not have a door. In addition, running along the lower part of the walls, between the buttresses and level with them, was an approximately 2.35-metre-high stone bench ending in a slope and separated from the pavement by a small curb [Figure 9]. Finally, it could be seen that the facade, built in ashlar, was covered with plaster, which was painted with a white-and-red design that simulated stonework.

A few years after the construction, Hisham I joined an ablutions room to the east facade, as the archaeologists' documentation has confirmed; this construction consumed part of the street and was only accessible from it. In the ninth century, during the reign of Emir 'Abd al-Rahman II, an entrance was opened in the free section of the facade,

Figure 9: Great Mosque of Cordoba. Archaeological remains of the stone bench leaned against the baseboard of the eighth–ninth-century mosque's east facade.

near that ablutions hall. Although the level of the street was raised almost to that of the interior floor of the prayer hall, a two-metre-high platform, with a flight of steps at each end, was built in front of the new door for ease of access.[53] This discovery was useful in determining what the exterior of the mosque looked like at its earliest stage and in confirming the early existence of the benches and platforms mentioned in tenth-century texts [Figures 10–11].

After the mid-tenth century, with the new extension completed, al-Hakam II radically altered the street in front of the east facade of the great mosque. Hisham I's ablutions room was pulled down, and a street – approximately twenty metres wide and paved with irregular slabs – was made, with the pavement raised enough to approach the level of the prayer hall floor. These works also emphasized the walkway (*dukkan*) running along the lower part of the facade. This was a platform made with ashlars in headers and stretchers (about three metres deep), whose height increased as it sloped down toward the river to the south. Steps to the southern doors were also built.[54] This last layout was found in excavations made by Velázquez Bosco at the beginning of the twentieth century, when the southern portals from the time of al-Hakam II came to light.[55] A similar structure was built on the facades of the last enlargement of the mosque, at the end of the tenth century.

Figure 10: Great Mosque of Cordoba. Archaeological remains of the ablution facility (*midaʾa*) built against the east facade by Hisham I (788–96).

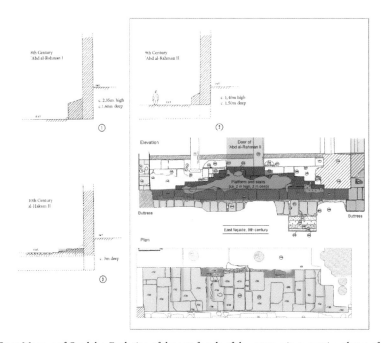

Figure 11: Great Mosque of Cordoba. Evolution of the east facade of the mosque in successive phases of construction from the eighth to the end of the tenth century. Plan and elevation of the reforms of the facade in the ninth century (according to Marfil 1999 and 2010).

Figure 12: Great Mosque of Cordoba. View of the west facade with the remains of the ancient stone sidewalk in 1954, on the occasion of the visit of a committee of prominent Muslims. Cordoba Municipal Archives, Photographs, ES.14021.AMCO/FO010101//A6-5/F12-18 (17).

A platform along the west facade also was documented when the modern walkways were demolished in 1928–30. The medieval platform was exposed in the area of the San Sebastian, or Viziers' door, as shown in old photographs [Figure 12].[56] The platform, made from sandstone slabs, was two metres deep and surrounded the buttresses, allowing pedestrians to walk next to the facade. By contrast, little is known about the exterior of the qibla wall in the first stage. A fragment from 'Abd al-Rahman II's qibla was found during excavations made by F. Hernández. The wall lacked buttresses, and the rectangular mihrab projection featured tiered courses of bossed ashlars, probably plastered like the rest of the facades described above.[57]

This archaeological data leads to the conclusion that the wide platform surrounding the building and separating it from the street was completed in the tenth century, at the same time as the environs of the mosque were cleared by pulling down adjoining buildings and widening the street. The platform, which was between two and three metres deep and rose to varying heights depending on the drop to the street, replaced the first small sloping benches adjoining the base of the walls, making the facades more monumental and slenderer. The mosque thus was surrounded by a large area that served to highlight its importance and to protect its holiness, isolating it from the built-up urban area.

Transformations and Continuity in the Surroundings of the Great Mosque of Cordoba After Its Conversion to a Cathedral

Esta es la mayor et más complida et más noble mezquita que los moros avían en España, et, loado a Dios, es agora eglesia et llámanla Sancta María de Cordova, et ofreciola el sancto rey don Ferrando a Sancta María cuando gano a Cordova de los moros.[58]

As the centuries passed, especially following the Christian conquest of the city in 1236 and the conversion of the great mosque into a cathedral, the walls and surroundings of the Islamic building were gradually transformed. According to the *First General Chronicle* of Alfonso X (*r.*1252–84), at the end of the thirteenth century the building was 'greatly abandoned' and in need of repair.[59] Initially, both the Spanish monarchs, following the example of the emirs and caliphs, and the Council of Cordoba were keen to preserve the cathedral and its environs. For example, in 1281, Alfonso X, aware of the deterioration of the urban area around the cathedral, ordered the demolition of the shops set up there and leaning against the walls, 'in its honour and to the great beauty of the town'.[60] Similarly, in 1523 the Council of Cordoba tried to prevent the bishop and chapter from carrying out work on the new cathedral, stating that 'what is being undone [in the mosque] is of such fine quality that cannot be remade to the same standard of perfection in which it was done'.[61]

The Cordoba cathedral was not the only example of this phenomenon. In 1395 the archbishop and chapter of Seville wrote:

In the interest of better decorum for their church, removed from all around the outside of the four sides of the Patio de los Naranjos many shops near to them… and surrounded it with a raised walkway on stone steps… also… that year the marble and chains were installed around Santa Maria de Sevilla.[62]

Later, in March 1593, the platforms adjoining the Door of Forgiveness (*Perdon* door) were demolished, 'where the fruit, ribbon and haberdashery shops stood, to make way for the steps seen today', according to a document [Figure 13].[63]

This eagerness to preserve the magnificence of a religious building inherited from the Muslims may be surprising. The reasons were not only religious, given that the buildings had been converted into cathedrals, but also aesthetic. An instance of Christians appreciating the beauty of the buildings appears in the chronicle of the archbishop of Toledo and first bishop of Cordoba Rodrigo Jiménez de Rada (*d.*1247), which tells of the Christian conquest of Cordoba and the impression made by the superb and unique building, the ancient great mosque, on all those attending its consecration. In his opinion, it was the most beautiful and largest of all the Arab mosques on the peninsula.[64]

Figure 13: Great Mosque of Seville (1169–98). View of the platform and benches around the courtyard walls. Left: east facade. Right: north facade, stone bench after the restoration to its original state.

This does not mean that the prayer hall and outer facades had remained unchanged. During the fifteenth and sixteenth centuries, the two entrances to the cathedral in the western facade were known as the 'Bishop Door' and the 'Palace Door' (Postigo del Obispo and Postigo de Palacio). They were used by the bishop to enter the building from his palace, which was in the former Umayyad palace (*al-qasr*) on the other side of the street.[65] In both cases, the portal was changed and different decoration added. To a certain extent, the use of both doors is a prolongation of the function of the facade in the Islamic era, as it held the passageways used by the emir or caliph to enter the *maqsura* from the palace (*sabat*).[66] The facades were not more radically altered until the eighteenth and nineteenth centuries, with rooms adjoining the east side and hiding all the original decoration of the doors, and a row of balconies built on the west section of the qibla wall [see Figures 5–6].[67]

Preserving the platforms and walkways along the facade, as well as the street around the building, once again became a topic of interest in the twentieth century, when the architects restoring the mosque-cathedral began to study it. Velázquez Bosco recovered and restored the platform at the southern ends of the east and west facades between 1893 and 1917, slightly lowering the height to make access to the building easier and to return the portals to their original size.[68] However, years later, since the height and width of the platforms had been altered,[69] and other socles had been added to the buttresses, it was believed that the platforms and socles were the result of successive modern reforms. Around 1929, work started on pulling down the walkways of the north wall and the northern part of the east and west facades. During the course of demolition, the remains of an original perimeter platform came to light in some places. The walls remained uncovered until the 1980s, which led to the deterioration of its lowest courses of ashlars. From the end of the 1980s to the beginning of the 1990s, the architects Ruiz Cabrero and Rebollo Puig, aware that the platform had a historical basis and that it was needed to protect and preserve the building, replaced and restored the walkways around the perimeter of the cathedral (higher in the south than in the north).[70]

Conclusions

The difference between the 'internal space' and the 'external spaces' of a Friday mosque like Cordoba's, in terms of usage and meaning, is often imprecise: courtyard and prayer hall, doors and thresholds, annex spaces and streets served as a venue for prayer, for reading the Qur'an, or for proclaiming the sovereign's authority. Both the facades, with their stone benches and sidewalks, and the vacant areas that surrounded the mosques partly shared its holiness, constituting a liturgical extension of the prayer hall. At the same time, these adjacent spaces and the adjoining structures could be considered not only mere transitional zones but also 'areas of respect', which secluded and enhanced the place of worship both physically, by separating the mosque from its urban surroundings, and metaphorically, by keeping it safe from any kind of pollution caused by everyday secular activities. The importance given to these 'respected' spaces adjoining the mosques is confirmed by the fact that Christian kings took measures to preserve them once the mosques had been converted into cathedrals. This is the reason why these environs in Cordoba and in Seville are still, at least in part, preserved.

At the same time, the walls and outer spaces of the Great Mosque of Cordoba proved an excellent location for propaganda, the ideal showcase for the ruling class to put forward their official, religious, and political messages to the public. It is probable that they would have served the same functions during the emirate of the eighth and ninth centuries, but few inscriptions documenting the early stages of the building are preserved. In contrast, a large part remains of the epigraphic programme of the tenth century, implemented both inside the prayer room and on the external walls. Thanks to these 'public texts',[71] and the fact that it is a freestanding monument, the Great Mosque of Cordoba became a basic emblem of the Umayyads of al-Andalus and the focal point of the capital, from a political and social point of view.

Ultimately, and to summarize, these liminal areas became relevant from several perspectives. First, in their spatial meaning, the Great Mosque of Cordoba and other urban mosques, as freestanding buildings surrounded by vacant areas, contradict the idea of dense and labyrinthine medieval Islamic cities, as described by western historiography in the past. Second, in their functional purposes these mosques were both liturgical spaces and urban areas, sharing in the everyday life of the city. And finally, they are relevant due to their ideological significance. As places for the dissemination of propaganda, mosques were closely linked to power and its public face.

Acknowledgements

This study is part of a project funded by the Spanish National I+D+i Plan (Research, Development and Innovation), HAR2013-45578-R.

Notes

* The diacritical marks for Arabic transliteration originally included in the article submitted in 2016, were later removed due to editorial requirements.

1 Seville's great mosques, although they are only partially preserved, are the only cases that could be comparable.
2 In Cordoba, Ibn al-ʿAbd al-Raʾuf (tenth century) wrote a treatise asking the 'secondary' muezzins to imitate the muezzin in the minaret. He stated that there should be muezzins in the souks and workshops, so that no one would forget to pray: 'Ibn al-ʿAbd al-Raʿuf, 'Traduction anotée et comentée des traités de hisba d' Ibn al-ʿAbd al-Raʿuf et de ʿUmar al-Garsifi', trans. Rachel Arié, *Hespéris-Tamuda* 1 (1960): 18–21; and Ibn al-ʿAbd al-Raʿūf, 'Risāla fī ādāb al-ḥisba wa-l-muḥtasib', in *Documents árabes inèdits sur la vie sociale et économique en Occident musulman au Moyen Age, Trois traités hispaniques de ḥisba (texte arabe)*, ed. Évariste Lévi-Provençal (Cairo: Publications de l'Institut français d'archeologie orientale du Caire, 1955), 70–76. The Seville *muhtasib*, Ibn ʿAbdun (thirteenth century) said that 'in the great mosque, there must be as many muezzins as doors, plus another two (one next to the imam and another in the courtyard… to let the faithful praying in the atriums repeat the *takbir* at the same time as the imam'. See Ibn ʿAbdūn, 'Risālah fī-l-qaḍāʾ wa-al-ḥisbah,' in *Documents inédits*, 21–23; and Ibn ʿAbdun, *Sevilla a comienzos del siglo XII: el tratado de Ibn ʿAbdun*, trans. Evariste Lévi-Provençal and Emilio García Gómez (Madrid: Monedo y Crédito, 1948), 82–83, 88.
3 Ibn ʿIdhari, *Al-Bayan al-Mugrib fi ajbar al-Andalus wa-l-Magrib*, 2 vols., ed. Reinhart Dozy (Beyrouth, 1948–51), 378. This ceremony of *iqama* was also held in Mecca. On the development of the call to prayer from the time of the Prophet, the way of doing it in Medina and Mecca, and the organisation of the muezzins (*muʾadhdhin*), see Johannes Pedersen, Rudolf Aernoud Kern, Ernst Diez, 'Masdjid', in *The Encyclopaedia of Islam,* 2nd ed. (Leiden: Brill, 1989), 663, 677; and Ian Keith Anderson Howard, 'The Development of the Adhan and Iqama of the Salat in Early Islam', *Journal of Semitic Studies* 26 (1981): 219–28. According to Ibn Abi Zayd al-Qayrawani, this second *adhan* was introduced by the Umayyad and was made in the same way as the first *adhan*, from the minaret; see Ibn Abi Zayd al-Qayrawani, *Risala fi-l-Fiqh, Compendio de derecho islámico,* trans. Jesús C. Riosalido (Madrid: Trotta, 1993), 83.
4 Susana Calvo Capilla, *Las Mezquitas de al-Andalus* (Almeria: Fundacion Ibn Tufayl, 2014), 175.
5 Calvo Capilla, *Las Mezquitas*, 240–48. A document from the mid-thirteenth century states that the mosque in Ceuta had a door of funerals (*bab al-janaʾiz*), where people took the coffins before nightfall, as well as a justice portal and another for teachers and students; see Halima Ferhat, 'Un nouveau document sur la grande mosque de Sabta au Moyen Age',

Hespéris-Tamuda 24 (1986): 11. According to Ibn 'Abdun, in the Great Mosque of Seville (the Umayyad Mosque, now under the church of El Salvador) there was a *mawdi' salat al-jana'iz* (a place for funeral prayers) in the *rihab* (parvis) and a door for the funeral prayers; see Ibn 'Abdun, 'Risalah fi-l-qada' wa-al-hisbah', in *Documents inédits arabes sur la vie sociale et économique en Occident musulman au Moyen Age: Trois traités hispaniques de hisba*, ed. Évariste Lévi-Provençal (Cairo: Publications de l'Institut français d'archeologie orientale du Caire, 1955), 32; and Ibn 'Abdun, *Sevilla*, 86–87.

6   Calvo Capilla, *Las Mezquitas*, 180–81. On women's religious practices, see Marion Holmes Katz, *Women in the Mosque* (Cairo: American University in Cairo, 2015).

7   This type of interpretation has been brought up for other Islamic monuments; see Oleg Grabar, *The Shape of the Holy: Early Islamic Jerusalem* (Princeton: Princeton University Press, 1996); Irene Bierman, 'The Art of Public Text: Medieval Islamic Rule', in *World Art: Themes of Unity in Diversity, Acts of the XXVI International Congress of the History of Art*, ed. Irving Lavin (Pennsylvania: Pennsylvania State University Press, 1989); Yasser Tabbaa, *The Transformation of Islamic Art during the Sunni Revival* (Seattle: University of Washington Press, 2001); Sheila Blair and Jonathan Bloom, 'Inscriptions in Art and Architecture', in *The Cambridge Companion to the Qur'an*, ed. Jane Dammen McAuliffe (Cambridge: Cambridge University Press, 2006); Dina M. H. Montasser, 'Modes of Utilizing Qur'anic Inscriptions on Cairene Mamluk Religious Monuments', in *Creswell Photographs Re-examined: New Perspectives on Islamic Architecture*, ed. Bernard O'Kane (Cairo: American University in Cairo Press, 2009); and Holly Edwards's general considerations in Holly Edwards, 'Text, Context, Architext: The Qur'an as Architectural Inscription', in *Brocade of the Pen: The Art of Islamic Writing*, ed. Carrol Garrett Fisher (East Lansing, Michigan: Kresge Art Museum, Michigan State University, 1991), 63–75.

8   *Tasliya* appears more frequently over the entrances on the eastern facade (at least three of these are preserved), as does verse 33:56. The *tasliya* also is seen in an inscription on the facade of the mihrab.

9   Ibn Baskuwal, *Kitab al-qurba ilà rabb al-'alamin, El acercamiento a Dios*, ed. and trans. Christina de la Puente (Madrid: Consejo Superior de Investigaciones científicas, 1995), 287; Arent Jan Wensinck, *A Handbook of Early Muhammadan Tradition: Alphabetically Arranged* (Leiden: E. J. Brill, 1927), 155; and Muslim ibn al-Hajjaj, *Sahih Muslim* (hadith collection), trans. Abdul Hameed Siddiqi (New Delhi: Islamic Book Service, 1984), 1:346 (nº 1538): 'Abu Usaid reported that the Messenger of Allah (may peace be upon him) said: When any one of you enters the mosque, he should say: "O Allah! open for me the doors of Thy mercy"; and when he steps out he should say: "O Allah! I beg of Thee Thy Grace."' A recent study of invocations on the Door of Perdon (Forgiveness) in the Almohad Great Mosque of Seville: Tom Nickson, '"Sovereignty belongs to God": Text, Ornament and Magic in Islamic and Christian Seville', *Art History* 38, no. 5 (2015): 838–61.

10 According to the chronicler Ibn Hayyan (eleventh century), in the spring of 974 (363), the chief judge of Cordoba ordered a proclamation to be read out at the doors of the great mosque, reminding the public of the 'situation of need and poverty' suffered by the poor and needy of the city, and thus asking for the obligation to the poor (*zakat*) not be forgotten. See Ibn Hayyan, *Muqtabis V*, ed. Pedro Chalmeta, Federico Corriente, and Mahmud Subh (Madrid: Instituto

Hispano-Árabe de Cultura, 1979), 149–50; and Ibn Hayyan, *Anales palatinos del califa de Córdoba al-Hakam II por Isa ibn Ahmad al-Razi (360–364H/971–975JC.)*, trans. E. García Gómez (Madrid: Sociedad de Estudios y Publicaciones, 1967), 189–90. For the second notice of the year 364/975, see Ibn Hayyan, *Al-Muqtabis fi ajbar balad al-Andalus (Muqtabis VII)*, ed. Abd al-Rahman Ali Hayyi (Beirut: Dar al-Taqafa, 1965), 233–34; and Ibn Hayyan, *Anales*, 275–76.

11 These were verses 40:3 and 40:12–14, 16–17. See Susana Calvo Capilla, 'Justicia, misericordia y cristianismo: una relectura de las inscripciones religiosas de la Mezquita de Córdoba en el siglo X', *Al-Qantara* 31, no. 1 (2010): 155–61 (see figure 1, gates 4 and 5, respectively).

12 Eschatological inscriptions from the Qur'an frequently are found on the portals of great mosques, including the Dome of the Rock in Jerusalem; see Grabar, *The Shape*, 63–68. This type of message is less common in the interior of the Great Mosque of Cordoba (Q. 41:30–32 on the facade of the *sabat*; Q. 3:4–8 and Q. 3:191–93 in the axial nave). On the other hand, divine reward and pity, as well as the resurrection of the body, were rejected by the heretical Masarri movement, as described in Miguel Asín Palacios, *Tres estudios sobre pensamiento y mística hispanomusulmanes* (Madrid: Hiperión, 1992), 120–25, 136–37; and Susana Calvo Capilla, 'El programa epigráfico de la Mezquita de Córdoba en el siglo X: Un alegato a favor de la doctrina malikí', *Qurtuba* 5 (2000): 23–24.

13 Q. 43:68–71, on portal 17, and Q. 3:191–92, on portal 14, respectively (see figure 1).

14 Q. 39:53–54 and Q. 14:52, on gate 16, and Q. 36:78–79, on gate 17, respectively. See T. O'Shaughnessy, *Muhammad's Thoughts on Death: A Thematic Study of the Quranic Data* (Leiden: Brill, 1969). Also see figure 1.

15 About the possibility that these inscriptions were not only apotropaic but also to be intoned aloud, see Edwards, 'Text, Context', 65; and Richard Ettinghausen, 'Arabic Epigraphy: Communication or Symbolic Affirmation', in *Near Eastern Numismatics, Iconography and History: Studies in Honor of George C. Miles*, ed. Dickran Kouymjian (Beirut: American University of Beirut, 1974), 309: 'there is considerable evidence that many Islamic inscriptions were not expected to be read in its literal sense but rather functioned in an imagistic or symbolic manner, affirming the belief of the patron as well as that of the viewer… The text would not necessarily be "read" in an academic sense but recalled and commented on orally.'

16 As we see in Ana Echevarría, *Almanzor: un califa en la sombra* (Madrid: Silex, 2011), 189–90.

17 Muhammad b. Masarra, considered to be the instigator of philosophical thought and mysticism in al-Andalus, followed the doctrine of free will (*qadarism*), spread in the east by the Mutalizites. The Mutalizites defended free will, or the capacity of humans to make choices, in opposition to religious determinism, which was the basic cornerstone of absolute power and the infallibility of the caliphs. Ibn Masarra's sect not only questioned the fundamental principles of the caliphate but also introduced an element of religious and social instability by breaking the community's doctrinal unity (*umma wahida*). The Mutalizites were accused of heresy and were persecuted by the religious authorities throughout the tenth century. See Maribel Fierro, *La heterodoxia en al-Andalus durante el período omeya* (Madrid: Instituto Hispano-Árabe de Cultura, 1987), 132–33; Calvo Capilla, 'El programa', 17–26; Dominique Sourdel, Ann Katharine Swynford Lambton, Frederick de Jong and Peter Malcolm Holt, "Khalifa", in *Encyclopaedia of Islam*, Second Edition, eds, Peri Bearman, Thierry Bianquis, Clifford Edmund Bosworth, Emeri Johannes van Donzel,

and Wolfhart Heinrichs (Leiden: Brill, 1978), 4:947–50; Nuha N. Khoury, 'The Meaning of the Great Mosque of Cordoba in the Tenth Century', *Muqarnas* 13 (1996): 84; Jan Van Ess, *Les prémices de la théologie musulmane* (Paris: Éditions Albin Michel, 2002), 101–12; and Susana Calvo Capilla, 'La ampliación califal de la Mezquita de Córdoba: Mensajes, formas y funciones', *Goya* 323 (2008): 89–106. Marín pointed out that *qadarism* arrived in al-Andalus in the ninth century. Since then, the defence of predestination was likely to have been part of the ideological programme of the Umayyad dynasty (the motto 'emir by divine will' was on 'Abd al-Rahman II's stamp), benefitting both the sovereigns and the intellectual elites who supported them. Manuela Marín, 'Una galería de retratos reales: los soberanos omeyas de al-Ándalus (siglos II/VIII–IV/X) en la cronística árabe', *Anuario de Estudios Medievales* 41, no. 1 (2011): 286–87; and Sarah Stroumsa, 'The Mu'tazila in al-Andalus: The Footprints of a Phantom', *Journal of Intellectual History of the Islamicate World* 2 (2014): 80–100.

18 Fierro, *La heterodoxia*, 161–70; and Echevarria, *Almanzor*, 212–13.

19 Janina M. Safran, 'The Politics of Book Burning in al-Andalus', *Journal of Medieval Iberian Studies* 6, no. 2 (2014): 152–54. All of the Arabic sources are cited in Calvo Capilla, 'Justicia', 160.

20 The reasons for the great mistrust that Christianity stirred in the jurists (*fuqaha*) and rulers were both theological, leading to controversial treatises condemning Christian dogma, and practical, due to the consequences it had in daily life. Years after the disturbances caused by the 'martyrs of Cordoba' had been quelled, at the end of the ninth century, many Christians in Cordoba still sought execution by disturbing public order. Cases of Muslims converting to Christianity and renouncing Islam were considered even more serious.

21 The rebellion led by 'Umar b. Hafsun, which held 'Abd al-Rahman III's authority in check until 928, was still recent when enlargement of the great mosque began. The heads of the ringleader and his sons were impaled on spikes and stayed for years before one of the palace doors, the waterwheel door (*bab al-sudda*). See Calvo Capilla, 'Justicia', 169–73.

22 Grabar, *The Shape*; and Oleg Grabar, *The Dome of the Rock* (Cambridge: Harvard University Press, 2006), 59–119 (where he used the expression 'talkative buildings'). Also on the inscriptions and their importance for the meaning and functions of the Dome of the Rock, see Marcus Milwright, *The Dome of the Rock and Its Umayyad Mosaic Inscriptions* (Edinburgh: Edinburgh University Press, 2016); and Gülru Necipoğlu, 'The Dome of the Rock as Palimpsest: "Abd al-Malik's Grand Narrative and Sultan Suleyman's Glosses"', *Muqarnas* 25 (2008): 17–105.

23 Calvo Capilla, 'El programa,' 165–78.

24 Yasser Tabbaa, 'The Transformation of Arabic Writing: Part 2, the Public Text', *Ars Orientalis* 24 (1994): 119–47; and Tabbaa, *The Transformation of Islamic Art*, 53–72.

25 Sebastián Herrero Romero, *Teoría y práctica de la restauración de la Mezquita-Catedral de Córdoba durante el siglo XX* (Madrid: E.T.S. Arquitectura, Universidad Politécnica de Madrid, 2015), 73.

26 The Holy Spirit (Espiritu Santo) and Palace (Postigo de Palacio) doors are the only entrances in the western wall to conserve fragments of original inscriptions. During the restoration of the San Ildefonso and Espiritu Santo doors, on this western facade, two new epigraphs

in Arabic were added in 1904. The two southern gates of the east facade were not restored. Calvo Capilla, 'El programa'.

27 For interesting remarks about the use of chrysography in Islamic epigraphy, see Alan George, 'Calligraphy, Colour and Light in the Blue Qur'an', *Journal of Qur'anic Studies* 11, no. 1 (2009): 95–125. In the arch of the St. Nicholas gate there are red traces on the inscription; see figure 1, gate 16.

28 This is a subject that has been treated for other examples and will be addressed here for the case of Cordoba.

29 Calvo Capilla, 'El programa', 180–81. Official discourses, such as this qadi's, continually refer to quotations from the Qur'an to argue any idea. See Linda G. Jones, *The Power of Oratory in the Medieval Muslim World* (Cambridge: Cambridge University Press, 2012). On the similarities among sermons, recitations, and inscriptions in using particular Qur'anic passages for political, ethical, or religious purposes in a public context, see Edwards, 'Text, Context', 67–70. There are also critical differences between their expressions, which are more dramatic and emotional in sermons and more devotional in recitations (*dhikr* and *du'a*).

30 The square, or atrium, of the Great Mosque of Cordoba appears, among others, in al-Maqqari, *Analectes sur l'histoire et la littérature des arabes d'Espagne par Almaccari (Nafh al-tib)*, partial edition by Reinhart Dozy (Leiden, 1855–61; Amsterdam, 1967), 1:365. For its presence in the local mosques, see al-Wansharisi, *Histoire et société en Occident musulman au Moyen Âge: Analyse du Miʿyar d'al-Wansarisi*, selected and trans. Vincent Lagardère (Madrid: Casa de Velázquez, 1995), 255 (nº 150). For Seville see Ibn Sahib al-Sala (d. after 1198), *Al-Mann bi-l-Imama*, ed. ʿAbd al-Hadi al-Tazi (Beirut: Dar al-Andalus, 1969), 474; and Ibn Sahib al-Salat, *Al-Mann bi-l-Imama, Bendiciones del imamnato (Historia del Imperio Almohade)*, trans. Ambrosio Huici Miranda (Valencia: Textos Medievales, 1987), 196 and 203.

31 Ibn Habib, ʿAbd al-Malik, *Kitab al-Wadiha (al-Wadiha fi al-sunan wa al-fiqh)*, ed. and trans. María Arcas Campoy (Madrid: Consejo Superior de Investigaciones científicas, 2002), 104.

32 Ibn Habib, *Kitab al-Wadiha*, 70. The Maliki jurists thought that the *fina'* belonged to the building it stood before, and so the owners could use the space as they saw fit, or build on it, provided it did not molest or harm the public. See Akel. I. Kahera and Omar Benmira, 'Damages in Islamic Law: Maghribi Muftis and the Built Environment (9th–15th Centuries C.E.)', *Islamic Law and Society* 5, no. 2 (1998): 148–50.

33 Several fatwas from tenth-century Cordoba respond to cases of this type: Al-Wansharisi/ Lagardère *Histoire*, 255–56 (nº 150, 153) and 346 (nº 239). The term *'sahat al-masjid'* is also used to designate the spaces around the Cordoba Mosque. See Ibn ʿIdhari, *Bayan*, 397; and Ibn ʿIdhari, *Histoire de l'Espagne Musulmane de la conquête au XIème siècle, Histoire de l'Afrique et de l'Espagne, intitulée Al-Bayano'l-Mogrib*, trans. Edmond Fagnan (Alger: P. Fontana & Cie, 1901–4), 2:240.

34 Ibn Hayyan, *Muqtabis V*, 259; Ibn Hayyan, *Crónica del Califa ʿAbderrahman III an-Nasir entre los años 912 and 942*, trans. María Jesús Viguera y Federico Corriente (Zaragoza: Anubar, 1981), 286–87; Ibn Hayyan, *Muqtabis VII*, 67, 70–71; and Ibn Hayyan, *Anales*, 89–90, 93.

35 Ibn Hayyan, *Muqtabis VII*, 233–34; and Ibn Hayyan, *Anales*, 275–76. Riots also took place there; see Ibn Hayyan, *Muqtabis VII*, 78; and Ibn Hayyan, *Anales*, 101, respectively.

36 Ibn ʿIdhari, *Bayan,* 234; and Ibn ʿIdhari, *Histoire,* 387.

37 Al-Maqqari, *Nafh,* 365.

38 For those of the Great Mosque of Cordoba, see Ibn al-ʿAbd al-Raʿuf, 'Risala fi adab al-hisba wa-l-muhtasib', in *Documents árabes inèdits sur la vie sociale et économique en Occident musulman au Moyen Age, Trois traités hispaniques de hisba (texte arabe),* ed. Lévi-Provençal (Cairo: I. F. A. O., 1955), 75; and Ibn al-ʿAbd al-Raʿuf, 'Traduction anotée', 21. For the *dakakin* of the Great Mosque of Seville, see Ibn ʿAbdun, *Risala,* 22; and Ibn ʿAbdun, *Sevilla,* 86–87.

39 Because [the vendors] 'think the mosques are shops', says Ibn al-ʿAbd Al-Raʿuf. See Ibn al-ʿAbd al-Raʿuf, *Risala,* 75–76; and Ibn al-ʿAbd al-Raʿuf, 'Traduction anotee', 21.

40 *Dukkan* is translated by Carole Hillenbrand in *The History of al-Tabari* as: 'a kind of wide bench, of stone or brick, generally built against a wall, upon which one sits'; according to Edward William Lane, *dukkan* is a shop in the market, a small booth raised over a platform or *mastabah.* See al-Tabari, *The History of al-Tabari, The Waning of the Umayyad Caliphate: Prelude to Revolution A.D. 738–745/A.H.121-127,* vol. 26, trans. Carole Hillenbrand (Albany: State Univ. of New York Press, 1989), 167; Edward William Lane, *Manners and Customs of the Modern Egyptians* (1860; Cairo: The American University in Cairo Press, 2014), 277; and Joseph Sadan, *Le mobilier au Proche-Orient médiéval* (Leiden: E.J. Brill, 1976), 123–24.

41 He resorted to doing so with the waqfs of other mosques, since those of the great mosque had been used. Ibn Rusd, *Fatawà,* ed. Ibn al-Táhir al-Talili, 3 vols. (Beirut: Dar al-Garb al-Islami, 1987), 1268, nº 419; Al-Wansharisi, *Al-Miʿyar al-muʿrib wa-l-jamiʿ al-mugrib ʿan fatawà ʿulamaʾ,* ed. Muhammad Hayyi (Rabat: Wizarat al-Awqaf wa-l-Suʾun al-Islamiyya, 1981), 7:465–66; and Ana María Carballeira Debasa, *Legados píos y fundaciones familiares en al-Andalus (Siglos IV/X–VI/XII)* (Madrid: CSIC, 2002), 94n74.

42 Ibn al-Abbar, *al-Takmila li-kitab al-sila: Diccionario biográfico,* 2 vols., ed. Francisco Codera (Madrid: Biblioteca Arábico-Hispánica IV–V, 1886), vol. 2, nº 197, 61: biography of Jalaf Allàh b. Yusuf b. Faraj al-Ansari of Cordoba.

43 The western angle of the Great Mosque of Damascus was called according to the name of those who frequented it in their ascetic practices. Daniella Talmon-Heller, *Islamic Piety in Medieval Syria: Mosques, Cemeteries and Sermons under the Zanguids and Ayyubids (1146–1260)* (Leiden and Boston: Brill, 2007), 78.

44 Al-Wansharisi, *Al-Miʿyar al-muʿrib,* 9:49–50. *Fatwa* issued by Abu al-Mutarrif al-Saʿbi (from al-Andalus, date uncertain).

45 Al-Wansharisi/Lagardère, *Al-Miʿyar al-muʿrib,* 256, nº 153.

46 Calvo Capilla, *Las Mezquitas,* 204, 570, 576–77.

47 Abu Bakr al-Turtusi, *Kitab al-hawadit wa-l-bidà, El Libro de las novedades y las innovaciones,* ed. and trans. María Isabel Fierro (Madrid: Consejo Superior de Investigaciones científicas, 1993), 309. In Damascus, the Umayyad Mosque built by al-Walid between 705 and 715 had an open space to the south of the qibla, bounded by a street with porticoes. The portico was used by the caliph to enter the mosque (through the qibla) from his palace, the Qubbat al-Jadraʾ (The Green Dome); see Finbarr Barry Flood, *The Great Mosque of Damascus* (Leiden: Brill, 2001), 139–58.

48 In the *ziyada,* next to the entrances, rooms and ablution fountains alternated with garden areas and other structures of unknown use. The section of the *ziyada* behind the qibla

wall was filled by rooms apparently reserved for the caliph, from where he could enter the *maqsura* through an open door next to the mihrab. Thomas Leisten, *Excavation of Samarra I. Architecture: Final Report of the First Campaign 1910–1912*, Bagdader Forschungen 20 (Mainz am Rhein: Philipp von Zabern, 2003), 51–55. Sources state that in Cairo there was a *mawdiʻ wasi,ʻ* or wide, open space with no permanent buildings, next to many of the great mosques, and the ʻAmr Mosque has several *rahba*s added between the eighth and ninth centuries. On the other hand, the ninth-century Ibn Tulun Mosque in the same city had a true *ziyada*, similar to those in Iraq and filled with ponds and various facilities. Bernard O'Kane, 'The *Ziyada* of the Mosque of al-Hakim and the Development of the *Ziyada* in Islamic Architecture', in *L'Egypte fatimide: son art et son histoire*, ed. Marianne Barrucand (Paris: Presses universitaires de Paris-Sorbonne, 1999), 152–53.

49   María Isabel Calero Secall and Virgilio Martínez Enamorado, *Málaga, ciudad de al-Andalus* (Málaga: Ágora, 1995), 208–9.

50   In Toledo, in the mosque converted to the church of El Salvador following conquest by the Christians, a wall has been excavated outside the southeast side (qibla), which may have been for this use. Calvo Capilla, *Las mezquitas*, 438–41.

51   Ibn ʻIdhari, *Bayan*, 2:240; and Ibn ʻIdhari, *Histoire*, 396–97.

52   Alberto J. Montejo Córdoba, 'El pabellón de abluciones oriental de la mezquita de Córdoba correspondiente a la ampliación de Almanzor', *Cuadernos de Madinat al-Zahra* 4 (1999): 209–31; and Rafael Pinilla Melguizo, 'Notas sobre las referencias textuales al pabellón de abluciones de Almanzor hallado recientemente en la mezquita de Córdoba', *Qurtuba* 3 (1998): 248–51.

53   It is unknown when the door was opened: before or after the extension to the prayer hall, ordered by the emir and inaugurated in 848. Neither is it known whether there were any doors in the east facade after the extension, as this section was below the sixteenth-century cathedral, and it is unlikely that there are any remains in the subsoil.

54   The ashlars of the platform, between the buttresses, were used in part by al-Mansur's architects as foundations for the naves added. P. Marfil Ruiz, 'Avance de resultados del estudio arqueológico de la fachada este del oratorio de ʻAbd al-Rahman I en la Mezquita de Córdoba', *Cuadernos de Madinat al-Zahra* 4 (1999): 175–207.

55   Antonio Fernández Puertas, *Mezquita de Córdoba: Su estudio arqueológico* (Córdoba: Editorial Universidad de Córdoba, 2015), 17–18, 84–98.

56   Pedro Marfil Ruiz, 'Las puertas de la Mezquita de Córdoba durante el Emirato Omeya' (Ph.D. diss., Universidad de Córdoba, 2010), 1:245–61.

57   Fernández Puertas, *Mezquita*, 108–12.

58   Don Juan Manuel (1282–1348), *El Conde Lucanor* (Madrid, 1988, chapter 41): 'This is the largest and most excellent and noblest mosque of the Moors in Spain, and, praise God!, now it is a church and it's called Saint Mary of Cordova, and it was offered by the holy king Ferdinand to Saint Mary when he captured Cordova from the Moors'. In this tale, the author recalls the extension *(añadimiento)* of al-Hakam II *(ziyadat al-hakam)*.

59   Alfonso X, *Primera Crónica General*, 734; and Manuel Nieto Cumplido, *Historia de la Iglesia de Córdoba: Reconquista y Restauración (1146–1326)* (Córdoba: Publicaciones del Monte de Piedad y Caja de Ahorros de Córdoba, 1991), 143.

60 'a honrra della é á gran postura de la villa.' Real Academia de la Historia, 'Documentos de Alfonso X el Sabio', in *Memorial Histórico Español, Colección de Documentos, Opúsculos y Antigüedades*, vol. 2 (Madrid: Real Academia de la Historia, 1851), n° 45–48 (n° 189). English version in Heather Ecker, 'The Great Mosque of Córdoba in the Twelfth and Thirteenth Centuries', *Muqarnas* 20 (2003): 113–41 (124; Doc. P); M. Nieto Cumplido, *Corpus mediaevale cordubense* (Córdoba: Publicaciones del Monte de Piedad y Caja de Ahorros de Córdoba, 1979–80), 2:n° 548, n° 624, n° 617; and Susana Calvo Capilla, 'Les alentours de la Mosquée de Cordoue avant et après la conquête chrétienne', *Al-Masaq: Islam and the Medieval Mediterranean* 15, no. 2 (2003): 101–17.

61 '[lo] que se desfaze es de calidad que no se podra volver a fazer en la bondad e pefiçion questa fecha.' Miguel A. Orti, 'Oposición del Cabildo municipal de Córdoba a la construcción del crucero de la Mezquita', *Boletín de la Real Academia de Córdoba* 71 (1954): 273–74.

62 'atendiendo al mayor decoro de su iglesia.' Alfonso Jiménez Martín, 'Las fechas de las formas. Selección crítica de fuentes documentales para la cronología del edificio medieval', in *La catedral gótica de Sevilla: Fundación y fábrica de la obra nueva*, ed. Alfonso Jiménez Martín, Antonio Collantes de Terán, Juan Carlos Rodríguez et al. (Seville: Secretariado de Publicaciones de la Universidad, 2007), 40. The item is taken from Ortiz de Zúñiga (1677). Concerning the 'steps' of Seville cathedral, mentioned by Miguel de Cervantes in one of his exemplary novels, *Rinconete y Cortadillo*, also see Alfonso Jiménez Martín, 'Restauración de dos fachadas de la Catedral de Sevilla (2006–2013)', in *XX edición del Avla Hernan Rviz. La Catedral entre 1434 y 1517: Historia y conservación* (Seville: Avla Hernan Rviz, 2013), 79–121. Some of the shops adjoining the cathedral were donated to the chapter by Alfonso X in 1254; see Manuel González Jiménez, ed., *Diplomatario andaluz de Alfonso X* (Sevilla: El Monte, Caja de Huelva y Sevilla, 1991), 154, doc. 143.

63 Document studied by Gestoso Perez in 1890, apud Jiménez Martín, 'Las fechas', 123; and Jiménez Martín, 'Restauración', 92. After the Lisbon earthquake in 1762, the chapter pulled down some of the medieval structures still adjoining the cathedral. Antonio Almagro, 'De mezquita a catedral. Una adaptación imposible', in *La piedra postrera: V centenario de la conclusión de la Catedral de Sevilla*, ed. Alfonso Jiménez (Sevilla: Sevilla Tvrris Fortissima, 2007), 9–45.

64 Rodrigo Ximenez de Rada, *Roderici Toletani antistitis opera* (Valencia: Anubar, 1968), 206. The *General Historia*, written at the time of Alfonso X, said that the mosque of Cordoba 'sobraua et vençie de afeyto et de grandez a todas las otras mezquitas de los alauares'. Alfonso X, *Primera Crónica General*, 734.

65 Manuel Nieto Cumplido, *La Catedral de Córdoba* (Córdoba: CajaSur, 1998), 153–54, 263.

66 Guadalupe Pizarro Berengena, 'Los Pasadizos Elevados entre la Mezquita y el Alcázar Omeya de Córdoba. Estudio arqueológico de los *sabatat*', *Archivo Español de Arqueología* 86 (2013): 233–49; and Calvo Capilla, 'Les alentours'. The *sabat* built during the caliphate period at the southern end of the west facade stood until the seventeenth century. Whether it was used by the bishops to enter the cathedral is unknown.

67 Ambrosio de Morales (m. 1591), who saw the qibla prior to Cardinal Salazar's reforms between 1738 and 1742, said that there was a marble slab with epigraphy in the area of the

mihrab projection. Ambrosio de Morales, 'Córdoba,' *Las Antigüedades de las ciudades de España* (Madrid, 1792), vol. X, chap. 39, 53.

68 Herrero Romero, *Teoría y práctica*, 69–78. The author has studied projects by Velázquez Bosco. See also Gabriel Ruiz Cabrero, 'La Mezquita-Catedral de Córdoba. Dieciséis proyectos de Velázquez Bosco', *Arquitectura* (Madrid, COAM) 256 (1985): 47–56; and Miguel Ángel Baldellou Santolaria, *Ricardo Velázquez Bosco*: [catálogo de la exposición]: diciembre 1990–febrero 1991 (Madrid: Ministerio de Cultura, 1990).

69 On the west facade, there was even a toilet built under the renewed platform. Many old photographs show the state of preservation of the facades and platforms in the second half of the nineteenth century: Herrero Romero, *Teoría y práctica*; and Marfil Ruiz, *Las puertas*, 'Fotografía historica de las puertas emirales de la mezquita,' 305–45.

70 Herrero Romero, *Teoría y práctica*, 250, 306–12.

71 Bierman, 'The Art,' 283–90; Tabbaa, 'The Transformation'; and Tabbaa, *The Transformation of Islamic*, 53–72.

Lahore's Badshahi Masjid: Spatial Interactions of the Sacred and the Secular

Mehreen Chida-Razvi

Introduction

In South Asia, where Muslim dynasties ruled over much of the region from 1206, when the Delhi Sultanate was established, until 1858, when the Mughal dynasty came to an abrupt end, the construction of *jami' masjids* took on great political and religious symbolic importance.[1] This importance stemmed from the fact that, during the entire period of Muslim rule in South Asia, those in power were a religious minority ruling over a non-Muslim majority population. As the ruling elite, the various sultanates of South Asia constructed Friday mosques throughout the cities they controlled, and while these structures had a religious function, they also very clearly proclaimed the might and power of their patrons.

Interestingly, when the Mughals (r.1526–1858), the most dominant of these Muslim dynasties, came to power, they were unique in just how little the emperors emphasized the construction of Friday mosques. Architecture of religion, power, and prestige was certainly a priority for the early Mughal rulers but did not include the construction of a *jami' masjid* until 1568, forty-two years after the founding of the empire. Instead, it seems that they were content to utilize those built by their Sultanate predecessors, even in their own capital cities. The Mughal court was peripatetic, and until 1648 four cities shared the title of 'imperial capital': Delhi, Agra, Lahore, and Fatehpur Sikri.[2] Of these four, the first to have an imperially commissioned Friday mosque was Fatehpur Sikri, where the third emperor, Akbar (r.1556–1605), constructed a grand *jami' masjid* in his new, purpose-built capital. Constructed between 1571 and 1574,[3] this was the first imperial *jami' masjid* of the Mughals. This act was not repeated until the reign of his grandson, Shah Jahan (r.1628–58), who ordered the construction of large imperial congregational mosques in Agra (1648) and Delhi (1650–56).

Lahore, on the other hand, did not receive such attention until the sixth emperor, Aurangzeb 'Alamgir (r.1658–1707), ordered the construction of the Badshahi Masjid [Figure 1].[4] Completed in 1674 and described as the most impressive building of 'Alamgir's reign,[5] this was the last of the great city *jami' masjids* constructed by the Mughals, despite the continued existence of the empire until 1858. While no longer designated as an imperial capital city when construction on the Badshahi Masjid began, Lahore retained great importance in the Mughal Empire due to its location and its position as a provincial capital. With a capacity of more than 60,000 people, this mosque was to remain the largest Muslim congregational space in South Asia until 1986, when the Faisal Mosque in Islamabad was completed.

Prior to the construction of the Badshahi Masjid, two other Mughal mosques had sequentially served as Lahore's congregational prayer space. The first was the Begum Shahi

Figure 1: The Badshahi Masjid, 1674. Photograph by the author.

Masjid, built by the mother of Emperor Jahangir (*r.*1605–27), Maryam Zamani, between 1611 and 1614. Her mosque was utilized in this capacity until it was replaced – in 1634–35, during the reign of Shah Jahan – by the larger, grander Mosque of Wazir Khan. The respective areas of these two mosques were much smaller than that of the Badshahi Masjid, whose courtyard measures 530 square feet (172 square metres). Their courtyards measure 128 feet by 82 feet (Begum Shahi Masjid) and 160 feet by 130 feet (Mosque of Wazir Khan).[6]

With the construction of the Badshahi Masjid, Lahore now had a large-scale, imperially patronized congregational mosque for the use of the Muslim population. During the period of Mughal control, there was never a question as to the functional use of the religious space or its surrounds. However, the declining political power of the emperor in Delhi, and the tumultuous political situation within the Punjab, meant that Lahore remained a Mughal city only until 1748, when it was captured by the Afghans. It was then taken by the Sikhs in 1758, becoming the capital of the Sikh Kingdom from 1801 until 1848, when the British deposed the last Sikh ruler, Dalip Singh, and took control of the city. Because Lahore was successively under the control of the Mughals, the Sikhs, and the British, the functional role of 'Alamgir's great *jami' masjid* fluctuated depending on who ruled the city, a result of the changing fortunes and religious affiliations of the city's political elite.

During each of these eras, the mosque and the eastern enclosure immediately adjacent to it – together referred to in this paper as the Badshahi Complex – were politicized, militarized, or both. But what of the intrinsic purpose of the mosque as a religious space during these periods? Whereas one assumes that a Friday mosque would continually occupy the role for which it was created – as a site for the Muslim community's religious practice and communal gatherings – the history of the urban context and of the functionality of the Badshahi

Complex reveals that this basic assumption can be called into question. What happened, for example, when purposeful actions were taken to disallow the use of the congregational mosque for worship and collective meeting? Or when this incredibly important symbolic space was removed from the population for which it was intended? Examining the spatial context of the Badshahi Complex during the Mughal, Sikh, and British eras, this paper will examine how the space was adapted, and its functionality altered, according to the political state of the city. It will demonstrate that the notion of sacrality in relation to the mosque became fluid, shifting according to the political ruling class of Lahore, and that the location of the Badshahi Complex, adjacent to the political heart of the city, further complicated the use of the space, completely blurring the lines between the sacred and the secular.

The Construction of the Badshahi Complex and Its Use in the Mughal Era

The great Badshahi Masjid was situated just to the west of the Shahi Qila (the Royal Fort), the political centre of the city [Figure 2], within the Walled City of Mughal Lahore. As the mosque had to be oriented toward qibla (i.e., toward the city of Mecca), which is to the west in South Asia, the prayer hall was constructed in the middle of the western wall of a large quadrangle which served as the mosque courtyard, with an impressive entrance gate

Figure 2: Satellite view of the Badshahi Masjid, Hazuri Bagh, and Shahi Qila, Lahore. Courtesy of Google Earth.

constructed directly opposite it in the eastern wall. Outside was another enclosed quadrangle which spanned the length between religious and royal complexes.

The masjid was constructed on a raised platform and thus was elevated from its surroundings, requiring visitors to climb a flight of 22 steps to reach the entrance gate. Once one passed through it and was within the mosque courtyard, the original ablutions fountain was visible at its centre while the prayer hall was at the opposite end, to the west [Figure 3].[7] *Chattri*-topped turrets rise from the four corners of the prayer hall itself, echoing the four extremely tall minarets that rise to a height of 54 metres from the corners of the mosque's enclosure walls.

At the same time as the mosque was constructed, the Alamgiri Gate of the Shahi Qila [Figure 4] was built directly opposite the entrance gate into the mosque compound [Figure 5]. The intervening space between these two gateways was created as an open, walled-in courtyard, with two smaller gateways built into the north and south walls. According to Latif, this space was referred to as the Aurangzeb Sarai;[8] while this is likely a later, anachronistic name given to the space, it will be referred to here with the same name when discussing this courtyard as it existed in the Mughal era. Jalal describes the *sarai* as it was first constructed as merely a 'walkway from the citadel to the mosque with *Sarai*'s on its northern side', referring to cells built into the northern wall that served as living quarters for guards.[9] This entire

Figure 3: The interior courtyard and prayer hall of the Badshahi Masjid, Lahore, 1674. Photograph by the author.

Figure 4: *Alamgiri Gate*, Lahore, 1673. Photograph by the author.

Figure 5: Satellite view of the Hazuri Bagh, with the entrance gate to the Badshahi Masjid opposite the Alamgiri Gate, Lahore. Courtesy of Google Earth.

spatial composition – from the Alamgiri Gate of the Fort in the east to the prayer hall of the Badshahi Masjid in the west – was clearly constructed as a single spatial unit, conceived as a symmetrical space centrally aligned along an east–west axis.[10]

The two entrance gates of this unit, the Alamgiri Gate and the entrance gate into the mosque courtyard, must have been intended to echo each other across the Aurangzeb Sarai, creating a strong and purposeful link between the newly constructed religious centre of Mughal Lahore and its political heart, the Shahi Qila. The *sarai* was therefore an inherently transitional space between these two centres of the city, blurring the lines between its secular and spiritual nuclei; this quality was exemplified both literally and figuratively by the two grand gateways of the fort and the masjid facing each other from opposite sides of the space. As highlighted by Suvorova, in a discussion of the topography of cities, gateways are inherently transitional spaces.[11] In this instance, however, it was the Aurangzeb Sarai that was the space of liminality between the religious and political centres of 'Alamgir's Lahore, while the gateways into each space signified one's stark physical arrival to and departure from these centres. As will be seen, this merging of political and religious space in the Badshahi Complex is something which has endured throughout its history, from the time of its construction until British control of the Punjab came to an end.

The masjid was completed in 1674; while 'Alamgir ordered its construction, the work was supervised and overseen by Fidai Khan Koka, 'Alamgir's foster brother, who was made governor of Lahore in order to oversee the building of the new Friday mosque.[12] The dates of construction and the fact that Koka was the supervisor of the work is known through one of the two inscriptions found on the entrance gate into the mosque courtyard – the other one being the *shahada*,[13] the Muslim profession of faith. Additionally, the *firman*, or royal decree, giving the directive to construct the mosque specified the following: that the location was to be the imperial capital of the province of Lahore, that the construction was by royal command, that thirty lakh rupees be given from the imperial treasury for the construction, and that the space be completed as soon as possible.[14]

The placement of the Badshahi Masjid made it distinctive in comparison to the other imperial Mughal *jami' masjids* in Fatehpur Sikri, Delhi, and Agra as it was constructed on the edge of the city rather than further within its confines. The precedent for the construction of imperial *jami' masjids*, established by Akbar with his patronage of the great religious complex at Fatehpur Sikri, and continued under Shah Jahan in the building of the *jami' masjids* in Delhi and Agra, was that the mosque be constructed in close proximity to the city's *qila*. Due to the existing topography of Lahore, keeping to this precedent meant that there were very few options for a space large enough to build the type of complex intended. The Shahi Qila, in relation to the rest of the Mughal Walled City of Lahore, was located at its northern extreme, directly on the banks of the Ravi River, which served as a natural boundary between the city and the surrounding country. This meant that for the masjid to be constructed in close proximity to the *qila* but remain within the city walls, options were limited to areas west, east, and south of the fort.

The Walled City, as constructed by 'Alamgir's great-grandfather, Akbar, took the shape of an irregular pentagon, with the Ravi River flowing against the northern walls of the Shahi Qila. Within the Walled City was a defined network of spaces and, by the end of Akbar's reign in 1605, the city had been divided into nine *guzars* (quarters), each of which was extremely dense as a result of its own urban development.[15] Such urban topography and layout meant that by the time of 'Alamgir's reign, large plots of land close to the *qila* were very few and far between. While the Italian traveller Niccolao Manucci reported that the site ultimately chosen for the construction of the masjid was that of Dara Shikoh's grand *haveli*, and that 'Alamgir destroyed it to make way for the mosque's construction,[16] his statement is not corroborated by other sources. Other interpretations include that when Aurangzeb confiscated Dara's holdings in Lahore, the proceeds of those holdings went toward the construction of the Badshahi Masjid,[17] or that the stones used for the mosque's construction were previously gathered by Dara Shikoh for his planned construction of a mausoleum for Mian Mir, his spiritual guide.[18]

However the Badshahi Masjid came to be located, its placement meant that it was constructed along the northwestern edge of the Walled City, immediately west of the Shahi Qila; thus, the mosque's northern and western enclosure walls merged with and became part of the city's own fortification walls.[19] Jalal calls attention to this unique aspect of the mosque's placement but finds an explanation in calling it a 'strategic blunder' due to the later uses to which the mosque compound was put as a result of its strategic position adjacent to the fort.[20] This explanation, however, can be offered only in hindsight once the history of the structure in the years between its construction and the modern era is known. When it was built, there was ample reason and justification for the mosque to be constructed where it was.

As today, when it was constructed the mosque was accessible only through its single entrance gate facing the fort; in order to access it, one first had to enter the Aurangzeb Sarai. The proximity of the Badshahi Masjid to the Shahi Qila was minimal, encompassing only the enclosed *sarai* between them. As emphasized above, this *sarai* was clearly utilized as a transitionary space when the mosque complex and the Alamgiri Gate were constructed, as it was the means through which one traversed between the political heart of Lahore to the new religious centre. Despite the extremely short distance, there was much pomp attached to the movement of the emperor when he attended prayers at the mosque. Latif writes that during the Mughal period it was

> thronged by the imperial cavalcade and vast bodies of armed retainers, who formed the king's procession, as the grand Seignior went to offer his prayers at the Royal Chapel, preceded by a cortege of mace-bearers, and followed by his omerahs, grandees and nobles ... From the King's apartments to the gate of the fortress a lane of several hundred soldiers formed, and through it His Majesty passed with all the pomp of an eastern sovereign.[21]

Additionally, the walkway needed to be continuously watered down because of the heat and dust.[22] A contemporary account of 'Alamgir's visits to the masjid is given by Jean-Baptiste Tavernier, whose 1676 account of his time in the Mughal Empire states:

When the Emperor goes to the mosque in his pallankeen one of his sons follows on horseback, and all the Princes and officers of the household on foot. Those who are Musalmans wait for him upon the top of the steps to the mosque, and when he comes out they precede him to the gate of the palace. Eight elephants march in front of him, four carrying two men each, one to guide the elephant, and the other seated on its back, bearing a standard attached to a hand pile. Each of the four other elephants carries a seat or kind of throne on its back, one of which is square, another round, one covered, and another closed with glass of many kinds.[23]

What is seen is that from the time of its construction, during the Mughal era of Lahore, the Badshahi Masjid and its wider surrounds were utilized for the purposes for which the spaces were constructed. The mosque compound was used for religious practice by the Muslim population of the city while the *sarai* served as a transitory space between the fort and the masjid. At the same time, the *sarai* was reflective of the liminality between the two areas, serving as a stage for the political performance of the great ceremonial processions that took place each time the emperor traversed it. In addition, the *sarai* was the threshold between the Walled City and the masjid, as the entrance gate to the latter was only accessible once the Aurangzeb Sarai had already been entered.

The Badshahi Complex in the Sikh Period[24]

When Lahore came under the control of the Sikhs, the use of the masjid and its surrounding spaces began to shift. The stability of the city had been challenged by the Sikh tribes after the death of the Mughal emperor Bahadur Shah in 1712, but their revolts were brutally put down and large numbers of their survivors retreated into the Punjab Hills. The period that followed was tumultuous for Lahore, with the raiding of the Punjab by Nadir Shah in 1738 and the series of invasions by Ahmad Shah Durrani between 1748 and 1756, during which time he captured Lahore and claimed it as part of his Afghan kingdom, subject to the government in Kabul. At the end of his 1756 campaign, Durrani left his son, Timur Shah, as the governor of Lahore province, and the latter undertook punitive missions against the Sikhs, who all the while had been carrying out raids throughout the Punjab. Timur Shah's retaliation culminated in the sacking of Amritsar and extensive damage to the Sikh holy sites there. The Sikhs fought back under the leadership of Jassa Singh and captured Lahore for the first time in 1757; they were driven out again, however, by the Marathas in 1758. The Sikhs again captured the city in 1764, at which time the Sikh Triumvirate of Gujar Singh, Lana Singh, and Sobha Singh was established, who together ruled Lahore. The era of Sikh rule that is most important to this study, however, is that of Ranjit Singh, who established control of Lahore in 1799 before being proclaimed Maharaja of the Sikh Kingdom in 1801.

As the political supremacy of the Sikhs became absolute, religious spaces were taken away from Muslims throughout the Sikh kingdom. Religious services could no longer be held within these spaces, and in some instances the sites were taken over for other uses; this was the fate of the Badshahi Masjid. While Chaghtai writes that it was around 1762 that the masjid began to be used by the Sikhs for military purposes,[25] Lafont states that it was in 1764 that the Sikh Triumvirate, recognizing the strategic placement of the mosque, turned it into a military building.[26] This was one of several Muslim monuments that were considered important both strategically, due to their location, and symbolically, because of their prestigious and symbolic nature; they were therefore appropriated by the Triumvirate for the Sikh state.[27] However, Ranjit Singh was responsible for the continued denial of the Badshahi Masjid and other religious spaces to the Muslim community. One such example given by William Moorcroft was the Great Mosque in Srinagar, which Ranjit Singh ordered to be shut so that large groups of Muslims could not assemble there and plot against him.[28]

The Badshahi Masjid was never overtly politicized during the Mughal era; this changed under Sikh rule. This shift is clear in Sohan Lal Suri's *Umdat-ul-Tawarikh*, a court history of Ranjit Singh, which states that before the maharaja ordered the mosque transformed into a storage site for powder and horse stables, he liked to hold court there.[29] The fact that political audiences and ceremonial activities were held within the masjid is indicative of just how far removed from its original purpose as a space of worship the mosque had become. By turning the Badshahi Masjid into a political and military space, Ranjit Singh negated the idea of liminality between the religious and political centres of Lahore, intended with the Mughal construction of the Badshahi complex.

Moorcroft was among those at Ranjit Singh's court who corroborated the uses to which the space was now put:

> The great square and buildings of the principle mosque have been converted into a place of exercise for his Sipahi infantry, and he has stripped the dome of the mausoleum of Asaf Jah, the brother of Nurjehan Begum, of its white marbles, to apply them to the erection of some insignificant apartments in the garden-court of the mosque.[30]

Another was Baron Charles Hugel, who said that Ranjit Singh 'has turned it to the best advantage, the north side of this strong building being made a portion of the city wall, and the mosque itself converted in to a barrack'.[31] In addition to the masjid's use as a site for military storage, stables for the cavalry horses, and barracks for soldiers, parts of it were also utilized as storage for powder magazines.[32]

Another way through which the use and spatial interactions of the wider complex of the Badshahi Masjid were altered at this time was the transformation of the Aurangzeb Sarai. The *sarai* retained its Mughal character and makeup until 1818, when Ranjit Singh constructed a formal garden in the middle of the space, which he renamed the Hazuri Bagh [see Figure 5].[33] At the same time, he ordered the construction of a three-story marble *baradari* in the centre of his new garden, two levels of which were above ground and one of which was subterranean. Today it stands as a single-story pavilion [Figure 6] with its subterranean chamber, the top story having been completely removed after it collapsed on July 19, 1932. The placement of this *baradari* meant that it was located directly between the entrance gate to the masjid and the Alamgiri Gate of the fort. With this construction and the transformation of the *sarai* into the Hazuri Bagh, the *sarai* shifted from being a transitional, performative space between the fort and the mosque, through which the ruler's procession would pass as he navigated between the political and religious centres of Mughal Lahore, to a place of ceremonial activity and courtly scenes. After it was built, the *baradari* served as a site for pleasure and courtly business for Ranjit Singh, where he would be joined by courtiers and soldiers; citizens were able to enter the Hazuri Bagh to watch the maharaja carry out affairs of state.[34] 'Hazuri Bagh' translates as 'Garden of Reception', and in essence the space was treated by Ranjit Singh and his successors as an extension of the fort, which was the usual site for the events now taking place in a more public arena.

No longer a place of transition, the Hazuri Bagh became a site for stationary events that emphasized the Sikh character of the space and the political supremacy of Sikh rule over Lahore and the Punjab. For example, it is written in the *Umdat-ut-Tawarikh* that on Ranjit Singh's return to Lahore on July 20, 1831, the first thing he did after entering the city gates

Figure 6: Ranjit Singh's Baradari, Hazuri Bagh, Lahore, 1818. Photograph by the author.

was seat himself in his pavilion in the Hazuri Bagh. While there, he received gifts and the presentation of various vakeels; he then welcomed the 'Captain Sahib' (Lieutenant-Colonel C. M. Wade) there rather than within the formal audience halls of the fort.[35] It therefore seems that there was a clear preference for holding such activities, presentations, and greetings in the more public space of the Hazuri Bagh rather than within the private setting of the fort. This preference is further indicated by the fact that six days later, Ranjit Singh again went to the Hazuri Bagh to receive a group of Englishmen in the *baradari* before taking them into the fort.[36]

Under Maharaja Ranjit Singh, we thus see that a complete transformation of the spatial unit comprised of the Badshahi Masjid, (now) Hazuri Bagh, and Alamgiri Gate took place. The liminal space of the Mughal Aurangzeb Sarai, existing between the political and religious centres of the city, was no longer present. Rather, the Badshahi Complex now served political functions; it can therefore be said that both the Hazuri Bagh and the masjid became extensions of the fort under Ranjit Singh. For the former this was due to the ceremonial activities and receptions which took place there, rather than in the pavilions created for such use within the fort; for the latter, the maharaja essentially viewed the masjid as an extended space of the fort – for the storage of military goods and equipment, as well as for living quarters for his soldiers and cavalry.

After the death of Ranjit Singh in June 1839, these spaces continued to be the site of political acts and provocation, and in fact they became sites for military engagements as well. Ranjit Singh had chosen his eldest son, Kharak Singh, as his successor; however, the latter was not equipped to rule, and the next several years saw internal fighting for the throne between different Sikh factions. During some of these struggles, the functionality of Badshahi Masjid and the Hazuri Bagh became more militarized, again due to the strategic location and proximity of these spaces to the fort. For example, in 1841, when Sher Singh, Ranjit Singh's second son, besieged the fort with approximately 30,000 troops to remove from power Kharak Singh's widow, Maharani Chand Kaur, his matchlock men occupied the tops of the masjid's minarets.[37] Shortly thereafter, further attacks on the fort were carried out with light guns mounted on the minarets.[38] As mentioned earlier, these towers reached a height of 54 metres and so gave an incredible advantage to the besiegers, who were able to strike above the walls and battlements of the fort. Furthermore, because the chattris surmounting the minarets had been weakened during an earthquake in 1840 and had been removed,[39] when Sher Singh placed his men atop the minarets their view and aim were not encumbered by the columns and domes of the chattris. The clear advantage that he had through his control of these spaces – which gave his soldiers the ability to fire directly down into the fort from the minarets of the mosque – indicates the strategic importance of the site. This importance was emphasized by Hira Singh's later utilization of the minarets when he too besieged the fort after the murders of Sher Singh and Dhian Singh, his uncle, in 1843. At that time, he placed light guns atop the minarets and wreaked havoc upon the opposing side, which controlled the fort, becoming the victor in this military engagement.

These individuals also used the Hazuri Bagh for political purposes during these tumultuous times. When Sher Singh was battling with the maharani for the Sikh throne and besieging the fort, he occupied the Hazuri Bagh, where he sat enthroned within the *baradari* and received those who came to swear their allegiance to him.[40] Once he officially occupied the Sikh throne, he, like Ranjit Singh before him, used the marble pavilion as a site for ceremonial and courtly activity. We see, then, the continued use of the Hazuri Bagh during the Sikh period as a political space, as an extension of the palatial–administrative fort space, rather than as a lead-in space to the religious complex or a transitional space between the two. The same thing occurred during Hira Singh's siege; he established his headquarters in the Hazuri Bagh pavilion, which was where the heads of the assassins who killed his uncle were laid at his feet after their capture and execution.[41]

The British Era and the Badshahi Complex

Sikh rule of Lahore came to an end after a lengthy period of uncertainty and internal fighting, culminating in the British officially annexing the city in March 1848. When this occurred, the Badshahi Masjid continued to be denied to the Muslim population for a period of time, due to the ongoing political turmoil and the continued recognition of its strategic location. The British retained the mosque as a military store, keeping powder magazines and creating a silkworm establishment on the mosque grounds.[42] Nevertheless, in December 1849, soon after the British annexation of the Punjab, the Muslim community formally petitioned the new rulers for the return of the masjid. It would take seven years for their wish to be granted.

During the time the masjid remained in use by the army, it was subject to various repairs deemed necessary by British officials. Those they wanted to carry out in 1850 highlight the fact that these officials did not have any real appreciation of the site as a religious space and that they viewed it as their personal property. This is exemplified by the following: when it became necessary to raise funds to undertake the intended work, they placed some of the mosque's red sandstone slabs for sale, much to the dismay of the local Muslim population.[43] This act indicates the mind-set of the British officials and government when it came to such historical monuments: their appropriation extended beyond the spaces they now controlled: they felt that the very fabric and materials of these structures were theirs to do with as they pleased. Additionally, the planned repairs were not intended for the benefit of the mosque or the Muslim community but rather were a direct result of the masjid continuing to be utilized by the British Army. This ownership was manifested not only through the persistent use of the space as a store but also with offices and residences placed within the mosque complex. Documentation relating to repairs indicates that restoration was undertaken only when parts of the building were literally falling apart. For instance, when part of a minaret's cladding fell off in February 1852, it landed on the roof of an 'Officer's quarters', after which the minaret facade was declared to be of danger to 'those living around it'.[44] The following month, written communications concerning the expenditure for the maintenance of the minarets to prevent a recurrence focused on prevention rather than on proper conservation. It was stated in no uncertain terms that the aim of the maintenance was for security reasons rather than restoration of the minaret facade to its original condition.[45] It is clear, then, that the mosque was viewed in very particular terms by the British as a strategic and official site for the army and not at all as a functional religious space.

Deliberations on whether the Badshahi Masjid should be returned to the Muslim population of Lahore took place between December 1849 and June 1856.[46] The discussions indicate that even if the mosque were to be returned to the Muslim community, its ultimate control would continue to reside with the British Army. For example, the conditions imposed by Sir Charles Napier early in these discussions,[47] in 1850, included a caveat that would have allowed the British to again deny Muslims access to the mosque if it were deemed necessary.[48] What exactly constituted a 'necessary' denial of the space was left ambiguous, arbitrary, and completely at the discretion of the commanding officer of the fort. This situation was seen as permissible because the British, like the Sikhs before them, considered the mosque to be an extended part of the fort, not a separate entity, and therefore under their continued jurisdiction. This was enshrined within the documentation formally returning the masjid to the local Muslim community.

At 5:30 a.m. on June 11, 1856, the mosque was officially given to the custodianship of Syed Hakim Wali Shah and Syed Buzurg Shah, to be reconsecrated for religious ritual and use, with an additional nineteen Muslim men named to a committee to oversee the repairs and alterations necessary at the site.[49] In the decree returning the mosque to the Muslim community, it was written:

> You shall be the custodians of the mosque and it will be essential and obligatory upon you to obey the orders that the Commandant of the Fort issues pertaining to the management of the Fort and the Hazuri Bagh.... And it should be borne in mind that the mosque will always remain under the mandate of the commanding officer of the Fort. Whenever the said officer may deem it necessary, he may prevent entry and exit of people from the mosque, and you shall maintain the respect and honour of the late Maharaja Ranjit Singh's Samadhi, situated near the mosque, in the same way as is in general essential for the sacred places of Hindus and Muslims and the tombs of Emperors and great men. Therefore this decree for the custodianship of the mosque is granted for you.[50]

When this handover occurred, the powder stores within the mosque were moved into new custom-built spaces within the fort,[51] but an April 18, 1856, letter on the upcoming transfer includes the request that the government's silkworm establishment (already within the mosque grounds) continue to be housed there.[52] This seems a minor request, but it can be considered a form of continuous claim of British ownership of the space, and of an intrinsic right to access the mosque whenever desired in order to check on their property – in every sense of the word. Additionally, the continued control over the site and ultimate authority of the British Army manifested itself in different ways. In a slightly earlier letter, dated April 5, 1856, in which conditions to accompany the formal handover were stated, one of the stipulations was:

> The Chief Commissioner will be solicited to cause such additional police precautions as he may deem necessary, to be taken by the Deputy Commissioner of the City to prevent unusually and dangerously large collections of Mahomedans from proceeding simultaneously to the Mosque and that due notice may be given on all Mahomedan festivals on which larger numbers than in general are likely to resort to the edifice, on order that suitable military arrangements may be effected.[53]

Another requirement from the same letter was that a sentry be posted and given a perfect view of the mosque, so that he could report unusual gatherings or anything out of the ordinary.[54] Clearly, then, in addition to the notion of ultimate authority over the Badshahi Masjid even after it was returned to the Muslim community of Lahore and reutilized for its original function as a place of worship, further controls were exerted in order to (at need) limit the number of people gathering there.

This control, authority, and continued monitoring of the religious space was also evident in more explicit physical ways when the mosque was returned to religious use. Before they handed over the site, the British tore down the eastern walls of the complex to either side of the entrance gate so that the enclosed courtyard could not be used as a stronghold against them [Figure 7].[55] In an even more overt statement of control, it was noted by the Commissioner and Superintendent of the Lahore Division that this removal of the eastern courtyard walls was completed so as to allow the guns of the fort easy access to the mosque courtyard if needed,[56] as standing permission was given for the fort's military commander to fire into the courtyard whenever there was a need to 'enforce obedience'.[57] The explicit statements that these orders and precautions were taken to prevent large groups of Muslims from gathering together raises the spectre of the underlying fear of revolt that the British officials continuously felt. In essence, however, through such actions the *being* of the mosque itself was denied, as a *jami' masjid* by its definition and nature was a place for the entire Muslim (male) population to gather together, to congregate. Despite the masjid having been returned to the Muslim community as functional space for religious practice, Muslim activity was monitored, restricted, and policed. In addition, through the removal of the eastern courtyard wall, the physical separation of space between the religious complex and the Hazuri Bagh – still also considered an extension of the fort – went beyond being blurred to being negated. Just as in the Sikh era, this resulted in the notion of liminality between these spaces, which was so clearly defined when they were initially created during the Mughal era, being eliminated.

Because the Badshahi Masjid remained under the military jurisdiction of the British Army, certain elements of control were left openly in place – beyond Napier's early edict and the other stipulations and acts discussed above. One example is that the two gateways into

Figure 7: Samuel Bourne, View of the Badshahi Masjid from the Lahore Fort, c.1863–64. Albumen Print, 22.1 x 29.1 cm. Courtesy of the Victoria & Albert Museum, London.

the Hazuri Bagh, the Alamgiri Gate and the entrance gate to the mosque, were deemed to be continually in need of guards. In a letter dated April 9, 1856, Major Paton, the Assistant Quarter Master General, writing to Brigadier Groves, commanding at Lahore, gave the following order: the Alamgiri Gate was to have a double sentry during the hours it was open (daybreak to sunset) and a single sentry when it was closed (sunset to daybreak); there were to be five guards at the north gate and five guards at the south gate to the Hazuri Bagh; and the entrance gate into the mosque courtyard was to be closed between sunset and daybreak.[58] This meant that access to the mosque remained restricted, both in the sense that people who wanted access to the Hazuri Bagh and the mosque needed to pass through guarded gates and because each of these gates was to be closed at sunset. This latter point was more problematic: one of the daily prayers, *isha*, would not have been able to be carried out within the mosque because it is proscribed to be performed at night – and therefore after sunset. The inherent problems with this scheme were recognized, as is evident in a letter dated almost a year later, on April 2, 1857, from the Military Secretary of the Chief Commissioner of Punjab to the Quarter-Master General of the army. It states that the gates into the 'masjid square' are to be blocked, leaving the Hazuri Bagh gates as the sole entrances to the mosque, and that hindrance to entering the site will not sit well with the local Muslim population; this was noted to be especially true if it was necessary for worshippers to request permission from guards to enter the space, which might very well lead to them not wanting to attend prayers at the masjid.[59] It was therefore suggested that nothing be put in place that would impede Muslim access to the site when they were coming to or leaving the mosque.[60] This resulted in a response, dated April 28, 1857, which states that unrestricted access to the mosque under *ordinary circumstances* was determined to be positive, and so the guards had been ordered to withdraw from the Hazuri Bagh gates. In order to ease access, the entrances into the masjid square, which were intended to be closed, were now to be left as they were.[61] The wording, however, still makes clear that if extraordinary circumstances were to take place, or if the Chief Officer of the fort decided that a particular gathering constituted such an event, the restrictions and additional guards would be employed.

What becomes evident from these various stipulations regarding the handover is that control of the mosque, including basic access, was a means through which the Muslim community itself was controlled. It was not magnanimity that prompted the British to return the mosque to the Muslims of Lahore: they had very clear political reasons for doing so. As noted by Jalal, the restoration was initiated purely on political grounds, as a gesture of goodwill intended to enable and enhance a positive relationship with the Muslim community.[62] Nevertheless, there seemed to be no contradiction in retaining ultimate authority over the site, keeping in place an ever-present threat to remove the right to worship, dismantling part of the grounds to be able to better aim guns into the courtyard, and policing the events which took place there.

The Badshahi Masjid is merely one example of the British government's management of Muslim space in South Asia. Due to the extent of their geographic and political control in the region, this was a widespread and systemic practice. A stark parallel can be seen in their handling of the *jami' masjid* in Delhi, a space that was imbued with even more religious and political symbolism because of both its location in the capital city and the timing of British intervention. In this instance it was the uprising of 1857 which precipitated the confiscation of the *jami' masjid* and its conversion into a military site.[63] This time, the urban fabric of the city was also altered, with the areas between the mosque gate and the Lal Qila (Red Fort) of Delhi destroyed.[64] Presumably this was a means through which the British government exerted control over and appropriated the urban centre; it was also politically and militarily expedient to have a clear sight line between these two spaces. The same concerns discussed above in relation to British fears of the Muslim community in Lahore were present in Delhi, only they were much more strongly felt after the uprising: it was believed that the *jami' masjid* would become a space for political gatherings and anti-British activity. Therefore, the British found it politically expedient to retain control of Delhi's Friday mosque spaces and to deny the Muslim population entry.[65]

This state of affairs persisted until 1860, when the British declared that if Delhi's Muslim community were to request restored access to the mosque, their request would be considered, provided that the managers selected were loyal to the British government and that only religious matters would be discussed and practiced within the mosque.[66] Further stipulations were put in place, including the placement of sentries at the mosque gates and the acknowledgment that if 'any sign of seditious behaviour' took place within the mosque grounds, such would be cause for the British government to confiscate the *jami' masjid*.[67] These were agreed to by the Muslims composing the managing board, and the mosque reopened as a place of worship for Delhi's Muslim population on November 28, 1862, albeit as a British-regulated space.[68]

Conclusion

By its nature, a *jami' masjid* is a congregational mosque, a place for a city's wider Muslim community to come together as one, to meet, discuss pertinent events, and worship. At its essence are also the political connotations attached to these sites, exemplified by the *khutba*, the political sermon read out in the name of a ruler. Historically, the *khutba* has had connotations of both political and social power, associations which were inherently tied up with the Friday mosque itself. With the Badshahi Masjid, however, the functional and political usage of the space shifted with the changing fortunes of the city. This resulted not only in its religious functionality being altered in the post-Mughal era, but also in a change in meaning for its role as a symbol of political power – the mosque now stood as a representation of the political power of Lahore's non-Muslim rulers. As Jalal states, 'The Badshahi Mosque is a monument whose political history suffices to be as profound, if not more so, as its architectural value.'[69] This statement nicely sums up the duality of the Badshahi Masjid and its surrounding spaces, as discussed in this chapter.

In exploring the Badshahi Masjid and Complex from the time of their construction in the Mughal era, through the Sikh period of rule in Lahore, and during control of the city by the British government, the liminality of these spaces becomes clear. When first constructed, the Badshahi Masjid was conceived as the largest congregational mosque within the Mughal Empire, built to accommodate the large number of worshippers in Lahore. At the same time, 'Alamgir ordered the construction of the Aurangzeb Sarai and the Alamgiri Gate of the Lahore Fort; these three spaces were conceived as one unit, with the *sarai* serving as a transitional and ceremonial space between the religious and political centres of the city. This altered quite drastically, however, when the Sikhs came to power.

During Sikh rule, for a period of 100 years, this Friday Mosque's innate function as a place of religious worship was denied; access to and usage of the congregational space by the city's Muslim population was severely restricted. It was the new government that had the supreme right and made the ultimate decision as to the activities for which the mosque complex was to be used and who had permission to enter it. The gates into the Hazuri Bagh, and therefore access to the mosque gateway, were closed off, and those who requested access were routinely challenged. The Aurangzeb Sarai, meanwhile, was transformed into the Hazuri Bagh and became the site of a three-story pavilion constructed by Maharajah Ranjit Singh, an overt claim of ownership by the Sikh ruler. Ultimately, the mosque itself was given over to the Sikh army for its use and the storage of ammunition, and the spaces in question were used to aid in advancing a Sikh framework of political power and capital.

In the British era the functionality of the mosque shifted yet again. The British Army was able to claim the mosque under their continued control even after it was returned to the Muslim population for worship, which obviously suited their desires. This was made clear by Napier, who wrote that the mosque was in 'the citadel and that the commandant must always have it under his control and deny access to it whenever he may think necessary'.[70] The actions taken by the British in returning the mosque to the Muslim community clearly made known the continued strategic importance of the site, as well as the politicization of the space. Despite Muslims now being able to again worship within the mosque, and their being financially responsible for its upkeep and conservation, ultimately the space remained under military control, and access was contingent upon the continued grace of the British government. Even in the following years, the Badshahi Masjid and its surrounds continued to be a flashpoint of political contention. In 1919, for example, Muslims were again denied the right to access the religious compound, and the mosque was subject to martial law when the British authorities thought that the Muslim communities were using it as meeting point to promote seditious behaviour against them.[71] Napier's 1850 caveat was clearly still valid at this time.

We can thus see the Badshahi Masjid and Complex as being reflective of shifting use, meaning, and symbolism. In discussing the liminality of these spaces, this chapter has explored how changes in politics and governmental rule impacted the usage of the mosque and its complex. As stated by Kavuri-Bauer, 'monuments are not stable and unchanging but dynamic spaces that can help us understand how political movements and social identities…have been forged through the imperatives of power, subjectivity and the spatial practices they influence'.[72] While this study has taken a temporal approach and has read the space of the Badshahi Complex as a single unit, it nonetheless becomes clear that the mosque, gateways, and *sarai*/Hazuri Bagh can also be seen in isolation as their own liminal spaces. Their individual meanings and usage can just as easily be discussed independently of each other, such was the importance of each element.

Even today, spatial ambiguity continues to exist around the Badshahi Complex. In the area immediately to the south of the mosque is the Heera Mandi (Diamond Market), established during the British period. This neighbourhood has been transformed into a very popular gastronomic hub, resplendent with restaurants. The most famous of these pride themselves on the view they afford overlooking the Badshahi Masjid, the enclosed Hazuri Bagh, and the Alamgiri Gate. Truly, throughout the history of the Badshahi Complex, the spatial lines between the sacred and the secular have been blurred beyond recognition.

Notes

1 In the context of this discussion, the term 'South Asia' refers to the geographic region encompassing present-day Afghanistan, Pakistan, India, Bangladesh, and parts of Tibet and Nepal.

2 Fatehpur Sikri was utilized as an imperial capital for a period of only fifteen years, from 1571 to 1585, after which the capital shifted between Lahore, Delhi, and Agra until the construction of Shahjahanabad, today's Old Delhi, which became the sole imperial capital in 1648.

3 Catherine Asher, *Architecture of Mughal India* (1992; repr., New Delhi: Cambridge University Press, 2015), 53.

4 The 'Badshahi Masjid' and the 'masjid' will be used interchangeably in this chapter in reference to this mosque.

5 Ebba Koch, *Mughal Architecture* (Munich: Prestel-Verlag, 1991), 129.

6 The measurements for these spaces are taken from Yasmeen Lari, *Lahore Illustrated City Guide, A Heritage Guidebook* (Karachi: Heritage Foundation Pakistan, 2003), 6.28, 6.32–3.

7 Twentieth-century renovations at the mosque created ablution halls along the eastern walls of the courtyard. See Ihsan Nadiem, *Lahore: A Glorious Heritage* (Lahore: Sang-e-Meel, 1996), 111.

8 Syad Muhammad Latif, *Lahore: Its History, Architectural Remains and Antiquities* (1892; repr., Lahore: Sang-e-Meel, 2005), 117.

9 Talha Jalal, *Memoirs of the Badshahi Mosque: Notes on History and Architecture based on Archives, Literature and Archaic Images* (Karachi: Oxford University Press, 2013), 31, 33.

10 Interestingly, this also means that the entirety of this spatial unit was qibla-oriented, a necessary feature for the mosque and therefore for the mosque complex. As a result, this entire space is skewed at a different angle from the rest of the Shahi Qila.

11 Anna Suvorova, *Lahore: Topophilia of Space and Place* (Karachi: Oxford University Press, 2011), 8–9, 35.

12 Rajmohan Gandhi, *Punjab: A History from Aurangzeb to Mountbatten* (New Delhi: Aleph Book Co., 2013), 53.

13 The foundation inscription reads: 'The mosque of the victorious and valiant king Muinuddin Muhammad Alamgir. Constructed and completed under the superintendence of the humblest servant of the royal household, Fidai Khan Koka, in 1084 A.H.' This translation is given in Latif, *Lahore*, 113, while both the Persian text and an English translation are given in M. Abdullah Chaghtai, *The Badshahi Masjid: History and Architecture* (Lahore: Pakistan Times Press, 1972), 12.

14 Chaghtai, *The Badshahi Masjid*, 11. At the time of writing, Chaghtai had in his possession a Persian manuscript that included copies of royal firmans, including that on the construction of the Badshahi Masjid. A picture of this firman can be found on page 10, and the Persian text and English translation can be found on page 11.

15 J. S. Grewal and Veena Sachdeva, 'Urbanization in the Mughal Province of Lahore', in *Five Thousand Years of Urbanization: The Punjab Region*, ed. Reeta Grewal (New Delhi: Manohar, 2005), 112; and Abdul Rehman, *Historic Towns of Punjab: Ancient and Medieval Period* (Lahore: Ferozsons Pvt. Ltd., 1997), 172–73. For a plan of the Walled City showing the division of the space into nine *guzars*, see Rehman, *Historic Towns of Punjab,* 173.

16 Niccolao Manucci, *Storia do Mogor*, 4 vols. (London: John Murray, 1907), 2:120. Manucci relates that by the time the order for the mosque's construction was given, the memory of Dara Shikoh had 'faded or been made to be forgotten'. Therefore, Aurangzeb ordered that his brother's palace close to the fort be destroyed and the new mosque constructed on the site.

17 Subash Parihar, 'Palace of Asaf Khan at Lahore', *Journal of Pakistan Historical Society* 32.1 (1984): 72.

18 Gandhi, *Punjab*, 54; and Latif, *Lahore*, 115.

19 Jalal, *Memoirs of the Badshahi Mosque*, 8.

20 Jalal, *Memoirs of the Badshahi Mosque,* 10.

21 Latif, *Lahore*, 117. Unfortunately, Latif does not provide his source for this description.

22 Ibid.

23 Jean-Baptiste Tavernier, *Travels in India by Jean-Baptiste Tavernier, Baron of Aubonne*, ed. William Crooke (London: Oxford University Press, 1925), 310–11. Contemporary Mughal descriptions of the Badshahi Masjid and the ceremonial activities that took place within the wider Badshahi Complex are lacking. While contemporary official and unofficial histories of 'Alamgir's reign have been consulted, the construction of the mosque and his visits to it do not feature in them. For a summary of sources for 'Alamgir's reign, see the Bibliographic Essay in Audrey Truschke, *Aurangzeb: The Life and Legacy of India's Most Controversial King* (Stanford: Stanford University Press, 2017), 111–15.

24 The history of Lahore and the rise and fall of the Sikh Kingdom is too detailed and complicated to enter into here, so only those aspects relevant to the current discussion have been noted. For further information on the historical and military background of these periods, a brief selection of sources to see includes: Latif, *Lahore*; Jean-Marie Lafont, *Maharaja Ranjit Singh: Lord of the Five Rivers* (New Delhi: Oxford University Press, 2002); Jagtar Singh Grewal, *The Sikhs of the Punjab* (Cambridge: Cambridge University Press, 1998); and Hari Ram Gupta, *History of the Sikhs* (New Delhi: Munshiram Manoharlal Publishers, 1978).

25 Chaghtai, *The Badshahi Masjid,* 36.

26 Lafont, *Mahraraja Ranjit Singh,* 37.

27 Lafont, *Mahraraja Ranjit Singh,* 69. Another such site was the Sonahri Masjid, but this mosque was returned to the Muslim community of Lahore during the reign of Ranjit Singh, at the request of General Allard. See page 37.

28 William Moorcroft and George Trebeck, *Travels in the Himalayan Provinces*, 2 vols. (London: John Murray, 1841), 2:120.

29 Chaghtai, *The Badshahi Masjid,* 36.

30 Moorcroft and Trebeck, *Travels*, 1:104–5.

31 Charles Hugel, *Travels in Kashmir and the Punjab*, trans. Major Thomas Best Jervis (Patiala: Languages Department, Punjab, 1970), 285.

32 Latif, *Lahore*, 115.

33 Lafont, *Mahraraja Ranjit Singh*, 97.

34 Nadiem, *Lahore*, 167.

35 Lala Sihan Lal Suri, *Umdat-ut-Tawarikh, Daftar III, Parts I–V, 1831–1839 A.D.,* trans. Vidya Sagar Suri (Delhi: S. Chand & Co., 1961), 62.

36 Suri, *Umdat-ut-Tawarikh*, 65.

37 Nadiem, *Lahore*, 113; and Latif, *Lahore*, 114.

38 Nadiem, *Lahore*, 113.

39 Latif, *Lahore*, 114.

40 Major G. Carmichael Smyth, *A History of the Reigning Family of Lahore, with some account of the Jumari Rajahs, the Sikh Soldiers and their Sirdars* (Delhi: Parampala Publishers, 1979), 48.; and Nadiem, *Lahore*, 168.

41 Ibid.

42 Chaghtai, *The Badshahi Masjid,* 38; and Jalal, *Memoirs of the Badshahi Mosque,* 82.

43 Nadiem, *Lahore*, 115. The outcry was such that further sales of the mosque's materials were halted.

44 Letter from Captain Baker, the Officiating Garrison Engineer Lahore, to Major Macpherson, Major of Brigade Lahore, dated February 10, 1852, Press List of Old Records, The British Records Office in the Punjab Secretariat, Lahore, no. 284. Transcribed and reproduced in Jalal, *Memoirs of the Badshahi Mosque*, 58, 85.

45 Letter to the Officiating Secretary to the Government of India from the Secretary to the Board of Administration, dated March 29, 1852, Press List of Old Records, The British Records Office in the Punjab Secretariat, Lahore, no. 301. Transcribed and reproduced in Jalal, *Memoirs of the Badshahi Mosque*, 58, 94–95.

46 Ibid., 4–5.

47 Napier was the Governor of Sindh from 1843 to 1847, after which he returned to England. He returned to India in 1849 and served as the British Army's Commander-in-Chief of the Northern Division in India for two years before again returning to England.

48 Chaghtai, *The Badshahi Masjid*, 39; and Jalal, *Memoirs of the Badshahi Mosque*, 8.

49 Chaghtai, *The Badshahi Masjid*, 39–40.

50 Jalal, *Memoirs of the Badshahi Mosque*, 22, 24. This translation of the original Urdu text is by Jalal. The original *sanad* is pictured on page 23. Jalal makes the point that the language in the original Urdu version is very patronizing, emphasizing the subservience of the Muslim community to the British government (see page 24). This decree is also given in Chaghtai, *The Badshahi Masjid*, 40, cited from West Pakistan Civil Secretariat Records, File L, page 3.

51 Chaghtai, *The Badshahi Masjid*, 39.

52 Letter from R. Temple, Esq. Secretary to the Chief Commissioner for the Punjab to Major Clarke, Offg. Commissioner and Superintendent, Lahore Division, dated April 18, 1856, Punjab Government Civil Secretariat, no. 848. Transcribed and reproduced in Jalal, *Memoirs of the Badshahi Mosque*, 119.

53 Letter from Major Paton, Assistant Quartermaster-General to The Commanding Officer at Lahore, dated April 5, 1856, Punjab Government Civil Secretariat, no. 158. Transcribed and reproduced in Jalal, *Memoirs of the Badshahi Mosque*, 122–23.

54 Jalal, *Memoirs of the Badshahi Mosque*, 123.

55 Nadiem, *Lahore*, 115; and Jalal, *Memoirs of the Badshahi Mosque*, 17.

56 Letter from the Commissioner and Superintendent of the Lahore Division to the Secretary of the Public Works Department, dated May 7, 1873, Punjab Government Civil Secretariat, no. 1281. Transcribed and reproduced in Jalal, *Memoirs of the Badshahi Mosque*, 141. A picture from the private collection of Bob Scoales is reproduced on page 63 and shows a better view of the mosque after the removal of this eastern courtyard wall.

57 Letter from Lt.-Col. Macphereson, Military Secretary to the Chief Commissioner, Punjab, to The Quartermaster-General of the Army, dated April 2, 1857, Punjab Government Civil Secretariat, no. 1178. Transcribed and reproduced in Jalal, *Memoirs of the Badshahi Mosque*, 128.

58 Letter to Brigadier Groves from Major Paton, dated April 9, 1856, Punjab Government Civil Secretariat, no. 167. Transcribed and reproduced in Jalal, *Memoirs of the Badshahi Mosque*, 113.

59 Letter from Lt.-Col. Macphereson, Military Secretary to the Chief Commissioner, Punjab, to The Quartermaster-General of the Army, dated April 2, 1857, Punjab Government Civil

Secretariat, no. 1178. Transcribed and reproduced in Jalal, *Memoirs of the Badshahi Mosque*, 126–29. This particular point is on page 128.

60 Jalal, *Memoirs of the Badshahi Mosque*, 126–29.

61 Letter from Lt.-Col. Macpherson, Military Secretary to the Chief Commissioner, Punjab, to The Quartermaster-General of the Army, dated April 2, 1857, Punjab Government Civil Secretariat, no. 1178. Transcribed and reproduced in Jalal, *Memoirs of the Badshahi Mosque*, 129. Only one sentry was to be kept within the Hazuri Bagh, to ensure that the *baradari* was not damaged. Emphasis added.

62 Jalal, *Memoirs of the Badshahi Mosque*, 4.

63 On the confiscation of the mosque from the Muslim population, see Mrinalini Rajagopalan, *Building Histories: The Archival and Affective Lives of Five Monuments in Modern Delhi* (Chicago and London: The University of Chicago Press, 2016), 89; and Santhi Kavuri-Bauer, *Monumental Matters: The Power, Subjectivity, and Space of India's Mughal Architecture* (Durham and London: Duke University Press, 2011), 54. On the changing function into a military site, see Kavuri-Bauer, *Monumental Matters*, 104; the mosque was used to house the Thirteenth Punjab Infantry.

64 Rajagopalan, *Building Histories*, 89.

65 Rajagopalan, *Building Histories*, 87, 89. The twentieth-century use of the *jami' masjid* of Delhi as a site from which to engage the population in discussions of nationalism and to critique colonial power, through which the mosque became symbolic of these politically charged ideas, is outside the scope of this discussion and so will not be touched on here. For further information, see Rajagopalan, *Building Histories*, 87–117; and Kavuri-Bauer, *Monumental Matters*, 134–35, 140–41.

66 Kavuri-Bauer, *Monumental Matters*, 104.

67 Kavuri-Bauer, *Monumental Matters*, 105–6.

68 Kavuri-Bauer, *Monumental Matters*, 105.

69 Jalal, *Memoirs of the Badshahi Mosque*, 1.

70 Napier's instructions are given in a letter from the Secretary to the Chief Commissioner in Lahore to Major General Gowan, dated February 18, 1856, Press List of Old Records, The British Records Office in the Punjab Secretariat, Lahore, no. 346. Transcribed and reproduced in Jalal, *Memoirs of the Badshahi Mosque*, 110.

71 Jalal, *Memoirs of the Badshahi Mosque*, 25–26.

72 Kavuri-Bauer, *Monumental Matters*, 2.

City as Liminal Space: Islamic Pilgrimage and Muslim Holy Sites
in Jerusalem during the Mamluk Period

Fadi Ragheb

Introduction

Islamic pilgrimage[1] represented an inextricable part of Jerusalem's history during the medieval period. As the first qibla in Islam, as the place where the Prophet Muhammad visited during his *isra'* (night journey), and as a city deeply connected to many biblical traditions and narratives, Jerusalem is considered the third holiest city of Islam. During the medieval period, its extolled status in the faith brought to Jerusalem many medieval Muslim pilgrims and visitors who travelled annually to the city from as far as India in the east and Islamic Spain in the west.[2] Pilgrims en route to the hajj in Mecca also stopped in Jerusalem to visit the city and its many Islamic holy sites before embarking upon the journey to the Hijaz, further increasing the number of annual Muslim visitors to the city.[3] Considering the sanctity of the Dome of the Rock and al-Aqsa Mosque, it was common during the medieval period for Muslim scholars, Sufis, and ordinary pilgrims to worship at the Haram al-Sharif complex. In fact, many famous Muslim figures, such as Abu Hamid al-Ghazali, Ibn 'Arabi, and Ibn Battuta, to name a few, visited Jerusalem during their lifetime and spent long periods contemplating the holy within the confines of the Haram.

Significantly, Islamic pilgrimage to Jerusalem increased during the Mamluk period (1250–1517). After the end of the Crusades, Mamluk rule over Jerusalem both stabilized life in the city[4] and revived the Islamic practice of visiting Jerusalem.[5] Pilgrims began to flock from across the Islamic world, visiting all the religious sites the city had to offer:

> The sanctity of the city attracted pilgrims from many distant parts, east and west. For people of all conditions in Syria and Palestine Jerusalem had long been a place of pilgrimage … For pilgrims further afield it was common practice to visit Jerusalem on the way to perform, or on the return from, the prescribed Hajj to Mecca. People stayed on then, to benefit from residing in the holy city, in a word, to be a *mujawir*, either for the remainder of their declining years or for a limited period, perhaps combined with some study.[6]

A major factor contributing to the increased number of Muslim pilgrims visiting Jerusalem during the Mamluk period was Sufi brotherhoods' attraction to the city, an aspect of Islamic pilgrimage that was reflected in the large number of religious buildings erected in the city by Mamluk authorities in order to accommodate Sufi and other pilgrims. Many mosques, madrasas, and Sufi convents and lodges (*khanqah*s, *zawiya*s, *ribat*s) were built during the Mamluk period to house and feed pilgrims; these religious buildings also provided pilgrims with sacred spaces in which to perform their rituals.[7]

Although Islamic pilgrimage to Jerusalem represented a major aspect of the city's Islamic character during the Mamluk period, this important religio-historical phenomenon has yet to receive the scholarly attention it deserves. While some studies have investigated Islamic worship in Jerusalem during the earlier Islamic period (638–1099),[8] the study of sacred spaces and Islamic pilgrimage to Jerusalem during the Mamluk period remains less explored.[9] Researching the era of Mamluk rule over Jerusalem is all the more compelling considering that this period produced the largest number of *Fada'il al-Quds* (Merits of Jerusalem) texts – medieval Islamic pilgrimage guides to Jerusalem – than any other period in Islamic history.[10]

Importantly, to a Muslim pilgrim visiting Jerusalem during the Mamluk period, the sacred was not limited to the Haram al-Sharif complex. While the Haram, with its Dome of the Rock (Qubbat al-Sakhra) and al-Aqsa Mosque, was the epicentre of Islamic presence in the city and the starting point for any Muslim visitor, Islamic pilgrimage routes in Jerusalem extended to a larger network of religious sites across and around the city's urban landscape. In fact, the *Fada'il al-Quds* guides reveal a longer pilgrimage route that extended Muslims' worship in the city to several holy sites outside the Haram, including the Tower of David, Jerusalem's walls, the Mount of Olives, and the Church of Mary. To a medieval Muslim pilgrim, therefore, the holy sphere was not limited to the boundaries of the Haram al-Sharif complex but extended into the city itself. As a result of the numerous Islamic sacred sites scattered throughout the city, the spaces delimiting the sacred Islamic landscape from the secular in Mamluk Jerusalem became less fixed, and, in turn, the city, it will be argued, became one large liminal space.[11]

Using the *Fada'il al-Quds* pilgrimage guides, this study will investigate the network of Islamic holy sites in Jerusalem that were visited by Muslims during the Mamluk period. After providing an overview of the *Fada'il al-Quds* literature, the study will, first, use the *Fada'il al-Quds* pilgrimage guides from the Mamluk period to describe the extolled status that Jerusalem holds in Islam and the ways in which the city in its entirety is one large sacred holy site. Second, by tracing the traditions in the *Fada'il al-Quds*, the study will delineate Jerusalem's Islamic holy sites on the Haram complex, before identifying sites located *outside* the Haram that Muslims visited and prayed at in the city. Third, the study will query the Islamic religious institutions built by Mamluk authorities to elucidate the extent to which the sacred sphere permeated the city, transformed its Islamic religious landscape, and blurred the city's liminal spaces during this period. Finally, the study will reveal how the phenomenon of blurred liminal spaces in Mamluk Jerusalem also existed in another important medieval Islamic city: Mecca. It will be shown how the pilgrimage sites of Mecca during the medieval period were similarly not restricted to the Ka'ba and the Haram, Mecca's religious epicentre, but also included numerous sacred places related to the Prophet, his family, and his Companions that were scattered throughout the city and its surrounding mountains.

Thus, this study will demonstrate how, just as was the case with medieval Mecca, the sacred in Mamluk Jerusalem transcended the Haram al-Sharif complex. Indeed, Islamic holy sites were located both inside and outside the Haram, rendering the boundaries between the sacred and the secular more fluid. As a result, Jerusalem during the Mamluk period became a wider liminal space, where the sacred to a Muslim did not cease to exist past the confines of the Haram al-Sharif but instead permeated the city.

Fada'il al-Quds (Merits of Jerusalem) Literature

The *fada'il* literature is a large corpus of Muslim writings from early to late medieval Islam. These writings were composed to extol the religious '*fadila*', the merit or excellence, of different topics, such as the Qur'an, the Companions of the Prophet, and Muslim cities.[12] The *fada'il* literature on Muslim cities constitutes a large group of the *fada'il* genre. A *fada'il* work on a city normally consists of Islamic traditions associated with the city and highlights its religious importance and sanctity in early and medieval Islam.[13]

The *fada'il* writings on Jerusalem, the *Fada'il al-Quds*, constitute a large part of the *fada'il* genre on Muslim cities. They are religio-historical writings on medieval Islamic Jerusalem that were composed to extol the 'merits of Jerusalem'[14] and to praise the religious and historical importance of the city in Islam.[15] The sources for the traditions within the *Fada'il al-Quds* are typically the Qur'an, *tafsir* (Qur'anic exegesis), hadith (the Prophet's sayings), and *athar* traditions (reports of the early Companions of the Prophet and early converts to Islam). The literature also includes *qisas al-anbiya'* (stories and legends of Biblical and Islamic Prophets), the *isra'iliyyat* traditions (Jewish folkloric and mythological accounts on the city), as well as *akhbar* reports (historical accounts from Islamic chroniclers and geographers on the history of Jerusalem). Therefore, as a large collection of both religious *and* historical traditions, the *Fada'il al-Quds* writings serve as a crucial literary source for the history of early and medieval Islamic Jerusalem.[16]

Most *Fada'il al-Quds* texts contain a similar basic outline of subjects, with only some minor differences in the order or classification of sections. Topics discussed include the general religious merits of Jerusalem; the reward of visiting and praying there; its role in the end of days; the founding of the city by David and Solomon; the story of the Prophet's nocturnal journey to Jerusalem (*al-isra'*) and his ascension to the heavens from there (*al-mi'raj*); the history of Jerusalem's conquest by the second caliph, 'Umar; the building of the Dome of the Rock by the Umayyad caliph 'Abd al-Malik ibn Marwan; reports on who from among the Companions and other pious figures visited the city; and the sanctity of many holy sites in and around the city.

While many *fada'il* works were written on Mecca, Medina, and other Islamic cities beginning in the eighth century, *fada'il* writings on Jerusalem appeared as late as the eleventh century.[17] This period produced two major *Fada'il al-Quds* accounts: Ibn al-Murajja's *Fada'il Bayt al-Maqdis* and al-Wasiti's *Fada'il al-Bayt al-Muqaddas*.[18] Importantly, these works were written before the Crusades, and yet they remained the major sources for later *Fada'il al-Quds* texts composed after the Crusader conquest of Jerusalem in 1099.

The second period in the writing of the *Fada'il al-Quds* began during the Ayyubid period (1171–1250), specifically after the capture of Jerusalem by Salah al-Din in 1187. During Ayyubid rule, writings on Jerusalem circulated to renew and emphasize the sanctity of the city in the Islamic consciousness in order to hold onto the city and protect it from Crusader attacks.[19] The two major works on the Merits of Jerusalem that were composed during the Ayyubid period are Abu al-Faraj 'Abd al-Rahman ibn 'Ali Ibn al-Jawzi's (1116–1201) *Fada'il al-Quds*, and Muhammad ibn 'Abd al-Wahid al-Maqdisi's (*d.*1245) *Fada'il Bayt al-Maqdis*.[20]

The *Fada'il al-Quds* literature entered its zenith after the end of the Crusades and during the Mamluk period (1250–1517). The *Fada'il al-Quds* from the Mamluk period are of particular interest due to their vast number and wide circulation. By the time the Crusades ended and Mamluk rule over Palestine stabilized in the early fourteenth century, the city experienced long periods of peace. These safer conditions naturally brought increased pilgrimage.[21] As a result, the *Fada'il al-Quds* genre reached its apogee during the Mamluk period, with the era producing no fewer than twenty different texts, composed by both Jerusalemite and non-Jerusalemite scholars. Although not all have survived, the number of *Fada'il al-Quds* pilgrimage guides composed reveals an increased awareness of Jerusalem's sacredness in Islam as well as a revived interest in pilgrimage to the city.[22] The rise of non-Jerusalemite authors also reflects the increasing number of pilgrims who travelled to Jerusalem from different parts of the Islamic world.

Furthermore, the Mamluk period produced some of the most famous *Fada'il al-Quds* works,[23] including Ibn al-Firkah's (1262–1329) *Ba'ith al-nufus ila ziyarat al-Quds al-mahrus*; Shihab al-Din al-Maqdisi's (*d.*1363) *Muthir al-gharam ila ziyarat al-Quds wa al-Sham*; Abu al-Nasr Taj al-Din 'Abd al-Wahhab ibn 'Umar al-Husayni al-Shafi'i's (*d.*1470) *al-Rawd al-mugharras fi fada'il al-Bayt al-Muqaddas*; Shams al-Din al-Suyuti's *Ithaf al-akhissa bi-Fada'il al-Masjid al-Aqsa* (1475); and Mujir al-Din's *al-Uns al-jalil bi-tarikh al-Quds wa al-Khalil* (1496).[24] By the sixteenth century, which coincided with the fall of Cyprus to the Ottomans in 1522 and the final end of the Crusader threat to the Muslim Near East, the *Fada'il al-Quds* genre had reached its peak and began to decline.[25]

Significantly, the *Fada'il al-Quds* guided Muslims around Jerusalem's sacred spaces, thus acting as pilgrimage guides. The sites listed in the literature include Muslim, Christian, and Jewish places, and the authors of the guides informed the Muslim pilgrim about the religious importance, function, and blessings attached to each site, including:

> The Merits of diverse sacred sites in and around the city (the two mosques, the twelve gates of Jerusalem, the Domes of the Ascension, of the Chain and of the Prophets, the Oratories of David, Zecharia, Mary and 'Umar, the Spring of Siloam, the Well of the Leaf, Bethlehem, Hebron etc.) [;] Traditions designed to *attract pilgrims and settlers to Jerusalem … [and] Importance of the visitation (ziyara) of al-Quds*, the value of prayer said in it.[26]

Additionally, as historical sources, the *Fada'il al-Quds* texts provide topographical, and even architectural, details for many of the sacred spaces in the city.[27] By tracing each place listed, along with the religious traditions, ceremonies, and blessings attached to it, one is able to extract from the *Fada'il al-Quds* literature a wealth of information on Jerusalem's sacred spaces and, in regards to the objective of this study, the itineraries of Muslim pilgrims visiting holy sites within and outside the Haram.

The Sanctity of Jerusalem in the *Fada'il al-Quds*

To a Muslim visiting Jerusalem during the medieval period, the abundance of Islamic traditions in the *Fada'il al-Quds* literature that extol the sanctity of the city as a whole blurs the borders that separate the sacred, represented by the Haram complex, from the city's more profane urban sphere [Figure 1]. Traditions such as Qur'anic verses, hadith sayings, biblical folklore, and *athar* transmissions sanctify the *entire* city and thus break down the rigid demarcations separating what in Jerusalem is sanctified and what is not. As a result, the exact boundaries that distinguish the sacred from the profane become increasingly ambiguous, if not fluid. Consequently, medieval Jerusalem becomes one large liminal space.

Figure 1: The view of Jerusalem and the Haram al-Sharif from the Mount of Olives. Photograph by Jennifer A. Pruitt.

Indeed, the *Fada'il al-Quds* literature provides to a Muslim a great number of Islamic traditions elevating the religious and spiritual importance of the city of Jerusalem as a whole. For example, almost all *Fada'il* guides begin with a simple praise of the city, listing all of Jerusalem's different names, with the authors of the *Fada'il* noting that 'it is apparent that an abundance of names [for a city] indicates the honour of that that is named'.[28] Several of these names, such as 'Iliya', 'Bayt al-Maqdis', and 'al-Quds', are rooted in the pre-Islamic history of the city. For example, traditions on the founding of Jerusalem by King David and his son Solomon are incorporated into the corpus and adopted by the Islamic tradition; these *isra'iliyyat* reports concerning such prominent Biblical-Islamic prophets further contribute to the city's sacred quality.[29] Moreover, the *Fada'il al-Quds* also relate traditions on Jerusalem's connection with Mecca and Medina.[30] This is most famously expressed in the Prophetic hadith tradition imploring Muslims to visit the three paramount mosques of Mecca, Medina, and Jerusalem:

> In a tradition on authority of Ibn 'Abbas it is related: The Prophet said, Ye shall set out only for three mosques, the Sacred Mosque [of Mecca], and the mosque of Medina, and the Mosque al-Aqsa. And a prayer in the Sacred Mosque is worth a hundred thousand prayers, and a prayer in my mosque is worth a thousand prayers, and a prayer in the Mosque al-Aqsa is worth ten thousand prayers.[31]

Jerusalem is also invoked in the Qur'an in Surat al-Isra', verse 17.1, which contains the account of the Prophet's *isra'* night journey to the city's 'al-Masjid al-Aqsa', perhaps the most famous Qur'anic verse that connects Islam with Jerusalem and sanctifies the city's position in the faith. Verse 17.1, which is included in every single *fada'il* work on the city, glorifies Prophet Muhammad's *isra'* to Jerusalem's al-Aqsa Mosque, the place from which, according to Islamic tradition, he also ascended to the Heavens during his *mi'raj*.[32] While it is true that the verse here refers only to 'al-Masjid al-Aqsa' (The Farthest Mosque) and not to 'Bayt al-Maqdis' or 'al-Quds', the Arabic names for the city of Jerusalem, nevertheless there is consensus among medieval Qur'anic exegetes that 'al-Masjid al-Aqsa' is in fact located in Jerusalem, thus imbuing the city with a special sanctified position in the Islamic tradition.[33]

Yet verse 17.1 is only one of several Qur'anic verses that sanctify the city as a whole; several verses cited in the *fada'il* literature extol Jerusalem's holiness, including verses 2.58, 7.21, and 21.71.[34] Furthermore, Jerusalem served as the first qibla in Islam, as the Prophet spent the first sixteen or seventeen months of his prophecy praying toward the city, an act that, according to Islamic tradition, all other prophets before Muhammad had done, and one that further adds to the city's sacredness:

> Abu 'l-Ma'ali relates on authority of Muhammad ibn Shihab az-Zuhri the following: Allah hath not sent a prophet to the earth since the descent of Adam (from Paradise) who hath not set as his point to face in prayer the Rock of Jerusalem. Our Prophet prayed thus for sixteen months.[35]

Many other traditions glorify the entirety of the city and, consequently, compel the Muslim visitor or pilgrim to enter a state of religious contemplation as he or she enters and visits Jerusalem. Such traditions further solidify the sacred position the city occupies in the Islamic tradition and thus engender a reverent state in the Muslim who passes through its many alleys, outside and inside the Haram. For example, the *fada'il* works tell that Jerusalem originated from and is connected to Paradise, whereby, for example, mercy, light, heavenly dew, and even verses of the Qur'an descend onto it from the heavens.[36] Another set of traditions revels in God's special bond with the city, positing that God has made a special place for it in His world.[37] Furthermore, many traditions connect Jerusalem with angels, who, for example, descend onto the city, pray around it, and bless those who visit and pray there.[38] Moreover, particularly numerous in the *Fada'il al-Quds* literature are the apocalyptic traditions connected with Jerusalem, especially its role on the Day of Judgment as the site where humankind will be rewarded or punished, where the separation of believer from sinner will take place, where the anti-Christ (*dajjal*) will appear, and where the eye of Moses will become visible. Jerusalem in these traditions is also the place to which Mecca will relocate at the end of the world.[39]

These numerous traditions enticed Muslims to visit Jerusalem, and the *Fada'il al-Quds* guides directly implore them to embark on pilgrimages to the city:

> On authority of Makhul it is reported: Who makes pilgrimage to Jerusalem by riding there, he shall enter Paradise carefully guided, and shall visit all the prophets in Paradise; and they shall envy him in his relationship with Allah. And whatever company sets forth to go to Jerusalem, there shall attend them ten thousand angels, interceding for them and praying for them, and serving as their agents, when they set out for Jerusalem.[40]

Other reports directly praise the religious merit of visiting, living, and dying in the city. For example, ample traditions describe the multiplying blessings of visiting the city;[41] the great rewards of praying in Jerusalem, such as the proliferation of the merit of each prayer (one prayer in Jerusalem, for example, may be worth a thousand prayers elsewhere); the remission of all sins; and the admission to Heaven for whomever prays there.[42] Many traditions state that in Jerusalem good deeds multiply, as do sins.[43] Other traditions report on the great blessings of living and dying in the city (for Jerusalemites are the 'neighbours of God' and whomever dies there is 'buried in the Heavens');[44] promise a great reward to whomever builds there;[45] extol the blessings of fasting and giving alms (*sadaqa*) there;[46] and tell of the great spiritual reward of calling for prayer in Jerusalem (*fi fadl al-adhan*).[47] Ultimately, the *Fada'il al-Quds* works implore Muslims to follow in the footsteps of famous pious men, such as the prophets, the *sahaba* (Companions of the Prophet), and the *tabi'un* (early followers of Islam), who visited, lived, and/or died in the city.[48]

The *Fada'il al-Quds* also inform Muslims of the great reward of stopping in Jerusalem en route to the hajj and entering the state of *ihram* – the hajj ritual of spiritual and bodily purification – at the gates of the city:

[I]n another citation from [Umm Salimah] it is related: The Apostle of Allah said, Who puts on the *ihram* in pilgrimage or pious visitation from Jerusalem, he is absolved from his sins as he was on the day his mother bore him.[49]

This annual Islamic ritual increased the number of pilgrims to Jerusalem during the medieval period; it also enhanced the sacredness of the city as a whole, as many Muslim pilgrims, intent on beginning the hajj, entered Jerusalem's gates in a state of spirituality (*ihram*), further adding to the sacred atmosphere that infused the city.

The diffusion of the sacred throughout the city is also evident in another much-cited tradition concerning a visit to Jerusalem in 636 by Ka'b al-Ahbar, an important authority on Judeo-Islamic traditions on the city.[50] A Jewish convert to Islam during the early period, Ka'b is one of the the the main sources, along with Wahb ibn Munabbih, of the *isra'iliyyat* traditions quoted in the *Fada'il al-Quds*.[51] This tradition reports how from the moment Ka'b entered the gates of the city, he remained silent, abstaining from speaking except in reciting the Qur'an and speaking God's name ('*amsaka 'an al-kalam fa-lam yatakallam illa bi-tilawat kitab Allah wa al-dhikr*').[52] While maintaining his spiritual state, he walked through Jerusalem, visited the Haram complex, prayed at the Sakhra, which is the holy rock upon which the Dome of the Rock was later built, and then left the city. When he was asked why he did not speak, Ka'b revealed that Jerusalem is a city where the reward of good deeds multiplies (as do the punishments of sins), and so it is best to remain in a spiritual state of silence while visiting the city.[53]

Ka'b's ritual of entering the city in a contemplative state of spirituality is supported in one of the Qur'anic verses on the sacredness of Jerusalem in Islam. Within the account of the Israelites' Exodus in Sura 2 of the Qur'an, verse 2.58 implores them to 'Enter the gate with heads bowed, and profess repentance, so that We may forgive your sins and increase the reward of the righteous'.[54] This verse is cited in several *Fada'il al-Quds* works as an indication of the sacred nature of the city and its surroundings, and as an admonition that Muslims should, just as Ka'b did, enter Jerusalem in a spiritual state of repentance and religious contemplation:

On authority of Ibn 'Abbas it is said: In the words of the Most High, 'And when We said, Enter this city', Jerusalem is meant. And, 'Eat of it bountifully as ye wish', is meant, the amount is at your volition. And, 'Enter the gate worshiping', is meant the gate of Jerusalem. And His expression 'Hittah' means, There is no god but Allah (*La ilah illa Allah!*), because it is a term which unburdens the load of sin.[55]

Therefore, according to the *Fada'il al-Quds* literature, Muslim pilgrims visiting the city should maintain a spiritual, contemplative state within its walls, a phenomenon that would further add to the element of sacredness permeating throughout the city.

Holy Sites on the Haram al-Sharif

The Dome of the Rock (Qubbat al-Sakhra) and al-Masjid al-Aqsa on the Haram complex remained the central focus of Muslim pilgrims to Jerusalem during the medieval period. The Haram complex is the Muslim epicentre within the city and the main destination of all Muslim visitors [Figure 2]. The *Fada'il al-Quds* guides provide a detailed pilgrimage plan to direct Muslim pilgrims around the Haram's labyrinth of Islamic religious sites, especially those within the Dome of the Rock and al-Aqsa Mosque [Figure 3].[56] According to the *Fada'il al-Quds* guides, a Muslim visitor should first enter the Dome of the Rock (where the sacred rock should be on the visitor's right side), then stop at the spot where people place their hands on the rock (but abstain from kissing it); the visitor should then, for the remission of sins, pray on the right and on the left side of the rock (but not on the rock itself).[57] Then

Figure 2: The Dome of the Rock on the Haram al-Sharif. Photograph by Jennifer A. Pruitt.

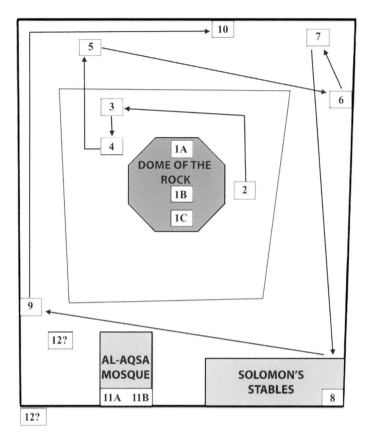

1. Dome of the Rock
     1A. Black Stone (al-Balata al-Sawda')
     1B. Maqam al-Nabi
     1C. Grotto Cave under Rock (al-Maghara)
   2. Dome of the Chain (Qubbat al-Silsila)
   3. Dome of the Prophet (Qubbat al-Nabi)
   4. Dome of the Ascension (Qubbat al-Mi'raj)
   5. Dome of Suleyman/Solomon's Chair (Kursi Sulayman)
   6. Gate of Mercy (Bab al-Rahma)
   7. Mihrab of Zecharia (Zakariyya)
   8. Mihrab of Mary (Maryam)
   9. Gate of Tranquility (Bab al-Sakina)
   10. Gate of Remission (Hitta)
   11. al-Aqsa Mosque
     11A. Mihrab 'Umar
     11B. Mihrab Mu'awiya
   12. al-Buraq station

Figure 3: Pilgrimage routes on the Haram al-Sharif Complex.

the pilgrim should proceed to the Black Stone (al-Balata al-Sawda'), pray there between two and four times, and recite supplications.[58] A visit to the Maqam al-Nabi, the place where Prophet Muhammad's footprints are believed to be engraved, comes next,[59] after which the pilgrim should proceed to the Cave under the Rock (al-Maghara) to pray and perform supplications.[60] Then the pilgrim should exit the Dome of the Rock and visit the Dome of the Chain (Qubbat al-Silsila), performing two or four prostrations there.[61] Next, the pilgrim should turn to the Dome of the Prophet (Qubbat al-Nabi),[62] then to the Dome of the Ascension (Qubbat al-Mi'raj),[63] followed by a stop at the Dome of Sulayman (named for the Umayyad Caliph Sulayman b. 'Abd al-Malik, who built it).[64]

On the Haram, the *Fada'il al-Quds* texts mention the Gate of Mercy (Bab al-Rahma)[65] and several mihrabs, such as Mihrab of Zecharia (Zakariyya)[66] and Mihrab of Mary (Maryam) (also referred to as Mahd 'Isa (Cradle of Jesus), where a Muslim should pray and recite the Sura of Maryam (Mary) from the Qur'an.[67] On the complex, the visitor should also stop by Solomon's Chair (Kursi Sulayman), which is situated next to the rocks near the Gate of the Tribes (Bab al-Asbat); supplications there, according to tradition, remit one's sins.[68] Another gate recommended to the pilgrim is Bab al-Sakina,[69] in addition to the Gate of Hitta.[70]

Next, the *Fada'il al-Quds* direct the Muslim pilgrim to enter al-Aqsa Mosque and to visit several places within it, including Mihrab 'Umar,[71] Mihrab Mu'awiya,[72] and other mihrabs.[73] Once the visitor exits al-Aqsa Mosque, he or she must visit the site where the Archangel Gabriel drilled a hole and tied down to it the Buraq flying beast of the *isra'* night journey outside the Gate of the Prophet (*al-mawdi' al-ladhi kharaqahu Jibril...wa rabata fihi al-Buraq kharij Bab al-Nabi*).[74] After completing the route around the Haram, the pilgrim is instructed by the *Fada'il al-Quds* to head outside the Haram and visit holy sites inside and around the city.

Holy Sites Outside the Haram

While the sacred spaces of the Haram complex comprised the routine, obligatory sites, the itinerary does not stop there. The *Fada'il al-Quds* guides also include destinations outside the Haram, further contributing to the fluidity of the sacred within Jerusalem and making it difficult for the Muslim visitor to discern a definitive boundary that separates the holy from the secular and the profane in the city. Since Muslims visiting the Haram are expected to be in a spiritual state, contemplating the holy, performing invocations, and reciting supplications at its various sites, it is obvious that the Haram complex is infused with the sacred. Yet this sacredness also continues *outside* of the Haram complex, in other holy sites located in and around the city.

After descending from the Haram, visitors are expected to head to Tur Zayta and al-Sahira, i.e., the Mount of Olives and the valley next to it (*'al-buqay' al-ladhi huwa ila janib al-Tur'*) [Figure 4].[75] According to the *Fada'il al-Quds* literature, the religious importance of the Mount of Olives lies in several traditions or events connected to the site that compel a Muslim visitor to include it in his or her pilgrimage itinerary around Jerusalem.

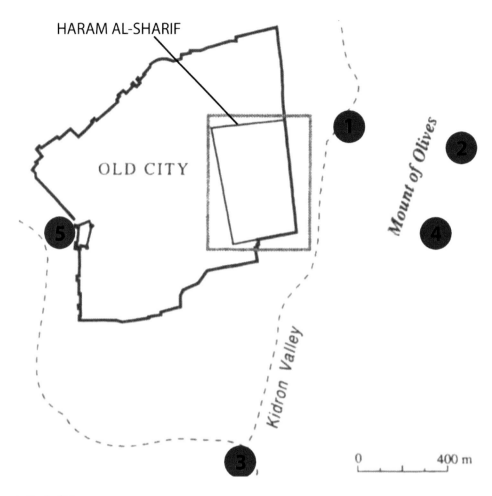

HARAM AL-SHARIF

OLD CITY

Mount of Olives

Kidron Valley

0   400 m

1. Tomb of Mary
2. Church of the Ascension
3. Spring of Siloam
4. Mount of Olives/al-Sahira
5. Tower of David (Mihrab Dawud)

Figure 4: Holy sites outside the Haram mentioned in the *Fada'il al-Quds*. Adapted and modified from Elad, *Medieval Jerusalem* (1999). (Reprinted with permission of publisher.)

First, the Mount of Olives is connected with verse 95.1 of the Qur'an, in which the word 'olive' (*al-zaytun*) has been interpreted by the *Fada'il* authors as referring to the Mount of Olives; second, it was the site from which, according to Islamic tradition, God raised Jesus before his resurrection; third, it is the place where the famous female mystic Rabi'a al-'Adawiyya was buried.[76] In his *al-Uns al-jalil*, Mujir al-Din al-'Ulaymi explicitly refers to her tomb as 'a pleasant place that is frequented by visitors' and mentions that it is located next to the site where Jesus was raised.[77] On the other hand, al-Sahira – next to the Mount of Olives, and cited in verse 79.14 ('*wa idha hum bi-'l-Sahira*') – is connected with events of the end of days, especially as the place where humankind will gather on the Day of Judgment ('*ard al-mahshar wa al-manshar*'):

> On authority of Khuleid ibn Du'laj, it is reported that Safiyyah, wife of the Prophet, went to Jerusalem and prayed there, and ascended the Mount of Olives and prayed there, and stood on the crest of the mount, and said, From this very place shall mankind be separated on the Resurrection Day unto Paradise and unto Hell-Fire.[78]

Part of the importance of the Mount of Olives within the Islamic tradition is its connection to Mary, mother of Jesus. In this regard, the Church of Mary (Kanisat Maryam), which allegedly houses Mary's tomb, is included in the *Fada'il* guides as one of the Muslim holy sites in Jerusalem.[79] It is important to note here that the Church of Mary is the same church that is called al-Kanisa al-Jismaniyya by some *Fada'il* authors.[80] It is also one of the sites at which the second caliph 'Umar b. al-Khattab prayed after Jerusalem was captured by the Arabo-Muslim armies during the mid-seventh century.[81] Some authors permit Muslims to pray at the church as long as certain rules are followed; for example, Muslims must first obtain permission from the church's Christian caretakers before praying inside,[82] although Muslims, as Amikam Elad states, 'did not heed these reservations, and continued to enter and pray at the Church of Mary.'[83] Another holy site located at the Mount of Olives and mentioned in the *Fada'il* literature is the Church of the Ascension. Referred to as Kanisat al-Tur, the Church of Ascension is recognized by some authors as the place where Jesus was resurrected.[84]

Intriguingly, another church mentioned by one author in connection to Mary is the Church of St. Anne. This church was built by Crusaders but was converted to a madrasa by Salah al-Din al-Ayyubi (Saladin) after his capture of Jerusalem; the madrasa was then named al-Madrasa al-Salahiyya, thus bearing Salah al-Din's name.[85] The author of *al-Mustaqsa fi fada'il al-Masjid al-Aqsa* states that Anne (Hanna), mother of Mary, was born and buried at the Church of St. Anne, which, he adds, was captured by the Ayyubid ruler and converted to the school that bears his name.[86] This madrasa is located outside the Haram complex, on its north side, and was a common destination for Sufi visitors.[87]

The sacred spaces that lie outside the Haram also extend south of the city. At the southern end of the Mount of Olives is the Spring of Siloam, 'Ayn Silwan. The *fada'il* literature extols the sanctity of the Spring of Siloam and includes it as part of the Muslim visitor's itinerary in Jerusalem. According to the *Fada'il* literature, the Spring of Siloam's religious importance lies in the tradition that Siloam's, along with the Spring of Zamzam in Mecca, is one of the springs of Paradise:

> On authority of Khalid ibn Ma'dan it is related: Zamzam and the spring of Siloam in Jerusalem are each a spring of Paradise. On his authority also: Two springs of Paradise in this world are Zamzam and Siloam.[88]

The Spring of Siloam is also the place where al-Khidr, a mystical figure in the Islamic tradition, bathes; according to certain traditions, Mary is also associated with this site.[89]

Another of the important Islamic sacred spaces located within the city is Mihrab Dawud. According to some traditions recorded in the *Fada'il al-Quds*, Mihrab Dawud lies in the citadel of the city, located at its western gates, near or at David's Tower.[90] The site is connected in the *Fada'il* literature with narratives on Jerusalem's establishment and its history under the reigns of David and Solomon.[91] The *Fada'il* traditions that sanctify Mihrab Dawud are sometimes cited early in the texts.[92] That references to these traditions on Mihrab Dawud precede those referring to holy sites in the Haram complex may indicate that Muslims should stop first at the western gates of the city, visit Mihrab Dawud, and assume a state of spiritual contemplation (through praying and performing supplications at the site) *before* entering the city and visiting the Haram. Following this itinerary, the sacred sphere in the city would begin immediately when Muslim pilgrims enter the city, and they persist in their state of spiritual contemplation while walking through the city towards the Haram complex. The sacred thus first appears to the Muslim immediately at the city gates – and not just only within the confines of the Haram – and thus removes any defined boundaries between the sacred (the Haram complex) and the profane (the rest of the city) within Jerusalem's walls.

Even Jerusalem's walls (*aswar Bayt al-Maqdis*) are sanctified in the Islamic traditions reported in the *Fada'il al-Quds* literature. The literature speaks of these walls and their construction by David and Solomon; it also provides certain supplications that Muslims should perform there, ones that were recited by Solomon himself.[93] Especially sacred is the eastern wall of Jerusalem (*sur Bayt al-Maqdis al-sharqi*), since, according to verse 57.13 of the Qur'an, it is this wall that separates the domain of mercy or Paradise (Jerusalem/the Haram) from Hell (Jahannam), which is identified as the valley lying east of the Haram:

> Then one should go to the Gate of Mercy and pray there, inside the wall. Then one should make invocation and ask Allah in this place for Paradise, and seek refuge in Him from Hell; and there will be granted more than that.

> And verily, the valley to the rear (of the eastern wall) is the Valley of Gehenna. And this is the place about which Allah said [verse 57.13]: 'And there shall be set between them a wall with a gate, on its inside Mercy, and without, in front of it, Punishment.'[94]

As a result, the sacredness of the walls that surround Jerusalem further extends the holy spaces outside the Haram, and into and around the city, all along its gates.

Mamluk Religious Buildings in and around Jerusalem: The Expansion of the Sacred Sphere

It is important to note that, in a departure from previous periods in Islamic history, Mamluk Jerusalem witnessed a high level of building activity by sultans, emirs, and other members of the Mamluk hierarchy. Many of these new buildings, such as madrasas, *zawiyas*, *khanqahs*, *ribat*s, and *turba* mausoleums, were religiously inspired and associated with pilgrims, travellers, and Sufi mystics; they also provided new sacred spaces for religious devotion, prayer, and ritual. In comparison to construction undertaken during pre-Mamluk periods, such as the Abbasid, Fatimid, Seljuk, and Ayyubid eras, Mamluk religious building programmes in Jerusalem transformed the city's Islamic landscape, thus further increasing the number of Islamic sacred spaces in Bayt al-Maqdis. Furthermore, these religious buildings were founded not only in and around the Haram complex but also deep within the urban quarters of the city and even outside Jerusalem's walls. Such extensive religious building throughout the city further blurred the liminal spaces that previously separated the sacred sphere from secular quarters.

Indeed, a brief survey of the limited religious building initiatives undertaken during the Abbasid, Fatimid, Seljuk, and Ayyubid periods in Jerusalem reveals the significant changes that the city experienced under the Mamluks. Prior to Mamluk rule, most religious architectural activity was limited to the Haram. Few religious buildings were erected outside the Haram and even fewer were built deep within the secular confines of the city.[95] For example, during Abbasid rule in Jerusalem (750–969) architectural restoration and maintenance activities were performed on the Haram, but 'little is known of construction outside the Haram at this time'[96] – we do know, for example, one mosque was founded during the early tenth century on the eastern side of the Church of the Holy Sepulchre.[97]

Similarly, during the Fatimid period (969–1071, 1098–99) the caliphs of Egypt continued to focus their building activity on the Haram complex (especially due to the earthquakes of 1016 and 1034), with the exception of a mosque erected near the Golden Gate and prayer areas for Sufis outside the northern walls of the Haram.[98] This trend continued during the very short reign of the Seljuks and Turkmen over the city (1071–98). Despite Jerusalem becoming more open to scholars under Seljuk rule,[99] the reign of the Seljuks brought almost no architectural activity, religious or secular, that is known from the literary sources or from architectural surveys of the city, save for an inscription indicating the founding of a mosque in 1089–90.[100]

The Crusader period during the twelfth century interrupted Islamic rule over Jerusalem for nine decades or so, until the city was recaptured in 1187 by Salah al-Din, the founder of the Ayyubid dynasty. The Ayyubid reign over the city lasted more than five decades (from 1187 until 1250). During this time, instability and fears of renewed Crusader invasions pervaded the history of the city. Although the Ayyubids undertook a sizeable religious building programme in the city – constructing madrasas, mosques, Sufi *zawiyas*, and *khanqahs* that catered to pilgrims and visitors – the number and size of these edifices are dwarfed by that which was built during the Mamluk period. Furthermore, most of the construction during the Ayyubid era took place on the Haram. As Robert Hillenbrand explains, Ayyubid Jerusalem 'served as a curtain-raiser for the thorough transformation which the city [of Jerusalem] experienced under the Mamluks, who systematically beautified it with dozens of new public buildings'.[101] Moreover, while the Ayyubids introduced to the city new forms of art and architecture, Ayyubid architecture, as Mahmoud Hawari notes, constituted a 'prelude' to the 'magnificent architecture' of the Mamluks.[102]

The Ayyubids did erect many significant religious edifices in the city. According to Hawari's survey of Ayyubid monuments in Jerusalem, 40 Ayyubid buildings and monuments are known to have been completed.[103] These building initiatives – including the re-Islamicization of the Haram's Dome of the Rock and al-Aqsa Mosque – were undertaken to Islamicize Jerusalem after nine decades of Christian Frankish rule.[104] Moreover, churches were converted to Islamic religious buildings, and, in some cases, material from Frankish buildings was recycled as spoils in new Ayyubid monuments.[105] Yet Ayyubid construction was mainly limited to the Haram and its immediate vicinity, in significant contrast to Mamluk religious building, which were located not only within the Haram but also around it and even outside the city's walls.[106]

While Ayyubid religious monuments served Muslim pilgrims in Jerusalem, the number and size of these projects pale in comparison to those undertaken by the Mamluks. For example, it is true that, as part of their Sunnification programme, the Ayyubids paid great attention to building tens of madrasas across Egypt and Greater Syria.[107] In Jerusalem, however, only six madrasas were built, with three of them located immediately outside the Haram, within the urban landscape of the city.[108] The Mamluks, on the other hand, managed to build 31 madrasas across the city, a significant leap in the establishment of an important religious institution that was attended by pilgrims, transient visitors, and residents of the city alike.[109] Similarly, while the Ayyubids had built only 5 *zawiyas* and 1 Sufi *khanqahs* (al-Khanqah al-Salahiyya), the Mamluks founded 30 *zawiyas*, 9 ribats, and 2 *khanqahs*.[110] In fact, under the Mamluks the total number of religious building projects doubled; in contrast to the 40 buildings and monuments erected by the Ayyubids, 86 buildings were constructed during the Mamluk period.[111]

Many of the building initiatives undertaken during the Mamluk period were established through waqf endowments made by the upper echelons of Mamluk society. During this period, many emirs chose to retire in or were exiled to Jerusalem.[112] Their contributions to the religious building projects in the city 'helped accommodate the increased Muslim presence' in the city and helped 're-establish the city as a pilgrimage centre for Muslims'.[113] Moreover, as successors to and banishers of the Crusaders in the Holy Land, the Mamluks dedicated great efforts to extolling the Islamic character of Jerusalem through religious building programmes:

[The Mamluks'] status as Muslim successors to the Crusaders obligated them to work energetically to glorify Jerusalem as a Muslim city. The Mamluks accomplished this objective by a massive building programme, adding religious places to the town, renovating and maintaining existing shrines, and destroying any offensive remnants of the previous Crusader culture.[114]

In particular, these buildings served the pilgrimage and Sufi communities that were present throughout the city. For example, 'about forty hospices (*ribat, khanqah, zawiya*) were established in Jerusalem in order to house Muslim pilgrims',[115] a total that accounts for all buildings and monuments in the city constructed during the Ayyubid period. Significantly, while most Ayyubid monuments were limited to the Haram, many of the new institutions erected during the Mamluk era were built or founded *outside* the Haram and around its perimeter within the city:

> Philanthropic institutions are typical of any reasonably large town of the period. What makes them exceptional in Jerusalem is their distinct relatedness to the Haram ... how intensively construction was concentrated at the north and west, town-side, borders of the Haram, either alongside the sanctuary itself or along the streets leading to it. In no other medieval Islamic town can one find such a conglomeration of religiously-inspired buildings.[116]

Indeed, many of these Mamluk institutions were located around the Haram complex, thus blurring the liminal spaces that demarcated where the sacred sphere of the Haram ends and the secular quarters of the city begin [Figure 5]. For example, many ribat hospices, which were major religious institutions established to house pilgrims, visitors, and mystic Sufis,[117] were founded immediately around the Haram complex, creating contiguous sacred spaces all along the perimeter of the complex. Along the western side of the Haram, for example, lies al-Ribat al-Mansuri of Sultan Qalawun, Ribat Kurt al-Mansuri, the Ribat of Women (Ribat al-Nisa'), Ribat al-Jawhariyya, and the Ribat al-Zamani.[118] On the north side of the Haram lies the Ribat of 'Ala' al-Din and the Ribat al-Maridini, a pilgrim hospice for visitors from Mardin, a city located southeast of Anatolia, along with al-Khanqah al-Dawadariyya.[119] The Zawiya al-Fakhriyya and the Zawiya al-Wafa'iyya are also located immediately around the Haram on the southwest and west sides of the Haram, respectively.[120]

Additionally, during the Mamluk period numerous madrasas were constructed, many of which were, and still are, located immediately outside the Haram and surrounding its perimeter. These religious institutions of learning were frequented by pilgrims, transient visitors, and residents of the city, even serving simultaneously as *zawiyas* or *khanqahs*. Some, such as Sultan Qaytbay's al-Madrasa al-Ashrafiyya, were built by sultans.[121] On the western side of the Haram, others included, for example, al-Madrasa al-Tankiziyya, al-Madrasa al-Khatuniyya, al-Madrasa al-Arghuniyya, al-Madrasa al-Hanbaliyya, al-Madrasa al-Muzhiriyya, and al-Madrasa al-'Uthmaniyya.[122] The north walls of the Haram were

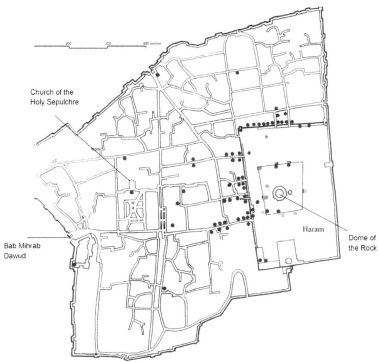

Figure 5: Islamic religious buildings erected during the Mamluk period outside the Haram in Jerusalem City. Reprinted with permission from Burgoyne, *Mamluk Jerusalem.*

also surrounded by madrasas, such as al-Madrasa al-Jawaliyya, al-Madrasa al-Karimiyya, al-Madrasa/Zawiya al-Aminiyya, al-Madrasa al-Sallamiyya, al-Madrasa al-Malikiyya, al-Madrasa al-Farisiyya, the Madrasa/Khanqah al-Is'irdiyya, and the Madrasa/Khanqah al-Basitiyya.[123]

Furthermore, many pilgrimage-related religious buildings were constructed deep within the urban quarters of the city, far from the Haram complex. Frequented by pilgrims and Sufis, these sites further rendered the liminal spaces separating the sacred from the secular more ambiguous. For example, in the northeast quarters of the city and north of the Haram is the Zawiya of Shaykh al-Bistami.[124] Similarly, west of the Haram and in the centre of the Old City stood al-Zawiya al-Qiramiyya and the Caravanserai of Sultan Barquq (previously the Wakala).[125] On the other hand, al-Zawiya al-Lu'lu'iyya is located northwest of the Haram, just south of the Damascus Gate (Bab al-'Amud).[126] Dar al-Qur'an of al-Sallamiyya, a Qur'an-teaching institution, and al-Madrasa al-Taziyya[127] both are located on the south side of the same *tariq* (road), while al-Madrasa al-Lu'lu'iyya is located west of the Haram in the centre of the Old City.[128] Other monuments located far from the Haram and in the urban landscape of the city include the *turba* mausoleum of Barka Khan and its mosque,[129] the Jaliqiyya Tomb,[130] and al-Kilaniyya Tomb, located west of the Haram along Tariq Bab al-Silsila (Road of Bab al-Silsila).[131] The Shaykhuniyya Zawiya was located near the Salahiyya Madrasa and the Ribat al-Hamawi in the Quarter of the Cotton Merchants west of the Haram.[132]

Moreover, the Mamluks even built religious institutions outside Jerusalem's walls. These buildings served pilgrims and visitors to the city. Such pilgrimage-related monuments outside the walls of Jerusalem included, to name a few, the Adhamiyya Zawiya, which occupied a cave under the Sahira cemetery north of the city,[133] and two *zawiyas* built outside the southern walls: Zawiyat Ahmad al-Balasi and Zawiyat Ibrahim al-Azraq.[134]

Considering the large number of pilgrims lodging, praying, and contemplating the sacred in the numerous religious institutions erected around the Haram, inside the city itself, and even outside its walls, it is evident that the Islamic character of Mamluk Jerusalem is far from restricted to the sites on the Haram. Instead, Jerusalem's sacred milieu would have flowed throughout the city during this period. Indeed, with the presence of many of these Islamic religious institutions scattered outside the Haram, in addition to the sacred sites cited in the *Fada'il al-Quds* in and around the city, it becomes clear to the medieval Muslim pilgrim that the sacred sphere expanded throughout and around Jerusalem, thus rendering the city one larger, liminal space.

City as Liminal Space: The Case of Mecca

The blurring of liminal spaces separating the sacred from the profane in Mamluk Jerusalem is also apparent in and comparable to the same phenomenon in Mecca. This blurring is even more evident in the holiest city in Islam, as Mecca is not only pivotal to the faith, as Islam's birthplace, the home of the Ka'ba, and the destination of the yearly hajj (as well as the 'umra, the lesser pilgrimage), but is also home to many secondary holy sites that are connected with the Prophet, the Companions, and the Four Rightly Guided Caliphs.[135] The city of Mecca, it will be argued, was also a place that transformed into one large sacred sphere during the medieval period.

Similar to Jerusalem, the city of Mecca as a whole is consecrated in Islam; traditions tell of how God has blessed Mecca and its surroundings.[136] One tradition states that God spoke to Adam after his descent from Paradise, stating, 'Adam, today have I sanctified Mecca and all that surrounds it, and it shall be sacred until the day of resurrection'.[137] Furthermore, Mecca's raison d'être, according to Islamic tradition, is the presence of the Ka'ba and al-Masjid al-Haram sanctuary, the Sacred Mosque, because, according to tradition, the Sacred Mosque antedates Mecca.[138]

Central to this sacred topography is, of course, the presence of the Ka'ba within the Sacred Mosque. The Ka'ba and the Black Stone (al-Hajar al-Aswad) lie at the centre of the complex, which, according to the Islamic narrative, is also a representation of God's throne on earth and even God's holy abode (Bayt Allah al-Haram).[139] The Ka'ba, which is associated with

Abraham as well as with Muhammad's early life and mission, lies at the centre of Islam. It is the qibla to which all Muslims turn during their daily prayers and the destination of pilgrims during the hajj season as well as throughout the year for the *'umra*. Furthermore, the Ka'ba is part of a cluster of holy sites within the sanctuary, including Maqam Ibrahim, the Spring of Zamzam, al-Hijr, and the adjacent Safa and Marwa promenade.[140] Each site is a stop along the pilgrim's journey through the complex; each represents and is connected to important Islamic figures, such as Adam, Abraham, Hajar, and Ismael, as well as to religious cosmology and pre-Islamic myths and legends.

Yet the sacred in Mecca is not limited to the quarters of the Sacred Mosque. Just as is the case with Jerusalem, the holy sphere in Mecca extends well beyond the boundaries of the Ka'ba and the Sacred Mosque, penetrating deep into the city itself and even further, past its geographical boundaries and into the surrounding mountains. As Francis Edward Peters has noted in his study of the hajj, and based on the sacred geography delineated in al-Azraqi's history of medieval Mecca, there are generally three layers of sacredness in Mecca:

> There was and is more than one holy domain at Mecca. At the heart of the present city, and of the settlement for as long as we have records, there is a holy building, the Ka'ba … The Ka'ba is in turn surrounded by two larger areas, both defined in the manner of a *temenos* and both marked by prohibited and privileged behaviour within them. The one immediately surrounding the Ka'ba is called the 'sacred shrine' (al-masjid al-Haram) and was regarded in Muslim times as a mosque. A third and far larger area, the true *Haram* and called simply by that name, extends well beyond the settled area of Mecca city and is defined by stone boundary markers (*ansab al-Haram*). This is the sacred territory prohibited to non-Muslims throughout its history.[141]

In other words, as in Jerusalem, the sacred in Mecca is not limited to al-Masjid al-Haram complex and its Ka'ba but extends in this case through three layers of geographical sacredness, stretching beyond the Haram and into the city and its environs, thus blurring liminal spaces in Mecca and even rendering them obsolete.

Beginning with the third, outermost layer of sacredness, the boundaries demarcating the sanctified territory around Mecca are the *miqat* boundaries. The *miqat*, marked by stations placed at these boundaries outside Mecca city, constitute the beginning of Mecca's *sacred* zone – the third, outermorst layer noted by Peters – and are important geographical locations for the pilgrim.[142] Once the pilgrim passes the *miqat*, he or she must enter *ihram*, a spiritual 'state of temporary consecration of someone who is performing the hadjdj or the 'umra; a person in this state is referred to as a *muhrim*'.[143] After passing this boundary point, and following major ablutions, prohibitions of certain conduct – swearing, shaving, cutting hair, and having sexual relations – are imposed on the *muhrim*.[144]

Once the pilgrim passes the *miqat* station and dons the *ihram*, he or she enters a spiritual state. As is the case in Jerusalem, pilgrims travelling to Mecca in the state of *ihram* become spiritual agents crisscrossing the city. Their new spiritual state 'symbolizes a separation from the world and [their] intention to be with God alone'.[145] Along with the performance of the hajj itself, the *ihram* symbolizes the unity of the Muslim community, just as the rites of the hajj decree an equality of all the *umma* in Mecca.[146]

It is also through the act of performing the hajj – by pilgrims in a spiritual state of *ihram* – that Mecca becomes a larger zone of sacredness. As they move towards the principal shrine, the Ka'ba, pilgrims spread the air of sanctity outward from the Sacred Mosque to the rest of the city, its outer boundaries, and 'over the very act of pilgrimage'.[147] As a result, drawing boundaries between the sacred and the profane in Mecca becomes difficult if not outright impossible; the city is engulfed in a sphere of holiness that buries any liminal spaces that may exist within and without the confines of the city.

Indeed, the hajj ritual, with its rites, routes, and sites, further blurs Mecca's liminal spaces. The performance of the hajj is not limited to the Sacred Mosque and its Ka'ba. The *manasik* rituals of the hajj include many holy sites located beyond the Ka'ba and the Sacred Mosque. Therefore, it is important to trace here the itinerary and all the sacred locations visited by the pilgrims during the hajj.

Taking place during the first two weeks of the month of Dhu al-Hijja, the hajj season constitutes an elaborate set of rites and rituals at different holy sites inside and outside Mecca city. After passing the *miqat* and entering the state of *ihram*, pilgrims enter the second sphere of sacredness, the precincts of al-Masjid al-Haram, and attend to the Ka'ba, the epicentre of Mecca and the first sphere of sacredness. Here pilgrims perform the *tawaf* circumambulation around it. They then pray two rak'as at Maqam Ibrahim, after which pilgrims traverse the Safa and Marwa promenade seven times. On the seventh of the month, they attend the *khutba* sermon in the Mosque of Mecca, and, on the eighth, the day of watering (*Yawm al-tarwiya*), pilgrims and their animals drink.[148]

Next, just as pilgrims to Jerusalem leave the Haram al-Sharif complex and visit sites outside its walls, pilgrims in Mecca leave the Ka'ba and the confines of the Sacred Mosque as they continue the hajj rituals outside the city. Immersed in *ihram*, they move eastward through the city until they reach Mina, where they spend the night of the eighth of Dhu al-Hijja.[149]

The next day, the pilgrims perform the most important rite in the hajj, the *wuquf* on the Mount of Mercy (Jabal al-Rahma) in the valley of 'Arafa. (This perhaps can be compared to the pilgrimage in Jerusalem, as Muslims in Jerusalem also exit the walled city and head eastward to visit the Mount of Olives.) It is during the *wuquf* that pilgrims pray to God and ask for the forgiveness of sins, just as Adam, according to the Islamic tradition, had done when he reunited with Eve after their expulsion from Paradise.[150] Next comes the *ifada*, retracing the road back to Mecca and entering the boundaries of al-'Alamayn (the Two Flags), after which pilgrims stop at Muzdalifa to perform the Maghrib and 'Isha' prayers.

On the morning of the tenth, *Yawm al-nahr*, pilgrims leave Muzdalifa and head to Mina, where they stay for three days. They engage in the practice of stoning the devil at Jamrat al-'Aqaba. This day also marks the Feast of Sacrifice, 'Id al-Adha. Pilgrims then enter Mecca city and perform another set of circumambulations around the Ka'ba, *tawaf al-ifada*, which concludes the hajj. Now the pilgrim can exit the state of *ihram*.[151] From the eleventh to the thirteenth of Dhu 'l-Hijja, pilgrims again visit Mina, where they stone the *jimar* once again. Finally, pilgrims return one last time to Mecca to perform *tawaf al-wida'* – the farewell circumambulation around the Ka'ba.[152]

Although the hajj itinerary takes the pilgrim to the Ka'ba and the Sacred Mosque and then out into the city and the mountains north of it, the pilgrim's spiritual journey in Mecca does not end here. After the farewell circumambulation, pilgrims are expected to begin a new set of *ziyara* visitations to holy sites in and around Mecca for the purpose of extracting the *baraka* blessing of each site. Indeed, Mecca and its surroundings are filled with secondary holy sites that further expand the sphere of the sacred in the city. These sites are associated with Prophet Muhammad, his family, his Companions, and the Rightly Guided Caliphs; some are also associated with the narratives of Islamic prophets.[153] The proliferation of these 'secondary' holy sites is a consequence of the presence of the Ka'ba and the Haram. As Peters remarks:

> The holiness of the central place, the chief shrine [the Ka'ba], inevitably extends itself over the city. This extended sacralization, taken in conjunction with the pragmatic reality that the pilgrim will spend some time in the city, leads to a *multiplication of secondary shrines* in the city and its environs.[154]

These secondary shrines surround the Sacred Mosque and even reach as far as the surrounding mountains, thus creating 'a porous barrier between the sacred and profane'.[155] Many pilgrims during the medieval period visited these sacred places during their hajj, 'umra, and *ziyara* visits around the city.[156]

Many of these sites, and pilgrims' visits to them, were recorded during the medieval period. For example, medieval works – such as al-Azraqi's ninth-century historical chronicle of Mecca, al-Harawi's twelfth-century guide for pilgrims and visitors, Ibn Jubayr's twelfth-century travelogue, and Ibn Battuta's accounts of his visits to Mecca during the Mamluk period – preserve the memory of the secondary sites scattered across Mecca that extended the pilgrim's itinerary. Their reports indicate that the sphere of the sacred stretched beyond the Ka'ba and the Sacred Mosque, and deep into Mecca city and its environs.[157]

Most prominent among the medieval reports are the abodes and shrines that are associated with the Prophet and his Companions,[158] to which al-Harawi refers to as 'blessed abodes in Mecca' ('*duyur mubaraka fi Makka*').[159] For example, the birthplace of the Prophet ('*mawlid rasul Allah*') is located in the Alley of the Birthplace of the Prophet ('*Ziqaq al-Mawlid*'). Accounts by al-Azraqi, Harawi, and Ibn Jubayr indicate that *ziyara*s were performed at this site.[160] Ibn Jubayr refers to it as the 'pious mausoleum' ('*al-turba al-tahira*'), where, he writes, a mosque stands.[161] Ibn Jubary adds that it was the abode of the Prophet's father, 'Abd Allah ibn al-Muttalib,[162] and a place where 'we benefited by the blessings of gazing at [the Prophet's] noble birthplace'.[163]

Other sacred sites marking the birthplaces of important Muslim figures are included in the *ziyara*s of pilgrims and visitors to the city. They include the *mawlid* (birthplace) of Abu Bakr which, according to the reports, is marked by a mosque (Mosque of Abu Bakr);[164] the *mawlid* of 'Umar ibn al-Khattab;[165] the *mawlid* of 'A'isha, the daughter of Abu Bakr and the wife of the Prophet;[166] and, most significantly, the abode of Muhammad's first wife Khadija ('Dar Khadija/Manzil Khadija'), which houses her birthplace as well as the birthplace of Fatima, the Prophet's daughter, and her two sons al-Hasan and al-Husayn.[167] The record provides detailed descriptions of the abode of Khadija and bestows great sanctity onto it, and both al-Azraqi and al-Harawi note that it serves as a mosque.[168] Besides being the birthplace of Khadija, it is also the place where Muhammad resided until his hijra, the place where all his children were born, and the place where Khadija died.[169] Within this site lie many sacred spots: for example, the Dome of Revelation (Qubbat al-Wahy), the *mawlid* of al-Hasan and al-Husayn, and a dome commemorating the birthplace of Fatima.[170] Ibn Jubayr indicates the blessings of these sites, where people pray and rest, and where, he writes, 'we wiped the cheeks on these sanctified birthplaces'.[171]

Other sacred abodes (*duyur mubaraka*) exist in and around Mecca. There is the much-reported Dar al-Khayzuran, where, according to Islamic tradition, the Prophet prayed secretly before publicly pronouncing his mission; it is also commemorated as the place where 'Umar ibn al-Khattab was converted to Islam, which, consequently, marks the public establishment and proselytization of Islam ('*mansha' al-Islam haythu aslama 'Umar ibn al-Khattab*').[172] Other sacred abodes include that of the Prophet's uncle al-'Abbas (Dar al-'Abbas) between al-Safa and al-Marwa, which, Ibn Battuta notes, was converted into a *ribat* hospice.[173] Furthermore, there is the abode of the cousin of the Prophet and the brother of 'Ali, the *dar* of Ja'far ibn Abi Talib.[174]

The medieval reports also list many sacred sites north of Mecca ('*bi-a'la Makka*'). At the time, many of these places were converted to mosques and were visited by pilgrims. For example, located at the Sheep Market (Suq al-ghanam) is Masjid al-Fath (Mosque of the Conquest), where, according to al-Azraqi, the Prophet had struck an accord with the people of Mecca on the day of his conquest of the city ('*baya'a al-nabiyy … al-nas bi-Makka yawm al-fath*').[175] Another mosque associated with the conquest of Mecca is a mosque in Dhi Tawa ('*Masjid bi-Dhi Tawa*'), where, it is reported, the Prophet had prayed on the day of his conquest of Mecca;[176] it is also, in Azraqi's account, the place where the Prophet stayed overnight when he performed the *'umra*.[177] Ibn Jubayr mentions that visitors receive *baraka* blessings at this mosque, as it is also connected with Abraham.[178] Other mosques north of Mecca that are associated with the Prophet and were visited by pilgrims include the Mosque of the Jinn (Masjid al-Jinn),[179] which is adjacent to the Mosque of the Tree (Masjid al-Shajara), yet another visited holy site.[180]

Moreover, according to the medieval record, in Mina, north of Mecca, lay many sacred sites and mosques, including sanctified places associated with the Prophet, his family, and his Companions. There is Dar Abu Bakr, to which al-Azraqi refers as Manzil Abu Bakr, although Ibn Jubayr mentions that its remains are buried ('*darisat al-athr*').[181]

There is also a mosque commemorating ʿAʾisha (Masjid ʿAʾisha), which is next to Miqat al-Maʿmarayn, and opposite her mosque is another associated with ʿAli ibn Abi Talib.[182] Another popular site in Mina is Masjid al-Khayf, which is referred to by al-Azraqi as Masjid Mina, where, it is believed, the Prophet stayed, and where 70 or more prophets had also prayed.[183] There is also Masjid al-Bayʿa, where, according to the sources, the Prophet conducted his first *bayʿa* pact with the people of Medina before the hijra.[184]

Other important holy places reported by the medieval sources include sites located in the mountains surrounding Mecca. The most important of these is Ghar Hiraʾ, the cave within the Mount of Hiraʾ, where the Prophet is believed to have meditated prior to his mission and the location at which he received his first revelation from Archangel Gabriel.[185] There is also Ghar Thawr, the cave within the Mount of Abu Thawr, where Muhammad and Abu Bakr found refuge during their hijra.[186] Moreover, the medieval reports indicate that there are many sacred graves of important figures in Islam at al-Jabbana cemetery, a place frequently visited by pilgrims.[187] Although it has been reported that many of these graves have disappeared, some, such as the Grave of Khadija and the Grave of the Abbasid Caliph al-Mansur, still existed at the time of the medieval writers' visits to the city.[188]

Finally, just as was the case in Jerusalem under the Mamluks, Mecca also witnessed the proliferation of religious institutions such as madrasas, *zawiyas*, ribats, and *khanqahs* during the Sunni revival period of the twelfth through the sixteenth centuries.[189] Many religious buildings associated with pilgrims, Sufis, and the *ʿulama* scholars were constructed around the Sacred Mosque,[190] thus further obfuscating the liminal spaces around the Haram. For example, Ibn Battuta reports that there was a large *zawiya* outside the Gate of Abraham designated for the Maliki imam.[191] He also reports on a large hospice, the Ribat al-Muwaffaq, which was located around the Sacred Mosque.[192]

Mecca, then, is another example of an Islamic city in which the liminal spaces dividing the sacred quarters of the Haram from the city's urban confines were far from fixed during the medieval period. Similar to Mamluk Jerusalem, medieval Mecca, with its three spheres of sacredness, its multitude of holy sites associated with the hajj, and the secondary shrines scattered across its surrounding region, constituted a larger holy sphere. Precisely designating where in Mecca a Muslim should have been aware of the sacred and where he or she could remove the cloak of spirituality would have been a difficult task. Just as was the case with Mamluk Jerusalem, the medieval city of Mecca thus became one large liminal space.

Conclusion

This study has attempted to demonstrate the ways in which, to a medieval Muslim pilgrim, the sacred sphere in Mamluk Jerusalem was present inside the Haram complex, immediately outside the Haram, deep within the confines of the city, and even outside the city's walls and in its surroundings. Using the *Fadaʾil al-Quds* pilgrimage guides dating from the Mamluk period, the study has shown that the entirety of the city is sacred and blessed in the Islamic tradition, and thus Muslims entering the city were obligated to be in a state of spiritual and religious contemplation. The study then traced in the *Fada'il al-Quds* the itinerary of a Muslim pilgrim around the city's holy sites. While the Haram complex represents the zenith of Islamic religiosity in the city, a further analysis of the guides indicates that the sacred to Muslim pilgrims did not stop once he or she left the Haram. Instead, the *Fada'il al-Quds* extol the holiness of several sites located outside the complex, including non-Muslim locations. Intriguingly, not only did these sites extend the Muslim sacred sphere beyond the Haram and into and around the city, but they also revealed that Jews, Muslims, and Christians shared sacred places in and around the city.[193] Such an interfaith itinerary must have been uncomfortable for conservative Mamluk jurists such as Ibn Taymiyya (1263–1328), who opposed not only pilgrimage to shrines, tombs, and churches but also Islamic pilgrimage to Jerusalem altogether.[194] Yet *ziyara* pilgrimage to Jerusalem would not only continue but also flourish in the centuries following the Mamluk period – especially during the early modern Ottoman era.

On the one hand, the Ottoman period experienced a decline in the composition of *Fada'il al-Quds* literature.[195] It has been argued that by the sixteenth century, which also coincided with the fall of Cyprus and the final end of the Crusader threat to the Muslim Near East, the *Fada'il al-Quds* writings on Jerusalem reached the end of their peak.[196] Thereon, the Fada'il al-Quds genre entered a phase of decline.[197] For example, in comparison to the many guides produced during the Mamluk period, only six *Fada'il al-Quds* works were composed during the Ottoman period.[198] However, what thrived in place of *Fada'il al-Quds* texts during this period is Arabo-Muslim travelogue literature on Jerusalem. These works were written by Muslim travellers who visited the city, toured the Holy Land, and worshipped at the many holy sites the area had to offer.[199] Interestingly, these travel writings on Jerusalem quoted extensively from the *Fada'il al-Quds* of the Mamluk period and thus helped preserve the traditions during the Ottoman centuries. The genre also continued to demonstrate the flourishing phenomenon of Islamic pilgrimage to Jerusalem in late medieval and early modern history.[200]

There are several important Arabo-Muslim travel accounts on Ottoman Jerusalem, whose authors visited and worshipped at the city's many Muslim holy sites.[201] The list includes the Damascene, distinguished scholar and Sufi, Shaikh 'Abd al-Ghani al-Nabulusi (1641–1731). al-Nabulusi authored the travelogue *al-Hadra al-unsiyya fi al-rihla al-Qudsiyya*, an important source on Ottoman Jerusalem.[202] In *al-Hadra al-unsiyya*, al-Nabulusi extensively recorded his entire visit to the city, and provided a detailed mosaic of religious life in late-seventeenth-century Ottoman Jerusalem.[203] al-Nabulusi's visit to Jerusalem not only helped preserve and continue the *Fada'il al-Quds* writings in his travel accounts, but also provided evidence of the flourishing of Islamic pilgrimage to Jerusalem and its abundant holy sites.[204] Moreover, visiting and worshipping at the many sacred spaces the city had to offer to Muslim pilgrims both inside and outside the Haram further continued the blurring of liminal spaces in the city during this period.

These Ottoman travellers to Jerusalem also demonstrated the necessity for building more religious institutions to accommodate their needs and help them fulfil their objective of performing pilgrimage in the city. As this study has shown, great religious building projects were undertaken earlier during the Mamluk era, which was shown to have eclipsed any Islamic building initiatives prior to this period. The scale of construction of madrasas, *khanqahs*, *zawiyas*, mausoleums, and mosques helped transform the Islamic religious landscape of the city. The upper echelons of Mamluk society had built tens of these institutions outside the Haram and within the urban landscape. These religious spaces were closely associated with visitors, pilgrims, and Sufi brotherhoods who lodged, prayed, and performed supplications while contemplating the sacred. The religious activities of Muslim pilgrims in these institutions across Jerusalem further extended the sacred sphere, well beyond the Haram and deep into the secular fabric of the city.

Finally, the study has shown that the phenomenon of blurred liminal spaces in Mamluk Jerusalem was also present in Mecca during the medieval period. Reports from medieval chronicles of Mecca, pilgrimage guides, and medieval travelogue literature on the city indicate that, in addition to holy sites associated with the hajj ritual, there were numerous secondary religious sites located within and beyond the Ka'ba and the Sacred Mosque. Visited by pilgrims and travellers alike, these holy sites were spread all around the city and even in the surrounding areas, further distorting any liminal spaces that may have existed between the sacred and the profane in Mecca city. As a result, medieval Mecca was also a city transformed into a wider liminal space, mirroring the Islamic religious landscape in Jerusalem during the Mamluk period.

Acknowledgements

This paper was first written through the generous funding of the Canadian Social Sciences and Humanities Research Council. I would like to thank my graduate supervisor, Professor Linda S. Northrup, for her support throughout my graduate studies – and especially for her very crucial seminars on everything Mamluk. I would like to thank Professor Walid Saleh for his encouragement as well, and particularly for directing my attention to the *Fada'il al-Quds* literature in his paleography seminar. Many thanks must also go to Drs. Suzan Yalman and A. Hilâl Uğurlu for convening a panel at MESA's 2016 annual meeting in Boston, where I had presented a version of this chapter. I would also like to thank Professor Simon Coleman for organizing the Pilgrimage Forum at the University of Toronto, where I had presented my research from this chapter on one very rainy afternoon. Special thanks should go to Dr. Michael Burgoyne, for taking the time out of his trip to Toronto to meet over coffee and discuss Mamluk Jerusalem, and for reading a draft of this chapter. Finally, I dedicate this chapter to my wife, Barbara, for her endless love, support, and encouragement throughout the many twists and turns that I have experienced (which she at times burdensomely shared!) during my long years of research and studies: to you I am forever grateful.

Notes

1 For an excellent introductory text on pilgrimage in history and across religions, see Simon Coleman and John Elsner, *Pilgrimage: Past and Present in the World Religions* (Cambridge, MA: Harvard University Press, 1995), especially the chapter on pilgrimage to Mecca, at 52–73; see also Ian Reader, *Pilgrimage: A Very Short Introduction* (Oxford: Oxford University Press, 2015); and Simon Coleman, 'Pilgrimage', in *The Blackwell Companion to the Study of Religion*, ed. Robert A. Segal (Oxford: Blackwell Publishing Ltd., 2006), 385–96. For an outstanding research companion to pilgrimage, see Linda Kay Davidson and Maryjane Dunn-Wood, *Pilgrimage in the Middle Ages: A Research Guide* (New York: Garland, 1993); and the comprehensive encyclopedia by Larissa J. Taylor, ed., *Encyclopedia of Medieval Pilgrimage* (Leiden: Brill, 2010). For a short, succinct introduction to and overview of pilgrimage in general, see Edith Turner, 'Pilgrimage: An Overview', in *Encyclopedia of Religion, Second Edition*, ed. Lindsay Jones (Detroit: Macmillan Reference, 2005), 10:7145–48, and sources in its bibliography. For the groundbreaking theoretical study on pilgrimage, see the seminal study of Victor Turner and Edith Turner, *Image and Pilgrimage in Christian Culture: Anthropological Perspectives* (New York: Columbia University Press, 1978), especially their chapter on theory of pilgrimage and the concepts of liminality and communitas, at 1–39; for a response to the Turners' framework on pilgrimage study, especially communitas, see the contributions in John Eade and Michael J. Sallnow, eds, *Contesting the Sacred: The Anthropology of Christian Pilgrimage* (New York: Routledge, 1991); for a recent overview of the debates on pilgrimage theory and the field, see Dionigi Albera and John Eade, 'International Perspectives on Pilgrimage Studies: Putting the Anglophone Contribution in Its Place', in *International Perspectives on Pilgrimage Studies: Itineraries, Gaps and Obstacles*, ed. Dionigi Albera and John Ease (New York: Routledge, 2015), 1–22. For a recent survey of Islamic pilgrimage, see Sophia Rose Arjana, *Pilgrimage in Islam: Traditional and Modern Practices* (London: Oneworld Publications, 2017); for a short overview of Islamic pilgrimage with a focus on pilgrimage to Mecca, see Richard Martin, 'Pilgrimage: Muslim Pilgrimage', in Jones, *Encyclopedia of Religion*, 10:7154–61; for a survey of Islamic pilgrimage to holy sites other than Mecca's, see Josef W. Meri, Werner Ende, Nelly van Doorn-Harder, et al., 'Ziyara', in *Encyclopaedia of Islam, Second Edition*, ed. Peri Bearman, Thierry Bianquis, Clifford Edmund Bosworth, et al., accessed October 26, 2018, http://dx.doi.org/10.1163/1573–3912_islam_COM_1390; Yousef (Josef) Meri, 'The Cult of Saints and Pilgrimage', in *The Oxford Handbook of the Abrahamic Religions*, eds Adam J. Silverstein and Guy G. Stroumsa (Oxford: Oxford University Press, 2015), 499–517. For studies on pilgrimage to Palestine and Syria, see Chester Charlton McCown, 'Muslim Shrines in Palestine', *Annual of the American School of Oriental Research in Jerusalem* 2–3 (1923): 47–68; Tewfik Canaan, *Mohammedan Saints and Sanctuaries in Palestine* (Jerusalem: Ariel Publishing House, 1927); Amikam Elad, *Medieval Jerusalem and Islamic Worship: Holy Places, Ceremonies, Pilgrimage*, 2nd ed. (Leiden: Brill, 1999); Andreas Kaplony, *The Haram of Jerusalem, 324-1099: Temple, Friday Mosque, Area of Spiritual Power* (Stuttgart: Franz Steiner, 2002); and Josef W. Meri, *The Cult of Saints among Muslims and Jews in Medieval Syria* (New York: Oxford University Press, 2002). For translated

accounts of pilgrimage, see *Palestine Pilgrims Text Society* (London: London Committee of the Palestine Exploration Fund, 1896–97), vols. 1, 3, and 10; Francis Edward Peters, *Jerusalem: The Holy City in the Eyes of Chroniclers, Visitors, Pilgrims, and Prophets* (Princeton: Princeton University Press, 1985); and Janin Hunt, *Four Paths to Jerusalem: Jewish, Christian, Muslim, and Secular Pilgrimages, 1000 BCE to 2001 CE* (Jefferson, N.C.: McFarland & Co., 2002). On the geography of Palestine and the translation of medieval geographers' and travellers' descriptions of Palestine, see Le Strange's indispensable work, Guy Le Strange, *Palestine under the Moslems: A Description of Syria and the Holy Land from A.D. 650 to 1500* (repr., Beirut: Khayats Oriental Reprints, 1965).

2   Elad, *Medieval Jerusalem*, 51–146; Michael Hamilton Burgoyne with additional historical research by Donald Sidney Richards, *Mamluk Jerusalem: An Architectural Study* (Essex: Published on behalf of the British School of Archaeology in Jerusalem by the World of Islam Festival Trust, 1987), 33[a, b], 61[a,b]; and Yehoshua Frenkel, 'Muslim Pilgrimage to Jerusalem in the Mamluk Period', in *Pilgrims and Travellers to the Holy Land*, ed. Bryan F. Le Beau and Menachem Mor (Omaha: Creighton University Press, 1996), 64, 70. On the debate regarding Jerusalem in lieu of Mecca as a hajj destination during the medieval period, see S. D. Goitein's summary in section A.I.6 of Shelomo Dov Goitein and Oleg Grabar, 'al-Kuds', in *Encyclopaedia of Islam, Second Edition*, accessed August 4, 2017, http://dx.doi.org/10.1163/1573-3912_islam_COM_0535.

3   Burgoyne, *Mamluk Jerusalem*, 61[b].

4   For Mamluk Jerusalem generally, see the following (representative but not exhaustive) list: Donald P. Little, '1260–1516: The Noble Sanctuary (*al-Haram al-Sharif*) under Mamluk Rule: History', in *Where Heaven and Earth Meet: Jerusalem's Sacred Esplanade*, ed. Oleg Grabar and Benjamin Z. Kedar (Austin: University of Texas Press, 2009), 176–87; Donald P. Little, 'Jerusalem under the Ayyubids and Mamluks', in *Jerusalem in History: 3,000 B.C. to the Present Day*, ed. Kamil J. Asali (London: Kegan Paul International, 1997), 177–99; al-'Arif, *al-Mufassal fi Tarikh al-Quds* (Jerusalem, 1961); Burgoyne, *Mamluk Jerusalem*; Michael H. Burgoyne, 'The Noble Sanctuary (*al-Haram al-Sharif*) under Mamluk Rule: Architecture', in Grabar and Zedar, *Where Heaven and Earth Meet*, 188–209; 'Ali al-Sayyid 'Ali, *al-Quds fi al-'asr al-Mamluki* (Cairo: Dar al-Fikr, 1986); David Ayalon, 'Discharge from Service, Banishments and Imprisonments in Mamluk Society', *Israel Oriental Society* 2 (1972): 324–49: Joseph Drury, 'Jerusalem during the Mamluk Period', in *The Jerusalem Cathedra: Studies in the History, Archaeology, Geography, and Ethnography of the Land of Israel*, ed. Lee I. Levine (Jerusalem: Yad Izhak Ben-Zvi Institute; Detroit: Wayne State University Press, 1981), 190–213; Yusuf Darwish Ghawanimah, *Tarikh Niyabat Bayt al-Maqdis fi al-'asr al-Mamluki* (Amman: Dar al-Hayah bi-Da'm min Jami'at al-Yarmuk, 1982); Ulrich Harmann, 'Mamluk Jerusalem', *Levant* 22 (1990): 149–53; Donald P. Little, 'The Governance of Jerusalem under Qaytbay', in *The Mamluks in Egyptian and Syrian Politics and Society*, ed. Amalia Levanoni and Michael Winter (Leiden: Brill, 2004), 143–61; Donald P. Little, 'Mujir al-Din al-'Ulaymi's Vision of Jerusalem in the Ninth/Fifteenth Century', *Journal of the American Oriental Society* 115.2 (1995): 237–47; Hatim Mahamid, 'Waqf, Education and Politics in Mamluk Jerusalem', *The Islamic Quarterly* 50.1 (2006): 33–57; Nimrod Lutz, *The Mamluk City in the Middle East: History, Culture, and the*

Urban Landscape (New York: Cambridge University Press, 2014), 47–68, which provides an architectural survey of Mamluk Jerusalem and its shared 'vernacular' architecture with other cities of Syria; Muhammad al-Hafiz Naqr, *Tarikh Bayt al-Maqdis fi al-'asr al-Mamluki* (Amman: Dar al-Bidayah, 2006); Robert Schick, 'Arabic Studies of Mamluk Jerusalem: A Review Article', *Mamluk Studies Review* 5 (2001): 159–68; and Francis Edward Peters, *Jerusalem and Mecca: The Typology of the Holy City in the Near East* (New York: New York University Press, 1986). For the Haram al-Sharif documents and their role in deciphering the legal, social, and urban history of Mamluk Jerusalem, see Linda S. Northrup and Amal A. Abul-Hajj, 'A Collection of Medieval Arabic Documents in the Islamic Museum at the Haram al-Sharif', *Arabica* 25 (1978): 282–91; Donald P. Little, *A Catalogue of the Islamic Documents from al-Haram al-Sharif in Jerusalem* (Beirut: Beiruter Texte und Studien, 1984), and his many other articles on the Haram documents in Donald P. Little, *History and Historiography of the Mamluks* (London: Variorum Reprints, 1986); Kamil J. Asali, *Watha'iq Maqdisiyah tarikhiyah ma'a muqaddimah hawla ba'd al-masadir al-awwaliyah li-tarikh al-Quds*, vol. 1 (Amman: al-Jami'ah al-Urduniyah, 1983); Wael Hallaq, 'The Qadi's Diwan (Sijill) before the Ottomans', *Bulletin of the School of Oriental and African Studies* 60 (1997): 415–36; Huda Lutfi, *Al-Quds al-Mamlukiyya: A History of* Mamluk *Jerusalem Based on the* Haram *Documents* (Berlin: Islamkundliche Untersuchungen, 1985); and Christian Müller, 'A Legal Instrument in the Service of People and Institutions: Endowments in Mamluk Jerusalem as Mirrored in the Haram Documents', *Mamluk Studies Review* 12.1 (2008): 173–91.

5 Burgoyne, *Mamluk Jerusalem*, 61[a–b]; Ghalib Anabsi, 'Popular Beliefs as Reflected in "Merits of Palestine and Syria" (*Fada'il al-Sham*) Literature: Pilgrimage Ceremonies and Customs in the Mamluk and Ottoman Periods', *Journal of Islamic Studies* 19.1 (2008): 59–71, 61; and Frenkel, 'Muslim Pilgrimage', 70–72. On the increase in the number of Muslim visitors from the Maghrib, see Yehoshua Frenkel, 'Muslim Travellers to Bilad al-Sham (Syria and Palestine) from the Thirteenth to the Sixteenth Centuries: Maghribi Travel Accounts', in *Travellers in Deserts of the Levant: Voyagers and Visionaries*, eds Sarah Searight and Malcolm Wagstaff (Durham: ASTENE, 2001), 109–20.

6 Burgoyne, *Mamluk Jerusalem*, 61[a–b].

7 Ibid., 33[a–b], and passim; and Frenkel, 'Muslim Pilgrimage', 72–76. See also Donald P. Little, 'The Nature of Khanqahs, Ribats and Zawiyas under the Mamluks', in *Islamic Studies Presented to Charles J. Adams*, eds Wael B. Hallaq and Donald P. Little (Leiden: Brill, 1991), 91–106.

8 See, most importantly, Elad, *Medieval Jerusalem*; and Kaplony, *The Haram of Jerusalem*.

9 Very few studies have focused on pilgrimage to Jerusalem during the Mamluk period: Frenkel, 'Muslim Pilgrimage'; Anabsi, 'Popular Beliefs'; and Canaan, *Mohammedan Saints and Sanctuaries in Palestine*. Other studies have mentioned Islamic pilgrimage to the city during this era only in passing or in a short survey of this phenomenon: Little, 'Jerusalem under the Ayyubids and Mamluks', 189–94; Little, 'The Noble Sanctuary', 178–80, 186; Burgoyne, *Mamluk Jerusalem*, 31, 61, and passim as part of his architectural survey of all Mamluk buildings; Peters, *Jerusalem and Mecca*, 176–79; Peters, *Jerusalem*, 379–426, where

Peters provides accounts of the city during the Mamluk period based on translations of European, Jewish, and Muslim chroniclers, pilgrims, and travellers, with the majority of the reports from the famous Mamluk chronicler of Jerusalem Mujir al-Din al-ʿUlaymi (on Mujir al-Din's chronicle, see *infra*, section II); Hunt, *Four Paths to Jerusalem*, 109–45, where the author includes mostly European and Jewish pilgrimage reports on the city during this period, with short accounts from Ibn Battuta's travelogue (123–24) and Mujir al-Din's chronicle (144–45); and Joseph Drory, 'Jerusalem During the Mamluk Period', in *The Jerusalem Cathedra: Studies in the History, Archaeology, Geography and Ethnography of the Land of Israel*, ed. Lee I. Levine, vol. 1 (Detroit: Wayne State University Press, 1981), 198–208. Meri, *Cult of Saints* does not deal extensively with Jerusalem, despite the rich reservoir of Islamic pilgrimage guides to the city, focusing instead on Syrian cities such as Damascus and Aleppo. I am currently writing a larger study of Islamic pilgrimage to Jerusalem during the Mamluk period.

10 For a discussion of the *Fadaʾil al-Quds* literature, see the next section, *infra*, and sources cited within that section.

11 On liminality as a theoretical tool for the study of pilgrimage experience, see Victor Turner and Edith Turner, *Image and Pilgrimage in Christian Culture*, 1–39, where the authors engage the concepts of ritual and initiation to describe the stage of liminality in a pilgrim's second of three phases of his or her sacred journey – separation, liminality, and reaggregation. The concept of liminality has also extended to other fields of the social sciences, including, for example, the study of landscapes and travel: see the contribtions to the volume by Hazel Andrews and Les Roberts, eds, *Liminal Landscapes: Travel, Experience and Spaces In-Between* (London: Routledge, 2012); for a recent collection of essays on spatio-temporal and symbolic experience of liminality in Late Antiquity, including liminal spaces in Late Antique cities, see Emilie M. van Opstall, ed., *Sacred Thresholds: The Door to the Sanctuary in Late Antiquity* (Leiden: Brill 2018). On liminality generally, see Bjørn Thomassen, 'Liminality', in *Routledge Encyclopedia of Social Theory*, eds Austin Harrington, Barbara Marshall and Hans-Peter Müller (New York: Routledge, 2006) 322[b]–323[a]; for a historical overview of the use of the term from Arnold van Gennep to the Turners and beyond, see also Bjørn Thomassen, 'The Uses and Meanings of Liminality', *International Political Anthropology* 2.1 (2009): 5–27; see also Denise A. Stodola, 'Liminality', in *Encyclopedia of Medieval Pilgrimage*, ed. Larissa J. Taylor (Leiden: Brill 2010) 334[b]–336[b].

12 Rudolf Sellheim, 'Fadila', in *Encyclopaedia of Islam, Second Edition*, accessed July 31, 2017, http://dx.doi.org/10.1163/1573-3912_islam_COM_0204.

13 See Kamil J. ʿAsali, *Makhtutat Fadaʾil Bayt al-Maqdis* (Amman: Manshurat Mujmaʿ al-Lugha al-ʾArabiyya al-Urduni, 1981), 2–3; and Gustave Edmund von Grunebaum, 'The Sacred Character of Islamic Cities', in *Melanges Taha Husain*, ed. A. Badawi, (Cairo: Dar al-maʾarif, 1962), 25–37.

14 Some studies translate the term *Fadaʾil al-Quds* as 'The Merits of Jerusalem'; see Emanuel Sivan, 'The Beginnings of the *Fadaʾil al-Quds* Literature', *Israel Oriental Studies* 1 (1971): 263–71. For the use of the translation 'Praises of Jerusalem', see Elad, *Medieval Jerusalem*, 6–22; and Moshe Sharon, 'The "Praises of Jerusalem" as a Source for the Early History of Islam', *Bibliotheca Orientalis* 46.1 (1992): 56–67.

15 There is a growing corpus of scholarship on *Fada'il al-Quds* literature. A major bio-bibliographical study that contributed to the accelerating process of editing and publishing the *Fada'il al-Quds* manuscripts is Kamil J. 'Asali's important bio-bibliographical work *Makhtutat Fada'il Bayt al-Maqdis*. For one of the earliest and most important studies of the literature, see Joachim Wilhelm Hirschberg, 'The Sources of Moslem Traditions Concerning Jerusalem', *Rocznik Orientalisticzni* 17 (1951–52): 314–50. See also Heribert Busse, 'Sanctity of Jerusalem in Islam', *Judaism* 17 (1968): 441–68; Emanuel Sivan, 'Le caractère sacre de Jerusalem dans l'Islam aux XIIe-XIIIe siecles', *Studia Islamica* 27 (1967): 149–82; and Sivan, 'The Beginnings of the *Fada'il al-Quds* Literature'. Other studies include important contributions by Amikam Elad, 'A Note on Some Traditions of *Fada'il al-Quds*', *Jerusalem Studies in Arabic and Islam* 14 (1991): 71–83; Amikam Elad, 'The History and Topography of Jerusalem during the Early Islamic Period: The Historical Value of *Fada'il al-Quds* Literature, a Reconsideration', *Jerusalem Studies in Arabic and Islam* 14 (1992): 41–70; and Elad, *Medieval Jerusalem*. Recent scholarship by Ofer Livne-Kafri has further contributed to the understanding of content, topics, and traditions within the literature: Ofer Livne-Kafri, 'The Muslim Traditions "In Praise of Jerusalem" (*Fada'il al-Quds*): Diversity and Complexity', *Annali* 58 (1998): 165–92; Ofer Livne-Kafri, '*Fada'il Bayt al-Maqdis* (The Merits of Jerusalem): Two Additional Notes', *Quaderni di Studi Arabi* 19 (2001): 61–70; Ofer Livne-Kafri, 'The Early Shi'a and Jerusalem', *Arabica* 48 (2001): 112–20; Ofer Livne-Kafri, 'Christian Attitudes Reflected in the Muslim Literature in Praise of Jerusalem', *Proch-Orient Chrétien* 54 (2004): 347–75; Ofer Livne-Kafri, 'On Muslim Jerusalem in the Period of its Formation', *Liber Annuus* 55 (2005): 203–16; Ofer Livne-Kafri, 'Jerusalem in Early Islam: The Eschatological Aspect', *Arabica* 53.3 (2006): 382–403; and Ofer Livne-Kafri, 'Jerusalem: The Navel of the Earth in Muslim Tradition', *Der Islam* 84.1 (2008): 46–72. See also Meir Jacob Kister's contributions to the study of Jerusalem and the *Fada'il al-Quds* literature: Meir Jacob Kister, 'You Shall Only Set out for Three Mosques', *Le Museon* 82 (1969): 173–96; Meir Jacob Kister, 'Comment on Antiquity of Traditions Praising Jerusalem', *Jerusalem Cathedra* 1 (1981): 185–86; Isaac Hasson, 'The Muslim View of Jerusalem – the Qur'an and Hadith', in *History of Jerusalem: Early Muslim Period, 638–1099*, eds Joshua Prawer and Haggai Ben-Shammai (New York: New York University Press, 1996), 349–85; Isaac Hasson, 'Muqadima', in Abu Bakr Muhammad ibn Ahmad al-Wasiti, *Fada'il al-Bayt al-Muqaddas*, ed. Isaac Hasson (Jerusalem: The Magnes Press, 1979); and Suleiman Mourad, 'The Symbolism of Jerusalem in Early Islam', in *Jerusalem: Idea and Reality*, eds Tamar Mayer and Suleiman A. Mourad (New York: Routledge, 2008), 86–102.

16 See Elad, *Medieval Jerusalem*, 6–22.

17 On the development of the genre, see Sivan, 'The Beginnings of the *Fada'il al-Quds*'.

18 Abu Bakr Muhammad ibn Ahmad al-Wasiti, *Fada'il al-Bayt al-Muqaddas*, ed. Isaac Hasson (Jerusalem: The Magnes Press, 1979); and Abu al-Ma'ali al-Musharraf Ibn al-Murajja al-Maqdisi, *Fada'il Bayt al-Maqdis*, ed. Ayman Nasr al-Din al-Azhari (Beirut: Dar al-Kutub al-'Ilmiyah, 2002).

19 On the Muslim ideological response to the Crusades, including the proliferation of *Fada'il al-Quds* literature, see the important work of Emanuel Sivan, *L'Islam et la Croisade, idéologie et propagande dans les réactions musulmanes aux Croisade* (Paris: Paris Librairie d'Amérique et d'Orient, 1968). For a chronological list of *Fada'il al-Quds* composed before, during, and after the Crusades, see 'Asali, *Makhtutat*, where the author provides a catalogue of *Fada'il*

al-Quds manuscripts from the early Islamic period to the Ottoman and modern periods; see also the informative discussion in Carole Hillenbrand, *The Crusades: Islamic Perspectives* (Edinburgh: Edinburgh University Press, 1999), 162–65, 175–80.

20 Abu al-Faraj ʿAbd al-Rahman ibn ʿAli Ibn al-Jawzi, *Fadaʾil al-Quds*, ed. Jibraʾil Sulayman Jabbur (Beirut: Dar al-Afaq al-Jadidah, 1979); and Muhammad ibn ʿAbd al-Wahid al-Maqdisi, *Fadaʾil Bayt al-Maqdis*, ed. Muhammad Mutiʿ al-Hafiz (Damascus: Dar al-Fikr, 1985).

21 See above, notes 5–7.

22 ʿAsali, *Makhtutat*, 41–114.

23 Most of the surviving works have been edited and published in the last two decades.

24 Burhan ad-Din ibn al-Firkah al-Fazari, *Baʿith al-nufus ila ziyarat al-Quds al-mahrus*, trans. Charles D. Matthews as *Palestine, Mohammedan Holy Land*, Part I (New Haven: Yale University Press, 1949); Abu al-Nasr Taj al-Din ʿAbd al-Wahhab ibn ʿUmar al-Husayni al-Shafiʿi, *al-Rawd al-mugharras fi fadaʾil al-bayt al-muqaddas*, ed. Zuhayr Ghanayim ʿAbd al-Latif (Amman: Dar Jarir lil-Nashr wa-al-Tawziʿ, 2009); Muhammad ibn Shihab al-Din al-Suyuti, *Ithaf al-akhissa bi-fadaʾil al-Masjid al-Aqsa*, ed. Ahmad Ramadan Ahmad (Cairo: al-Hayʾah al-Misriyah al-ʿAmmah li-al-Kitab, 1982); and Mujir al-Din ʿAbd al-Rahman ibn Muhammad al-ʿUlaymi, *al-Uns al-jalil bi-tarikh al-Quds wa al-Khalil*, ed. Muhammad Bahr al-ʿUlum (Najaf, Iraq: al-Matbaʿa al-Haydariyya, 1968), vol. 1. After the end of the Mamluk period and during the beginning of the Ottoman period, a work was composed in 948/1541 by Muhammad ibn Muhammad ibn Khidr al-Maqdisi, *al-Mustaqsa fi Fadaʾil al-Masjid al-Aqsa*, ed. Mashhur al-Habbazi (Jerusalem: Bayt al-Shiʿr al-Filastini, 2008).

25 ʿAsali, *Makhtutat*, 9.

26 Sivan, 'The Beginnings of the *Fadaʾil al-Quds*', 266–67. Emphasis added.

27 This is discussed in more detail in the section 'Holy Sites on the Haram al-Sharif', *infra*. See Elad's discussion of the historical value of the literature and of how his study used the *fadaʾil* literature to reconstruct the early Islamic history of Jerusalem and to trace pilgrims' itinerary in the city, whereby the *Fadaʾil al-Quds* literature provides ample information concerning holy sites scattered inside and outside the Haram: Elad, *Medieval Jerusalem*, 6–22, 78–146.

28 '*Kathrat al-asmaʾ tadullu ʿala sharaf al-musamma*': al-Husayni al-Shafiʿi, *al-Rawd al-mugharras*, 28. Different names include 'Iliyaʾ', 'Bayt al-Maqdis', 'Ur Shalim', and 'al-Quds'; see Suyuti, *Ithaf al-akhissa*, 93–94; Shihab al-Din Ahmad ibn Muhammad Ibn Hilal al-Maqdisi, *Muthir al-gharam ila ziyarat al-Quds wa al-Sham*, ed. Ahmad al-Khutaymi (Beirut: Dar al-Jil, 1994), 190; and ʿUlaymi, *al-Uns al-jalil*, I, 6–7.

29 Traditions relating to the building of Jerusalem by David and Solomon are abundant in the *Fadaʾil al-Quds* works. Some are derived from biblical narratives, but many are also mythological. Regardless of each tradition's source or its veracity, all of them point to the association of Jerusalem with the prophets (of Islam) and, therefore, to its sacredness: see, for example, al-Husayni al-Shafiʿi, *al-Rawd al-mugharras*, 34–36, 41–43, 47–51; Suyuti, *Ithaf al-akhissa*, 101, 103, 106, 128, 129; Ibn al-Firkah, *Baʿith al-nufus*, 3–7; Ibn Hilal al-Maqdisi, *Muthir al-gharam*, 132–33, 135–39, 143–53; ʿUlaymi, *al-Uns al-jalil*, I, 7–8, 113–24, 238–39; and Ibn Khidr al-Maqdisi, *al-Mustaqsa fi fadaʾil al-Masjid al-Aqsa*, 41–51.

30 Ibn al-Firkah, *Ba'ith al-nufus*, 2–3; Ibn Hilal al-Maqdisi, *Muthir al-gharam*, 131–32; al-Husayni al-Shafi'i, *al-Rawd al-mugharras*, 33–34; Suyuti, *Ithaf al-akhissa*, 98–99; 'Ulaymi, *al-Uns al-jalil*, I, 7; and Ibn Khidr al-Maqdisi, *al-Mustaqsa*, 38 (that the Ka'ba was built from stones of Tur Zayta [i.e., the Mount of Olives in Jerusalem]).

31 '*La tashudda al-rihal illa li-thalathat masajid: Masjid al-Haram wa Masjidi hatha wa al-Masjid al-Aqsa*' (translation by Matthews of Ibn al-Firkah, *Ba'ith al-nufus*, 4); al-Wasiti, *Fada'il al-Bayt al-Muqaddas*, 3–5, nos. 1–4; Ibn al-Murajja, *Fada'il Bayt al-Maqdis*, 101–5; Ibn al-Jawzi, *Fada'il al-Quds*, 96; Diya' al-Din Muhammad ibn 'Abd al-Wahid al-Maqdisi, *Fada'il Bayt al-Maqdis*, ed. Muhammad Muti' al-Hafiz (Damascus: Dar al-Fikr, 1985), 39–44; Ibn Hilal al-Maqdisi, *Muthir al-gharam*, 207; al-Husayni al-Shafi'i, *al-Rawd al-mugharras*, 95; Suyuti, *Ithaf al-akhissa*, 97–98; 'Ulaymi, *al-Uns al-jalil*, I, 230–32; and Ibn Khidr al-Maqdisi, *al-Mustaqsa*, 41.

32 '*Subhan al-ladhi asra bi-'abdihi laylan min al-Masjid al-Haram ila al-Masjid al-Aqsa al-ladhi barakna hawlahu*': al-Wasiti, *Fada'il al-Bayt al-Muqaddas*, 102, no. 165, 95–101, nos. 155–59, 162; Ibn al-Murajja, *Fada'il Bayt al-Maqdis*, 330, 356, 363, 441; Ibn al-Jawzi, *Fada'il al-Quds*, 84; Ibn al-Firkah, *Ba'ith al-nufus*, 31; Ibn Hilal al-Maqdisi, *Muthir al-gharam*, 69; al-Husayni al-Shafi'i, *al-Rawd al-mugharras*, 62; Suyuti, *Ithaf al-akhissa*, 95; 'Ulaymi, *al-Uns al-jalil*, I, 226 (here the author emphasizes that even if there were no other blessing on the city, this Qur'anic verse on its own is enough ('*law lam yakun lahu fadila ghayr hathihi al-aya la-kanat kafiya*'); and Ibn Khidr al-Maqdisi, *al-Mustaqsa*, 107. For the *isra'* narrative, see Frederick S. Colby, *Narrating Muhammad's Night Journey: Tracing the Development of the Ibn 'Abbas Ascension Discourse* (Albany: SUNY Press, 2008).

33 See, for example, Abu Ja'far Muhammad ibn Jarir al-Tabari, *Tafsir al-Tabari: Jami' al-bayan 'an ta'wil ay al-Qur'an*, ed. 'Abd Allah ibn 'Abd al-Muhsin al-Turki, v. 14 (Riyadh: Dar 'Alam al-Kutub, 2003), 420; Abu Mansur Muhammad ibn Muhammad ibn Mahmud al-Maturidi, *Tafsir al-Qur'an al-'azim, al-musamma, Ta'wilat ahl al-Sunnah*, ed. Fatimah Yusuf al-Khaymi, vol. 3 (Beirut: Mu'assasat al-Risalah, 2004), 133; Abu al-Hasan 'Ali ibn Muhammad ibn Habib al-Mawardi, *al-Nukat wa-al-'uyun, tafsir al-Mawardi*, ed. al-Sayyid ibn 'Abd al-Maqsud ibn 'Abd al-Rahim, vol. 3 (Beirut: Dar al-Kutub al-'Ilmiyah, Mu'assasat al-Kutub al-Thaqafiyah, 1992), 226; Abu al-Fida' Isma'il ibn 'Umar ibn Kathir al-Qurashi, *Tafsir al-Qur'an al-'azim*, ed. Sami ibn Muhammad al-Salamah, vol. 5 (Riyadh: Dar Tibah, 1997), 5; and Jalal al-Din 'Abd al-Rahman ibn Abi Bakr al-Suyuti, *al-Durr al-manthur fi al-tafsir al-ma'thur wa-huwa mukhtasar tafsir turjuman al-Qur'an*, vol. 4 (Beirut: Dar al-Kutub al-'Ilmiyah, 2000), 258. Some exegetes even interpret the term 'al-Masjid al-Aqsa' as 'Bayt al-Maqdis', the Arabic term for Jerusalem; see, for example, al-Maturidi, *Ta'wilat ahl al-Sunnah*, 3:133; Ibn Kathir, *Tafsir al-Qur'an al-'azim*, 5:5; and al-Suyuti, *al-Durr al-manthur*, 4:258. As Heribert Busse has noted, 'Bayt al-Maqdis' can indicate three meanings, one of them being the city of Jerusalem: 'first [meaning], the Jewish Temple and its successor, the Temple Mount (*al-haram al-sharif*) with the Dome of the Rock and the Aqsa Mosque ...; second, *the city of Jerusalem*; third, the holy land (*al-ard al-muqaddasa*) as a whole'; see Heribert Busse, 'Jerusalem', in *Encyclopaedia of the Qur'an*, ed. Jane Dammen McAuliffe (Leiden: Brill Academic Publishers, 2003), accessed July 29, 2017. Original emphasis. While the term could refer to the Temple Mount/al-Haram al-Sharif complex

and/or to Jerusalem, the location of the Haram complex that houses al-Masjid al-Aqsa in Jerusalem gave (and continues to give) the city as a whole a special sanctity that attracted Muslim pilgrims and visitors to its quarters throughout the medieval period.

34 For 2.58, see, for example, Ibn al-Murajja, *Fada'il Bayt al-Maqdis*, 184–85; Ibn al-Firkah, *Ba'ith al-nufus*, 23; Ibn Hilal al-Maqdisi, *Muthir al-gharam*, 65; Suyuti, *Ithaf al-akhissa*, 96; and Ibn Khidr al-Maqdisi, *al-Mustaqsa*, 72–73, 181. For 5.21, see Ibn al-Murajja, *Fada'il Bayt al-Maqdis*, 351, 356; Ibn Hilal al-Maqdisi, *Muthir al-gharam*, 68; Suyuti, *Ithaf al-akhissa*, 96; and Ibn Khidr al-Maqdisi, *al-Mustaqsa*, 181. For 21.71, see al-Wasiti, *Fada'il al-Bayt al-Muqaddas*, 51–52, no. 78, 68, no. 109; Ibn al-Murajja, *Fada'il Bayt al-Maqdis*, 356; Ibn al-Jawzi, *Fada'il al-Quds*, 140; Diya' al-Din al-Maqdisi, *Fada'il Bayt al-Maqdis*, 58; Ibn Hilal al-Maqdisi, *Muthir al-gharam*, 72, 73, 217; 'Ulaymi, *al-Uns al-jalil*, I, 239; and Ibn Khidr al-Maqdisi, *al-Mustaqsa*, 56, 181. On Jerusalem in the Qur'an, see Hasson, 'The Muslim View of Jerusalem'.

35 Ibn al-Firkah, *Ba'ith al-nufus*, 18 (translation by Matthews); al-Wasiti, *Fada'il al-Bayt al-Muqaddas*, 51, no. 78, 138–39, no. 140; Ibn al-Murajja, *Fada'il Bayt al-Maqdis*, 123–24; Ibn al-Jawzi, *Fada'il al-Quds*, 114; Diya' al-Din al-Maqdisi, *Fada'il Bayt al-Maqdis*, 53–56; Ibn Hilal al-Maqdisi, *Muthir al-gharam*, 214–16; al-Husayni al-Shafi'i, *al-Rawd al-mugharras*, 60–61, 133, 134; Suyuti, *Ithaf al-akhissa*, 103, 106, 133; 'Ulaymi, *al-Uns al-jalil*, I, 232, 239, 292; and Ibn Khidr al-Maqdisi, *al-Mustaqsa*, 101.

36 al-Wasiti, *Fada'il al-Bayt al-Muqaddas*, 43, no. 59; Ibn al-Murajja, *Fada'il Bayt al-Maqdis*, 198–99, 200, 316; Ibn al-Jawzi, *Fada'il al-Quds*, 139; Diya' al-Din al-Maqdisi, *Fada'il Bayt al-Maqdis*, 58-59 (tradition referring to the Rock [*al-sakhra*]); Ibn al-Firkah, *Ba'ith al-nufus*, 28, 29, 140; Ibn Hilal al-Maqdisi, *Muthir al-gharam*, 221, 259; al-Husayni al-Shafi'i, *al-Rawd al-mugharras*, 57–58, 60; Suyuti, *Ithaf al-akhissa*, 101; 'Ulaymi, *al-Uns al-jalil*, I, 228, 232, 238–39; and Ibn Khidr al-Maqdisi, *al-Mustaqsa*, 175–76, 182.

37 al-Wasiti, *Fada'il al-Bayt al-Muqaddas*, 21–22, nos. 24–25, 22–23, nos. 27–28; Ibn al-Murajja, *Fada'il Bayt al-Maqdis*, 29, 30, 138, 199, 207, 360; Ibn al-Jawzi, *Fada'il al-Quds*, 84, 95; Diya' al-Din al-Maqdisi, *Fada'il Bayt al-Maqdis*, 58–59; Ibn al-Firkah, *Ba'ith al-nufus*, 28, 29–30, 33, 34; Ibn Hilal al-Maqdisi, *Muthir al-gharam*, 251 (God speaking to the Rock); al-Husayni al-Shafi'i, *al-Rawd al-mugharras*, 57, 58; Suyuti, *Ithaf al-akhissa*, 101, 104, 105, 109, 137; 'Ulaymi, *al-Uns al-jalil*, I, 227, 228, 229, 239, 240, 241; and Ibn Khidr al-Maqdisi, *al-Mustaqsa*, 176, 177–78, 182.

38 al-Wasiti, *Fada'il al-Bayt al-Muqaddas*, 29, no. 39, 30, no. 40, 138–39, no. 140; Ibn al-Murajja, *Fada'il Bayt al-Maqdis*, 217, 354, 357, 359; Ibn al-Jawzi, *Fada'il al-Quds*, 85–86, 88–89; Diya' al-Din al-Maqdisi, *Fada'il Bayt al-Maqdis*, 46–47; Ibn al-Firkah, *Ba'ith al-nufus*, 5, 28–29; Ibn Hilal al-Maqdisi, *Muthir al-gharam*, 221–22, 223; al-Husayni al-Shafi'i, *al-Rawd al-mugharras*, 57, 61, 63; Suyuti, *Ithaf al-akhissa*, 102–3; 'Ulaymi, *al-Uns al-jalil*, I, 238, 239; and Ibn Khidr al-Maqdisi, *al-Mustaqsa*, 175, 179, 180.

39 al-Wasiti, *Fada'il al-Bayt al-Muqaddas*, 22, no. 26, 40, no. 55, 102, no. 165; Ibn al-Murajja, *Fada'il Bayt al-Maqdis*, 51, 287–94, 297–313, 326–29, 358; Ibn al-Jawzi, *Fada'il al-Quds*, 94, 136; Diya' al-Din al-Maqdisi, *Fada'il Bayt al-Maqdis*, 49–51, 59, 61–62, 69, 70–71; Ibn al-Firkah, *Ba'ith al-nufus*, 16, 28, 30–31; Ibn Hilal al-Maqdisi, *Muthir al-gharam*, 69, 219–21, 230–36; al-Husayni al-Shafi'i, *al-Rawd al-mugharras*, 57, 59, 60, 61–62, 63, 165–66, 267;

Suyuti, *Ithaf al-akhissa*, 99, 102–3, 107, 109, 133-134, 153; 'Ulaymi, *al-Uns al-jalil*, I, 227, 228, 232, 240, 241, 244–45, 267–68; and Ibn Khidr al-Maqdisi, *al-Mustaqsa*, 175, 177, 179, 180, 181, 182.

40 Ibn al-Firkah, *Ba'ith al-nufus*, 11 (translation by Matthews).

41 al-Wasiti, *Fada'il al-Bayt al-Muqaddas*, 28–29, nos. 38–39; Ibn-Murajja, *Fada'il Bayt al-Maqdis*, 225–30, 330-33, 347–48, 348–49; Ibn al-Jawzi, *Fada'il al-Quds*, 85–86, 88–89; Diya' al-Din al-Maqdisi, *Fada'il Bayt al-Maqdis*, 39–44, 49–51; Ibn al-Firkah, *Ba'ith al-nufus*, 5, 10, 11; Ibn Hilal al-Maqdisi, *Muthir al-gharam*, 207-10, 223; al-Husayni al-Shafi'i, *al-Rawd al-mugharras*, 57, 68–69, 96–98, 103, 104, 106; Suyuti, *Ithaf al-akhissa*, 101–2, 138, 153; 'Ulaymi, *al-Uns al-jalil*, I, 229, 231, 233, 238; and Ibn Khidr al-Maqdisi, *al-Mustaqsa*, 177, 178.

42 al-Wasiti, *Fada'il al-Bayt al-Muqaddas*, 29, no. 39; Ibn-Murajja, *Fada'il Bayt al-Maqdis*, 347–48, 349–50, 353; Diya' al-Din al-Maqdisi, *Fada'il Bayt al-Maqdis*, 49–51, 52–53; Ibn al-Firkah, *Ba'ith al-nufus*, 4–7, 10–11, 32–33; Ibn Hilal al-Maqdisi, *Muthir al-gharam*, 199–204; al-Husayni al-Shafi'i, *al-Rawd al-mugharras*, 62, 104, 105, 111–17; Suyuti, *Ithaf al-akhissa*, 108, 121, 138–39; 'Ulaymi, *al-Uns al-jalil*, I, 228–30, 240–41; and Ibn Khidr al-Maqdisi, *al-Mustaqsa*, 178, 181.

43 al-Wasiti, *Fada'il al-Bayt al-Muqaddas*, 24, no. 31; Ibn-Murajja, *Fada'il Bayt al-Maqdis*, 295–97; Ibn al-Jawzi, *Fada'il al-Quds*, 91; Ibn Hilal al-Maqdisi, *Muthir al-gharam*, 205–7; al-Husayni al-Shafi'i, *al-Rawd al-mugharras*, 123–24; Suyuti, *Ithaf al-akhissa*, 143–44; and 'Ulaymi, *al-Uns al-jalil*, I, 230.

44 al-Wasiti, *Fada'il al-Bayt al-Muqaddas*, 24–25, no. 32, 40, no. 54, 46, no. 64, 46–47, no. 66, 47, no. 67, 59, no. 92; Ibn-Murajja, *Fada'il Bayt al-Maqdis*, 213–16, 272–76, 324–25, 353; Ibn al-Jawzi, *Fada'il al-Quds*, 90, 129–30; Ibn al-Firkah, *Ba'ith al-nufus*, 21, 25, 29, 28, 34; Ibn Hilal al-Maqdisi, *Muthir al-gharam*, 243–44, 246–49; al-Husayni al-Shafi'i, *al-Rawd al-mugharras*, 57, 69–71; Suyuti, *Ithaf al-akhissa*, 102, 103, 109, 146; 'Ulaymi, *al-Uns al-jalil*, I, 232, 233, 235, 239, 241; and Ibn Khidr al-Maqdisi, *al-Mustaqsa*, 176.

45 Ibn al-Murajja, *Fada'il Bayt al-Maqdis*, 223; Ibn Hilal al-Maqdisi, *Muthir al-gharam*, 229, 262; al-Husayni al-Shafi'i, *al-Rawd al-mugharras*, 57; Suyuti, *Ithaf al-akhissa*, 146; and 'Ulaymi, *al-Uns al-jalil*, I, 233.

46 Ibn al-Murajja, *Fada'il Bayt al-Maqdis*, 342–43, 345; Ibn al-Firkah, *Ba'ith al-nufus*, 13, 14; Ibn Hilal al-Maqdisi, *Muthir al-gharam*, 245–46; al-Husayni al-Shafi'i, *al-Rawd al-mugharras*, 127, 129; Suyuti, *Ithaf al-akhissa*, 146; and 'Ulaymi, *al-Uns al-jalil*, I, 235.

47 Ibn al-Murajja, *Fada'il Bayt al-Maqdis*, 209–10; Diya' al-Din al-Maqdisi, *Fada'il Bayt al-Maqdis*, 93; Ibn al-Firkah, *Ba'ith al-nufus*, 13, 32; Ibn Hilal al-Maqdisi, *Muthir al-gharam*, 245; al-Husayni al-Shafi'i, *al-Rawd al-mugharras*, 131; Suyuti, *Ithaf al-akhissa*, 147; and 'Ulaymi, *al-Uns al-jalil*, I, 234.

48 See, for example, the long lists of prophets, companions, early followers, and other religious scholars and pious men (and women, such as some of the wives of the Prophet and the mystic Rabi'a al-'Adawiyya) who visited, lived, and/or died in the city: Ibn al-Murajja, *Fada'il Bayt al-Maqdis*, 284–87; Ibn Hilal al-Maqdisi, *Muthir al-gharam*, 269–366; al-Husayni al-Shafi'i, *al-Rawd al-mugharras*, 233–41; Suyuti, *Ithaf al-akhissa*, 222–23; and Ibn Khidr al-Maqdisi, *al-Mustaqsa*, 93–112, 183–93.

49 Ibn al-Firkah, *Ba'ith al-nufus*, 13 (translation by Matthews); al-Wasiti, *Fada'il al-Bayt al-Muqaddas*, 61, no. 97; Diya' al-Din al-Maqdisi, *Fada'il Bayt al-Maqdis*, 87–88; al-Husayni al-Shafi'i, *al-Rawd al-mugharras*, 57, 72–73; Suyuti, *Ithaf al-akhissa*, 151–52; and 'Ulaymi, *al-Uns al-jalil*, I, 231–32.

50 Marcus Schmitz, 'Ka'b al-Ahbar', in *Encyclopaedia of Islam, Second Edition*, accessed July 31, 2017, http://dx.doi.org/10.1163/1573-3912_islam_SIM_3734.

51 See Georges Vajda, 'Isra'iliyyat', in *Encyclopaedia of Islam, Second Edition*, accessed July 31, 2017, http://dx.doi.org/10.1163/1573-3912_islam_SIM_3670, and sources listed therein; for biblical prophets in the Islamic tradition and corpus, see also part II in Robert Tottoli, *Biblical Prophets in the Qur'an and Muslim Literature* (Richmond, Surrey: Curzon Press, 2002). For Ka'b and Wahb ibn Munabbih's roles in transmitting the *isra'iliyyat* traditions, see Tottoli, *Biblical Prophets*, 86–96, 138–40.

52 al-Wasiti, *Fada'il al-Bayt al-Muqaddas*, 60–61, no. 96; Ibn al-Murajja, *Fada'il Bayt al-Maqdis*, 295–96; Ibn Hilal al-Maqdisi, *Muthir al-gharam*, 205–6; and al-Husayni al-Shafi'i, *al-Rawd al-mugharras*, 123.

53 al-Wasiti, *Fada'il al-Bayt al-Muqaddas*, 60–61, no. 96; Ibn al-Murajja, *Fada'il Bayt al-Maqdis*, 295–96; Ibn Hilal al-Maqdisi, *Muthir al-gharam*, 205–6; and al-Husayni al-Shafi'i, *al-Rawd al-mugharras*, 123.

54 *The Qur'an*, trans. Tarif Khalidi (London: Penguin Classics, 2008), 8–9: '*Udkhulu al-bab sujjadan wa qulu 'hitta' naghfiru lakum khatayakum*'.

55 Ibn al-Firkah, *Ba'ith al-nufus*, 21–22 (translation by Matthews); Ibn al-Murajja, *Fada'il Bayt al-Maqdis*, 184–85; Ibn Hilal al-Maqdisi, *Muthir al-gharam*, 65–66; al-Husayni al-Shafi'i, *al-Rawd al-mugharras*, 180; Suyuti, *Ithaf al-akhissa*, 202–4; and Ibn Khidr al-Maqdisi, *al-Mustaqsa*, 73. See Elad, *Medieval Jerusalem*, 114–15.

56 For a description of a Muslim pilgrim's itinerary on the Haram complex during the pre-Crusader period, see Elad, *Medieval Jerusalem*, 78–130.

57 al-Wasiti, *Fada'il al-Bayt al-Muqaddas*, 17–19, nos. 19–22, 75, no. 120, 76, no. 123; Ibn al-Murajja, *Fada'il Bayt al-Maqdis*, 81–82; Ibn al-Jawzi, *Fada'il al-Quds*, 120, 139–40; Diya' al-Din al-Maqdisi, *Fada'il Bayt al-Maqdis*, 56–59, 86, 142; Ibn al-Firkah, *Ba'ith al-nufus*, 14–18; Ibn Hilal al-Maqdisi, *Muthir al-gharam*, 251; al-Husayni al-Shafi'i, *al-Rawd al-mugharras*, 133–34, 137–39, 150, 152; Suyuti, *Ithaf al-akhissa*, 159; 'Ulaymi, *al-Uns al-jalil*, I, 229, 236, 242; and Ibn Khidr al-Maqdisi, *al-Mustaqsa*, 67.

58 al-Wasiti, *Fada'il al-Bayt al-Muqaddas*, 90, no. 146; Ibn al-Murajja, *Fada'il Bayt al-Maqdis*, 83–84; Ibn al-Firkah, *Ba'ith al-nufus*, 18; Ibn Hilal al-Maqdisi, *Muthir al-gharam*, 255–56; al-Husayni al-Shafi'i, *al-Rawd al-mugharras*, 161; Suyuti, *Ithaf al-akhissa*, 162–63; and 'Ulaymi, *al-Uns al-jalil*, I, 236.

59 Ibn al-Murajja, *Fada'il Bayt al-Maqdis*, 86–88; Ibn Hilal al-Maqdisi, *Muthir al-gharam*, 264; al-Husayni al-Shafi'i, *al-Rawd al-mugharras*, 138; Suyuti, *Ithaf al-akhissa*, 134; and Ibn Khidr al-Maqdisi, *al-Mustaqsa*, 67.

60 Ibn al-Murajja, *Fada'il Bayt al-Maqdis*, 85–86; Ibn al-Firkah, *Ba'ith al-nufus*, 16–17; Ibn Hilal al-Maqdisi, *Muthir al-gharam*, 264; al-Husayni al-Shafi'i, *al-Rawd al-mugharras*, 130, 150; Suyuti, *Ithaf al-akhissa*, 134, 160–61; 'Ulaymi, *al-Uns al-jalil*, I, 242–43; and Ibn Khidr al-Maqdisi, *al-Mustaqsa*, 68–69.

61 al-Wasiti, *Fada'il al-Bayt al-Muqaddas*, 73–75, no. 119; Ibn al-Murajja, *Fada'il Bayt al-Maqdis*, 83–92; Ibn al-Jawzi, *Fada'il al-Quds*, 83; Ibn al-Firkah, *Ba'ith al-nufus*, 21; al-Husayni al-Shafi'i, *al-Rawd al-mugharras*, 175–76; Suyuti, *Ithaf al-akhissa*, 159, 170; and 'Ulaymi, *al-Uns al-jalil*, I, 273.

62 al-Wasiti, *Fada'il al-Bayt al-Muqaddas*, 73–75, no. 119; Ibn al-Murajja, *Fada'il Bayt al-Maqdis*, 94–101; Ibn al-Firkah, *Ba'ith al-nufus*, 19, 20–21; al-Husayni al-Shafi'i, *al-Rawd al-mugharras*, 170; and Suyuti, *Ithaf al-akhissa*, 173, 200.

63 Ibn al-Murajja, *Fada'il Bayt al-Maqdis*, 92–94; Ibn al-Jawzi, *Fada'il al-Quds*, 119; Ibn al-Firkah, *Ba'ith al-nufus*, 19; Ibn Hilal al-Maqdisi, *Muthir al-gharam*, 257; al-Husayni al-Shafi'i, *al-Rawd al-mugharras*, 170; Suyuti, *Ithaf al-akhissa*, 171, 172, 173; and 'Ulaymi, *al-Uns al-jalil*, I, 236, 297.

64 al-Husayni al-Shafi'i, *al-Rawd al-mugharras*, 170; and Suyuti, *Ithaf al-akhissa*, 173.

65 This gate is the one referred to in the Qur'anic verse 57.13: '*Fa-duriba baynahum bi-surin lahu babun batinahu fihi al-rahmatu wa zahiruhu min qiblihi al-'adhab.*' See al-Wasiti, *Fada'il al-Bayt al-Muqaddas*, 36–37, no. 47; Ibn al-Jawzi, *Fada'il al-Quds*, 138; Ibn al-Firkah, *Ba'ith al-nufus*, 19; Ibn Hilal al-Maqdisi, *Muthir al-gharam*, 19, 22; al-Husayni al-Shafi'i, *al-Rawd al-mugharras*, 49, 170, 179; Suyuti, *Ithaf al-akhissa*, 197–98; and 'Ulaymi, *al-Uns al-jalil*, I, 280.

66 Ibn al-Murajja, *Fada'il Bayt al-Maqdis*, 97; Ibn al-Firkah, *Ba'ith al-nufus*, 19; al-Husayni al-Shafi'i, *al-Rawd al-mugharras*, 180; and Suyuti, *Ithaf al-akhissa*, 195–96.

67 Ibn al-Murajja, *Fada'il Bayt al-Maqdis*, 97; Ibn al-Firkah, *Ba'ith al-nufus*, 20; al-Husayni al-Shafi'i, *al-Rawd al-mugharras*, 180; Suyuti, *Ithaf al-akhissa*, 196, 204; and 'Ulaymi, *al-Uns al-jalil*, I, 140, 273, 296.

68 Ibn al-Murajja, *Fada'il Bayt al-Maqdis*, 97; Ibn al-Jawzi, *Fada'il al-Quds*, 149; Ibn al-Firkah, *Ba'ith al-nufus*, 19; al-Husayni al-Shafi'i, *al-Rawd al-mugharras*, 180; Suyuti, *Ithaf al-akhissa*, 197; and 'Ulaymi, *al-Uns al-jalil*, I, 123.

69 Ibn al-Murajja, *Fada'il Bayt al-Maqdis*, 97; Ibn al-Firkah, *Ba'ith al-nufus*, 19; al-Husayni al-Shafi'i, *al-Rawd al-mugharras*, 180; Suyuti, *Ithaf al-akhissa*, 205; and 'Ulaymi, *al-Uns al-jalil*, I, 280.

70 Ibn al-Murajja, *Fada'il Bayt al-Maqdis*, 97; al-Husayni al-Shafi'i, *al-Rawd al-mugharras*, 180; Suyuti, *Ithaf al-akhissa*, 205; and 'Ulaymi, *al-Uns al-jalil*, I, 280.

71 Ibn al-Murajja, *Fada'il Bayt al-Maqdis*, 97; Ibn al-Firkah, *Ba'ith al-nufus*, 19; al-Husayni al-Shafi'i, *al-Rawd al-mugharras*, 180; and Suyuti, *Ithaf al-akhissa*, 196.

72 Ibn al-Murajja, *Fada'il Bayt al-Maqdis*, 97; Ibn al-Firkah, *Ba'ith al-nufus*, 19; al-Husayni al-Shafi'i, *al-Rawd al-mugharras*, 180; and Suyuti, *Ithaf al-akhissa*, 197.

73 Suyuti, *Ithaf al-akhissa*, 197.

74 Ibn al-Murajja, *Fada'il Bayt al-Maqdis*, 98; Ibn al-Jawzi, *Fada'il al-Quds*, 119; Diya' al-Din al-Maqdisi, *Fada'il Bayt al-Maqdis*, 77; Ibn al-Firkah, *Ba'ith al-nufus*, 25; al-Husayni al-Shafi'i, *al-Rawd al-mugharras*, 180; and Suyuti, *Ithaf al-akhissa*, 197.

75 al-Wasiti, *Fada'il al-Bayt al-Muqaddas*, 47–48, 55, 87–88, nos. 69–70, 84, 142–43; Ibn al-Murajja, *Fada'il Bayt al-Maqdis*, 98–100; Ibn al-Jawzi, *Fada'il al-Quds*, 70–71; Ibn al-Firkah, *Ba'ith al-nufus*, 6, 17, 21, 25; Ibn Hilal al-Maqdisi, *Muthir al-gharam*, 78–79; al-Husayni al-Shafi'i, *al-Rawd al-mugharras*, 181–82; Suyuti, *Ithaf al-akhissa*, 97, 221; 'Ulaymi, *al-Uns al-jalil*, I, 167, 266, 292; and Ibn Khidr al-Maqdisi, *al-Mustaqsa*, 38, 111. For these sites in

the pre-Crusader period and their connection to Islamic pilgrimage, see Elad, *Medieval Jerusalem*, 141–46.

76 See also al-Wasiti, *Fada'il al-Bayt al-Muqaddas*, 47–48, nos. 69–70; Ibn al-Murajja, *Fada'il Bayt al-Maqdis*, 70–71; Ibn al-Jawzi, *Fada'il al-Quds*, 70–71; Ibn al-Firkah, *Ba'ith al-nufus*, 20; Ibn Hilal al-Maqdisi, *Muthir al-gharam*, 78–79 (Jesus raised from Mount of Olives); al-Husayni al-Shafi'i, *al-Rawd al-mugharras*, 181–82; Suyuti, *Ithaf al-akhissa*, 97, 221; 'Ulaymi, *al-Uns al-jalil*, I, 167 (Jesus raised from Mount of Olives), 266 (it is the location of Rabi'a al-'Adawiyya's tomb); and Ibn Khidr al-Maqdisi, *al-Mustaqsa*, 38, 111–12 (Jesus raised from Mount of Olives).

77 'qabr Rabi'a al-'Adawiyya 'ala ra's Jabal Tur Zayta bi-jiwar mas'ad Sayyidina 'Isa…wa huwa makan ma'nus yuqsad li-'l-ziyara.' See 'Ulaymi, *al-Uns al-jalil*, I, 292.

78 al-Firkah, *Ba'ith al-nufus*, 6 (translation by Matthews), 25; al-Wasiti, *Fada'il al-Bayt al-Muqaddas*, 48, no. 71; Ibn al-Murajja, *Fada'il Bayt al-Maqdis*, 322–24; and Ibn Hilal al-Maqdisi, *Muthir al-gharam*, 241–42. See also Elad, *Medieval Jerusalem*, 141–44.

79 al-Wasiti, *Fada'il al-Bayt al-Muqaddas*, 49, 73; Ibn al-Jawzi, *Fada'il al-Quds*, 121; Diya' al-Din al-Maqdisi, *Fada'il Bayt al-Maqdis*, 86; Ibn Hilal al-Maqdisi, *Muthir al-gharam*, 293; Suyuti, *Ithaf al-akhissa*, 213–14 (he mentions that Muslims should not visit this site, but, according to Elad, Muslims continued to enter and pray at this church; see Elad, *Medieval Jerusalem*, 139); 'Ulaymi, *al-Uns al-jalil*, I, 116–17, 171; and Ibn Khidr al-Maqdisi, *al-Mustaqsa*, 107.

80 Suyuti, *Ithaf al-akhissa*, 213; 'Ulaymi, *al-Uns al-jalil*, I, 116–17, 171 (here the author states also that David was buried at this church); and Ibn Khidr al-Maqdisi, *al-Mustaqsa*, 107.

81 Ibn Khidr al-Maqdisi, *al-Mustaqsa*, 107.

82 Ibid., 107–9 (here the author stipulates four conditions that must be satisfied for a Muslim to be permitted to pray in a church). See also Elad, *Medieval Jerusalem*, 139.

83 Elad, *Medieval Jerusalem*, 139.

84 Suyuti, *Ithaf al-akhissa*, 213–14; and 'Ulaymi, *al-Uns al-jalil*, I, 170.

85 On the Church of St. Anne and its conversion to al-Madrasa al-Salahiyya, see Dan Bahat, *The Carta Jerusalem Atlas*, tran. Shlomo Ketko, 3rd ed. (Jerusalem: Carta, 2011), 115, 116, 127, 140.

86 'Wa wulidat Hanna Maryam…wa dufinat fi manziliha, wa banu 'alayha kanisa 'azima wa hathihi al-kanisa akhadhaha al-Malik al-Nasir Salah al-Din ibn Ayyub hina futihat Bayt al-Maqdis wa summiyat bi-'l-Madrasa al-Salahiyya wa huwa makan tu'azzimuhu al-Nasara.' See Ibn Khidr al-Maqdisi, *al-Mustaqsa*, 109–10.

87 Bahat, *The Carta Jerusalem Atlas*, 125, 127.

88 Ibn al-Firkah, *Ba'ith al-nufus*, 23 (translation by Matthews).

89 al-Wasiti, *Fada'il al-Bayt al-Muqaddas*, 45, no. 62, 91, no. 148; Ibn al-Jawzi, *Fada'il al-Quds*, 97–98; Ibn al-Firkah, *Ba'ith al-nufus*, 23, 35; Ibn Hilal al-Maqdisi, *Muthir al-gharam*, 182, 250; Suyuti, *Ithaf al-akhissa*, 211–12; and Ibn Khidr al-Maqdisi, *al-Mustaqsa*, 113–14. See also Elad, *Medieval Jerusalem*, 80–81.

90 Elad, *Medieval Jerusalem*, 131–32. 'Ulaymi, in his *al-Uns al-jalil*, states that Mihrab Dawud, where the Caliph 'Umar prayed when he entered Jerusalem, is located at the gate of the city, in the citadel ('wa mada nahwa Mihrab Dawud wa huwa al-lathi 'ala bab al-balad fi al-qal'a'). See 'Ulaymi, *al-Uns al-jalil*, I, 256.

91 See Elad, *Medieval Jerusalem*, 131–37; and ʿUlaymi, *al-Uns al-jalil*, I, 256.

92 al-Wasiti, *Fadaʾil al-Bayt al-Muqaddas*, 13, no. 13, 44, no. 61, 49, no. 73; Ibn al-Murajja, *Fadaʾil Bayt al-Maqdis*, 54–55; Ibn al-Jawzi, *Fadaʾil al-Quds*, 97, 120–121, 123; Ibn Hilal al-Maqdisi, *Muthir al-gharam*, 155; Suyuti, *Ithaf al-akhissa*, 195; and ʿUlaymi, *al-Uns al-jalil*, I, 256.

93 al-Wasiti, *Fadaʾil al-Bayt al-Muqaddas*, 6–7, no. 5; Ibn al-Murajja, *Fadaʾil Bayt al-Maqdis*, 9–13; Ibn Hilal al-Maqdisi, *Muthir al-gharam*, 140; and Suyuti, *Ithaf al-akhissa*, 191–94.

94 Ibn al-Firkah, *Baʿith al-nufus*, 19 (translation by Matthews); verse 57.13: '*fa-daraba baynahum bi-surin lahu babun batinuhu fihi al-rahma wa zahiruhu min qibalihi al-ʿadhab*': al-Wasiti, *Fadaʾil al-Bayt al-Muqaddas*, 14, nos. 14, 15, 15-16, no. 17; Diyaʾ al-Din al-Maqdisi, *Fadaʾil Bayt al-Maqdis*, 44–46; Ibn al-Firkah, *Baʿith al-nufus*, 19; Ibn Hilal al-Maqdisi, *Muthir al-gharam*, 75–76; al-Husayni al-Shafiʿi, *al-Rawd al-mugharras*, 179; Suyuti, *Ithaf al-akhissa*, 197–98; and ʿUlaymi, *al-Uns al-jalil*, I, 227. On Bab al-Rahma separating Jerusalem from the Valley of Hell, east of the city, see Elad, *Medieval Jerusalem*, 102–4.

95 Burgoyne, *Mamluk Jerusalem*, 46[b].

96 Ibid., 46[a–b].

97 Ibid., 46[b].

98 Ibid., 46[b]–47[a].

99 Abdul Aziz Duri, 'Jerusalem in the Early Islamic Period 7th–11th Centuries AD', in Asali, *Jerusalem in History*, 119–20.

100 Burgoyne, *Mamluk Jerusalem*, 47[a].

101 Robert Hillenbrand, 'Preface' in *Ayyubid Jerusalem: The Holy City in Context 1187–1250*, eds Robert Hillenbrand and Sylvia Auld (London: al-Tajir Trust, 2009), ix[a].

102 Mahmoud Hawari, 'Ayyubid Monuments in Jerusalem', in Hillenbrand and Auld, *Ayyubid Jerusalem*, 216[b].

103 Hawari, 'Ayyubid Monuments in Jerusalem', 216[b]. According to Hawari, only twenty-two buildings have survived; five were rebuilt or restored.

104 Carole Hillenbrand, 'Ayyubid Jerusalem: A Historical Introduction', in Hillenbrand and Auld, *Ayyubid Jerusalem*, 19[b].

105 Hillenbrand, 'Ayyubid Jerusalem', 19[b]. On a survey of Crusader *spoila* reused in Ayyubid monuments, see also Finbarr Barry Flood, 'An Ambiguous Aesthetic: Crusader *Spolia* in Ayyubid Jerusalem', in Hillenbrand and Auld, *Ayyubid Jerusalem*, 202–15.

106 See Hawari's survey of monuments in Hawari, 'Ayyubid Monuments in Jerusalem', which is based on his larger study: Mahmoud Hawari, *Ayyubid Jerusalem (1187–1250): An Architectural and Archaeological Study* (Oxford: Archaeopress, 2007). See, for example, his map of monuments on p. xx of his monograph, which shows that Ayyubid building activity concentrated on or around the Haram.

107 Hawari, 'Ayyubid Monuments in Jerusalem', 219[b].

108 The six are al-Madrasa al-Salahiyya, al-Madrasa al-Afdaliya, al-Madrasa al-Maymuniyya, al-Qubba al-Nahawiyya, al-Madrasa al-Badriyya, and al-Madrasa al-Muʿazzamiyya; the three located within the urban confines of the city are al-Salahiyya (established by converting the Crusader Church of St. Anne), al-Madrasa al-Maymuniyya (the former Church of St. Mary Magdalene, north of the city near Bab al-Sahira/Herod's Gate), and al-Madrasa al-Badriyya (on the west side of Tariq al-Qirami): see Hawari, 'Ayyubid Monuments in Jerusalem', 220[a]–230[b]; and Little,

'Jerusalem under the Ayyubids and the Mamluks', 180–81. The limited number of madrasas built by the Ayyubids was no doubt due to the instability Jerusalem experienced during this time, a result of continuous fears of Crusader efforts to recapture the city, which limited Muslim resettlement. Also note the short period (five decades or so) during which the Ayyubids reigned over the city.

109 See Burgoyne, *Mamluk Jerusalem*, 68[b]–69[a]. Also, see the discussion below on Mamluk building.

110 See Hawari's survey of Ayyubid monuments in Hawari, 'Ayyubid Monuments in Jerusalem' (although only two *zawiyas* have survived). For Mamluk religious building in the city, see the table provided in Burgoyne, *Mamluk Jerusalem*, 69[a].

111 Harawi, 'Ayyubid Monuments in Jerusalem', 216[b], map on 217[a]; and Burgoyne, *Mamluk Jerusalem*, 68[b]–69[a]. It must be stated, however, that the Ayyubids ruled the city for just over half a century, and the Mamluks controlled it for more than two and a half centuries, which contributed not only to the larger number of projects undertaken by the Mamluks but also to the architectural transformation of the city, including its religious landscape.

112 Little, 'Jerusalem under the Ayyubids and Mamluks', 189; Drory, 'Jerusalem During the Mamluk Period', 196; and Ayalon, 'Discharge from Service'.

113 Little, 'Jerusalem under the Ayyubids and Mamluks', 191.

114 Drory, 'Jerusalem During the Mamluk Period', 198.

115 Frenkel, 'Muslim Pilgrimage', 73, 74–83; and Burgoyne, Mamluk *Jerusalem*, 63[b] and passim.

116 Burgoyne, *Mamluk Jerusalem*, 33[a–b]. Burgoyne's architectural survey of all Mamluk buildings indicates that religious institutions were erected throughout the city, outside the Haram; see, for example, the map locating these religious buildings: Burgoyne, *Mamluk Jerusalem*, 35, fig. 2. There are religious institutions as far north in the city as the Damascus Gate and as far west as 'Aqabat al-Khanqah, near the Church of the Holy Sepulchre. There is also another as far south as Harat al-Yahud.

117 Little, 'Jerusalem under the Ayyubids and Mamluks', 191.

118 al-Ribat al-Mansuri (Burgoyne, *Mamluk Jerusalem*, 129–40; Little, 'Jerusalem under the Ayyubids and Mamluks', 191; and Drory, 'Jerusalem During the Mamluk Period', 204); Ribat Kurt al-Mansuri (Burgoyne, *Mamluk Jerusalem*, 144–53; Little, 'Jerusalem under the Ayyubids and Mamluks', 189; and Drory, 'Jerusalem During the Mamluk Period', 204); the Ribat of Women (Ribat al-Nisa') (Burgoyne, *Mamluk Jerusalem*, 240–43); Ribat al-Jawhariyya (Burgoyne, *Mamluk Jerusalem*, 555–67); and Ribat al-Zamani (Burgoyne, *Mamluk Jerusalem*, 572–78).

119 Ribat of 'Ala' al-Din (Burgoyne, *Mamluk Jerusalem*, 117–26); Ribat al-Maridini (Burgoyne, *Mamluk Jerusalem*, 412–14); and al-Khanqah al-Dawadariyya (Burgoyne, *Mamluk Jerusalem*, 154–65; and Little, 'Jerusalem under the Ayyubids and Mamluks', 192).

120 Burgoyne, *Mamluk Jerusalem*, 258–69, 456–59.

121 Ibid., 589–605; and Little, 'Jerusalem under the Ayyubids and Mamluks', 188.

122 al-Madrasa al-Tankiziyya (Burgoyne, *Mamluk Jerusalem*, 223–39; and Little, 'Jerusalem under the Ayyubids and Mamluks', 192); al-Madrasa al-Khatuniyya (Burgoyne, *Mamluk Jerusalem*, 343–55; and Little, 'Jerusalem under the Ayyubids and Mamluks', 191); al-Madrasa al-Arghuniyya (Burgoyne, *Mamluk Jerusalem*, 356–67; and Little, 'Jerusalem under the Ayyubids and Mamluks', 189); al-Madrasa al-Hanbaliyya (Burgoyne, *Mamluk Jerusalem*, 437–42; and

Little, 'Jerusalem under the Ayyubids and Mamluks', 189); al-Madrasa al-Muzhiriyya (Burgoyne, *Mamluk Jerusalem*, 579–88; and Little, 'Jerusalem under the Ayyubids and Mamluks', 189–90); and al-Madrasa al-'Uthmaniyya (Burgoyne, *Mamluk Jerusalem*, 544–54; Little, 'Jerusalem under the Ayyubids and Mamluks', 191; and Drory, 'Jerusalem During the Mamluk period', 205).

123 al-Madrasa al-Jawaliyya (Burgoyne, *Mamluk Jerusalem*, 201–10); al-Madrasa al-Karimiyya (Burgoyne, *Mamluk Jerusalem*, 211–18); al-Madrasa/Zawiya al-Aminiyya (Burgoyne, *Mamluk Jerusalem*, 249–57); al-Madrasa al-Sallamiyya (Burgoyne, *Mamluk Jerusalem*, 299–307; and Little, 'Jerusalem under the Ayyubids and Mamluks', 191); al-Madrasa al-Malikiyya (Burgoyne, *Mamluk Jerusalem*, 308–18); al-Madrasa al-Farisiyya (Burgoyne, *Mamluk Jerusalem*, 337–42); and the Madrasa/Khanqa al-Basitiyya (Burgoyne, *Mamluk Jerusalem*, 519–25).

124 Burgoyne, *Mamluk Jerusalem*, 419–23.

125 Ibid., 476–78, 479.

126 Ibid., 434–36.

127 Ibid., 380–83, 399–411.

128 Ibid., 424–33.

129 Ibid., 109–16.

130 Ibid., 184–91.

131 Ibid., 325–36.

132 Ibid., 70[a]. The Mamluks also built mausoleums that were frequented by pilgrims. Many of them were also located away from the Haram. These include the Tomb of Shaykh 'Ali Ardabili, located east of the city in Bab al-Rahma (Golden Gate) Cemetery (this did not survive, however); the *turba* mausoleum of Amir Qansuh al-Yahayawi, north of the cemetery outside of the Golden Gate east of the Haram (ibid., 70[b]); and the Kubakiyya *turba* mausoleum in the Mamilla Cemetery (ibid., 85[b]). Furthermore, the Mamluk sultan al-Nasir Muhammad ibn Qalawun built a mosque in the citadel near Jaffa Gate (ibid., 85[b]), while the first Mamluk ruler, Baybars, had erected a caravanserai northwest of the city, the Khan al-Zahir, which also included a mosque (ibid., 85[b]–86[a]).

133 Ibid.

134 Ibid., 69[b].

135 For Mecca and the hajj, see Arent Jan Wensinck, Jacques Jomier, and Bernard Lewis, 'Hadjdj', in *Encyclopaedia of Islam, Second Edition*, accessed May 6, 2017, http://dx.doi.org/10.1163/1573-3912_islam_COM_0249; William Montgomery Watt, Arent Jan Wensinck, Clifford Edmund Bosworth, Richard Bayly Winder and David A. King, 'Makka', in *Encyclopaedia of Islam, Second Edition*, accessed May 6, 2017, http://dx.doi.org/10.1163/1573- 3912_islam_COM_0638; Robert R. Bianchi, 'Hajj', in *The Oxford Encyclopedia of the Islamic World. Oxford Islamic Studies Online*, accessed June 25, 2017, http://www.oxfordislamicstudies.com/article/opr/t236/e0289?_hi=2&_pos=1; and Gerald Hawting, 'Pilgrimage', in McAuliffe, *Encyclopaedia of the Qur'an*, vol. 4, 91–100, accessed June 25, 2017, http://go.galegroup.com/ps/retrieve.do?resultListType=RELATED_DOCUMENT&userGroupName=utoronto_main&inPS=true&contentSegment=9789047403791&prodId=GVRL&isETOC=true&docId=GALE|CX2686400494. The most important contribution to the study of Mecca and the hajj in recent times is by far the scholarship of Francis Edward Peters; see Francis Edward Peters, 'Mecca',

in *The Oxford Encyclopedia of the Islamic World. Oxford Islamic Studies Online*, accessed May 6, 2017, http://www.oxfordislamicstudies.com/article/opr/t236/e0522?_hi=3&_pos=3; his classic study, Francis Edward Peters, *The Hajj: The Muslim Pilgrimage to Mecca and the Holy Places* (Princeton: Princeton University Press, 1994); and his excellent comparative study of Jerusalem and Mecca, Francis Edward Peters, *Jerusalem and Mecca*. For the most recent collection of studies on the hajj, see Eric Tagliacozzo and Shawkat M. Toorawa, eds, *The Hajj: Pilgrimage in Islam* (New York: Cambridge University Press, 2016). For the hajj during the period under investigation, see 'Abd Allah 'Aqil 'Anqawi, 'The Pilgrimage to Mecca in Mamluk Times', *Arabian Studies* 1 (1974): 146–70.

136 Juan E. Campo, 'Visualizing the Hajj: Representations of a Changing Sacred Landscape Past and Present', in Tagliacozzo and Toorawa, *The Hajj*, 272.

137 Campo, 'Visualizing the Hajj', 272, citing al-Kisa'i, *The Tales of the Prophets of al-Kisa'i*, trans. W. M. Thackston Jr. (Chicago: Kazi Publications, 1997); see also the multitude of traditions on the sanctity of Mecca and its holy sites in al-Azraqi, *Akhbar Mecca*, vol. 1.

138 Peters, *The Hajj*, 10.

139 Campo, 'Visualizing the Hajj', 272.

140 Peters, *The Hajj*, 9–19; for Maqam Ibrahim, see Meir Jacob Kister, 'Makam Ibrahim', in *Encyclopaedia of Islam, Second Edition*, accessed June 25, 2017, http://dx.doi.org/10.1163/1573-3912_islam_SIM_4815; and Meir Jacob Kister, 'Maqam Ibrahim, a Stone with an Inscription', *Museon: Revue d'Etudes Orientales* 84 (1971): 477–91.

141 Peters, *The Hajj*, 11. See also Campo, 'Visualizing the Hajj', 271–72. For al-Azraqi's sacred geography of Mecca, see Oleg Grabar, 'Upon Reading al-Azraqi', *Muqarnas* 3 (1985): 1–7.

142 The *miqat* stations are actual geographical locations outside Mecca. There are different *miqats* for different pilgrims, grouped according to which route they take to Mecca. For example, those travelling from Syria, Egypt, or the west visited the *miqat* stands at al-Juhfa (although now it has changed to Rabigh) (they could also, as stated earlier, enter the *ihram* state in Jerusalem); for those coming from Iraq, stations are located at Dhat 'Irf in the northeast of Mecca. It is also here that the male pilgrim dons the special garb of the hajj, the *izar* and *rida'* (no special garment is needed for women pilgrims). See Arent Jan Wensinck and Jacques Jomier, '*ihram*', in *Encyclopaedia of Islam, Second Edition*, accessed June 25, 2017, http://dx.doi.org/10.1163/1573-3912_islam_SIM_3506; and Wensinck, Jomier, and Lewis, 'hajj'.

143 Wensinck and Jomier, '*ihram*'; Wensinck and King, 'miqat', in *Encyclopaedia of Islam, Second Edition*, accessed June 25, 2017, http://dx.doi.org/10.1163/1573-3912_islam_COM_0735; and Peters, *Jerusalem and Mecca*, 109.

144 See Wensinck and Jomier, '*ihram*'; and Peters, *The Hajj*, 119, for list of interdictions.

145 Wensinck and Jomier, '*ihram*'.

146 Ibid.

147 Peters, *Jerusalem and Mecca*, 68.

148 Wensinck and Jomier, 'Hadjdj'; and Shawkat M. Toorawa, 'Performing the Pilgrimage', in Tagliacozzo and Toorawa, *The Hajj*, 222–28.

149 Wensinck and Jomier, 'Hajdj'.

150 See Campo, 'Visualizing the Hajj', 272.

151 Wensinck and Jomier, 'Hadjdj'.

152 Ibid.

153 It is important to note that many of these sites were preserved until the advent of puritanical Wahabism and the Saudi capture of the Hijaz. The new rulers in the twentieth century began to demolish sites in the name of *tawhid*, ending the practice of *ziyara* to shrines and rituals of *tabarruk*. See Ziauddin Sardar, *Mecca The Sacred City* (London: Bloomsbury, 2015), 343–63; see also Meri, Ende, van Doorn-Harder, et al., 'Ziyara'; and Yusuf Raghda al-'Amili, *Ma'alim Makkah wa-al-Madinah bayna al-madi wa-al-hadir* (Beirut: Dar al-Murtada, 1997), 181–91.

154 Peters, *Jerusalem and Mecca*, 123. Original emphasis; see also 18: 'the hajji in Mecca was escorted around some of the historical and sacred sites connected with the Prophet and the birth of Islam'.

155 Ibid., 64–65.

156 Ibid., 141.

157 For the main medieval sources on the hajj and its sites, see the indispensable chronicle of Mecca by the third-/ninth-century Aba al-Walid Muhammad ibn 'Abd Allah al-Azraqi, *Akhbar Makka wa ma ja'a fiha min al-athar*, ed. Rushdi al-Salih Malhas (Beirut: Dar al-Andalus, 1969); the important guide to pilgrimage dating to the Ayyubid period, Abu al-Hasan 'Ali ibn Abi Bakr al-Harawi, *Kitab al-isharat ila ma'rifat al-ziyarat*, ed. Janine Sourdel-Thomine (Damas: Institut Français de Damas, 1953); and the travels of Ibn Jubayr, *Tadhkirah bi-al-akhbar 'an ittifaqat al-asfar (Rihlat Ibn Jubayr)*, ed. Dar Sadir (Beirut: Dar Sadir, 1964). For an account of Mecca during the Mamluk period, see the famous travels of Ibn Battuta, *Tuhfat al-nuzzar fi ghara'ib al-amsar wa-'aja'ib al-asfar (Rihlat Ibn Battutah)*, ed. Abu al-Muzaffar Sa'id ibn Muhammad al-Sinnari (Damascus and Cairo: Dar al-Kitab al-'Arabi, 2012). For a modern travelogue of Mecca and Medina and the history of the Hijaz, see Muhammad Labib al-Batanuni, *al-Rihlah al-Hijaziyah li-wali al-ni'm al-haj 'Abbas Hilmi Basha al-thani khidiw Misr* (Cairo: Matba'at al-Jamaliyah, 1329 [1911]).

158 Peters, *Jerusalem and Mecca*, 141.

159 Harawi, *Kitab al-isharat*, 87 (translations in this section are by the author of this chapter).

160 Azraqi, *Akhbar Makka*, 2:198–99; Harawi, *Kitab al-isharat*, 87; and Ibn Jubary, *Rihlat Ibn Jubayr*, 91–92, 141.

161 Ibn-Jubayr, *Rihlat Ibn Jubayr*, 91–92.

162 Ibid., 141.

163 Ibid., Ibn Jubayr, *Rihlat Ibn Jubayr*, 92 ('*wa nafa'ana bi-barakat mushahadat mawlidihi al-karim*').

164 Harawi, *Kitab al-isharat*, 87; and Ibn Jubayr, *Rihlat Ibn Jubayr*, 93: at the far south of Mecca ('*wa bi-jihat al-masfal wa huwa akhir al-balad*').

165 Harawi, *Kitab al-isharat*, 87.

166 Ibid., 87.

167 Azraqi, *Akhbar Makka*, 2:199 (refers to it as 'manzil Khadija'); Harawi, *Kitab al-isharat*, 87; Ibn Jubayr, *Rihlat Ibn Jubayr*, 141–42; and Ibn Battuta, *Rihlat Ibn Battuta*, 127.

168 Azraqi, *Akhbar Makka*, 2:199 (Azraqi reports that the mosque was built by the first Umayyad Caliph, Mu'awiya); and Harawi, *Kitab al-isharat*, 87.

169 Ibid., 87 ('*al-bayt al-ladhi sakanahu rasul Allah … wa fihi waladat awladaha minhu. Wa bihi tuwuffiyat, wa lam yazal bihi al-nabi ila an hajara wa huwa al-an masjid*').

170 Azraqi, *Akhbar Makka*, 2:199; Ibn Jubary, *Rihlat Ibn Jubayr*, 91, 127, 141–42.

171 Ibn Jubary, *Rihlat Ibn Jubayr*, 142 ('*masahna al-khudud fi hadhihi al-masaqit al-mukarrama*').

172 Ibid., 145; Azraqi, *Akhbar Makka*, 2:200 (al-Azraqi writes that it is next to the Safa); and Harawi, *Kitab al-isharat*, 87.

173 Ibn Battua, *Rihlat Ibn Battutat*, 128; and Harawi, *Kitab al-isharat*, 87.

174 Ibn Jubayr, *Rihlat Ibn Jubayr*, 93.

175 Azraqi, *Akhbar Makka*, 2:201; and Harawi, *Kitab al-isharat*, 87.

176 Harawi, *Kitab al-isharat*, 87; and Ibn Jubayr, *Rihlat Ibn Jubary*, 85.

177 Azraqi, *Akhbar Makka*, 2:203; he states that Masjid bi-Dhi Tawa is located between the graveyard of Mecca (al-Jabbana) and al-Hashas.

178 Ibn Jubayr, *Rihlat Ibn Jubary*, 85.

179 Azraqi, *Akhbar Makka*, 2:200–01; Harawi, *Kitab al-isharat*, 87; and Ibn Jubary, *Rihlat Ibn Jubayr*, 88.

180 Azraqi, *Akhbar Makka*, 2:201; and Harawi, *Kitab al-isharat*, 87.

181 Ibn Jubayr, *Rihlat Ibn Jubayr*, 92; al-Azraqi, *Akhbar Makka,* 2:173; and Harawi, *Kitab al-isharat*, 87 (he states that it is located in what is called Dar al-Darb).

182 Harawi, *Kitab al-isharat*, 84; and Ibn Jubayr, *Rihlat Ibn Jubayr*, 90.

183 Azraqi, *Akhbar Makka*, 2:173–74, 181–84; Harawi, *Kitab al-isharat*, 84; and Ibn Jubayr, *Rihlat Ibn Jubayr*, 137–38.

184 Harawi, *Kitab al-isharat*, 87; and Ibn Jubayr, *Rihlat Ibn Jubayr*, 136. Mina is also home to Masjid al-'Ayshuma, where it is also believed that the Prophet rested (al-Azraqi, *Akhbar Makka*, 2:174); another Mina mosque, Masjid al-Dhabh li-Isma'il or Manhar al-Dhabih, is associated with Abraham's attempt to sacrifice Ismael and also holds a rock that is associated with the Prophet (al-Azraqi refers to this place as Masjid al-Kabsh). See Azraqi, *Akhbar Makka*, 2:175; Harawi, *Kitab al-isharat*, 84; and Ibn Jubayr, *Rihlat Ibn Jubayr*, 137.

185 Azraqi, *Akhbar Makka*, 2:7, 204; and Ibn Jubayr, *Rihlat Ibn Jubayr*, 90–91, 138.

186 Azraqi, *Akhbar Makka*, 2:7; and Ibn Jubayr, *Rihlat Ibn Jubayr*, 93.

187 Ibn Jubayr, *Rihlat Ibn Jubayr*, 87; and Ibn Battuta, *Rihlat Ibn Battuta*, 128.

188 Ibn Battuta, *Rihlat Ibn Battuta*, 128.

189 Peters, *Jerusalem and Mecca*, 116–17.

190 Ibid.

191 Ibn Battuta, *Rihlat Ibn Battuta*, 126–27.

192 Ibid., 127.

193 This reflects Josef Meri's conclusion in his study of medieval pilgrimage in Syria. See Meri, *The Cult of Saints*, 287.

194 Ahmad ibn 'Abd al-Halim Ibn Taymiyya, 'Qa'ida fi Ziyarat Bayt al-Maqdis', in *Majmu'at al-Rasa'il al-Kubra li-Ibn Taymiyya* (Cairo, 1905); and Charles D. Matthews, 'A Muslim Iconoclast on the Merits of Jerusalem and Palestine', *Journal of the American Oriental Society* 56 (1936): 1–21. On the phenomenon and law of *ziyara* with an emphasis on Egypt, see

Christopher Taylor, *In the Vicinity of the Righteous: Ziyara and the Veneration of Muslim Saints in Late Medieval Egypt* (Leiden: Brill, 199), 62–79.

195 Asali, *Makhtutat fada'il Bayt al-Maqdis*, 6–9.

196 For the decline in number of *Fada'il al-Quds* texts during the Ottoman period, see ibid., 115.

197 Ibid., 9.

198 One of these is in Turkish, and, so far, only two have been published: Muhammad ibn Muhammad ibn Khidr al-Maqdisi, *al-Mustaqsa fi fada'il al-Masjid al-Aqsa*, ed. Mashhur al-Habbazi (Jerusalem: Bayt al-Shiʻr al-Filastini, 2008); Mustafa Asʻad al-Luqaymi, *Lata'if uns al-jalil fi taha'if al-Quds wa-al-Khalil*, ed. Khalid ʻAbd al-Karim al-Hamshari (Acre: Mu'assasat al-Aswar, 2001). See Asali, *Makhtutat fada'il Bayt al-Maqdis*, 115–121.

199 Abdul-Karim Rafeq, 'Ottoman Jerusalem in the Writings of Arab Travellers', in *Ottoman Jerusalem, The Living City: 1517–1917*, eds Sylvia Auld and Robert Hillenbrand (London: Altajir World of Islam Trust, 2000).

200 Rafeq, 'Ottoman Jerusalem', 63–64; Anabsi, 'Popular Beliefs', 61.

201 Rafeq, 'Ottoman Jerusalem'; I'm currently in the process of writing a larger study on Islamic pilgrimage to Jerusalem during the Ottoman period.

202 ʻAbd al-Ghani, al-Nabulusi, *al-Hadra al-unsiyya fi al-rihla al-Qudsiyya*, ed. Akram Hasan al-ʻUlabi (Beirut: al-Masadir, 1990). For an overview on al-Nabulusi's life and career, see Samer Akkach, *ʻAbd al-Ghani al-Nabulusi: Islam and the Enlightenment* (Oxford: Oneworld, 2007); and on his travels to Ottoman Jerusalem, see Rafeq, 'Ottoman Jerusalem', 64–66.

203 For example, see his visits to the Haram and its many holy sites: al-Nabulusi, *al-Hadra al-unsiyya*, 96–140.

204 Rafeq, 'Ottoman Jerusalem', 65.

Section II

Creating New Destinations, Constructing New Sacreds

Sanctifying Konya: The Thirteenth-Century Transformation of the Seljuk Friday Mosque into a 'House of God'

Suzan Yalman

The Friday Mosque of Konya, known after the legendary Anatolian Seljuk sultan 'Ala al-Din Kayqubad (*r.*1220–37) as the 'Alaeddin Mosque' (Alaeddin Camii), sits atop the citadel mound known similarly as the 'Alaeddin Hill' (Alaeddin Tepesi), in the heart of the old city of Konya [Figure 1]. Following classical Islamic models, the mosque is located near the remains of the Seljuk citadel palace, on the ancient acropolis, and has a commanding view of the city. Its striped marble masonry (*ablaq*) is a striking presence amid the city's skyline. As the mosque originally was without a minaret, its most prominent feature must have been the conical dome of the dynastic tomb of the Seljuk sultans, said to have been covered with blue tiles.[1] Until the early twentieth century, the converted Church of St. Amphilochius, later known as 'Plato's Mosque' (Eflatun Mescidi), stood behind the mosque, further up the hill.[2]

Figure 1: Konya, Friday ('Alaeddin') Mosque, general view of north facade. Photograph by the author.

This paper examines the role of the Friday Mosque in shaping the city of Konya, which served as the capital of the Anatolian Seljuk Sultanate (*c*.1081–1308). As the principal mosque of Konya, the Alaeddin Camii must have enjoyed a key role as the central mosque of the Seljuk Sultanate; however, scholars have noted that it 'has stood for centuries as no more than a curious mélange of disparate architectural elements and styles'.[3] Built in the twelfth century under Mas'ud (*r*.1116–55) and Qilij Arslan II (*r*.1155–92), and expanded in the first decades of the thirteenth century by 'Izz al-Din Kayka'us (*r*.1211–19) and 'Ala al-Din Kayqubad (*r*.1220–37), the Konya Friday Mosque appears to lack a coherent architectural programme and has been the subject of numerous studies that attempt to understand the sequence of its construction. According to the inscriptional programme that will be discussed below, Kayka'us took the building from *masjid* to *jami'*, and Kayqubad 'completed' the project, to which he referred with the unprecedented term 'house of God' (*bayt Allah*). What did this terminology signify? What does it imply about the fashioning of Konya at the time? Understanding the thirteenth-century renovation of the building in the context of such terminology will help shed light on the liminal dynamics between the Friday mosque and the city of Konya, as well as the sultans' ambitions for reshaping and sanctifying their capital.

Introducing the Site

The Konya Friday Mosque has a hypostyle plan with rows parallel to the qibla wall [Figure 2]. The non-centralized asymmetrical design of the building indicates interventions over the centuries. The northern and eastern walls help to create a courtyard; however, unlike those within most hypostyle mosques, this is not a central courtyard but appears to be a forecourt with two tomb towers. The mosque's overall construction is an early example of a mixture of stone and brick made by different craftsmen. On the north facade, the *ablaq* masonry combines two different colours of marble; this technique was commonly used in Syria as a framing device on mihrabs and portals. These frames also incorporate cursive inscriptions, which announce the different stages of construction [Figures 3–7].[4]

Over the course of the twentieth century, many scholars studied the Alaeddin Camii in terms of its plan, architecture, decoration, and inscriptions. These include early Orientalists such as Clément Huart, Friedrich Sarre, and, later, Michael Meinecke, as well as Turkish scholars such as Zeki Oral, Mehmet Önder, İbrahim Hakkı Konyalı, Doğan Kuban, Haluk Karamağaralı, Yılmaz Önge, Erol Yurdakul, and Canan Parla, among others.[5] In more recent decades, Scott Redford and Neslihan Asutay-Effenberger have been interested in the archaeology of the site.[6] Remzi Duran has published the Seljuk inscriptions from Konya, and Yaşar Erdemir has provided a comprehensive overview of the scholarship on the Alaeddin Camii and its tombs.[7] More recently, Richard McClary has offered his suggestions regarding the incomplete tomb tower in the mosque courtyard.[8]

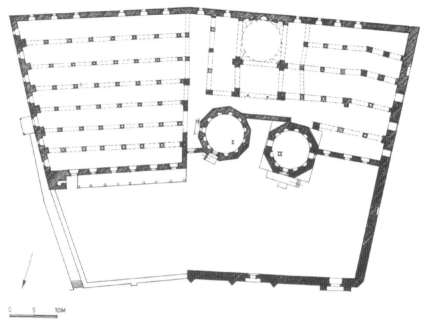

Figure 2: Konya, Friday Mosque, plan of the complex. After Redford, 'The Alaeddin Mosque in Konya Reconsidered'.

Figure 3: Konya, Friday Mosque, north facade, text panel with evidence of tampering. Photograph by the author.

Figure 4: Konya, Friday Mosque, north facade, text panel for *jāmiʿ* by Kaykaʾus. Photograph by the author.

Figure 5: Konya, Friday Mosque, north facade, main portal with *ablaq* interlace and text panel for *bayt Allah*. Photograph by the author.

Figure 6: Konya, Friday Mosque, north facade, main portal, detail of text panel for *bayt Allah*. Photograph by the author.

Although there is a need for an updated review of the literature and a fresh assessment of the archaeological information that might be gleaned during the constant restoration and renovation of the site, this would require a monograph and is beyond the scope of this chapter. For the purposes of the present volume, I focus on the thirteenth-century phase of expansion – which created a liminal space between the mosque and the city – as a way of examining the broader urban context and the dynamic relationship between the mosque and the city of Konya. As I will demonstrate, by imbuing the mosque with new meaning, the Seljuk sultans hoped to transform it into a pilgrimage destination, and thereby to sanctify their capital.

A Traveller's Impressions

At the turn of the twentieth century, the British politician Earl Percy (1871–1909), who travelled to Anatolia, described the Konya Friday Mosque as follows:

It is of great size, oblong in shape, and commands a magnificent panorama of the town. The interior is curious, the spacious hall containing about sixty marble columns of a grayish-blue colour, some of them plain, and some fluted or decorated with the love-knot pattern so familiar in the Armenian churches of Ani. One has a long inscription in the

Figure 7: Konya, Friday Mosque, north facade, text panel for *jāmiʿ* by Kayqubad in elaborate star-shaped frame, with a more modest panel naming the supervisor and architect to the right. Photograph by the author.

Greek character near the base, and there are traces of the obliteration of a similar record on another. The *mimber*, or pulpit, is of wood, exquisitely carved, and the fine Mihrab, is adorned with Persian tiles, or with paintings ingeniously designed to conceal the fact that many of the plaques have been picked out and sold, a fate which has also befallen some of the carpets, of which there was formerly a large and valuable collection in the mosque. The same artifice, instances of which may also be seen at Constantinople, has been employed on the walls, and at a little distance it is difficult to detect the fraud. In a small chamber opening on the right aisle are a row of seven or eight catafalques of the Sultans covered with green cloth.[9]

In a departure from our contemporary preconceptions about the mosque, Percy describes the building as of 'great size' and having a commanding view of the town, pointing to the importance of the 'gaze' from the citadel. Inside, he notes 'sixty' spoliated columns, particularly remarking on knotted columns that remind him of Ani, as well as those with preserved or obliterated Greek inscriptions [Figure 8]. Along with such reused architectural fragments, the 'curious' interior also included an 'exquisitely carved' minbar and a 'fine' mihrab, 'adorned with Persian tiles' [Figure 9]. As a comment on the building's state of neglect, Percy elaborates on the fact that some of the tiles and the carpets had been looted and sold on the art market.[10] The tiles had been replaced with 'paintings ingeniously designed to conceal the fact [...]'. Finally, Percy remarks that in a 'small chamber opening on the right aisle', one could visit the 'catafalques of the Sultans' [Figure 10]. This statement indicates that, at the time of his visit, one could access the upper chamber of the dynastic tomb tower from inside the mosque. This is no longer the case, as the connection between the mosque and the tomb tower was severed, and the buildings were returned to their original, separate state during modern restorations.

Percy's comments regarding access to the small chamber that housed the sultans' cenotaphs indicate that at the turn of the twentieth century part of the ritual of going to the mosque included paying homage to the Seljuk sultans. One wonders, what was the case during the

Figure 8: Konya, Friday Mosque, view of eastern hypostyle section with spoliated columns. Photograph by the author.

Figure 9: Konya, Friday Mosque, view of dome over *mihrab* with twelfth-century minbar. Photograph by the author.

Figure 10: Konya, Friday Mosque, dynastic tomb tower, view of tile-clad cenotaphs of the Seljuk sultans. Photograph by the author.

Seljuk period? When did visitation of the Seljuk tombs begin? Was it related to the architectural development of the site? As we shall see, the architectural and ritual developments were intended to add sanctity to the site. For Konya, formerly called Iconium, a central Anatolian town that did not boast an illustrious history, these developments were meant to sanctify the city and thereby to boost the claims of Rum Seljuk rulers for the capital of their empire.

In addition to Percy's comments on looting, alterations over the course of centuries indicate some of the difficulties of studying this site. The Friday Mosque is situated on an ancient mound that dates back millennia and at different times experienced serious structural issues that required frequent interventions, particularly during the Ottoman era.[11] In the twentieth century as well as in more recent decades, the mosque has continued to undergo extensive renovations.[12] Despite the increasingly invasive modern interventions that threaten our understanding of the history of the building, foundation inscriptions shed light on the phases of construction under the Seljuk sultans.

The Epigraphic Sequence

The epigraphic evidence indicates that the building of the Konya Friday Mosque likely commenced under the Seljuk sultan Mas'ud (r.1116–55). The earliest extant date (1155) comes from the minbar and thus refers to the reign of Mas'ud, yet the name and titles mention his son Qilij Arslan II (r.1155–92), who may have assumed the throne at the time of the minbar's completion by the craftsman Mengi Birti al-Haji al-Akhlati. The extant 'exquisite' woodwork that Percy noted, still in situ, also includes Qur'anic inscriptions. In this way, the twelfth-century building seems to have been completed by Mas'ud's son Qilij Arslan II, whose name also appears on the first tomb tower added next to the mosque.[13]

In the thirteenth century, during a second Seljuk phase of building, the Friday Mosque was enlarged considerably. Qilij Arslan's grandsons 'Izz al-Din Kayka'us (r.1211–19) and 'Ala al-Din Kayqubad (r.1220–37) expanded the structure and added the courtyard as well as another tomb tower that was left incomplete, which created a complex and awkward plan. Curiously, this expansion project appears to be the highlight of mosque patronage for both of these sultans, whose reigns are considered a 'golden age' for the Seljuks of Rum. The epigraphic evidence that documents this phase of construction comes from several inscription panels situated on the newly created northern wall of the mosque.[14] As has been previously noted by scholars, these are damaged in specific areas that have to do with the name of the sultan and therefore indicate tampering intended to 'update' the information with the name of the later sultan, i.e., 'Ala al-Din Kayqubad.[15] According to the discernible texts, Kayka'us was responsible for a mosque and a tomb – the terminology goes from *masjid* to *jami'* – and Kayqubad 'completed' the project, which was referred to in unprecedented terms as a 'house of God' (*bayt Allah*) [Figures 3–7]. I will return to this terminology below.

Apart from the textual evidence, we cannot securely attribute architectural developments to Kayka'us or Kayqubad's patronage specifically. Examining the building with this epigraphic information in mind, scholars in the twentieth century made different suggestions about the sequence of construction.[16] The larger hypostyle area with spoliated columns seems to be the earliest part of the mosque.[17] To this, the first dynastic tomb tower with a conical dome was added; originally this was not part of the mosque – as described by Percy – but stood nearby [Figures 2 and 11]. At a later date, most likely during the second phase of construction, the complex was expanded significantly. The orientation of the building changed: the northern facade became the main facade and was highlighted with *ablaq* masonry. The section with the dome in front of the mihrab was likely added at this time; the new portal appears to be aligned with this space. The dome and the mihrab were originally covered with turquoise and black mosaic tilework, which remains visible despite later damage and renovations. To the west of this domed unit was an awkward, small hypostyle area, which is usually described as the 'sultan's lodge' due to its proximity to the Seljuk palace pavilion that was likely accessible through the western portals of the mosque.[18]

In addition to the sultans, other noteworthy figures were involved in the Konya Friday Mosque project. As we shall see, inscriptions name Ayaz as the *waqf* administrator, or supervisor (*mutawalli*), with the latest such inscription providing the date of completion as 617 according to the Islamic calendar (1220).[19] In a smaller inscription next to a larger panel [Figure 7], his name appears together with that of a Damascene architect, Muhammad bin Khawlan

Figure 11: Konya, Friday Mosque, view of courtyard with tomb towers. Photograph by the author.

al-Dimashqi, who would later build the Aksaray Sultan Han.[20] The thirteenth-century epigraphic programme also includes a round tile with the signature of Karim al-Din Ardishah, most likely indicating his role as a ceramic artist [Figure 12].[21] Though little is known of the latter two individuals (beyond the epigraphic evidence), the multiple origins of the artists, including an Arab from Damascus and an artist who signed his name in Persian (the other inscriptions are in Arabic), reflect the diverse background of artists patronized in the Rum Seljuk realm.

The employment of artists from different regions, who brought their own know-how to the Konya Friday Mosque, does seem to indicate that there were certain references and grander aims in mind during the second building phase. Gülru Necipoğlu has commented on the addition of a dome in front of the mihrab as a possible connection to the Seljuk reconstruction of the Friday Mosque of Isfahan. This would be 'a means of proclaiming themselves as legitimate heirs to their cousins in Iran, as did Rāvandī's early thirteenth-century history, which refers to the Sultan of Rūm as the fruit of the Great Seljuq family tree'.[22] In addition to Isfahan, the dome might also be connected to the dome in front of the mihrab in the Great Mosque of Damascus. In fact, considering that the architect in charge of the Konya project was Damascene, and that the enlargement of the Isfahan mosque itself coincided with repairs to the Umayyad Mosque carried out by the Great Seljuks under Malik

Figure 12: Konya, Friday Mosque, north facade, ceramic inscription naming Kayqubad and artist. Photograph by the author.

Shah, connections to both Isfahan and Damascus are possible. Moreover, it is important to note that besides the quotation of the dome, the mosque in Konya does not incorporate the most noteworthy Seljuk innovation in Isfahan: the centralized courtyard and four-iwan plan. The hypostyle plan and forecourt are more reminiscent of Damascus. The absence of the four-iwan plan in Anatolian mosques is often ascribed to the harsh climate, but this cannot be the only reason, as the region features plenty of Seljuk madrasas and other buildings (including Kayka'us's hospital in Sivas) that have a four-iwan plan with an open court. While the Konya mosque did eventually acquire a court, this was not a central courtyard. Perhaps it was too difficult to incorporate a four-iwan plan into an expansion project that needed to take into account – among other factors – the dynastic tomb tower, which would require it to negotiate the space offered by the site itself.

A Closer Reading: From Mosque to 'House of God' (*bayt Allah*)

Let us return to some of the texts for a close reading of the expansion project. The northern enclosure wall of the Konya Friday Mosque created a liminal space between the mosque and the city, the purpose of which is open to interpretation. I believe that the foundation inscriptions inserted into this wall, announcing the different stages of construction, acted as a 'public text', a term developed by Irene Bierman for Fatimid epigraphy.[23] The tampered text framed by elegant Syrian strapwork reads [Figure 3]:

[1] The construction of this masjid and purified tomb was ordered by
[2] the [Victorious] Sultan ['Izz] al-Dunya wa'l-Din Father of Conquest
[3] Kay[ka'us] son of the Martyred Sultan Kaykhusraw son of Qilij Arslan
[4] Victorious Commander of the Believers under the supervision of the slave Ayaz the Atabek in the year 616.[24]

This informative panel tells us that Kayka'us ordered the construction of 'this masjid', in addition to a 'purified tomb' (*turba al-mutahhara*), under the supervision of his emir Ayaz, the *atabeg* (tutor of princes). As there is no reference to the existing masjid, Kayka'us appears to be claiming to establish a new building; this kind of bold formulation was common at the time. Another inscription by Kayka'us refers to the building as a Friday Mosque (*jami'*) [Figure 4].[25]

What is more interesting and puzzling is the reference to the 'purified tomb' (*turba al-mutahhara*), which seems to harken to that of the Prophet Muhammad in Medina. For the 'pure garden' (*rawda al-mutahhara*) is a sacred space, located between the house of the Prophet and his minbar, that had paradisiacal associations.[26] This area can itself be considered a liminal space within the Prophet's mosque, as it was originally a zone between what might be seen as the public and private spheres of the Prophet, his pulpit and the rooms of his wives. Although the notion is controversial, some pilgrims believe that prayers offered in this section of the mosque have more value.

What was intended with the Seljuk reference? To which tomb did it refer? The word is in the singular (not dual or plural). Like the masjid, did it refer to the existing tomb tower? Is it possible that the refurbishment of the tomb tower was ordered during the reign of Kayka'us? Perhaps the ceramic artist Karim al-Din Erdishah began working on the cenotaph tiles at this time. Or, alternatively, did the tomb refer to the now-incomplete marble tomb tower? Many scholars attribute the latter tower to Kayka'us because of the mention of a *turba* in this inscription and because of the trilobed frame around it, which is similar to the frame without a text on the incomplete tomb tower itself. Did Kayka'us initially intend the tower for himself, and the project was abandoned when he died and was buried in Sivas, as argued? Maybe Kayqubad meant to use it for himself afterward; however, he also died unexpectedly, from poisoning.

Whatever the exact original intent, the terminology of the 'purified tomb' in the 'public text' and the reference to the Prophet's tomb indicate an effort to imbue the funerary space of the Seljuk dynasts with sanctity, regardless of whether these were in one shared or two separate towers. The title that Kayka'us uses for his father, 'the Martyred Sultan' (*al-sultan al-shahid*), signifies the new status that Kaykhusraw (*r.*1192–96, 1205–11) gained following his 'martyrdom' at Alaşehir (ancient Philadelphia) during the Seljuk confrontation with the Laskarids in 1211. Such terms resonate with religious and paradisiacal symbolism that paralleled efforts to sanctify the architectural space.

In fact, what may have bolstered such claims was the recovery of Kaykhusraw's body, much like a saint's relic, from the Laskarids.[27] For, as the Seljuk historian Ibn Bibi (active *c.*1285) informs us, Kayka'us and his emir, Sayf al-Din Ayaba, went to great pains to recover the sultan's body and bring it back to Konya, where it was ceremonially interned in the dynastic tomb tower.[28] Furthermore, despite Ibn Bibi's mention of burial, the remains of Seljuk sultans are known to have been mummified; this is yet another important indicator of the necessity of *preserving* ancestral memory.[29]

> Then they brought the body of the sultan to Konya and buried [it] next to his ancestors and father and brother. The next day, the Sultan visited the tomb of the sultans. He ordered the collection of thirty thousand dinars along with what the Rum malik sent. Some of it he separated for the inhabitants and poor. And some he sent to the *zawiya*, convents and pious places. And he dispatched the remainder around the country until it was scattered to the worthy and lords of science and masters of certainty. He had a mounted guard on duty. [Since that day] until the present, in this manner, they arrange a horse with trappings and red satin every day of summons [i.e., Fridays].[30]

Ibn Bibi's narrative reveals that in addition to the interment, which was celebrated with charitable acts across the Seljuk realm, new rituals were created to commemorate 'the Martyred Sultan' every Friday, the weekly day of gathering for the congregation at the Friday Mosque itself. In this way, the rituals further underscored and enhanced the visual signifiers – both epigraphic and spatial – that claimed sanctity for the dynasty.

Whatever enmity may have existed between the two brothers, Kayka'us and Kayqubad, due to their intense fight for the throne following the death of their father, their reverence for him must have been a shared feeling. Ibn Bibi tells a poignant story of how, as young boys, they cried after him when he was deposed and forced into exile.[31] Thus, it should come as no surprise that when we turn to the foundation inscription naming Kayqubad above the new main portal on the northern facade of the Friday Mosque, which was overseen by the same emir Ayaz and completed only a year later, we see echoes of the same terminology [Figures 5–6]:

[1] In the name of God (*Allah*) and peace be upon the Messenger of God (*rasul Allah*). This House of God (*bayt Allah*) was completed by the Magnificent Sultan 'Ala al-Dunya [2] wa'l-Din Father of Conquest Kayqubad son of the Exalted Martyred Sultan (*al-sultan al-sa'id al-shahid*) Kaykhusraw son of Qilij Arslan son of Mas'ud [3] Victorious Commander of the Faithful by the hand of the poor slave requiring the grace of God, Ayaz Supervisor (*mutawalli*) the Atabek, year 617.[32]

Within the formulaic nature of the 'public text' that mostly repeats itself, we notice Kaykhusraw's martyrdom underlined further with the title 'the Exalted Martyred Sultan' (*al-sultan al-sa'id al-shahid*). What really stands out, however, is the first line, which not only mentions God and the Prophet Muhammad but also defines the building with the unusual term *bayt Allah* (House of God).

Although the term came to be used generically during the Ottoman era (Baytullah is even used as a proper name in Turkey today), in the medieval period it was usually synonymous with the Ka'ba in Mecca, the point to which Muslims turn five times a day in prayer and visit during the hajj, a pilgrimage that forms one of the five tenets of Islam.[33] The only other site that had associations with the term was the Dome of the Rock in Jerusalem, linked with the Prophet Muhammad's ascension to heaven (*mi'raj*).[34] From this context, it becomes evident that the selected terminology in the Konya Friday Mosque had symbolic meaning that would link the city of Konya to one of the holy cities of Islam: Mecca and Medina or Jerusalem.[35] Thus, although the building may not resonate with the modern viewer, Kayqubad's use of the term *bayt Allah* in fact implies bold claims for the renovation project he took over from Kayka'us to complete. For this reason, while understanding the intended meaning of the term 'House of God' is not easy, the references imply an assertion of sanctity for the Friday Mosque – and ultimately for the city of Konya.

Liminality and the Konya 'Complex'

The additional sacred status sought with the term *bayt Allah* – as opposed to *jami'* – appears to be related specifically to the expansion project and, therefore, spatially to the liminal zone between the two mosque phases. Why? What was significant or unique about this transformation? The renovation transformed the buildings into a 'complex', creating a new multifunctional identity that integrated the mosque and tombs.

Intriguingly, in speaking of different functions, Neslihan Asutay-Effenberger hypothesizes that the sultans used the Friday Mosque for instructional purposes.[36] One of the earliest charitable foundation (waqf) records from the Seljuk period (1202, Altunaba) mentions in passing a 'royal madrasa' (madrasa-yi sultani) in the citadel area; however, we have no further information about the establishment and exact location of this important institution.[37] The idea is tempting, but in that case it is curious that the term was not recorded among the numerous inscriptions from the building. Further complicating the matter, comments made by the fourteenth-century hagiographer Aflaki about Jalal al-Din Rumi's father, Baha al-Din Valad (d.1228), and his arrival in Konya conflict with the information in the waqfiyya: 'Thus he alighted at the Altunpa Madrasa. And they relate that in Konya there was not yet any other madrasa, and the ramparts of the city had not been built.'[38] This may indicate that the city did not enjoy a separate freestanding madrasa building in the early thirteenth century but made use of the Friday Mosque and palace for educational purposes.

If we leave the madrasa discussion aside and return to the buildings for which we have evidence, the 'function' of the new bayt Allah seems to be related to the enclosure of the tomb towers and the development of the new courtyard. The inclusion of a tomb structure within a mosque space was most unusual for its time. While tombs were incorporated into other structures, such as hospitals (e.g., Gevher Nesibe in Kayseri), the complex created by bringing together a mosque and a tomb was novel within Islamic architecture. This set an important precedent that would be emulated by the Seljuks and their successors. A remarkable example of Seljuk female patronage of a funerary mosque complex was commissioned by Mahpari Khatun in Kayseri.[39] However unusual the complex was for Islamic architecture at the time, the tomb of Mahpari Khatun, which employed a reused sarcophagus lid as a cenotaph, also indicates that Seljuk patrons were aware of regional and international customs – Byzantine emperors and Norman kings were known to use sarcophagi for their burials.[40] The Seljuks were no doubt conscious, too, of church burials like the local example of the early Cappadocian church father, Amphilochius (d. after 394), located just above the Friday Mosque on the citadel mound.[41]

For dynastic burials in particular, one might also argue that the funerary mosque complex had parallels in the greater geographical context of Rum: dynastic burials in churches were a well-known feature in Christendom, the most famous example nearby being the Church of the Holy Apostles in Constantinople. Moreover, the twelfth-century dynastic mausoleum in the Pantokrator Monastery, in the same city, was a relatively recent example that seemed to provide a source of inspiration for Byzantine empires in exile following the Fourth Crusade (1204) – namely, the Laskarids in Nicaea (1204–61) and the Grand Komneni in Trebizond (1204–1461).[42] Thus, while this particular combination was unexpected in the Islamic context, the trend set in Constantinople and emulated in Nicaea and Trebizond must have been familiar to the Rum Seljuks, especially considering the Seljuk visits to the city of Constantinople by Qilij Arslan II and Giyath al-Din Kaykhusraw.[43]

Famous examples of Great Seljuk royal tombs, such as that of Sultan Sanjar (r.1118–57) in Merv – also with a turquoise dome – indicate that the tomb tower tradition was well known by the Seljuks of Rum. For this reason, I would argue that it was not necessarily the architectural form itself but the concept of a collective dynastic 'shrine' that may have inspired the Seljuks. As Redford previously remarked, the 'glorification of the Rum Seljuk dynasty was to have been a principal aim of this complex'.[44] Speaking of form, in Konya the Seljuks brought together different resources available to them: the Persian ceramic and tomb tower traditions coupled with the Armenian/Georgian conical dome, the Syrian masonry and mosque plan type, Roman and Byzantine spolia, and Arabic epigraphy. Whatever the source of inspiration may have been, thanks to inscriptions, this new concept and complex – the dynastic tomb enshrined within the mosque – was labelled with terms laden with Islamic meaning.

Along with the new vocabulary introduced into the epigraphic programme that seemed to highlight sacred references, the reconceptualization of the Konya Friday Mosque with noticeably new features, such as the prominent use of striped *ablaq* masonry on the northern facade of the building, indicates the intentional incorporation of a new *visual* vocabulary as a signifier of the new function of the building. The visitor to the renewed site would enter through the new portal of the building, framed with Syrian-style masonry and topped by the *bayt Allah* inscription [Figures 5–6].[45] Stepping into the courtyard, the visitor would then walk between the two tomb towers in order to access the new domed mihrab area [Figure 11].[46] Although some scholars thought of this space as the earlier part of the structure, Doğan Kuban and Haluk Karamağaralı demonstrated that it was part of the thirteenth-century refurbishment.[47] As do the novel masonry framing devices, the tile decoration also indicates a new decorative programme that highlighted the areas of the building that gained meaning with its new function. In addition to the ceramic tiles of the dynastic tomb tower were the mosaic tiles of the mihrab and dome area [Figures 9–10].[48]

Pilgrimage and the Shrine of the Seljuk Dynasty

Let us return to the question of *bayt Allah*: what was meant by this term and what was the intended use of the liminal space? The combination of a mosque with tomb towers seems to indicate that the latter somehow augmented the significance of the mosque. This is evident from the earlier discussion on the pointed selection of the term 'purified tomb' (*turba al-mutahhara*), which echoes references to the Prophet's tomb in Medina. Similarly, the saintly status given to Kaykhusraw with his martyrdom, the return of his body in the manner of a saint's relic, the celebration of his burial, and the rituals developed around his commemoration, such as weekly Friday visitations, seem to indicate a desire to create a dynastic cult.

Spatially speaking as well, the focus of this cult was the dynastic tomb of the Seljuk sultans. The enclosing of the towers into the courtyard of the mosque created a new liminal zone. The encouragement of visitation and the creation of rituals regarding death and commemoration transformed the space into a saintly shrine. Eventually, with others wanting to follow the Seljuk example, the courtyard became filled with many graves (which have been removed in the modern era).[49]

In contemporary cultural history parlance, the kind of act that creates a sacred space is referred to as 'hierotopy'.[50] Intriguingly, the example given by Alexei Lidov, the scholar who coined the term, refers to Jacob and the biblical House of God:

> In the biblical story the description of the hierotopic project starts with Jacob's awakening. Inspired by his dream-vision, he begins to create a sacred space, which would convert a particular place into *'the House of God and the gate of heaven'*. He takes the stone that has been his pillow, sets it up as a monument, and pours oil on it. Jacob also renamed the place and took special vows. So, Jacob and all his successors – creators of churches and shrines, created a particular spatial milieu.[51]

In Konya, Kayqubad's 'hierotopic project' of the *bayt Allah* was not significantly different. The impact was such that, in the later thirteenth century, Ibn Bibi relates that the power of and reverence for the Seljuk dynastic shrine (*gunbadkhane-yi salatin*) saved the city and prevented the walls from being demolished completely by the Mongol forces.[52] We also learn that the supporters of the usurper Jimri asked for the banner of Kayqubad from the tomb tower, which was important for claiming legitimacy.[53] By the turn of the twentieth century, although the Seljuks had faded into history and the building was in a state of disrepair, their memory remained, for the dynastic 'shrine' was still accessible through the mosque itself – as described by Percy above.

With the focus on the dynastic tombs in all of these accounts, it becomes evident that the Konya Friday Mosque – and thereby Konya – was meant to become a destination for pilgrimage. The cult of saints and the related practices of safeguarding relics and visiting sacred sites had a very long history in Anatolia. In his seminal essay on this topic, 'Pilgrimage in Medieval Asia Minor', Clive Foss outlined the traditions during the medieval era. In his conclusion, he also addressed the Muslim period, mentioning the report of al-Harawi (*d.*1215), the author of a pilgrimage guide, concerning the Church of St. Amphilochius in Konya, which contained the tomb of the ancient philosopher Plato.[54] This brings up an intriguing question that is difficult to address with limited information: was there a relationship between this church, dedicated to the Cappadocian church father St. Amphilochius and housing the remains of Plato, and the Friday Mosque or new 'House of God'? The significance of Plato, known as Aflatun in the Islamic world, and the development of a Plato cult in the Konya region at the time is a complicated topic that I have explored elsewhere.[55] For our purposes here, I will ask: was the Konya *bayt Allah* an alternative to the nearby pilgrimage site of Amphilochius/Plato, or was it meant to combine complementary visitations? The Ka'ba, the Prophet's Mosque, and the Dome of the Rock were all essential destinations for pilgrimage, each one with a collection of major and minor loci to visit. Among these, associations with the Ka'ba – i.e., claiming to be the direction in which prayers were offered – is most unusual.[56]

Given the new visual vocabulary and the fact that the architect was from Damascus, however, references to Syria and Jerusalem may have been likely as well. These do not appear to be simply stylistic borrowings. Were they signs of deference or alliance? Or, alternatively, were they part of a 'competitive discourse', reflecting the nature of Seljuk–Ayyubid relations? In the context of the Crusades and counter-Crusades in the Eastern Mediterranean, did the Anatolian branch of the Seljuks hope to claim legitimacy as 'fruit of the Great Seljuq family tree'?[57]

Transforming Konya into a new pilgrimage destination would go hand in hand with the fostering of other shrines and pilgrimage sites by the Seljuks, especially in frontier regions – for example, the tomb of Sayyid Battal Ghazi, an Umayyad warrior-hero, 'discovered' by a Seljuk queen mother, as well as the 'Companions of the Cave' (Ashab al-Kahf), Qur'anic saints associated with the Seven Sleepers in Christianity, developed by a regional governor serving under both Kayka'us and Kayqubad in present-day Afşin, Elbistan.[58] Writing about the latter, Oya Pancaroğlu states that '[t]he development of this cult site in the early thirteenth century exemplifies Rum Seljuk galvanization of sacred topography in conjunction with the consolidation of frontier territories'.[59] In the case of Ashab al-Kahf, there existed already the well-known site in Ephesus; therefore, the destination in Elbistan was a part of a new phenomenon. As Pancaroğlu articulates:

> In the twelfth and thirteenth centuries, it was another set of historical circumstances – the unfolding of geo-strategic rivalries at the eastern fringes of Anatolia between the Seljuks of Rum and the Ayyubids of Syria – that provided the impetus for the re-localization of the Companions' Cave in tandem with political appropriation of geographic marginality.[60]

In my opinion, the 'hierotopic project' of nurturing the Seljuk dynastic cult and the 'shrine' associated with it in Konya as a locus of pilgrimage fits into this greater narrative of Seljuk–Ayyubid 'geo-strategic rivalries' outlined by Pancaroğlu. As with Sayyid Battal Ghazi and the Seven Sleepers, so, too, with the tomb of Plato and the *bayt Allah*, the Seljuks were creating their own pilgrimage destinations. Referencing the Ka'ba, to which all Muslims are obliged to turn for their prayers and to which they travel during their lifetimes, the Konya *bayt Allah* claimed a new identity, not only for the Friday Mosque but also for Konya, the capital or *dar al-mulk*, that reflected the growing imperial ambitions of the Rum Seljuk sultans.

Sanctifying the City of Konya: Kayqubad's Reestablishment of the City

The new status sought for the Friday Mosque through the liminal space that enclosed the 'sacred' tomb tower(s) of the deified sultans helped sanctify the city of Konya. As scholars have pointed out, some cities, like Jerusalem, are 'sacred' by birth, whereas others need to equip themselves to become so.[61] Robert Ousterhout describes this phenomenon in relation to Constantinople and to the importance of imported relics in sanctifying the city.[62] I believe this was the case for Konya, too – i.e., that the Seljuks were hoping to amplify the status of the city, especially in the aftermath of 1204, when they began to have greater 'geo-strategic' aspirations.

In this historical context, renovating the Friday Mosque was an important component of re-establishing the city. As a model, I find Eric Ivison's argument concerning the Byzantine case particularly useful. Ivison states, 'the restoration of urban churches could also be included under the rubric of "rebuilding" a city' in Byzantium.[63] He adds that while 'evidence for wall construction suggests that the Byzantine concept of "rebuilding" a city meant, at least in the first instance, work on the fortifications', 'the restoration of urban churches could also be included under the rubric of "rebuilding" a city'.[64] In addition to this example from neighbouring Byzantium, the central role of the congregational Friday mosque (*jami'*) in the legal definitions of an Islamic city should also be noted.[65] Within this framework, which points to the key role of the 'rebuilding' of the Friday Mosque in 'rebuilding' Konya, perhaps it is not surprising that this curious expansion project was the highlight of mosque patronage for Kayka'us and Kayqubad. This kind of transformation was likely the case in the twelfth century too, with the initial establishment of the mosque and the city under sultans such as their grandfather, Qilij Arslan II, as well.

In the thirteenth century, Kayka'us may have been the initial visionary to 'build' the Friday Mosque and the *turba al-mutahhara* (as he claims in the text panel), transforming the building from a *masjid* to a *jami'*, as we have seen from the inscriptions on the northern facade. He is also the sultan named on a wooden Qur'an stand from the mosque, now housed in the Turkish and Islamic Arts Museum in Istanbul (inv. no. 247).[66] Still, the epigraphic evidence makes clear that Kayqubad played a vital role in the 'completion' of the project, as demonstrated by the term *bayt Allah*. Given this final stamp on the new complex, it is understandable that the mosque and hill bear his name today: 'Alaeddin Camii' or 'Alaeddin Tepesi'.

What was remarkable about Kayqubad's involvement in the Friday Mosque was that it did not constitute a single event – or simply the 'completion' of a project started by his brother – but became part of a greater transformation of the whole city. Ibn Bibi reports that soon after ascending to the throne, Kayqubad decided that the Seljuk capital was in need of new fortifications around the city. He dedicates a short chapter in his oeuvre to the planning and building of the Konya walls.[67] Given the dates of the transition of power from Kayka'us to Kayqubad, which coincided with the dates on the Friday Mosque, these walls were likely to have been built in tandem with the renovation of the Friday Mosque.

Interestingly, Ayaz *mutawalli*, whose name, curiously, was spelled as either Ayaz or Ayas in the Friday Mosque, was also responsible for one of the gates of Konya (Ayaz Kapısı).[68] This Ayaz was likely the loyal servant, mentioned by Ibn Bibi, who accompanied Kayka'us and Kayqubad's father, Kaykhusraw, during his years of exile.[69] His experience in building projects is known from an inscription recorded during the rebuilding of the Sinop walls.[70]

It is possible that he came from an Artuqid background and gained experience with the rebuilding of the Amid/Diyarbakır walls, which might explain his working relationship with the architect, Muhammad bin Khawlan al-Dimashqi.[71] Ayaz provides an important example of sultans delegating their projects to trusted officials. Given that his name appears prominently in the *bayt Allah* inscription, with a line (right above the new portal) dedicated to his 'poor' self, Ayaz must have enjoyed a significant position as *atabeg* in addition to his role as a supervisor of major civic projects. His important stature raises the question of his involvement in Kayqubad's other extensive patronage in the city. For, in addition to the Konya Friday Mosque and city walls, Kayqubad is known to have invested in engineering works related to the control of water, repaired Qilij Arslan II's palace, and built a new hospital near the citadel.[72] These were all in addition to other projects that Kayqubad patronized across the Seljuk Sultanate.

While surveys often relegate the Anatolian or Rum Seljuks to the status of a marginal medieval Islamic state, Kayqubad's contemporaries, as well as his successors, recognized the importance of his policies and achievements. He built on the empire that his predecessors had tried to expand and consolidate, venturing across the Black Sea into the Crimea. Beyond his political agenda, he was constantly involved in promoting urban civilization through architectural projects. City walls (e.g., Konya and Alanya), urban and suburban palaces (e.g., Konya and Kubadabad), mosques (Konya), and agricultural establishments (e.g., Alanya Hasbahçe) were all part of his extensive architectural patronage. The connections among these works were further enhanced by roads, bridges, caravanserais (e.g., Aksaray Sultan Han), and ports (Alanya), creating an urban and extra-urban network. Moreover, people travelling – from court members to armies, couriers, merchants, nomads, pilgrims, and refugees – used this infrastructure, bringing life to old towns, encouraging new settlements, and thus contributing to an urban matrix. All of this activity helped transform Asia Minor, once the periphery and frontier of Byzantium, into a centre of civilization, with artists, scholars, and Sufi mystics flocking to the court in Konya.[73]

Understanding the greater context of Kayqubad's long reign and his architectural patronage is important in shedding light on the developments in Konya. Unfortunately, today many works are no longer standing. In addition to the Church of St. Amphilochius (Eflatun Mescidi), other structures that have not survived include Kayqubad's city walls, waterworks, and hospital. However, fortunately, the city walls are known – from travellers' accounts and from illustrations – for being built mostly from spolia and for incorporating both spoliated and purpose-carved life-size statuary that usually is not associated with orthodox Muslim patrons. As discussed by Redford and Yalman, the decorative programme of the walls incorporated a repertoire of inscriptions and images that addressed audiences from both East and West.[74] Although the initial foundations of the Seljuk capital were established in the twelfth century, especially under sultans like Qilij Arslan – as exemplified in the Konya Mosque as well – in the thirteenth century the territorial expansion of the sultanate necessitated a refurbished capital to stake new claims.

Toward a Conclusion: Konya as City of God

Similar to the Seljuk development of rival pilgrimage centres and 'geo-strategic' aspirations, as articulated by Pancaroğlu, Seljuk investments in Konya and expansion of the Friday Mosque, which created a new liminal space that included the dynastic 'shrine', reveal their imperial ambitions. The new vocabulary – the term 'House of God' (*bayt Allah*), used to describe the renovated Konya Friday Mosque completed under Kayqubad – seems to have been a daring statement, reflecting the reconceptualization of the site. Moreover, in my opinion, the renovation of the Konya Friday Mosque and the construction of city walls should be examined together, as the sultan's project to refashion the Seljuk capital into a city worthy of his ambitions.

In the aftermath of 1204, with Byzantium in exile, Kayqubad was vying for the legacy of Constantinople, or 'New Rome', as 'Sultan of Rum', i.e., Rome. Thus, it is perhaps not surprising that we find similarities in the artistic patronage and signs of power among rulers competing with each other at the time. Livia Bevilacqua compares the Laskarid capital of Nicaea with Capua, developed by the Holy Roman Emperor Frederick II Hohenstaufen (*r.*1220–50).[75] Interesting parallels existed between Frederick and Kayqubad as well.[76] Given this competition on the international stage, especially with Constantinople but also with the Ayyubids, who had control over Jerusalem and Damascus – cities with an ancient and sacred pedigree – Kayqubad tried to refashion the capital of Konya. Together with the wall project, the rebuilding of the mosque, as in Ivison's model, enhanced the status of the city. If we take Ivison's comment to reflect a standard for rebuilding a city, Kayqubad seems to have been aiming even beyond that in his efforts to create not only a new city but also a pilgrimage destination. To this end, the 'House of God' served to transform Konya into a 'City of God'.

In the context of Seljuk Anatolia, which had a largely Christian population at the time, it might be useful to consider the concept of the biblical 'House of God' in addition to the Islamic *bayt Allah,* already noted as a term for the Ka'ba or Jerusalem. Interestingly, as a reference to the Temple, this 'House of God' redirects our gaze to Jerusalem. At a time of Crusades and counter-Crusades, such an indication is unsurprising. The Crusaders were inspired by the Dome of the Rock, which they referred to as 'Temple of the Lord' (*Templum Domini*).[77] Upon their return, the impact of the actual city of Jerusalem is also evident in Europe, particularly in the conceptualization of similar ideals and the formulations of the City of God and the city as Heavenly Jerusalem.[78] Thus, whether or not the Seljuks were aware of the famous *City of God* by Saint Augustine (*d.*430), the political context of European Cities of God, as well as Constantinople as a Heavenly Jerusalem, must have been familiar concepts. Such eschatological overtones are evident in a rare extant Qur'anic fragment from the Konya walls: 'And those that believe, and do deeds of righteousness – those are the inhabitants of Paradise; there they shall dwell forever' (2:82).[79] The selected verse reflects the Seljuks underlining their 'righteousness' through the 'deed' of the city walls. These pious works ensured the sultan's place in the afterlife and helped create a paradisiacal city, a *bayt Allah* or Heavenly Jerusalem.

Epilogue: Shifts in Sacred Topography

In an encomium for Konya, written sometime after Sultan 'Ala al-Din Kayqubad's death, Sultan Valad (*d.*1312), son of the renowned mystic Mawlana Jalal al-Din Rumi (*d.*1273), praised the Rum Seljuk *dar al-mulk* in familiar symbolic terms. Unlike the *bayt Allah*, Mecca and the Ka'ba are mentioned openly:[80]

> O Konya, full of cavalry soldiers (*sipahi*)
>> You are the throne (*takhtgah*) of the territories of Rum (*khata-yi rum*)
> Every city (*shahr*) is grand like an emir
>> You are the head of cities like a king (*shah*)
> Every citadel (*qal'a*) is a luminous star
>> You are the head of stars like the moon (*mah*)
> Since His Highness our King (*shah*) selected you
>> You are the Mecca and the Ka'ba divine.[81]

In Sultan Valad's medieval symbolism of the ideal city or the City of God, the *shah* mentioned was not the Rum Seljuk sultan but Mawlana Jalal al-Din, who had suggested that Konya be called 'City of the Friends of God'.[82] As visually documented in the sixteenth century by Matrakçı Nasuh (*d.*1564), the polymath who accompanied the Ottoman Sultan Süleyman (*r.*1520–66) on his eastern campaigns, the locus of pilgrimage in Konya was subsequently transferred from the walled-in hilltop of Alaeddin and Aflatun to Mawlana's extra-muros shrine, thereby transforming Kayqubad's 'City of Sultans' into the 'City of Saints'.[83] In fact, Nasuh reports that Süleyman visited Mawlana's tomb on his way back to Istanbul; however, there is no mention of any other site.[84] Evidently the Ottomans no longer needed the Seljuks for their own legitimacy.[85] Thus, while the vision of the Seljuk sultans – to transform Konya into a pilgrimage city – did succeed, ultimately it is no longer the dynastic tomb of the sultans but the shrine of Jalal al-Din Rumi that is the heart of Konya today.

Notes

1 İbrahim Hakkı Konyalı, *Abideleri ve Kitabeleri ile Konya Tarihi* (1964; repr., Ankara: Enes Kitap Sarayı for Konya Büyükşehir Belediyesi, 1997), 577.

2 For the Church of St. Amphilochius that later became Eflatun Mescidi, see Semavi Eyice, 'Konya'nın Alaeddin Tepesinde Selçuklu Öncesine Ait Bir Eser: Eflâtûn Mescidi', *Sanat Tarihi Yıllığı* 4 (1970–71): 269–302.

3 Scott Redford, 'The Alaeddin Mosque in Konya Reconsidered', *Artibus Asiae* 51 (1991): 54.

4 For the inscriptions, see Clément Huart, *Épigraphie arabe d'Asie Mineure* (Paris: Lemaire, 1895); Julius H. Löytved, *Konia: Inschriften der seldschukischen Bauten* (Berlin: Verlagsbuchhandlung von J. Springer, 1907); Zeki Oral, 'Konya'da Alaeddin Cami ve

Türbeleri', *Yıllık Araştırmalar Dergisi* 1 (1957): 45–62; Konyalı, *Konya Tarihi*, 293–317; Redford, 'The Alaeddin Mosque in Konya Reconsidered', appendix, 73–74; Remzi Duran, *Selçuklu Devri Konya Yapı Kitâbeleri* (Ankara: Türk Tarih Kurumu Basımevi, 2001), 36–45; and Remzi Duran, 'Konya Alaeddin Camisi Kitabeleri', *Anadolu Selçukluları ve Beylikler Dönemi Uygarlığı*, eds Ali Uzay Peker and Kenan Bilici, 2 vols. (Ankara: T. C. Kültür ve Turizm Bakanlığı Yayınları, 2006), 2:23–30.

5 See Huart, *Épigraphie arabe d'Asie Mineure*; Löytved, *Konia*; Friedrich Sarre, *Denkmäler persischer Baukunst* (Berlin: E. Wasmuth, 1910); and Michael Meinecke, *Fayencedekorationen seldschukischer Sakralbauten in Kleinasien*, 2 vols. (Tübingen: Verlag Ernstwasmuth, 1976). See also Oral, 'Konya'da Alaeddin Cami ve Türbeleri', 45–62; Mehmet Önder, *Mevlana Şehri Konya (Tarihi Kılavuz)* (Konya: Yeni Kitap Basımevi, 1962); Konyalı, *Konya Tarihi*; Doğan Kuban, 'Konya Alâeddin Camisi', *Anadolu-Türk Mimarisinin Kaynak ve Sorunları* (Istanbul: İstanbul Teknik Üniversitesi Mimarlık Fakültesi, 1965), 114–20; Haluk Karamağaralı, 'Konya Ulucâmii', *Rölöve ve Restorasyon Dergisi* 4 (1982): 121–31; Yılmaz Önge, 'Konya Alaeddin Camii'nin Çinili Mihrabı', *Önasya* 4.41 (1969): 10–11; Erol Yurdakul, 'Konya Alaeddin Camii 1971 Yılı Avlu Kazısında Yeni Buluntular', *Ön Asya* 6.69 (1971): 8–9; Erol Yurdakul, '1978 Yılına Kadar Alaeddin Camii'nde Yapılan Onarımlar', *XIII. Vakıf Haftası Kitabı*, eds İbrahim Ateş, Sadi Bayram, and Mehmet Narince (Ankara: Vakıflar Genel Müdürlüğü Yayınları, 1996), 125–70; and Canan Parla, 'I. Alâeddin Keykubad Dönemi Yapılarında Biçim ve Estetik', 3 vols. (PhD diss., Hacettepe University, 1997), 352–400, 722–26.

6 See Redford, 'The Alaeddin Mosque in Konya Reconsidered', 54–74; and Neslihan Asutay-Effenberger, 'Konya Alaeddin Camisi Yapım Evreleri Üzerine Düşünceler/Some Remarks on the Building Phases of the Alaeddin Mosque in Konya', *METU JFA* 23.2 (2006): 113–22.

7 Duran, *Selçuklu Devri Konya Yapı Kitâbeleri*, 36–45; and Yaşar Erdemir, *Alâeddin Camii ve Türbeleri* (Konya: T.C. Konya Valiliği İl Kültür ve Turizm Müdürlüğü, 2009), 39–69, 242–51.

8 See Richard P. McClary, *Rum Seljuq Architecture, 1170–1220: The Patronage of Sultans* (Edinburgh: Edinburgh University Press, 2017), 164–68.

9 Henry Algernon George Percy, *Highlands of Asiatic Turkey* (London: E. Arnold, 1901), 28–29.

10 For more on the carpet market, see Ayşin Yoltar-Yıldırım, 'Seljuk Carpets and Julius Harry Löytved-Hardegg: A German Consul in Konya in the Early 20th Century', in *Thirteenth International Congress of Turkish Art: Proceedings*, eds Géza Dávid and Ibolya Gerelyes (Budapest: Hungarian National Museum, 2009), 747–57.

11 See Mahmut Akok, 'Konya Şehri İçindeki Alâeddin Tepesinde Türk Tarih Kurumu Adına Yapılan Arkeolojik Kazıların Mimari Buluntuları', *Belleten* 39 (1975): 217–24.

12 For a summary of earlier work, see Mustafa R. Abicel, 'Konya Alaeddin Camii'nde Yapılan Onarımlar ve Zemin Güçlendirme Çalışmaları ile Alaeddin Tepesinin Sorunları', *Vakıflar Vakıf Haftası Dergisi* 5 (1987): 27–51.

13 For the minbar, see Oral, 'Konya'da Alaeddin Cami ve Türbeleri', 52–56; Konyalı, *Konya Tarihi*, 309–12; and Erdemir, *Alâeddin Camii ve Türbeleri*, 149–67. For further reading on the Qilij Arslan tomb tower and cenotaph inscriptions, see Orhan Cezmi Tuncer, *Anadolu Kümbetleri*, 3 vols. (Ankara: Güven Matbaası, 1986), 1:178–86; Hakkı Önkal, *Anadolu*

Selçuklu Türbeleri (Ankara: Atatürk Kültür Merkezi Yayını, 1996), 185–90; and Kerim Türkmen, 'Konya Sultanlar Türbesi İçerisindeki Sandukalar Üzerinde Yer Alan Kitabeler', *Konya Kitabı (Özel Sayı – Arıklara Armağan)* 10 (2007): 665–72.

14 See, in particular, Oral, 'Konya'da Alaeddin Cami ve Türbeleri', 45–62; Konyalı, *Konya Tarihi*, 293–308; Redford, 'The Alaeddin Mosque in Konya Reconsidered', appendix, 73–74; Duran, *Selçuklu Devri Konya Yapı Kitâbeleri*, 36–45; and Erdemir, *Alâeddin Camii ve Türbeleri*, 110–25.

15 See Oral, 'Konya'da Alaeddin Cami ve Türbeleri', 59n3; Redford, 'The Alaeddin Mosque in Konya Reconsidered', 71n49; Duran, *Selçuklu Devri Konya Yapı Kitâbeleri*, 37–39; and Erdemir, *Alâeddin Camii ve Türbeleri*, 120–21.

16 See note 3 above. For a more complete overview of the scholarship and bibliography, see Erdemir, *Alâeddin Camii ve Türbeleri*, 39–69, 242–51.

17 For further reading on the phenomenon of *spolia* in Anatolia, see Ivana Jevtić and Suzan Yalman, eds, *Spolia Reincarnated: Afterlives of Objects, Materials, and Spaces in Anatolia from Antiquity to the Ottoman Era* (Istanbul: ANAMED, 2018).

18 The sequence of construction and attribution to sultans have been debated over the decades. See Redford, 'The Alaeddin Mosque in Konya Reconsidered', 54–74; Asutay-Effenberger, 'Some Remarks on the Building Phases of the Alaeddin Mosque in Konya', 113–22; and Erdemir, *Alâeddin Camii ve Türbeleri*, especially 226–37. For further reading, see above, note 16. For a more unusual recent suggestion, see Sotiris Voyadjis and Petros Kapsoudas, 'Osmoses of the Persian, Syrian, and Byzantine Building Techniques in the Lands of the Rum: The Case of the so-called Alaeddin Camii in Konya and Its Collection of Marble Spolia', accessed March 21, 2019, https://www.academia.edu/38059888/Osmoses_of_the_Persian_Syrian_and_Byzantine_building_techniques_in_the_lands_of_the_Rum._The_case_of_the_so-called_Alaeddin_Camii_in_Konya_and_its_collection_of_marble_spolia.

19 See Zeki Sönmez, 'Anadolu Selçuklularında Atabeylik, Atabey Esededdin Ayaz ve 13. Yüzyıl Mimarisine Katkıları', in *Antalya V. Selçuklu Semineri Bildirileri* (Antalya: Antalya Valiliği, 1998), 4–11; and Mehmet Ali Hacıgökmen, 'Türkiye Selçuklu Devlet Adamlarından Esededdin Ayaz', *Türkiyat Araştırmaları Dergisi* 27 (2010): 471–88.

20 For the architect, see Konyalı, *Konya Tarihi*, 298; and Zafer Bayburtluoğlu, *Anadolu'da Selçuklu Dönemi Yapı Sanatçıları, Anadolu'da Selçuklu Dönemi Yapı Sanatçıları* (Erzurum: Atatürk Üniversitesi Yayınları, 1993), 90–1. For the Sultan Han, see Kurt Erdmann, *Das anatolische Karavansaray des 13. Jahrhunderts,* 2 vols. (Berlin: Verlag Gebr. Mann, 1961), 1:89.

21 See Konyalı, *Abideleri ve Kitabeleri ile Konya Tarihi*, 303, 311; and Bayburtluoğlu, *Anadolu'da Selçuklu Dönemi Yapı Sanatçıları*, 90–91.

22 Gülru Necipoğlu, 'Anatolia and the Ottoman Legacy', *The Mosque: History, Architectural Development and Regional Diversity,* eds Martin Frishman and Hasan-Uddin Khan (London and New York: Thames and Hudson, 1994), 142.

23 'For the Fatimids, every written sign in the public space was a public text: an officially sponsored writing addressed to a public audience which continuously reminded the viewers of the official Fatimid position'. Irene Bierman, *Writing Signs: The Fatimid Public Text* (Berkeley and Los Angeles: UC Press, 1998), 1.

24 [1] *Amara bi-binai hadha'l-masjid wa'l-turba al-mutahhara [2] al-sultan al-[ghalib 'Izz] al-Dunya wa'l-Din abu 'l-fath. [3] Kay[ka'us] al-sultan al-shahid Kaykhusraw bin Qilij Arslan [4] nasr amir al-mu'minin bi-tawalli al-'abd Ayaz al-Atabeki min sana sitta'ashra wa sitt mi'a.* Duran, *Selçuklu Devri Konya Yapı Kitâbeleri,* 37–39. See above, note 15.

25 Ibid., 36–37.

26 For 'pure garden' (*rawda al-mutahhara*), see Nebi Bozkurt, 'Ravza-i Mutahhara', *Türkiye Diyanet Vakfı İslam Ansiklopedisi,* 34:475. See also Louis Massignon, 'La rawda de Medine: cadre de la meditation musulmane sur le destinee du prophete', in *Opera Minora,* ed. Youakim Moubarac (Liban: Dar al-Maaref, 1960), 3:286–315.

27 See Zeynep Oğuz Kursar, 'Sultans as Saintly Figures in Early Ottoman Royal Mausolea', in *Sacred Spaces and Urban Networks,* eds Suzan Yalman and A. Hilâl Uğurlu (Istanbul: ANAMED, 2019).

28 There are many editions of Ibn Bibi's history. For the original and full text of the manuscript, see Ibn Bibi (el-Hüseyn b. Muhammed b. 'Ali el-Ca'feri er-Rugedi), *El-evamirü'l-'ala'iyye fi'l-umur'l-'ala'iyye,* facsimile edition (hereafter 'facs. ed.'), ed. Adnan Sadık Erzi (Ankara: Türk Tarih Kurumu Basımevi, 1956), fol. 132–33. Although Erzi – the scholar who published the facsimile edition – began to prepare a critical edition, only one volume was published. See Ibn Bibi, *El-evamirü'l-'ala'iyye fi'l-umur'l-'ala'iyye* (hereafter, 'critical ed.'), eds Necati Lugal and Adnan Sadık Erzi (Ankara: Türk Tarih Kurumu Basımevi, 1957), 1:190. For the modern Turkish translation of the full facsimile edition, see Ibn Bibi, *El Evamirü'l-Ala'iye fi'l-Umuri'l-Ala'iye* (hereafter 'Selçukname'), trans. Mürsel Öztürk, 2 vols. (Ankara: T.C. Kültür Bakanlığı Yayınları, 1996), 1:154.

29 See Faruk Sümer, 'The Seljuk Turbehs and the Tradition of Embalming', *Atti del secondo congresso internazionale di arte turca (Venezia 26–29 settembre 1963)* (Naples: Instituto universitario orientale, 1965), 245–48.

30 Ibn Bibi, facs. ed., fol. 132–33; Ibn Bibi, critical ed., 1:190; and Ibn Bibi, *Selçukname,* 1:154.

31 See Ibn Bibi, facs. ed., fol. 38.

32 [1] *Bism Allah w'al-salam 'ala rasul Allah tamma hadha bayt Allah al-sultan al-mu'azzam 'Ala al-Dunya [2] wa'l-Din abu 'l-fath Kayqubad ibn al-sultan al-sa'id al-shahid Kaykhusraw bin Qilij Arslan bin Mas'ud [3] nasr amir al-mu'minin 'ala yad al-'abd al-faqir al-muhtaj ila rahmat Allah Ayaz Mutawalli al-Atabeki sana sab'a ashra wa sitt mi'a.* Redford, 'The Alaeddin Mosque in Konya Reconsidered', appendix, 73; and Duran, *Selçuklu Devri Konya Yapı Kitâbeleri,* 41–42.

33 Oral noted the unusual nature of this term as well. See Oral, 'Konya'da Alaeddin Cami ve Türbeleri', 58.

34 For further reading on the *bayt Allah* for both the Ka'ba and the Dome of the Rock, see Gülru Necipoğlu, 'The Dome of the Rock as Palimpsest: 'Abd al-Malik's Grand Narrative and Sultan Süleyman's Glosses', *Muqarnas* 25 (2008): 17–105.

35 See Uri Rubin, 'The Ka'ba: Aspects of Its Ritual Functions and Position in Pre-Islamic and Early Islamic Times', *Jerusalem Studies in Arabic and Islam* 8 (1986): 97–131; and Meir Jacob Kister, 'Sanctity Joint and Divided: On Holy Places in the Islamic Tradition', *Jerusalem Studies in Arabic and Islam* 20 (1996): 18–65. I thank Sabiha Göloğlu for sharing her thoughts and references on the Ka'ba and the Mosque of the Prophet.

36 See Asutay-Effenberger, 'Konya Alaeddin Camisi Yapım Evreleri Üzerine Düşünceler', 118–19, 122.

37 Osman Turan, 'Selçuk Devri Vakfiyeleri I: Şemseddin Altun–Aba Vakfiyesi ve Hayatı', *Belleten* 11 (1947): 197–236.

38 Shams al-Din Ahmad Aflaki, *The Feats of the Knowers of God: Manaqeb al-'arefin*, trans. John O'Kane (Leiden and Boston: Brill, 2002), 23.

39 Redford, 'The Alaeddin Mosque in Konya Reconsidered', 72.

40 Suzan Yalman, 'Chapter 10: The "Dual Identity" of Mahperi Khatun: Piety, Patronage and Marriage across Frontiers in Seljuk Anatolia', in *Architecture and Landscape in Medieval Anatolia, 1100–1500*, eds Rachel Goshgarian and Patricia Blessing (Edinburgh: Edinburgh University Press, 2017), 237. Redford has noted that reused sarcophagi also show Seljuk awareness of the past and the original function of these pieces. See Scott Redford, 'The Sarcophagus as *Spolium*: Examples from Thirteenth-Century Konya', in *Spolia Reincarnated: Afterlives of Objects, Materials, and Spaces in Anatolia from Antiquity to the Ottoman Era*, eds Ivana Jevtić and Suzan Yalman (Istanbul: ANAMED, 2018), 195–209.

41 See Eyice 'Eflâtûn Mescidi', 269–302.

42 Antony Eastmond, *Art and Identity in Thirteenth-Century Byzantium: Hagia Sophia and the Empire of Trebizond* (Aldershot, England and Burlington, VT: Ashgate/Variorum, 2004), 54.

43 A number of Byzantine and Syriac authors recorded the visits to Constantinople of Seljuk sultans. For Qilij Arslan, see Alexander D. Beihammer, 'Defection across the Border of Islam and Christianity: Apostasy and Cross-Cultural Interaction in Byzantine-Seljuk Relations', *Speculum* 86.3 (2011): 634–39. For Kaykhusraw's time in Constantinople during his exile, see Ibn Bibi, facs. ed., fols. 52–58. See also Dimitri Korobeinikov, 'A Sultan in Constantinople: The Feasts of Ghiyath al-Din Kay-Khusraw I', in *Eat, Drink, and Be Merry (Luke 12:19): Food and Wine in Byzantium: Papers of the 37th Annual Spring Symposium of Byzantine Studies, in Honour of Professor A.A.M. Bryer*, eds Leslie Brubaker and Kallirroe Linardou (Aldershot, England and Burlington, VT: Ashgate, 2007), 93–108.

44 Redford, 'The Alaeddin Mosque in Konya Reconsidered', 69.

45 Originally, the entrance seems to have been through a double stairway of the kind that is common to many Anatolian tomb towers as well as the kiosk mosques of royal caravanserais. See an early photograph by John Henry Haynes in Robert G. Ousterhout, *John Henry Haynes: A Photographer and Archaeologist in the Ottoman Empire, 1881–1900* (Istanbul: Cornucopia Books, 2011), 54, pl. 34. I thank Scott Redford for pointing out this image. This feature raises questions regarding what was under the stairs that are difficult to answer without further archaeological research: was there possibly a crypt? Or could there have been a fountain, as at the later Aydinid Isa Bey Mosque (1374) in Ayasoluk, which was also built by a Damascene architect? For findings in the courtyard, see Yurdakul, 'Konya Alaeddin Camii 1971 Yılı Avlu Kazısında Yeni Buluntular', 8–9. For more on Syrian architecture of the period, see Stephennie Mulder, *The Shrines of the 'Alids in Medieval Syria: Sunnis, Shi'is and the Architecture of Coexistence* (Edinburgh: Edinburgh University Press, 2014).

46 On stylistic grounds, Richard McClary has recently suggested that the incomplete tomb tower dates from the 1240s and was left in this state due to disruptions following the Seljuk defeat by the Mongols at the Battle of Kösedağ in 1243. See McClary, *Rum Seljuq*

Architecture, 1170–1220, 164–68. I am more inclined to think it was conceptualized together with the northern facade but left incomplete due to the unexpected deaths of the sultans involved. Whatever the exact date, most scholars would likely agree that the marble tower was intended for a member of the Seljuk dynasty. For this reason, I consider the two towers together as part of the dynastic cult. While it is conceivable that the incomplete tower was meant to house another body, we have no record of this.

47   Önder, *Mevlana Şehri Konya*, 91–105. See also Kuban, 'Konya Alâeddin Camisi', 114–20; and Karamağaralı, 'Konya Ulucâmii', 121–31.

48   The dating for the ceramics in the complex has been a matter of debate. Given similarities to the tile that has the signature of Kerim al-Din Ardishah, he may have been responsible for the refurbishment of the cenotaph tiles in the dynastic tomb tower (*c.*1220). Meinecke suggests a date in the 1230s for the mosaic tilework in the mihrab and dome area, based on stylistic comparisons with the mosaic faience work at the Sırçalı and Karatay Madrasas from later decades. See Meinecke, *Fayancedekorationen seldschukischer Sakralbauten in Kleinasien*, 1:35–45, 2:212–33. Also see Şerare Yetkin, *Anadolu'da Türk Çini Sanatının Gelişmesi* (Istanbul: İstanbul Üniversitesi Edebiyat Fakültesi Yayınları, 1986), 44–47; and Rüçhan-Oluş Arık, *Tiles: Treasures of Anatolian Soil Tiles of the Seljuk and Beylik Periods* (Istanbul: Kale Group Cultural Productions, 2008), 42–43. Within discussions of tilework, I have not seen any commentary on the dating for the turquoise blue tiles formerly covering the Qilij Arslan tomb tower, which would have made a striking impression on the viewer. Were these from the twelfth or thirteenth century? Could this tile-clad dome have been a source of inspiration for later important examples in Anatolia, such as the Mawlana tomb tower in Konya (1273 with later additions) or the early Ottoman Green Tomb in Bursa (1421)?

49   For graves found in the courtyard, see Yurdakul, 'Konya Alaeddin Camii 1971 Yılı Avlu Kazısında Yeni Buluntular'.

50   For 'hierotopy', see Alexei Lidov, 'Hierotopy: The Creation of Sacred Spaces as a Form of Creativity and Subject of Cultural History', in *Hierotopy: Creation of Sacred Spaces in Byzantium and Medieval Russia*, ed. Alexei Lidov (Moscow: Progress-tradition, 2006), 32–58; and Alexei Lidov, 'Creating the Sacred Space: Hierotopy as a New Field of Cultural History', in *Spazi e Percorsi Sacri*, eds Laura Carnevale and Chiara Cremonesi (Padua: Libreriauniversitaria.it, 2015), 61–90.

51   Lidov, 'Hierotopy', 33. Emphasis added.

52   Ibn Bibi, facs. ed., fol. 626; and Ibn Bibi, *Selçukname*, 2:151.

53   Ibn Bibi, facs. ed., fol. 696; and Ibn Bibi, *Selçukname*, 2:209.

54   See Clive Foss, 'Pilgrimage in Medieval Asia Minor', *Dumbarton Oaks Papers* 56 (2002): 150. See also Ali ibn Abi Bakr Harawi, *A Lonely Wayfarer's Guide to Pilgrimage (Kitab al-isharat ila ma'rifat al-ziyarat)*, trans. J. W. Meri (Princeton: Darwin Press, 2004), 152.

55   This is a topic that I have explored separately. For further reading, see Suzan Yalman, 'From Plato to the *Shahnama*: Reflections on Saintly Veneration in Seljuk Konya', in *Sacred Spaces and Urban Networks*, eds Suzan Yalman and A. Hilâl Uğurlu (Istanbul: ANAMED, 2019), 119–40. I link this Konya cult with the activity of the mystic philosopher Suhrawardi *al-maqtul* (d. 1191) in Anatolia. See also Suzan Yalman, "Ala al-Din Kayqubad Illuminated: A Rum Seljuq Sultan as Cosmic Ruler', *Muqarnas* 29 (2012): 168–69.

56 Moreover, what is perhaps even more noteworthy is the fact that the Amphilochius/Plato tomb was located behind the qibla wall of the Friday Mosque; therefore, Muslim prayers would have been offered in this direction. Alternatively, some scholars have suggested that chapels in Seljuk citadels were reserved for the Christian members of the harem. V. Macit Tekinalp, 'Palace Churches of the Anatolian Seljuks: Tolerance or Necessity?' *Byzantine and Modern Greek Studies* 33.2 (2009): 148–67.

57 Necipoğlu, 'Anatolia and the Ottoman Legacy', 142.

58 Zeynep Yürekli, *Architecture and Hagiography in the Ottoman Empire: The Politics of Bektashi Shrines in the Classical Age* (Farnham, England and Burlington, VT: Ashgate, 2012); and Oya Pancaroğlu, 'Caves, Borderlands and Configurations of Sacred Topography in Medieval Anatolia', *Mésogeios* 25–26 (2005): 249–81.

59 Pancaroğlu, 'Caves, Borderlands and Configurations', 266.

60 Ibid., 265.

61 Gerhard Wolf, 'Between Distance and Proximity: Religious Architecture versus Sacred Topography. Sites, Non-sites and Landscapes' (paper, Synagogue, Church, Mosque conference, Swedish Research Institute, Istanbul, November 17, 2017); and Méropi Anastassiadou, 'Sacred Spaces in a Holy City: Crossing Religious Boundaries in 20th Century Istanbul', (lecture, Koç University Social Sciences and Humanities Seminar Series, Istanbul, February 20, 2018).

62 Robert G. Ousterhout, 'The Sanctity of Place and the Sanctity of Buildings: Jerusalem versus Constantinople', in *Architecture of the Sacred: Space, Ritual, and Experience from Classical Greece to Byzantium*, ed. Bonna D. Wescoat and Robert G. Ousterhout (Cambridge and New York: Cambridge University Press, 2012), 281–306; and Robert G. Ousterhout, 'Constructing and Deconstructing Sacred Space in Byzantine Constantinople', in *Sacred Spaces and Urban Networks*, eds Suzan Yalman and A. Hilâl Uğurlu (Istanbul: ANAMED, 2019), 89–104.

63 Eric Ivison, 'Urban Renewal and Imperial Revival in Byzantium (730–1025)', *Byzantinische Forschungen* 26 (2000): 7.

64 Ivison, 'Urban Renewal and Imperial Revival in Byzantium', 7.

65 See Baber Johansen, 'The All-Embracing Town and its Mosques: *al-miṣr al-ǧāmīʿ*', *Revue de l'Occident Musulman et de la Méditerranée* 32 (1981–82): 99–100.

66 Seracettin Şahin, *The Museum of Turkish and Islamic Arts: Thirteen Centuries of Glory from the Umayyads to the Ottomans* (New York: Blue Dome Press, 2009), 125–29.

67 Ibn Bibi, facs. ed., fol. 252–56.

68 Ayaz's is the only extant dated inscription from the Konya walls and is fragmentary: 'by the hand of (*ʿala yad*) the overseer (*mutawallī*) Ayaz, year 618'. See Duran, *Selçuklu Devri Konya Yapı Kitâbeleri*, 68.

69 Ibn Bibi reports that Ayaz had served Kaykhusraw faithfully, being exposed to much hardship during the sultan's exile. Ibn Bibi, facs. ed., fol. 236.

70 For the inscription with the name Ayaz (or rather Ayas) in Sinop, see Scott Redford, *Legends of Authority: The 1215 Inscriptions of Sinop Citadel, Turkey* (Istanbul: Koç University Press, 2014), 146–47, 228–30.

71 See above, note 19. For the Artuqid context, also see Yalman, "Ala al-Din Kayqubad Illuminated", 168–69.

72 For this and what follows, see Parla, 'I. Alâeddin Keykubad Dönemi Yapılarında Biçim ve Estetik'; and Suzan Yalman, 'Building the Sultanate of Rum: Memory, Urbanism and Mysticism in the Architectural Patronage of Sultan 'Ala al-Din Kayqubad (r. 1220–37)', (PhD diss., Harvard University, 2011), especially chapter 3.

73 In addition to note 72 above, for a general overview of the period, see Osman Turan, *Selçuklular Zamanında Türkiye* (1971; repr., Istanbul: Ötüken, 2004); Claude Cahen, *The Formation of Turkey: The Seljukid Sultanate of Rum: Eleventh to Fourteenth Century*, trans. P. M. Holt (1988; repr., Harlow, England: Pearson Education Limited, 2001); Emine Uyumaz, *Sultan I. Alâeddîn Keykubad Devri Türkiye Selçuklu Devleti Siyasî Tarihi (1220–1237)* (Ankara: Türk Tarih Kurumu Basımevi, 2003); and Andrew C. S. Peacock and Sara Nur Yıldız, eds, *The Seljuks of Anatolia: Court and Society in the Medieval Middle East* (London and New York: I. B. Tauris, 2013).

74 Scott Redford, 'Seljuks of Rum and the Antique', *Muqarnas* 10 (1993): 148–57; Redford, 'The Sarcophagus as *Spolium*', 195–209; and Suzan Yalman, 'Repairing the Antique: Legibility and Reading Seljuk *Spolia* in Konya', in *Spolia Reincarnated: Afterlives of Objects, Materials, and Spaces in Anatolia from Antiquity to the Ottoman Era*, eds Ivana Jevtić and Suzan Yalman (Istanbul: ANAMED, 2018), 211–33.

75 Livia Bevilacqua, '*Spolia* on City Gates in the Thirteenth Century: Byzantium and Italy', *Spolia Reincarnated: Afterlives of Objects, Materials, and Spaces in Anatolia from Antiquity to the Ottoman Era*, eds Ivana Jevtić and Suzan Yalman (Istanbul: ANAMED, 2018), 173–94.

76 See Yalman, "Ala al-Din Kayqubad Illuminated", especially 151–59.

77 Necipoğlu, 'The Dome of the Rock as Palimpsest', 56.

78 See Keith D. Lilley, 'Cities of God? Medieval Urban Forms and Their Christian Symbolism', *Transactions of the Institute of British Geographers, New Series* 29.3 (2004): 296–313.

79 Duran, *Selçuklu Devri Konya Yapı Kitâbeleri*, 68. See *The Koran Interpreted*, trans. Arthur John Arberry (1955; repr., New York: Collier Books, Macmillan Publishing Company, 1986), 38.

80 See Sunil Sharma, 'The City of Beauties in Indo-Persian Poetic Landscape', *Comparative Studies of South Asia, Africa and the Middle East* 24.2 (2004): 73–81.

81 *Divanı Sultan Veled*, ed. Feridun Nafiz Uzluk (Istanbul: Uzluk Basımevi, 1941), 462.

82 Aflaki, *The Feats of the Knowers of God*, 181.

83 For the topographical illustration of Konya, see Nasuhu's – Silahi (Matrakçı), *Beyan-i Menazil-i Sefer-i 'Irakeyn-i Sultan Süleyman Han*, ed. Hüseyin Yurdaydın (Ankara: Türk Tarih Kurumu Basımevi, 1976), fol. 17a.

84 Nasuh, *Beyan-i Menazil-i Sefer-i 'Irakeyn-i Sultan Süleyman Han*, 284 and fol. 107a.

85 The Ottoman dismissal of the Seljuk past is overtly stated in an inscription in the Topkapı Palace in Istanbul: '*Bu reşk-i Kisrâ Tâk-i Sultânî/Yanında Keykubâdun kasrı kaldı köhne bir hargâh*'. Abdurrahman Şeref, 'Topkapu Saray-i Humayunu', *Tarih-i Osmani Encümeni Mecmuası* 283, as cited in Redford, 'The Alaeddin Mosque in Konya Reconsidered', 70. I am similarly indebted to Gülru Necipoğlu for this reference. The Ottoman memory of the Seljuks is an extensive topic to which I hope to return in the future.

Inviolable Thresholds, Blessed Palaces, and Holy Friday Mosques: The Sacred Topography of Safavid Isfahan

Farshid Emami

In the seventeenth century, the city of Isfahan, the royal seat of the Safavid dynasty (1501–1722), was home to two congregational mosques: one was old, the other new. The Old Mosque (*masjid-i kuhna*) lay at the core of the walled town, in the vicinity of an urban square known as the Maydan-i Harun-i Vilayat or the Old Maydan (*maydan-i kuhna*). Originally built in the eighth century, the Old Mosque took its distinctive form in the late-eleventh and early-twelfth centuries under the Great Seljuks (1040–1157), when its monumental domes and iwans were erected [Figure 1]. The new congregational mosque, which became known as the Shah Mosque (*masjid-i shah*), was built eight centuries later (c.1611–38) [Figure 2]. Located on the south side of the city's new plaza, Maydan-i Naqsh-i Jahan (Image-of-the-World Square), it was the last and greatest monument built in Isfahan by the Safavid ruler Shah Abbas I (r. 1587–1629).

Modified and expanded over the ages, the Old Mosque was imbued with historical memories, bearing the marks of shifting architectural tastes, sectarian divides, and fluctuations of power. Emanating from a singular imperial vision, the Shah Mosque, by contrast, projected a coherent statement in both aesthetic and political terms. Constructed when the Safavid Empire was at the apogee of its power, it embodied and represented the newly gained might of the Twelver Shi'i polity in the form of a quintessentially Islamic building type – a Friday mosque.

These two congregational mosques were products of different contexts and temporalities, but in the seventeenth century, with the development of Isfahan under Shah Abbas, they became integrated into a unified urban system [Figure 3]. Following the establishment of the dynastic seat of the Safavid ruling household in the Naqsh-i Jahan garden, Isfahan's urban centre shifted southward to the Maydan-i Naqsh-i Jahan. In the meantime, with the construction of extramural gardens and neighbourhoods on the banks of the Zayanda Rud (the river that flows in the south of Isfahan) a bipolar urban structure emerged: the pre-Safavid walled town became known as the 'old city' (*shahr-i kuhna*), its central plaza as the 'old *maydan*' (*maydan-i kuhna*), and its congregational mosque as the 'old mosque' (*masjid-i kuhna* or *masjid-i jami'-i atiq*).

Situated along the city's old and new public squares, and linked via a two-kilometre-long covered market (the grand bazaar), the dual Friday mosques of seventeenth-century Isfahan were the most conspicuous emblems of its dichotomous physical structure – a duality that carried a wide range of social and political connotations. From an ideological perspective, what differentiated the new congregational mosque was its sectarian ethos: as staunch

Figure 1: Old Friday Mosque (*masjid-i jami'*), Isfahan, aerial view. Photograph: Reza Nur Bakhtiar, after *Isfahan, muza-yi hamisha zinda* (Shahrdari-yi Isfahan, 1993), 16.

Figure 2: Aerial view of the Safavid Congregational Mosque (Shah Mosque). After Henri Stierlin, *Ispahan, image du paradis* (Geneva: Sigma, 1976).

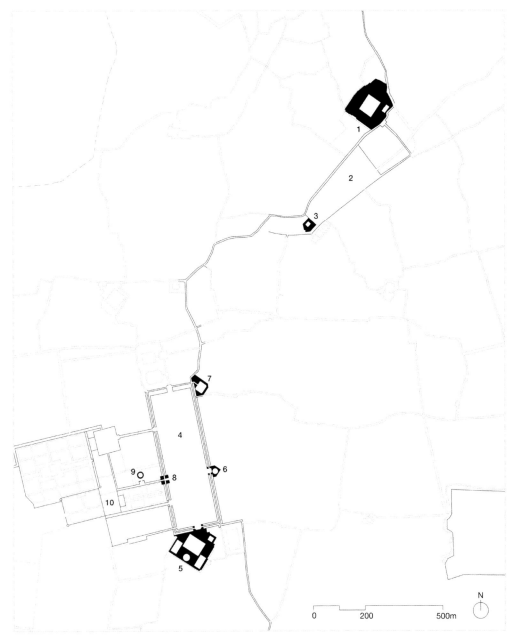

Figure 3: Map of the urban core of Isfahan in the seventeenth century, showing the main elements of the city and the location of the two congregational mosques: (1) Old Friday Mosque; (2) Maydan-i Harun-i Vilayat (Old Maydan); (3) Harun-i Vilayat Shrine; (4) Maydan-i Naqsh-i Jahan; (5) Shah Mosque (New Congregational Mosque); (6) Shaykh Lutfallah Mosque; (7) Mulla Abdallah Madrasa; (8) Ali Qapu; (9) Tawhidkhana; (10) Palace Complex (Dawlatkhana). Plan: Farshid Emami.

upholders of Twelver Shiʻism, the Safavids propagated their creed through myriad measures ranging from forceful conversion and sponsorship of clergy to the construction of Shiʻi shrines. And yet, although these policies had been pursued since the proclamation of Shiʻism as the state religion by Shah Ismaʻil (*r.*1501–24), the charismatic founder of the dynasty, the Shah Mosque of Isfahan was in all likelihood the first monumental mosque sponsored by a Safavid ruler that was officially designated for the performance of Friday prayer; during the first century of Safavid rule, an unsettled clerical debate over the permissibility of Friday prayer in the absence of the awaited Twelfth Imam apparently had hindered the Shiʻi shahs from sponsoring congregational mosques.[1] The Shah Mosque, however, was not meant to be an ecumenical venue of worship: its epigraphic programme included an unprecedented number of hadith (recorded sayings of the Prophet Muhammad and imams) proclaiming specifically Shiʻi tenets of faith. Hovering above the Safavid capital, the new congregational mosque was erected to unify Isfahan – and by extension the Safavid dominions – under the banner of a state-sponsored orthodox version of Shiʻism.

These aspirations were only partially realized. Over the course of the seventeenth century, the debate over the legality of Friday prayer was never truly settled, and the project of crafting a monolithic state religion based on a clerical interpretation of Shiʻism was faced with crises and resistance, particularly in the metropolitan context of Isfahan.[2] Despite the grandeur of its opulent rival, the age-old congregational mosque remained 'resilient'.[3] Ultimately, in the popular parlance, the Safavid Friday mosque became known as *masjid-i shah* (the shah's mosque) or *masjid-i abbasi* (the mosque of [shah] Abbas) rather than *masjid-i jami'* (congregational mosque), as the building was named in its inscriptions and in contemporary written sources.[4]

This essay explores the conceptions and material expressions of sacredness, urbanity, and liminality in Safavid Isfahan. It situates the Friday mosques of seventeenth-century Isfahan in the city's sacred topography, demonstrating how sectarian beliefs, imperial visions, and social processes shaped and refashioned their meanings and functions. In Safavid Isfahan, I contend, the experience and perception of the Friday mosque were affected and transformed by an increasing physical and functional demarcation between the domain of worship and that of ordinary urban existence. The physical delineation of the Friday mosque from surrounding urban spaces, together with the incorporation of Shiʻi relics, texts, and practices in mosques and the broader urban landscape, gave the sacred topography of Isfahan a distinctive character, which was particularly manifest in the symbolic and architectonic significance of transitional spaces and thresholds as venerated liminal sites.[5]

The Shaykh Lutfallah Mosque and the Sacred Sites of the Maydan-i Naqsh-i Jahan

The Shah Mosque is not a freestanding monument but rather an integral component of an enormous urban ensemble, the Maydan-i Naqsh-i Jahan, which informs its experience as a religious foundation. Moreover, the congregational mosque was neither the most sacred, nor the only sanctuary of the square. Prior to its construction, work had begun on a single-domed mosque known as the Shaykh Lutfallah Mosque (completed *c.*1595–1618). To fully appreciate the peculiarities of the Shah Mosque's architecture and the ideological, social and urban processes that underpinned its construction, it is thus essential to examine the form and function of the sacred structures around the Maydan-i Naqsh-i Jahan, and particularly the Shaykh Lutfallah Mosque, which was the first designated venue of congregational prayer in the royal plaza.

A colossal rectangular square (measuring 508 by 160 metres), the Maydan-i Naqsh-i Jahan consists of an open-air field – used for equestrian exercises, royal ceremonies, and various social activities – surrounded by a double row of shops on the ground floor topped by balconied chambers [Figure 4].[6] To the north lies the Qaysariyya (royal market), whose portal marks the longitudinal axis of the square. On the western side, closer to the south, stands the Ali Qapu (Lofty Gate), a five-story cubical tower, which functioned as the main gateway to the palace complex (*dawlatkhana*), and contained ornate reception halls overlooking the plaza and the royal precinct. (The pillared hall [*talar*] of the Ali Qapu and its masonry base were

Figure 4: Aerial view of the Maydan-i Naqsh-i Jahan, looking south from above the Qaysariyya market. Photograph: Reza Nur Bakhtiar, after *Isfahan, muza-yi hamisha zinda*, 34.

added later, in the 1640s).[7] The first monumental sanctuary on the perimeter of the plaza, the Shaykh Lutfallah Mosque, was erected opposite the Ali Qapu. Built adjacent to a now-lost madrasa, it was named after the eponymous Shi'i jurist Shaykh Lutfallah al-Maysi al-Amili (*d. c.*1622), who taught and led prayers in the mosque-cum-madrasa complex [Figure 5].

Written sources suggest that except for the Shah Mosque, which was a later addition to the initial blueprint, the Maydan-i Naqsh-i Jahan and its three principal monuments – the Qaysariyya, Ali Qapu, and Shaykh Lutfallah Mosque – were laid out in the mid-1590s; Shah Abbas inaugurated the complex in 1602, shortly after the official transfer of the Safavid capital from Qazvin to Isfahan in 1598, although construction work on the Ali Qapu and Shaykh Lutfallah Mosque continued until circa 1615 and 1618 respectively.[8] A passage in the chronicle by Fazli Beg Khuzani indicates that the construction of the Shaykh Lutfallah Mosque was begun in the same period together with other major components of the Safavid urban plan for Isfahan.[9] Fazli reports that in 1002 H (1593–94), Shah Abbas, who had brought Shaykh Lutfallah from Qazvin to Isfahan, asked the cleric to oversee the construction of the mosque, set a stipend for worshippers and ascetics (*zuhhad*), and perform Friday prayer and other obligatory duties (*fara'iz*) upon the mosque's completion.[10] Likewise, a late-seventeenth-century biography states that Shaykh Lutfallah believed in the obligatory status (*wujub 'ayni*) of Friday prayer for all Shi'i Muslims during the occultation of the Twelfth Imam – a fairly rare opinion among Shi'i clerics at the time – and that he performed Friday prayer in the mosque-cum-madrasa that the shah had built for him.[11] These references corroborate the insights gleaned from an Arabic epistle titled *Risalat al-I'tikafiyya* (Treatise on Seclusion), penned by Shaykh Lutfallah himself, confirming that the mosque was originally built for the Shi'i jurist.[12]

More importantly, these sources debunk the common interpretation of the Shaykh Lutfallah Mosque as a private royal chapel.[13] In its original conception, the intended congregation of the Shaykh Lutfallah Mosque consisted of the transplanted Shi'i community, who had moved to Isfahan along with the Safavid ruling household. This can be deduced from a passage in the above-mentioned epistle by Shaykh Lutfallah, which relates that Shah Abbas had told him: 'I want to build you a congregational mosque facing my abode, which can fit from a thousand to two thousand people, that Turkmens (*al-atrak*), slaves (*al-'abid*), and every other willing person including myself, may come to you'.[14] In keeping with the reforms of the age of Shah Abbas, the mosque was meant to provide a venue for instructing the Qizilbash warriors (Turkmen tribesmen who were instrumental in the rise and establishment of the Safavid state) and *ghulams* (military/administrative recruits of Georgian, Circassian, or Armenian origin) in the proper normative practices of Shi'ism. It is likely that Shaykh Lutfallah's stricter stance on the performance of Friday prayer made him particularly fit to fulfil this royal mandate; following Shaykh Lutfallah as a religious leader meant that the Qizilbash were obliged to attend the weekly Friday prayer and its accompanying sermon (*khutba*) held in the royal mosque located across the palace complex [Figure 6].

The ideological intent of the Shaykh Lutfallah Mosque is reflected in the content and tone of its epigraphy. The inscriptions include quotations from the Qur'an and hadith

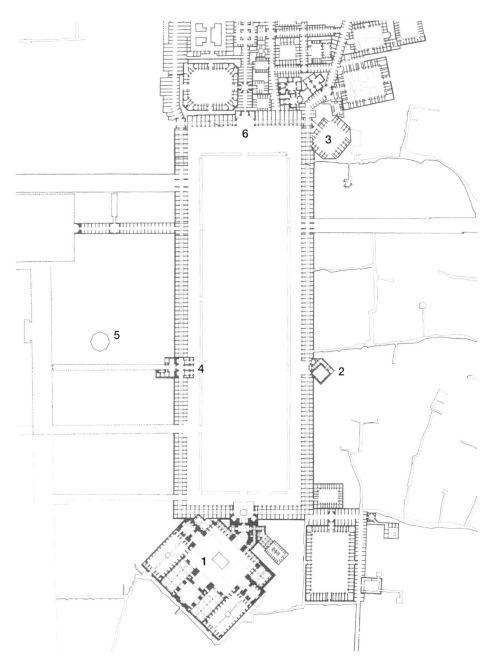

Figure 5: Plan of the Maydan-i Naqsh-i Jahan. (1) Shah Mosque (*masjid-i shah*); (2) Shaykh Lutfallah Mosque; (3) Mulla Abdallah Madrasa; (4) Ali Qapu; (5) Tawhidkhana; (6) Qaysariyya Portal. Plan after Nader Ardalan and Laleh Bakhtiar, *The Sense of Unity: the Sufi Tradition in Persian Architecture* (Chicago: University of Chicago Press, 1973), 98.

Figure 6: Shaykh Lutfallah Mosque, Exterior View from the Maydan. Photograph by the author, 2013.

that highlight the virtues of building and visiting mosques and brim with themes of repentance and salvation. The inscription that encircles the interior of the drum, for instance, quotes the entire Sura al-Jumu'ah (Friday, 62), which contains an unequivocal mandate for believers on the performance of Friday prayer, while another inscription above the row of windows consists of a number of hadith by the Prophet Muhammad and the sixth Shi'i imam Ja'far al-Sadiq (*d*.765) on the rituals and merits of visiting mosques [Figure 7]. The theme of salvation through the intercession of the imams, on the other hand, is expressed in two poems inscribed on opposing walls inside the domed hall. These Arabic poems, which were composed by Shaykh Lutfallah and his more illustrious contemporary cleric and polymath Shaykh Baha'i (Baha al-Din al-'Amili, *d*.1621), invoke the 'fourteen infallibles' (the Prophet Muhammad, his daughter Fatima, and the twelve imams), seeking God's mercy on the Day of Judgment for the 'sinful' composers of the verses (i.e., Baha'i and Lutfallah).[15] The theme of seeking God's forgiveness is also expressed in the pious phrases that accompany the signatures of two other individuals who were involved in the making of the mosque, namely the architect Muhammad Riza and the calligrapher Ali Riza Abbasi.[16] Together, the inscriptions underscore the role of the imams as mediators of God's grace, while highlighting mosque visitation and the performance of Friday prayer as religious practices prescribed by the very same holy figures. There is

Figure 7: Shaykh Lutfallah Mosque, view of the domed hall. Photograph by the author, 2014.

no hint in the inscriptions that the Shaykh Lutfallah Mosque was intended to function as a royal chapel. Through its decorative and epigraphic programme, the mosque evokes a harmonious universe of eternal bliss, where God's mercy is attainable by all members of the Shi'i community through normative pious practices, repentance, and the mediation of the Prophet and the imams.

Yet as Rula Abisaab has noted, the Shaykh Lutfallah Mosque soon began to trigger a controversy in the bipolar socio-urban structure of Safavid Isfahan. The objection was voiced by local Isfahani notables – traditional Shi'i community leaders revered as *sayyids* or descendants of the Prophet Muhammad.[17] These dissenters, who resided in vicinity of the Old Maydan and were associated with the Old Friday Mosque, questioned the suitability of the Shaykh Lutfallah Mosque to the performance of religious duties such as *i'tikaf* (seclusion), which were traditionally performed in congregational mosques. In his pejorative and fairly extensive epistle (*Risalat al-I'tikafiyya*), Shaykh Lutfallah argued that the newness of the mosque did not negate its congregational status (*al-jami'iyat*), and stated that the mosque is known in the popular parlance as the 'new congregational mosque' built for him by the shah.[18]

A close inspection of the architectural form of the Shaykh Lutfallah Mosque reveals that the cleric's assertion cannot be dismissed as a hyperbolic statement. The mosque's capacity for convening a fairly large congregation becomes clear if we consider that it consisted of more than a mere domed chamber. For instance, often overlooked is the fact that the mosque contained another prayer hall in the basement [Figure 8]. Built on a nine-bay plan and resting on four piers, this additional space was likely conceived as a *shabistan* (night-time hall) where, according to a mid-seventeenth-century dictionary, 'dervishes and others would pray and sleep at night'.[19] In addition to providing a protected space for prayer and sojourn during the winter or at night, the basement also increased the mosque's capacity for congregational prayer. If a sermon was delivered in the main prayer hall, one would have been able to listen to it in the lower level as well (there are three apertures in the floor). Further space for worshipers was provided in the upper-floor gallery, above the L-shaped corridor. One must also take into account the now-lost madrasa, which seems to have been located on the southeastern side of the domed hall.[20] With these additional spaces, the complex could accommodate a fairly large congregation of up to 1,000 people, as mentioned in Lutfallah's treatise and required by traditional Islamic law for Friday prayer.

Obviously, the Shaykh Lutfallah Mosque was not meant to attract the city's entire population, but neither was it a private oratory.[21] Its overall form can be described as an interpretation of the multifunctional mosques common in the fourteenth and fifteenth century in Anatolia and Iran, which were typically centred around a domed hall (rather than a courtyard) and often were known as *jami'* mosques. The best-known extant examples of this type are the Green Mosque (Yeşil Cami) in Bursa (1419–21) and the Blue Mosque (*masjid-i kabud* or *muzaffariyya*) in Tabriz (1465).[22] An intermediary building in terms of transfer of design was likely the Ali Mosque (*c.*1522), which was constructed in the first quarter of the sixteenth century in the vicinity of the Shrine of Harun Vilayat on the Old Maydan of Isfahan.[23] One formal element that makes the Shaykh Lutfallah Mosque akin to the Green Mosque of Bursa is the inclusion, in the upper-floor gallery, of an ornate balcony overlooking the main domed hall in the qibla direction. The balcony is the only portion of the gallery that bears tile decoration, suggesting that, as in the Green Mosque of Bursa, it likely functioned as a kind of 'royal loggia'.[24]

Another feature that distinguishes the Shaykh Lutfallah Mosque from its precedents is the configuration of its liminal zone – the transitional spaces between the square and the main prayer hall. In contrast to the U-shaped 'vestibule' of the Blue Mosque of Tabriz, here the auxiliary side spaces are arranged along an L-shaped corridor, while another hallway on the southwestern side likely led to the now-lost madrasa. The corridor conceals the shift in orientation from the square to the domed chamber, which is oriented toward the qibla (the holy shrine in Mecca) and is entered through a doorway facing the mihrab (the prayer niche on the qibla wall) [Figure 8]. The bent corridor acts as a liminal site in both temporal and spatial terms: it delays the instant of encounter with the mosque, while further accentuating the passage from the profane arena of the plaza to the sacred domain of worship. Passing through the fairly dark, low-vaulted corridor, the prayer hall would appear as a mysterious, unworldly locus where light, filtered through patterned screens, moves on vegetal scrolls that fill the glazed tiles covering the walls.

On a broader urban scale, the Shaykh Lutfallah Mosque was in dialogue with the Ali Qapu, manifesting the deepening link between orthodox Shi'i religiosity and Safavid kingship. The pairing of these monuments, nevertheless, does not signify the juxtaposition of opposites,

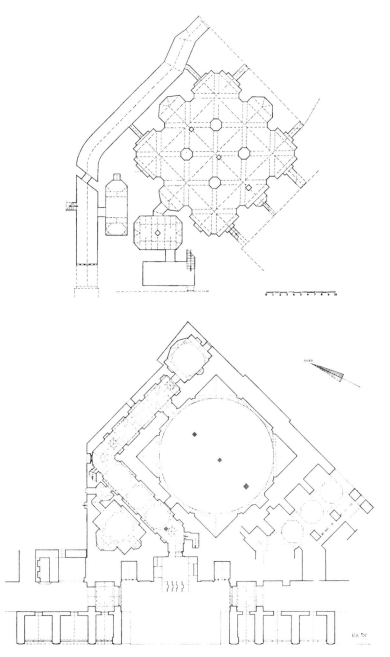

Figure 8: Shaykh Lufallah Mosque, plans of the first floor (below) and the basement (*shabistan*) (above). After Mario Ferrante, 'La Mosquee de Saih Lutfallah a Ispahan: relevés planimétrique', in Giuseppe Zander, ed., *Travaux de restauration de monuments historiques en Iran*, IsMEO Reports and Memoirs 6 (1968).

for the Ali Qapu too was a sacred building. Writing in 1617, the Italian traveller Pietro Della Valle described the Ali Qapu as a 'much venerated' site, and referred to a 'wooden threshold', on which nobody steps, adding that 'on certain occasions they kiss it as if it is sacred'.[25] Half a century later, the French jewel merchant and traveller Jean Chardin made a similar observation, noting that no one would step on this inviolable threshold, which he described as being made of green porphyry, and even the shah would dismount before passing through the gateway.[26] It appears that the threshold, in its initial wooden form or later stone incarnation, was a relic from a Shi'i shrine. According to nineteenth-century sources, the door of the Ali Qapu was brought from the shrine of Imam 'Ali ('Ali b. Abi Talib, the first Shi'i imam, d.661) in Najaf, and in one of the rooms there was a chest that contained a cloak and a Qur'an manuscript attributed to the imams.[27] Shi'i shrines are often called *dargah* (gateway) or *astana* (threshold), terms that underscore the role of the imams and their descendants as mediators of divine grace. Safavid sources referred to Shah Abbas as 'dog of the threshold of [Imam] 'Ali (*kalb-i astan-i 'Ali*). The sacred relic turned the threshold of the Ali Qapu into a site of veneration, creating a liminal locus that demarcated the plaza from the blessed abode of the shah.

Beyond the perimeters of the Maydan, the link between the Ali Qapu and the Shaykh Lutfallah Mosque extended to another institution: the Tawhidkhana (Hall of Unity), a twelve-sided domed building located off the alleyway running behind the Ali Qapu [Figure 9]. Set in a courtyard surrounded by rooms, it served as a communal prayer hall, where the ritual of *dhikr* (literally, 'remembrance', a form of Sufi prayer that involves repetition of a litany) was performed according to the custom of the Safaviyya order known as *halqa-yi tawhid* (circle of unity).[28] The first Safavid monarch, Shah Isma'il, was the hereditary spiritual leader (*shaykh*, *murshid-i kamil*) of the Safaviyya Sufi order (founded by the eponymous Sufi Shaykh Safi, d.1334), and Safavid rulers were revered as leaders of the order throughout the reign of the dynasty. As Kishwar Rizvi has noted, the Tawhidkhana closely resembles the Jannatsara (Hall of Paradise), an octagonal building erected around 1540 at the shrine of Shaykh Safi in Ardabil, suggesting that similar rituals were performed in both structures.[29] Indeed, the Sufi chantry appears to have been a fixture of Safavid royal ensembles: according to *Dastur al-Muluk*, an early eighteenth-century treatise of administration, when the shah was not in residence in Isfahan, a separate tent was set up for the Tawhidkhana in the imperial encampment.[30]

In Safavid Isfahan, the Tawhidkhana was the locus of a weekly pious ritual. Nicolas Sanson, a French missionary who visited the Safavid capital in the second half of the seventeenth century, refers to the Tawhidkhana as the 'mosque of the palace', noting that every Thursday members of the Safaviyya order gathered there to pray for the prosperity of the king.[31] This practice is confirmed by *Tazkirat al-Muluk* (Memorial for Kings), another Safavid state manual, which traces the custom back to the time of Shaykh Safi.[32] In addition to resident dervishes, the Thursday evening ritual was attended by state officials who had been 'honoured to wear the *taj* [Safavid hat]'; those who had performed this service, would also send 'a cash payment as votive offering (*nazr*)'.[33] On the following day, though, all were to attend Friday prayer at the Shaykh Lutfallah Mosque, complementing their Sufi devotion with normative worship.

Figure 9: Aerial view showing the Tawhidkhana and Ali Qapu, with the Shaykh Lutfallah Mosque in the background. Photograph: Reza Nur Bakhtiyar, after *Isfahan, muza-yi hamisha zinda.*

The axis formed by the Ali Qapu and these dual houses of worship – the Shaykh Lutfallah Mosque and Tawhidkhana – thus represented and embodied the varied forms of piety from which the Safavids drew their legitimacy [Figure 9]. The Tawhidkhana, which also served as an asylum (*bast*) for criminals and fugitives, was located within the shah's living quarters, signifying the sanctity of the Safavid ruler as the hereditary spiritual master of a Sufi order and a divinely sanctioned monarch whose abode is the locus of blessing and protection. But the devotion to the shah as the 'perfect guide' (*murshid-i kamil*) had to be complemented by proper religious practices. This balance was achieved not only by the state-sponsoring of Shi'i clerics and the promotion of orthodoxy – as epitomized by the construction of the Shaykh Lutfallah Mosque – but also through public proclamation of the (likely fabricated) descent of the Safavid shahs from the Shi'i imams: the Arabic foundation inscription of the Shaykh Lutfallah Mosque particularly highlights the holy lineage of Shah Abbas and his efforts to revive the sectarian religion (*madhab*) of his saintly ancestors.[34] Here, the titles and benedictions of a typical foundation inscription are given a decidedly Shi'i tenor, centred on the name of Shah Abbas in both verbal syntax and visual configuration [Figure 10].[35] Inscribed exactly above the mosque's entrance, the shah's name gives the doorway of the Shaykh Lutfallah Mosque the character of a sacred threshold; like the revered stone installed across from the square at the Ali Qapu, the name of Shah Abbas turns the mosque into a blessed sanctuary (*masjid al-mubarak*). As earthly embodiments of divine blessing, such material objects and public texts created a sacred realm that was constantly animated through rituals and pious actions.

And yet, this seemingly inclusive approach to variegated forms of religiosity – the world where the shah, Sufis, and clerics were all involved in the formation of a spiritual domain – was soon to give way to growing royal support for orthodoxy and legalism, which gradually transformed the religious landscape of Safavid Isfahan in favour of normative religious

Figure 10: Entrance Portal of the Shaykh Lutfallah Mosque. Photograph by the author, 2014.

practices. The first manifestation of this trend was the construction of the Mulla Abdallah Madrasa in the northeast corner of the Maydan-i Naqsh-i Jahan.[36] Completed between 1598 and 1600, the madrasa was built for the teaching of the cleric Abdallah Shushtari (d.1612), demonstrating that the shah intended to turn the royal square into a centre of Shiʻi learning, a trend which culminated in the construction of a monumental Friday mosque on the south side of the plaza.

Safavid Congregational Mosque

The Shaykh Lutfallah Mosque was an integral component of the socio-religious programme of the Maydan-i Naqsh-i Jahan, representing the first attempt to shift Isfahan's religious centre from the Old Maydan and its congregational mosque to the Safavid royal square. Nevertheless, while the Shaykh Lutfallah Mosque was used and perceived as a venue for Friday prayer, its form fell short of a full-fledged congregational mosque (*jamiʻ*) as epitomized by the Old Mosque of Isfahan. The lack of direct correspondence between the architectural form of the Shaykh Lutfallah Mosque and the shifting political realities and theological debates was likely one of the reasons that prompted the construction of a monumental congregational mosque officially designated for the performance of Friday prayer. Unlike the Shaykh Lutfallah Mosque, which is referred to as a 'blessed mosque' (*al-masjid al-mubarak*) in the foundation inscription, the Shah Mosque is unequivocal in the public proclamation of its primary function: An Arabic foundation inscription, carved in mosaic tiles on the mosque's portal, refers to the building as a 'congregational mosque' (*al-masjid al-jamiʻ*) ordered by Shah Abbas. Another inscription, installed above the doorway upon the project's completion, explicitly proclaims the mosque as a *jamiʻ* for 'the performance of Friday prayer according to its conditions'.[37]

In his annal for 1611–12 (1020 H), the court chronicler Iskandar Beg Munshi gives a fairly long account of why Shah Abbas decided to build 'a lofty mosque in the vicinity of the [Maydan-i] Naqsh-i Jahan in Isfahan':

> While with [the construction of] lofty buildings, delightful admirable mansions, ambergris-scented soul-lifting gardens, canals, and orchards, he had transformed the City of Rule, Isfahan, into a model of paradise, yet, though he had built a sublime mosque [i.e., the Shaykh Lutfallah Mosque] and a madrasa [i.e., the Mulla Abd Allah Madrasa] on the eastern and northern sides of the Maydan-i Naqsh-i Jahan, they looked low (*past*) in relation to his sublime aspiration (*himmat*). So his mind dwelled on the thought that now that the city of Isfahan with its exquisite edifices, gardens, Qaysariyya, and caravanserais was the envy of cities – and the proof of [the Quranic verse] 'Eram, the possessor of sturdy buildings the like of which have never been created in the land' (88:8–9) – the mosques, madrasas, and shrines of his excellency should also be the loftiest of mosques and shrines (*buqa'*) in Iran, and to resemble in ornamentation (*zinat*) and purity (*safa*) the Bayt

al-Maʿmur [heavenly prototype of the Kaʿba, the holy shrine in Mecca] and Masjid al-Aqsa ['the farthest mosque' in Jerusalem].[38]

According to Iskandar Beg, after surveying the square, the shah chose the south side, where there was a caravanserai, which was demolished to make room for the mosque. Iskandar Beg's narrative is echoed by Fazli, who relates that the shah drew up plans for a new Friday mosque 'for there was a mosque opposite the Ali Qapu for the teaching of Shaykh Lutfallah, but no counterpart for the Qaysariyya'.[39] (The five-sided recess in front of the mosque's portal mirrors the forecourt of the Qaysariyya market on the north side of the plaza.) These passages make clear that there was a distinction between sacred and secular aspects of urban development, as well as a need for functional and aesthetic balance in the urban design of the square. Furthermore, the reference to the Kaʿba and its heavenly prototype suggests the degree of holiness that the Friday mosque was meant to project. The new congregational mosque was intended to bestow on the central plaza of the Safavid capital an enhanced sense of normative piety, creating an iconic, spectacular sanctuary befitting the massive scale and imperial status of Isfahan [Figure 11].

The decision to construct the Shah Mosque came at a time when the Safavid empire was at the apogee of its prosperity and territorial expansion. Safavid forces had vanquished the Uzbeks in the province of Khurasan, retaking the cities of Mashhad and Herat, and the campaigns against the Ottomans, in 1602–03 and 1607–08, had returned the province of

Figure 11: Elevated view of the Shah Mosque. Photograph: Reza Nur Bakhtiyar, after *Isfahan, muza-yi hamisha zinda*, 15.

Azerbaijan and the Caucasus to Safavid control.[40] In 1611, when the new congregational mosque was commissioned, the political situation was radically different from the early 1590s, when the development of Isfahan had begun. The Safavids now ruled over an expansive centralized empire on a par with the Mughals and Ottomans. As the empire grew in size and power, so too did the scope of the architectural programme for the capital.

From a theological perspective, the construction of a monumental Friday mosque at the heart of the Safavid capital reflects a new phase in the evolution of the Shi'i discourse on the legality of Friday prayer. During the medieval period, the majority of Shi'i theologians opined that Friday prayer is not permissible in the absence of the immaculate imam or his deputy (na'ib). But the clerical discourse began to change after the rise of the Safavid dynasty, the first Islamic polity since the early medieval period to embrace Twelver Shi'ism as state religion.[41] The Shi'is, who had long been a minority, could now benefit from imperial patronage. The first earnest attempts to legitimize and 'revive' Friday prayer were made during the reign of Shah Tahmasp (r.1524–76), although the enterprise was vehemently opposed by some jurists, and the debate continued in the seventeenth century.[42] Unlike Shaykh Lutfallah, for instance, Shaykh Baha'i maintained that Friday prayer is not obligatory in the absence of the imam and is permissible only if a jurist (faqih) leads the prayer.[43] The statement in the Shah Mosque's inscription – 'the performance of Friday prayer according to its conditions' – likely reflects this intermediate position. In addition to drafting the endowment deed of the mosque, Shaykh Baha'i, who was the *shaykh al-Islam* (chief jurist) of Isfahan from 1600 until his death in 1621, was responsible for calculating the direction of qibla (orientation of Mecca) and perhaps certain other aspects of the mosque's design, although his role is shrouded in myth and the scope of his involvement remains uncertain.[44]

The embracing of Friday prayer after a century of antinomian practices does not mean that the Shah Mosque was devoid of Shi'i forms of piety. According to Chardin, relics of Shi'i imams, including a blood-stained shirt attributed to Imam Husayn (grandson of the Prophet Muhammad and the third Shi'i imam) were kept in a closet above the mihrab (prayer niche) of the mosque.[45] The incorporation of relics at the focal site of the mosque gave it an added layer of sanctity, while reminding worshippers of the most significant event in Shi'i Islam: the martyrdom of Imam Husayn at the battle of Karbala in 680. Moreover, it appears that in the seventeenth century the Shah Mosque was popularly known as the mosque of the 'Lord of the Age' (sahib al-zaman), the epithet of the Twelfth Imam (the Mahdi).[46] This dedication justified the presence of a Friday mosque in the Shi'i capital, for eventually, emerging from the occultation, the Mahdi would lead the prayer in the Friday mosque.

The sectarian ethos of the Shah Mosque is also manifest in its epigraphic programme, which is remarkable for its extensive and unprecedented use of hadith.[47] The longest inscription in the mosque, which runs the entire length of the qibla dome and iwan, quotes from the *Manaqib* (virtues) by Ibn al-Maghazili (d.1090–91), a Sunni author active in Iraq, who wrote this book on the virtues of the *ahl al-bayt* (family of the Prophet). Likewise, the interiors of the lateral domes are inscribed with hadith quoted from the *Musnad*, a canonical collection compiled by Ahmad ibn Hanbal (d.855), the founder of one of the four major Sunni schools of jurisprudence.[48] That the inscriptions were primarily drawn from Sunni – rather than exclusively Twelver Shi'i – collections of hadith discloses the polemical intent of the epigraphy: the goal was to convince the Sunnis of the validity of the Safavids' Shi'i creed through the former's own canonical sources. The primary audience of the epigraphic programme of the Shah Mosque, therefore, was much broader than that of the Shaykh Lutfallah Mosque, and included the Sunni inhabitants of Safavid territories and the neighbouring empires.[49] To the lay populace, on the other hand, the visual presence of Arabic in these monumental inscriptions lent an aura of authority to the Shi'i claims. Here, the sayings of the Prophet Muhammad and the imams were visually on a par with Qur'anic verses – a distinction less apparent to the Persian-speaking local population, for whom Arabic was primarily the language of scripture.

While relics and inscriptions gave a sectarian bent to an otherwise primordial Islamic building, the architectural form of the Shah Mosque referenced established emblems of Turco-Mongol power. With four axial iwans and a domed sanctuary on the qibla side, the overall design of the Shah Mosque is commonly regarded as the culmination of the four-iwan typology [Figure 12]. Although the roots of the four-iwan scheme can be traced to the early twelfth century – the nearby Old Mosque of Isfahan is considered the first example – the Shah Mosque is particularly akin to the monumental Friday mosques of the Timurid period (c.1370–1505), particularly the Friday Mosque of Samarkand (popularly known as the Bibi Khanum Mosque), built by the order of Turco-Mongol warlord Timur (r.1370–1405), as well as the Gawharshad Mosque at Mashhad and at Herat, which were completed in the first quarter of the fifteenth century under Timur's successor, Shahrukh, and sponsored by his consort Gawharshad. Combining the massive scale of courtyard-centred hypostyle mosques of the early Islamic period with the monumentality and royal associations of an architectural language centred on domes and iwans, these post-Mongol mosques set a new benchmark for imperial patronage. The link between the Shah Mosque and the Bibi Khanum Mosque are evident in their principal formal features: with the exception of the flanking courtyards, the main components of the Shah Mosque – the monumental entrance portal and the dual domed chambers behind the lateral iwans – can be seen in the Timurid Friday Mosque of Samarkand.[50] One feature that makes the Safavid mosque distinct is the integration of these elements into a layout that exudes a heightened sense of harmony and cohesion: the underlying geometry of the mosque's design is clearly the result of a sophisticated process.[51]

This morphological reference to an iconic Timurid model was likely a conscious choice, for no other mosque is known to have been based on the layout of the Bibi Khanum Mosque.[52] By evoking an architectural scheme associated with Timur, Shah Abbas thus consciously aimed to link his imperial persona to the epitome of a world conqueror in Islamic West Asia. The quest for new sources of legitimacy in Timurid models was likely necessitated by the emerging realities of the empire, as it is also reflected in the historiography of the age of Shah Abbas.[53] The formal affinity with Timurid monuments did not go unnoticed by contemporary visitors. To the poet Bihishti of Herat, who visited Isfahan in the 1630s,

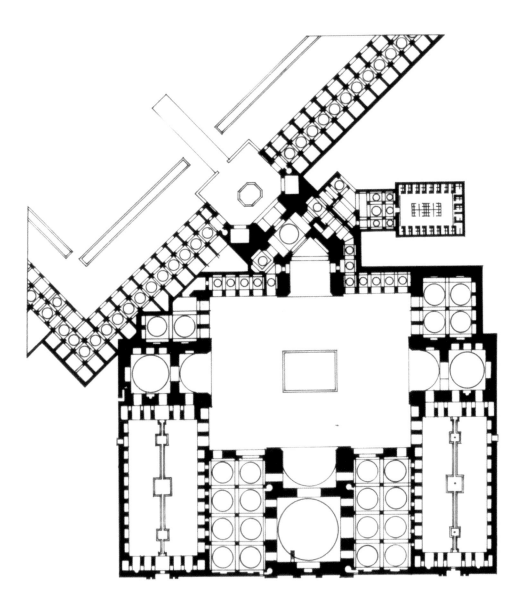

Figure 12: Plan of the Shah Mosque of Isfahan. Drawing: Keith Turner after Henri Stierlin, courtesy of MIT Libraries, Aga Khan Documentation Center.

for instance, the design (*tarh*) of the Shah Mosque was based on the (Friday) mosque of Herat.[54] The monumental form and glazed tile revetments likely evoked a Timurid idiom in the mind of the Herati poet.

Another feature that differentiates the Shah Mosque from its precedents is the variegation and segregation of the covered spaces that surround the courtyard. Indeed, despite its resemblance to Timurid prototypes in terms of enormousness, decoration, and overall morphology, the plan of the Shah Mosque retains little trace of the hypostyle model. The difference becomes evident if one compares the blueprint of the Gawharshad Mosque at Mashhad with that of the Shah Mosque: the former appears like a hypostyle mosque, with iwans inserted at the centres of the four sides of the courtyard.[55] By contrast, aside from the two-pillared halls that flank the domed sanctuary, the Shah Mosque does not contain a continuous hypostyle area around the courtyard. Rather, it reads more as a series of self-contained halls, clustered around the cruciform axes formed by the four iwans. It appears that only the domed sanctuary and its side halls were intended for the performance of Friday prayer per se. The two courtyards, a novel feature of the mosque's design, are commonly assumed to have functioned as madrasas, with the two domed chambers behind the side iwans probably conceived as lecture halls.[56] The extensive use of hadith in their inscriptions surely lent a scholastic aura to the lateral dome chambers. But it was only in the nineteenth century that the flanking courtyards became known specifically as distinctive madrasas; originally, these courtyards lacked the essential component of a madrasa: rooms (sing. *hujra*) for student residents.[57] (Residential cells are arranged in the upper floor around the central courtyard.) A study of the mosque's plan suggests that the twin courtyards were rather conceived as counterparts for the two winter prayer halls (sing. *shabistan*) located to the north of the lateral domed halls.[58] Featuring water canals punctuated by basins, these verdant open-air spaces provided pleasant venues for prayer, and perhaps theological debate, during the summer.[59] If this hypothesis is correct, it was the cyclical passage of seasons, rather than a strict functional programme, that underlay this peculiar spatial configuration.

The extant copy of the Shah Mosque's endowment deed (*vaqfnama*), originally drawn up in 1614 by Shaykh Baba'i, reveals that the entire mosque complex was meant to function as an educational institution.[60] Among the 77 employees of the mosque listed in the deed are 9 teachers and 37 students.[61] The students were to receive a daily stipend (*vazifa*) from the mosque's endowed properties on the condition that they kept the rooms occupied at all times.[62] Seventeenth-century sources indicate that the scheme laid out in the deed was implemented. A chronicle of the reign of Shah Abbas's successor, Shah Safi (r.1629–42), refers to reciters of the Qur'an (*huffaz*), teachers (*mudarrisin*), and students (*tullab*) who resided in the mosque.[63] Chardin reports that the lateral iwans were filled with books used for teaching, and that the upper-story rooms were occupied by students and teachers.[64] Another chronicle alludes to a certain poet-cum-tailor who lived in the mosque (*masjid-i jami'-i shahi*) for more than 24 years.[65] The 'congregational mosque' was not solely used for prayer or teaching; it was a living space for those supported by its endowments.

Another feature that sets the Shah Mosque apart from the monumental Friday mosques of the Ilkhanid and Timurid periods is the orientation of the courtyard. At least from the early thirteenth century (notably, in the early thirteenth-century Friday mosque at Varamin), monumental congregational mosques in Iran and central Asia were marked by an emphasis on the elongated axis leading from a colossal portal to the qibla wall. In the Shah Mosque, this established orientation is reversed: it is the massive size of the iwan and its pair of minarets, visible from the vestibule, rather than the courtyard's orientation, that marks the qibla direction. This peculiar orientation was likely devised to retain the mosque's view in the backdrop of the Maydan-i Naqsh-i Jahan, for it leads to a closer clustering of domes, iwans, and minarets, which in turn gives a more harmonious profile to the building. One can discern a novel quality in the way in which the tile-clad domes and minarets of the mosque appear on the city's skyline. This is a monument laid out with respect to its visual presence in the city: it provides a carefully designed backdrop for the royal plaza, while creating a monumental silhouette for Safavid urban developments in Isfahan. In this regard, the Shah Mosque – with its vast interior spaces and outward display of domes and minarets – bears a resemblance to sixteenth-century Ottoman imperial mosques, whose splendour had more to do with projecting the might of the empire than with the liturgical requirements of congregational prayer.[66] The design of the Shah Mosque combines references to various old and new models, aspiring to outshine preceding and contemporary examples.

It was under the successors of Shah Abbas that the new congregational mosque began to play a prominent role in Safavid practices of kingship, as evident in the ceremonies that followed the accession of Shah Safi in 1629. According to a chronicle, a few days after succeeding his grandfather, the new shah wore the belt and sword of Shah Isma'il and ascended the throne in the Ali Qapu, while music was played at the royal music-house (naqqara-khana). On the following Friday, Shah Safi ordered a gathering at the Shah Mosque (masjid-i shahi), and Mir Damad (Muhammad Baqir al-Astarabadi, d.1631), who had succeeded Shaykh Baha'i as the shaykh al-Islam of Isfahan, delivered an eloquent sermon (khutba) in the name of the recently enthroned shah.[67] The congregational mosque thus played its main political function in Islamic cultures: the place where the khutba is delivered in the name of the ruler. A few days later, on the 40th day following the death of Shah Abbas, ordinary people ('avam al-nas) gathered again at the royal congregational mosque (masjid-i jami'-i shahi), where more than 2000 plates of food were distributed.[68] This event demonstrates how the enormous mosque could accommodate a large population: unlike the Shaykh Lutfallah Mosque, which was built for a limited congregation, the Shah Mosque provided an arena for staging the state's benevolence toward a broader spectrum of the populace. The construction of a monumental Friday mosque around Isfahan's royal plaza allowed the Safavid kings to project an augmented sense of power, bolstering their claims as legitimate Islamic rulers in the eyes of their own subjects as well as their regional Sunni rivals.

The Portal: The Mosque and the Square

Judging from the date of the foundation inscription (1616), the portal was the first component of the Shah Mosque to be completed; it was erected many years before the mosque itself was finished in its entirety [Figure 13]. As the main entrance to the mosque, the portal not only provided a threshold between the plaza and the house of worship but also was one of the most conspicuous visual elements of the Maydan-i Naqsh-i Jahan: rising 29 metres above the ground, the portal is flanked by two 34-metre-high minarets. The portal's visual prominence is further amplified by its opulent decoration: marble dadoes, mosaic tiles, and semi-dome filled with *muqarnas*.

The main inscription on the portal, which runs along its border, contains declarations of Shi'i beliefs in a number of hadith attributed to the Prophet Muhammad. Executed in large white Thuluth script on a cobalt blue background, the epigraphic band is a salient visual element of the portal, legible from afar. In a versified description of the mosque, the seventeenth-century poet Mir Nijat likened these inscription bands to strands of hair (*khat*) on the sides of the beloved's face.[69] The inclusion of the hadith by the Prophet Muhammad ('I am the City of Knowledge and 'Ali is its Gate') indicates that the inscription was specifically designed for the mosque's doorway.[70] The same hadith is repeated in another pair of inscriptions on the sides of the portal. The gate mediates between the worldly terrain of the public square and the holy realm of the mosque, just as Imam 'Ali mediates between believers and the Prophet, and by extension the divine.

The epigraphic and iconographic elements of the mosque's portal reveal that it was a symbolic structure whose meaning went beyond a mere gateway. This is especially reflected in the artisanal quality of the silver doors. Measuring 4.30 metres high by 1.60 metres wide and faced with silver, the door is a fine work of craftsmanship.[71] The poetic inscription gives the year 1046 H (1636–37), indicating that it was made during the reign of Shah Safi.[72] The sixteen-verse poem extols the shah and the mosque, comparing the door to that of the Ka'ba.[73]

This door has just been opened in Isfahan
To all the seekers of spiritual favour (*ahl-i niyaz*).[74]

A similar sense is conveyed in a contemporary literary piece that refers to the door of the mosque as a 'gate of purity' (*bab al-safa*) and describes it as 'a golden door open to everyone like the door of [divine] mercy' and as 'a response for the seekers [of spiritual grace]'.[75]

The symbolic significance of the portal is further amplified by its iconography. Above the doorway is an intricate tile mosaic panel depicting a pair of peacocks flanking a vase [Figure 14]. Other pairs of peacocks and parrots appear on the sidewalls of the portal, above the foundation inscription. The motif had already appeared in the shrine of Shaykh Safi at Ardabil and the shrine of Imam Riza at Mashhad, the two most sacred sites of the Safavid territories.[76] But the pair of peacocks on the Shah Mosque was probably modelled after those that appear on the portal of the Harun Vilayat shrine (completed in 1513 under Shah Isma'il), a major site of pilgrimage in the Old Maydan.[77] It appears that the overall form of

Figure 13: Portal of the Shah Mosque on the Maydan-i Naqsh-i Jahan. Photograph: Daniel C. Waugh, 2010, courtesy of MIT Libraries, Aga Khan Documentation Center.

Figure 14: Mosaic tile panel on the portal of the Shah Mosque, showing confronted peacocks flanking a vase. Photograph by the author, 2014.

the Maydan-i Naqsh-i Jahan was based on that of the Old Maydan, but rather than the Old Friday Mosque, a Shi'i shrine served as the model for the portal of the Shah Mosque.

Although the image of peacock has a long lineage as symbol of both paradise and royalty, its consistent use in this particular form and place in Safavid-sponsored buildings suggests that it was meant to signify the dynasty's dual claims to divine and earthly authority.[78] Also noteworthy is the representation of living creatures (peacocks and parrots) on the portal of a mosque; while these motifs were common in Shi'i shrines, there seems to be no evidence of their appearance in mosques, where representations of living forms were commonly eschewed. Although animals are also depicted in the inner parts of the mosque, the presence of the pair of peacocks on the gateway has an added significance. It is as if the portal is not necessarily part of the mosque proper but rather an extension of the Maydan – a revered locus in its own right – imbued with the sacred aura of a Shi'i shrine. As a mediating zone, the portal blends and demarcates the mosque and the plaza at the same time. It extends the sacred domain of the mosque into the profane space of the square while highlighting the transition from one realm to the other. In this sense, the gateway of the Shah Mosque assumes a quality akin to the sacred threshold of the nearby Ali Qapu. According to the 1614 endowment deed, the Shah Mosque was indeed meant to function as a refuge or *bast* for criminals, replicating the model established in the Ali Qapu/Tawhidkhana ensemble.[79]

In the Safavid congregational mosque, however, liminality is not solely defined through a mere threshold, but also through a sequence of articulated spaces experienced over time. This transitional zone is often noted for the manner in which it conceals the 45-degree shift of axis from the square to the mosque [Figure 12]. From the sand-covered area of the Maydan-i Naqsh-i Jahan, one would first enter a forecourt – a five-sided recess carved out of the square's enclosing building mass – which is further separated from the square by a low parapet. Featuring a pool at its centre, the forecourt creates a spatial node – a moment to pause before stepping inside the sanctuary. Beyond the doorway lies a domed vestibule, whence one could view the main dome and iwan, framed in the arched opening of the north iwan. To reach the inner courtyard, however, one should pass through either of the two corridors that branch off from the sides of the vestibule. It is at the end of these low-vaulted, fairly dark passages that the luminous courtyard and its glistering main iwan are revealed again to the visitor [Figure 15]. Together, the monumental gateway and this articulated transitional zone have a profound impact on the experience of the mosque. If the portal – with its inscriptions, silver-faced doors, and paired peacocks – sets up a holy threshold, the sequential liminal zone creates spatial and temporal distance between the mosque and the square. Passing through this transitional zone dramatizes the encounter with the mosque's inner sanctuary and augments its sense of sanctity.

Figure 15: View of the south iwan of the Shah Mosque. Photograph by the author, 2005.

The Mosque and the City

The study of the Shah Mosque in the context of the Maydan-i Naqsh-i Jahan indicates how its meaning and perception were formed in relation to its surrounding sacred sites. But at a broader urban scale, the Shah Mosque was also in dialogue with the Old Mosque. As mentioned before, the ambivalent 'congregational' status of the Safavid mosque – built as the new Friday mosque of the city yet primarily associated with royalty – stemmed, to a large extent, from the presence of the Old Mosque, which in fact never lost its status as the chief Friday mosque of Isfahan. A comparison of the two mosques reveals how the Friday mosque and its liminal zones took on new meanings in Safavid times.

In its enduring status, the Old Mosque of Isfahan does not represent an exceptional case. As Lisa Golombek notes with regards to fifteenth-century Herat, despite political fluctuations, extramural expansions, and the erection of loftier mosques, the old Friday mosques at the historic cores of cities in Iran and Central Asia had often remained 'resilient'.[80] In Isfahan too the perpetual vitality of the city's historic core was largely due to the presence of the Old Friday Mosque. One might suggest that had the Old Mosque not existed, the new developments of the age of Shah Abbas would have utterly outshined the pre-Safavid walled town.

The 'resurgence' of the Old Mosque occurred soon after the completion of the Shah Mosque. Chardin's description portrays the mosque as a vibrant scene of social and pious activities in the second half of the seventeenth century. During this period, the official *imam jum'a* (Friday prayer leader) of Isfahan, Muhammad Taqi Majlisi (*d.*1659), was not stationed in the Shah Mosque – the royal congregational mosque – but rather in the Old Mosque, where he held teaching sessions as well. Revered as a saint by the populace, Majlisi was eventually buried in the precinct of the Old Mosque, and his tomb became (and remains to this day) a site of pilgrimage. As Kathryn Babayan notes, Majlisi belonged to a cast of clerics who, in the hope of converting the masses to the Shi'i cause, attempted to incorporate Sufism and aspects of popular piety into mainstream Twelver Shi'i discourse. Unlike many of his fellow clerics, for instance, he was not opposed to the use of tobacco (*qalyan*). In an age when Sufi beliefs and practices were increasingly under attack, figures like Majlisi came to defend it.[81] If the Safavid mosque was primarily intended to provide a stage for royal ceremonies and project a state-sanctioned orthodox narrative of Shi'ism, the Old Friday Mosque, integrated in the urban fabric and social life of the old city, had come to accommodate a broader range of popular forms of Shi'i piety.

As commonly noted, in the first centuries after the advent of Islam, the mosque was not perceived as a holy locus per se but rather as an urban centre, a meeting place for the nascent Islamic community where social and political activities were conducted along with communal prayer. From the outset, the Friday mosque was the site of day-to-day – and at times contentious – social activities. Storytellers often performed in Friday mosques, a practice disapproved by many jurists.[82] The famed theologian Ghazali (Abu Hamid Muhammad b. Muhammad al-Tusi, *d.*1111), for instance, wrote that it is not permissible 'to gather a crowd around oneself and narrate stories in mosques or sell charms or other objects'. In his opinion, 'one must expel those who tell stories in mosques if the contents of the stories are not what is found in dependable books of religious tradition, or are not accurate.[83] Such statements are indicative of the range of activities that were common in medieval mosques. Wandering dervishes and ordinary wayfarers also could take up residence in mosques. The addition of low-vaulted, enclosed halls for wintertime or night-time sojourns (*bayt al-shata'* or *shabistan*) was one of the main formal features that altered the morphology of Friday mosques in the post-Mongol era.

It was often the courtyard of the Friday mosque that provided an arena for nonreligious social practices. The courtyard of the congregational mosque of Kufa, built in the eighth century, for example, also functioned as the city's main market.[84] Surrounded by arcades, the enclosed courtyards of Friday mosques resemble urban plazas. The urban significance of the mosque courtyards is also reflected in the way they are integrated into broader city structures. Accessed from multiple entrances and located at physical cores of settlements, the courtyards of many congregational mosques were the primary open-air plazas in cities.[85]

Accessed from multiple gateways dispersed along its perimeter, the Old Friday Mosque of Isfahan epitomizes such blending of the mosque's courtyard and the urban fabric [Figure 16].

Figure 16: Aerial view of the Old Friday Mosque of Isfahan. Photograph: courtesy of University of Chicago, Oriental Institute, AE 589.

185

Judging from the inscriptions, the mosque's multiple gateways were erected or repaired through the ages, although some may have remained from the original hypostyle mosque. In the second half of the nineteenth century, the mosque had at least eight functioning gates.[86] Unlike the Shah Mosque, the Old Mosque does not feature any particularly monumental gateway infused with symbolic meaning; all the gates are of relatively similar size and significance. Rather than define a threshold, the gates of the Old Mosque function as nodes, merging the mosque in the city's network of alleyways.[87] The primary passage to the mosque from the Old Maydan is through the covered lanes of the bazaar, and most of the gateways open directly onto a hypostyle hall. Likewise, the mosque does not feature any conspicuous high elements that would stand out on the city's skyline. To the visitor entering the complex through its expansive halls, the courtyard appears as a vast urban space. The manner in which the courtyard was traversed on a daily basis made it more similar to the surrounding urban fabric.

A very different situation prevails in the experience of the Shah Mosque. The primary message of the Safavid Friday mosque arises from the manner in which it is set in a geometricized urban plaza. This positioning dictates certain ways of experiencing the monument: To the beholder standing in the Maydan-i Naqsh-i Jahan, the mosque first appears as a cluster of off-centre domes and minarets in the background of the south facade. Moreover, as discussed above, the passage from the square to the inner courtyard of the mosque is through an articulated transitional zone. Experienced in relation to the enormous space of the plaza, the courtyard of the mosque provides a stricter sense of enclosure and an aura of sanctity. This juxtaposition vacates the Shah Mosque from the kind of urbanity that characterizes medieval Friday mosques, and further augments its sense of holiness.

Conclusion

Seventeenth-century Isfahan reveals several new developments in the conception and perception of the Friday mosque as well as the relationship between sacred and profane domains and the role of the liminal spaces that mediated between them. The study of the sacred topography of the Maydan-i Naqsh-i Jahan indicates that the Safavid royal ensemble was permeated with a sense of sanctity derived from relics and the role of the Shi'i imams as mediators of divine grace. Sectarian forms of piety were not only manifest in the incorporation of sacred material objects in public buildings, but also in seemingly profane aspects of urban development. In 1604, for instance, Shah Abbas endowed the revenue from all the commercial structures surrounding the Maydan-i Naqsh-i Jahan to Shi'i *sayyids* in the cities of Medina and Najaf.[88] This dedication made it seem as if the entire project was primarily driven by pious intentions. These diverse devotional practices paint a complex picture of the relationship between religious and secular agendas in Safavid Isfahan.

At the same time, the meaning and function of the Friday mosque were affected by the emergence and expansion of a public sphere in Safavid Isfahan, a process that led to a heightened demarcation between the domain of normative religious practice and that of ordinary urban existence. The physical manifestation of this development, too, can be seen in the Maydan Naqsh-i Jahan: The Shah Mosque is situated on the south side; the centre of urban and social life was in the north side, where the markets and coffeehouses were located. The rise and expansion of novel spaces and modes of urban existence – in coffeehouses, markets, and gardens – not only affected the uses of the mosque as a social space, but also imparted a higher degree of sanctity on the house of worship in relation to the surrounding urban landscape. Unlike a typical medieval town, in Isfahan the loci of normative religious activities had become more and more segregated from the domain of mundane social life. The storytellers who were despised by Ghazali for performing in mosques were now provided with a permanent stage in coffeehouses – their space of performance had become disassociated from official religious spaces. Ghazali, however, would not have been entirely pleased in Safavid Isfahan, for storytellers continued to narrate their stories in coffeehouses, keeping popular forms of piety alive and arousing the ire of Shiʻi theologians, who referred to the establishments as 'schools of Satan' and 'houses of sedition'. In early modern Isfahan, the coffeehouse, rather than the Friday mosque, was the most contested social space.[89]

Considering this broader urban setting, one can discern how the architecture of Shaykh Lutfallah Mosque and the Shah Mosque shaped and reflected this emerging configuration of social and religious spheres. The elaborate liminal zones of these mosques did not merely mediate between the domain of worship and the profane sphere, but also manifested the growing separation between them. Obviously, functional segregation was not absolute (the Shah Mosque was also a site of living), but compared to the medieval period the Friday mosque was largely vacated of day-to-day social affairs. What ultimately unified Safavid Isfahan, it appears, were symbols and material objects of Shiʻi devotion: the blood-stained shirt of Imam Husayn, the sacred threshold of the Ali Qapu, the paired peacocks on the portal of the Shah Mosque, and the inscribed name of the Safavid shah as holy descendant of the imams. Traversing the domains of urban life and official religious practices, these material and visual emblems of holiness were the primary focus of pious sentiments and rituals for the majority of the populace. The Friday mosque, bestowed with a heightened sense of sanctity, was merely a component of this variegated sacred landscape.

Acknowledgements

An earlier version of this chapter was presented at the Mesa 2016 Annual Conference in Boston, where it received valuable feedback from the audience. I would like to thank A. Hilâl Uğurlu and Suzan Yalman for their efforts in editing this volume. I am also grateful to the anonymous reader for the helpful comments on a draft of this chapter.

Notes

1   For an overview of the opinions on the legality of the Friday prayer in Safavid times, see Andrew J. Newman, 'Fayd al-Kashani and the Rejection of the Clergy/State Alliance: Friday Prayer as Politics in the Safavid Period', in *The Most Learned of the Shiʿa: The Institution of the Marjaʾ Taqlid*, ed. Linda S. Walbridge (Oxford: Oxford University Press, 2001), 34–52. Also see Devin J. Stewart, 'Polemics and Patronage in Safavid Iran: The Debate on Friday Prayer during the Reign of Shah Tahmasb', *Bulletin of the School of Oriental and African Studies* 72.3 (October 2009): 425–57. A comprehensive study is offered in Rasul Jaʿfariyan, *Din va siyasat dar dawra-yi safavi* (Qum: Intisharat-i Ansariyan, 1991), 121–80. For an overview of early Safavid architecture, see Sussan Babaie, 'Building on the Past: The Shaping of Safavid Architecture, 1501–76', in *Hunt for Paradise: Court Arts of Iran, 1501–76*, eds Jon Thompson and Sheila Canby (London: The British Museum and The Asia Society, 2003), 27–47.

2   For a study, see Kathryn Babayan, *Mystics, Monarchs and Messiahs: Cultural Landscapes of Early Modern Iran* (Cambridge: Harvard University Press, 2002).

3   I borrow the concept of resilience from Lisa Golombek, 'The Resilience of the Friday Mosque: The Case of Herat', *Muqarnas* 1 (1983): 95–102.

4   Since the 1979 revolution in Iran, the mosque is officially called *masjid-i imam* (Imam's mosque). Seventeenth-century Safavid sources discussed in this essay refer to the mosque as *masjid-i shahi* or *masjid jamiʿ shahi*. An Arabic inscription on a portal of the mosque, dated 1078 H (1667–68), mentions '*jamiʿ kabir al-aʿzam al-shahi al-ʿabbasi al-safavi*'. From the early nineteenth century onward, the mosque was simply known as *masjid-i shah* (Shah Mosque).

5   Earlier studies of the Shah Mosque have dealt with its construction history, epigraphic programme, and royal associations. See André Godard, 'Isfahan', *Athar-e Iran, annales du service archeologique de l'Iran* 2 (1937), 107–16; Arthur Upham Pope, 'The Safavid Period', in *A Survey of Persian Art*, eds Arthur Upham Pope and Phyllis Ackerman, 14 vols. (London: Oxford University Press, 1938), 3:1165–1225, esp. 1185–89; Lisa Golombek, 'The Anatomy of a Mosque', in *Iranian Civilization and Culture*, ed. Charles J. Adams (Montreal: Institute of Islamic Studies, McGill University, 1973), 5–14. Also see Sussan Babaie, 'Sacred Sites of Kingship: the Maydan and Mapping the Spatial-spiritual Vision of the Empire in Safavid Iran', in *Persian Kingship and Architecture: Strategies of Power in Iran from the Achaemenids to the Pahlavis*, eds Sussan Babaie and Talinn Grigor (London: I.B. Tauris, 2015), 175–218. The Old Mosque of Isfahan has primarily been examined from an archaeological perspective, with a focus on its Seljuk-era constructions. The most comprehensive archeological study is Eugenio Galdieri, ed., *Iṣfahān: Masǧid-i Ǧumʿa*, 3 vols. (Rome: IsMEO, 1972–1984). For an art historical discussion, see Oleg Grabar, *The Great Mosque of Isfahan* (New York: New York University Press, 1990).

6   For an archaeological study of the Maydan-i Naqsh-i Jahan, see Eugenio Galdieri, 'Two Building Phases of the Time of Sah ʿAbbas I in the Maydan-i Sah of Isfahan, Preliminary Note', *East and West* 20.1/2 (1970): 60–69.

7   On the construction history of the Ali Qapu, see Eugenio Galdieri, *Esfahan, ʿAli Qapu: An Architectural Survey* (Rome: IsMEO, 1979).

8   On the construction history of the Maydan-i Naqsh-i Jahan see Robert D. McChesney, 'Four Sources on Shah 'Abbas's Building of Isfahan', *Muqarnas* 5 (1988): 103–34, which offered a textual basis for the two-phase scheme of construction suggested by Galdieri in the above-mentioned publication. See also Stephen Blake, *Half the World: The Social Architecture of Safavid Isfahan, 1590–1722* (Costa Mesa, CA: Mazda Publishers, 1999) and Sussan Babaie, *Isfahan and Its Palaces: Statecraft, Shi'ism and the Architecture of Conviviality in Early Modern Iran* (Edinburgh: Edinburgh University Press, 2008), 85–112.

9   Fazli b. Zayn al-Abidin Khuzani Isfahani, *A Chronicle of the Reign of Shah 'Abbas*, vol. 3 of *Afzal al-Tavarikh*, ed. Kioumars Ghereghlou (Cambridge, UK: Gibb Memorial Trust, 2015), 617–18 and 146, where the author explicitly asserts that the mosque was built for the teaching of Shaykh Lutfallah. For a discussion, see Charles Melville, 'New Light on Shah 'Abbas and the Construction of Isfahan', *Muqarnas* 33 (2016): 155–76, esp. 162–3. The earliest date given in the mosque's inscriptions is 1011 H (1602–3), which appears on a single tile that is reportedly installed in the mihrab in the mosque's basement and was originally part of the main facade; see Mario Ferrante, 'La Mosquée de Saih Lutfallah a Ispahan: Relevés planimétrique', in ed. Giuseppe Zander, *Travaux de restauration de monuments historiques en Iran* (Rome: IsMEO, 1968), 426n1. This date has been wrongly assumed to indicate the commencement of the project. The foundation inscription gives the date 1012 H (1603–4), but, judging by epigraphic evidence, work on internal decoration continued until 1028 H (1618–19); this date is inscribed inside in the mihrab niche in the main domed hall, alongside the signature of the architect. The inscriptions of the Shahyh Lutfallah Mosque are transcribed in Lutfallah Hunarfar, *Ganjina-yi asar-i tarikhi-yi Isfahan* (Isfahan: Saqafi, 1965), 401–15.

10 Fazli, *Chronicle*, 146.

11 Abd Allah Afandi al-Isbahani, *Riyad al-'ulama'wa hiyad al-fudala'*, ed. Ahmad al-Husayni, 6 vols. (Qum: Maktabat Ayat Allah al-Mar'ashi al-'Ammah, 1982–83), 4:417.

12 For an edited version of the text, see Shaykh Lutfallah al-Maysi, 'Risalat al-I'tikafiya', in *Miras-i Islami-yi Iran*, ed. Rasul Ja'fariyan (Qum: Kitabkhana-yi Ayat Allah Mar'ashi Najafi, 1994), 316–37. The implications of the treatise were first analysed on the basis of a manuscript version of the text in Rula Jurdi Abisaab, *Converting Persia: Religion and Power in the Safavid Empire* (London: I.B. Tauris, 2004), 82–87. Among previous studies of the Shaykh Lutfallah Mosque, see Blake, *Half the World*, 147–50; Babaie, *Isfahan and Its Palaces*, 96–98; and Sheila Canby, *Shah 'Abbas: The Remaking of Iran* (London: British Museum Press, 2009), 28–33.

13 The origin of the interpretation of the Shaykh Lutfallah Mosque as a private chapel or oratory, repeated in popular and scholarly works alike, can be traced back to the writing of Arthur U. Pope in *A Survey of Persian Art*. Noting that Shah Abbas built the mosque 'in honour of his saintly father-in-law', Pope stated that 'it served as *his own private chapel*, and from the Ali Qapu he needed only to cross the maydan to say his prayers' [emphasis added]. See Pope, 'Islamic Architecture, L. Safavid Period', in Pope and Ackerman, *A Survey of Persian Art*, 2:1189.

14 Shaykh Lutfallah al-Maysi, 'Risalat al-I'tikafiya', 336. Translated in Abisaab, *Converting Persia*, 84.

15 Hunarfar, *Ganjina*, 412–15. These poems frame the middle bays on the northwest and southeast sides of the domed hall. What further unites the two inscriptions is that

they are the only inscriptions on the mosque that bear the signatures of the otherwise unknown calligrapher Baqir Banna. While thematically similar, these two Arabic poems are composed in different rhymes and meters. It is likely that one poem was composed as a response (*nazira* or *javab*) to the other. As Rasul Ja'fariyan notes, it appears that the two clerics enjoyed a respectful, amicable relationship. The poems by Baha'i and Lutfallah might have been recited during sermons or nighttime vigils held in the mosque during the Ramadan. Not all members of the congregation understood the erudite Arabic verses in entirety, to be sure, but the repetition of the names of the imams in rhythmic phrases surely induced a sense of religiosity in the audience, a mood that conformed to Shah Abbas's goal of providing a place of worship for the Shi'i community of Turkmens and slaves.

16   In the inscription that encircles the drum, the signature of Ali Riza is followed by the Arabic phrase 'May God forgive his sins' (*ghafara Allahu zunubihi*). Likewise, in his signature, which is written in the cursive Nasta'liq script in two cartouches on the inner walls of the mihrab, the architect Muhammad Riza refers to himself as poor (*faqir*) and lowly (*haqir*), 'in need of God's mercy' (*muhtaj bi-rahmat-i khuda*). While such expressions of humility had long been an established practice, they take on a new meaning in the context of Shaykh Lutfallah Mosque alongside other inscriptions.

17   In a manuscript of Shaykh Lutfallah's treatise, the names of Mirza Muhammad Amin and his son are given as lowly people (*adhyal*) among the notables of Isfahan, who had questioned the congregational status of the Shaykh Lutfallah Mosque. See Shaykh Lutfallah al-Maysi, 'Risalat al-I'tikafiya', 334. Interestingly, the same Muhammad Amin is mentioned in Junabadi's chronicle as a *naqib* (community leader), one of the Isfahani notables who were suspicious of the building activities of Shah Abbas in the Old Maydan. See McChesney, 'Four Sources on Shah 'Abbas's Building of Isfahan', 112.

18   Shaykh Lutfallah al-Maysi, 'Risalat al-I'tikafiya', 335–36.

19   Muhammad Husayn b. Khalaf-i Tabrizi, *Burhan-i qati'*, ed. Muhammad Mu'in (Tehran: n.p., 1951), s.v. '*shabistan*'. The dictionary was completed in 1062 H (1651–52) in the Deccan region in South Asia.

20   Originally known as Khvaja Malik Madrasa, the building was probably built during the reign of Shah Tahmasp (*r.*1524–76). The madrasa of Khvaja Malik must have been a sizable structure: according to the chronicler Natanzi, on one occasion before the development of the Maydan, Shah Abbas ascended to the roof of the madrasa of 'Khvaja Malik Mustawfi that is located opposite the Naqsh-i Jahan Garden' to watch ceremonies in the Maydan. See Mahmud ibn Hidayat Allah Afushta'i Natanzi, *Nuqavat al-asar fi zikr al-akhyar: dar tarikh-i Ṣafaviyya*, ed. Ihsan Ishraqi (Tehran: 'Ilmi va Farhangi, 1994), 539.

21   Babaie, *Isfahan and Its Palaces*, 97, suggests that the form of the Shaykh Lutfallah Mosque represents an interpretation of the *maqsura*, a screened area reserved for the prince in front of the mihrab of a Friday mosque. This hypothesis does not consider the mosque's typological pedigree and presumes a princely function for the mosque, which is not supported by any epigraphic or textual evidence.

22   See Sheila S. Blair and Jonathan M. Bloom, *The Art and Architecture of Islam, 1250–1800* (New Haven: Yale University Press, 1994), 50–51; and Robert Hillenbrand, *Islamic*

Architecture: Form, Function, and Meaning (New York: Columbia University Press, 1994), 122. The same layout is repeated in the so-called Masjid-i Shah in Mashhad.

23 The domed sanctuary of the Ali Mosque features an underground prayer hall and an upper-floor gallery. For architectural drawings of the Ali Mosque, see Kambiz Haji-Qassemi, ed., *Ganjnameh: Cyclopaedia of Iranian Islamic Architecture*, vol. 2, 'Mosques of Esfahan' (Tehran: Shahid Beheshti University, 1996), 142–49.

24 The royal balcony is discussed in Babaie, 'Sacred Sites of Kingship', 198. It is likely that the upper floor was also used by women, as is evident from a number of early Safavid paintings. The earliest extant mosque to incorporate an upper-floor gallery is the fourteenth-century Friday mosque of Yazd.

25 Pietro della Valle, *Viaggi di Pietro della Valle, il Pellegrino*, ed. G. Gancia, 2 vols. (Brighton, England, 1843), 1:458–59. I am grateful to Martina Rugiadi for her help in translation.

26 Jean Chardin, *Voyages de Chevalier Chardin, en Perse et en autres lieux de l'Orient*, ed. Louis-Mathieu Langlès, 10 vols. (Paris: Le Normant, Imprimeur-libraire, 1810–11), 7:368–69.

27 Muhammad Mahdi b. Muhammad Riza al-Isfahani, *Nisf-i jahan fi ta'rif al-Isfahan*, ed. Manuchihr Sutuda (Tehran: Ta'yid, 1961), 39; and Sayf al-Dawla Sultan Muahammad, *Safarnama-yi Makka ma'ruf bi safarnama-yi Sayf al-Dawla*, ed. Ali Akbar Khudaparast (Tehran: Nashr-i Nay, 1985), 361–62. According to Muhammad Mahdi, on 21 Ramadan (the date of the martyrdom of Imam 'Ali), people of Isfahan gathered at the Ali Qapu to make sweetmeats like halvah as votive offering (*nazr*). See also Hunarfar, *Ganjina*, 420–21.

28 As Gülru Necipoğlu has noted, the earliest reference to the Tawhidkhana is in the chronicle of Iskandar Beg, indicating that the foundation of the building and its associated rituals date from the time of Shah Abbas. Gülru Necipoğlu, 'Framing the Gaze in Ottoman, Safavid, and Mughal Palaces', *Ars Orientalis* 23 (1993), 322n33.

29 Kishwar Rizvi, *The Safavid Dynastic Shrine: Architecture, Religion and Power in Early Modern Iran* (London: I. B. Tauris, 2011), 130 and 83–93 (on the Jannatsara). Interestingly, at the shrine at Ardabil, the Jannatsara was paired with the Dar al-Hadith (hall for the study of hadith), a building dedicated to the study of religious law according to Shi'i sources. This pairing is akin to the arrangement of the Tawhidkhana and Shaykh Lutfallah Mosque/Madrasa in Isfahan. For a different interpretation of the Jannatsara, see Sheila Blair, *Text and Image in Medieval Persian Art* (Edinburgh: Edinburgh University Press, 2014), 250–53. Blair argues that the Jannatsara was originally built as the tomb of Shah Isma'il.

30 Mirza Rafi'a Jaberi Ansari, *Dastur al-Moluk: A Safavid State Manual*, trans. Willem Floor and Mohammad H. Faghfoory (Costa Mesa, Calif.: Mazda Publishers, 2006), 50.

31 Nicolas Sanson, *Voyage, ou, Relation de l'etat present du royaume de Perse* (Paris, 1694), 40–41. Sanson also refers to the *pish-namaz* (prayer leader) of the court, suggesting that, at least in the late seventeenth century, communal prayer was held within the palace complex.

32 Vladimir Minorsky, trans., *Tadhkirat al-Muluk: A Manual of Safavid Administration (circa 1137/1725)* (London: 'E. J. W. Gibb memorial', Luzac & co., 1943), 33, 55. Cited in Rizvi, *Safavid Dynastic Shrine*, 130.

33 Jaberi Ansari, *Dastur al-Moluk*, 50.

34 Hunarfar, *Ganjina*, 402.

35 On the Shaykh Lutfallah Mosque's foundation inscription, see Sheila Blair, *Islamic Inscriptions* (New York: New York University Press, 1998), chap. 2.

36 Fazli, *Chronicle*, 244.

37 For transcription of these inscriptions, see Hunarfar, *Ganjina*, 427–33.

38 Iskandar Beg Munshi, *Tarikh-i 'alam-ara-yi 'Abbasi*, 2 vols, ed. Iraj Afshar (Tehran: Amir Kabir, 2003), 2:831. This is a modified translation offered in McChesney, 'Four Sources on Shah 'Abbas's Building of Isfahan', 111.

39 Fazli, *Chronicle*, 617–18; and Melville, 'New Light', 170.

40 See Andrew Newman, *Safavid Iran: Rebirth of a Persain Empire* (London: I. B. Tauris, 2006), 52–53. For a study of sociopolitical reforms and transformations of the Safavid household under Shah Abbas I, see Sussan Babaie et al., *Slaves of the Shah: New Elites of Safavid Iran* (London: I.B.Tauris, 2004).

41 For a comprehensive study of the still-contested debate over the legality of Friday prayer, see Ja'fariyan, *Din va siyasat dar dawra-yi safavi*, 121–80. Ja'fariyan lists more than one hundred treatises written in Safavid times on the issue of Friday prayer. By the closing years of the seventeenth century, the dispute was not completely settled; new epistles were written declaring the performance of Friday prayer *haram* (unlawful). See ibid., 607.

42 The chief proponent of the revival of Friday prayer in the first half of the sixteenth century was Muhaqqiq al-Karaki (Hasan b. Ja'far al-Karaki, d. 936), one of the first Shi'i clerics from the Arab lands to join the Safavid court.

43 On Shaykh Baha'i's life and career, see Devin J. Stewart, *Encyclopedia Iranica*, s.v. 'Kaskul-e Shaikh Baha'i'. Also see Andrew J. Newman, 'Towards a Reconsideration of the Isfahan School of Philosophy: Shaykh Baha'i and the Role of the Safawid Ulama', *Studia Iranica* 15 (1986): 165–99. A native of Jabal 'Amil, a region in what is today south Lebanon, Shaykh Baha'i emigrated to Safavid lands at a young age along with his father after the latter's mentor and friend was executed by the Ottomans. See Devin J. Stewart, 'An Episode in the 'Amili Migration to Safavid Iran: Husayn b. 'Abd al-Samad al-'Amili's Travel Account', *Iranian Studies* 39, no. 4 (2006): 481–508.

44 From the late nineteenth century onward, in the popular imagination, Shaykh Baha'i has become known as the mastermind of the Safavid master plan for Isfahan, and the Shah Mosque in particular. Shi'i scholars like Shaykh Baha'i were definitely instrumental in the building of the Shah Mosque by providing the legal framework for the construction of a congregational mosque and devising its epigraphic contents. However, there is no explicit evidence in contemporary sources on Shaykh Baha'i's direct engagement in architectural production. Nevertheless, the sources describe him as a polymath knowledgeable in mathematics and geometry, among other non-theological sciences. He had authored treatises on mathematics and his notebooks contain solutions for geometric constructions, many of which might have been applicable to architecture.

45 Chardin, *Voyages*, 7:349–50.

46 Adam Olearius, *The Voyages and Travels of the Ambassadors Sent by Frederick, Duke of Holstein*, trans. John Davies (London: printed for John Starkey, and Thomas Basset, 1699), 221; cited in Blake, *Half the World*, 144.

47 The implications of the inscriptions are studied in Gülru Necipoğlu, 'Qur'anic Inscriptions on Sinan's Imperial Mosques: A Comparison with Their Safavid and Mughal Counterparts', in *Word of God – Art of Man: The Qur'an and its Creative Expressions*, ed. Fahmida Suleman (Oxford: Oxford University Press, 2007), 88–93. For a study focused on the aesthetic features of the inscriptions, see Sheila Blair, 'Inscribing the Square: The Inscriptions on the Maidan-i Shah in Isfahan', in *Calligraphy and Architecture in the Muslim World*, ed. Mohammad Gharipour and Irvin Cemil Schick (Edinburgh: Edinburgh University Press, 2013), 13–28.

48 For the inscriptions, see Hunarfar, *Ganjina*, 438–41, 449–51.

49 The inscriptions of the Shah Mosque thus contrast with the epigraphy of the Shaykh Lutfallah Mosque, which is primarily concerned with the performance of prayer and the intercession of the imams for salvation. The audience for the latter was clearly a community of Shi'i believers rather than a broader populace.

50 Golombek, 'The Anatomy of a Mosque', 8.

51 For a discussion of the underlying geometry of the Shah Mosque, see Kambiz Nava'i and Kambiz Haji Qassemi, *Khisht va khiyal* (Tehran: Surush, 2011), 136–43, where the authors postulate that the overall layout of the mosque was derived from a series of pentagons.

52 Golombek, 'The Anatomy of a Mosque', 8.

53 See Sholeh A. Quinn, *Historical Writing during the Reign of Shah 'Abbas, Ideology, Imitation and Legitimacy in Safavid Chronicles* (Salt Lake City: University of Utah Press, 2000), esp. chap. 4.

54 Abd-allah Sani Bihishti Haravi, *Nur al-mashriqayn: safarnama-yi manzum az 'ahd-i Safavi*, ed. Najib Mayil Haravi (Mashhad: Astan-i Quds-i Razavi, 1998), 218.

55 The predominance of the hypostyle plan also can be seen in the Old Friday Mosque of Isfahan, which will be discussed in the last section of this chapter.

56 Golombek, 'The Anatomy of a Mosque', 8.

57 There is indeed no epigraphic evidence that the twin courtyards functioned as madrasas. Judging from the inscriptions, the courtyards, or at least their tile decorations, were finished much later, in the second half of the seventeenth century, under Shah Sulayman.

58 The function of the covered spaces as winter prayer halls are highlighted in Muhammad Hasan Jabiri Ansari, *Tarikh-i Isfahan va Ray va hamah-i jahan* ([Isfahan]: Husayn Imadzada, 1942–43), 362. Unlike the two eight-bay halls that flank the dome sanctuary, these halls were lower than the courtyard and entirely enclosed, which made them more suitable for use in winters. The larger eastern hall has been entirely reconstructed since the French architect Pascal Coste surveyed the mosque in 1840.

59 These features are depicted in the earliest survey of the mosque, which was made by Coste in April 1840 and is now preserved in Marseille, Bibliothèque de l'Alcazar (former Bibliothèque municipale), Ms. 1132, fol. 3–4. The plan later appeared in Pascal Coste, *Monuments modernes de la Perse, mesurés, dessinés et décrits par Pascal Coste* (Paris, 1867).

60 See Abd al-Husayn Sipanta, *Tarikhcha-yi awqaf-i Isfahan* (Isfahan: Intisharat-i Idara-yi Kull-i Awqaf, Mantaqa-yi Isfahan, 1967), 50–62. For a study, see Robert D. McChesney, 'Waqf and Public Policy: The Waqfs of Shah 'Abbas, 1011–1023/1602–14', *Asian and African Studies* 15 (1981): 165–90, esp. 178–81.

61 A useful summary is provided in Blake, *Half the World*, 146–47.

62 Sipanta, *Tarikhcha-yi awqaf-i Isfahan*, 61.

63 Muhammad Husayn al-Husayni al-Tafrishi, *Tarikh-i Shah Safi*, ed. Mohsen Bahramnezhad (Tehran: Miras-i Maktub, 2010), 138.

64 Chardin, *Voyages*, 7:351.

65 Vali Quli ibn Davud Quli Shamlu, *Qisas al-khanqani*, ed. Hasan Sadat Nasiri, 2 vols. (Tehran: Sazman-i Chap va Intisharat-i Vizarat-i Farhang va Irshad-i Islami, 1992–95), 2:135.

66 See Gülru Necipoğlu, *The Age of Sinan: Architectural Culture in the Ottoman Empire* (London: Reaktion Books, 2005).

67 Muhammad Ma'sum b. Khajigi Isfahani, *Khulasat al-siyar*, ed. Iraj Afshar (Tehran: 'Ilmi, 1989), 37–39.

68 Ibid., 41. The distribution of food at the Shah Mosque after the death of a Safavid ruler had apparently become a ritual. A later Safavid source reports that the same practice was performed after the death of Shah Sulayman. See Hunarfar, *Ganjina*, 660.

69 Mir Abd al-Ma'ali Nijat Isfahani, 'Vasf-i Isfahan', ed. Aḥmad Gulchin Ma'ani, in *Majmu'a Maqalat-i Kungiri-yi Jahani-yi Buzurgdasht-i Isfahan*, ed. Fazlullah Salavati (Tehran: Intisharat-i Ittila'at, 2006), 367–76.

70 Blair, 'Inscribing the Square', 24. Blair suggests that the text might have been devised by Shaykh Baha'i.

71 See James W. Allan, 'Silver Door Facings of the Safavid Period', *Iran* 33 (1995): 123–37.

72 Hunarfar, *Ganjina*, 433–34.

73 This reference to the Ka'ba may also have a sectarian connotation. In Shi'i narratives, Imam 'Ali is said to have been born in the Ka'ba.

74 *Baz shud chun bi tazagi in dar/Dar Sifahan bi ruy-i ahl-i niyaz.* Hunarfar, *Ganjina*, 433–34.

75 Aqa Mansur [Simnani], 'Dastur al-amal-i sayr-i Isfahan', ed. Muhammad Taqi Danishpazhuh, *Farhang-i Iran-zamin* 18 (1971): 213–43, at 228.

76 Pope, 'The Safavid Period', 1185.

77 It has been suggested that the Old Maydan was the model for the Maydan-i Naqsh-i Jahan, and that its overall form followed that of the Old Maydan. If this was the case, then it is not surprising that the portal of the new mosque was modelled on the main portal of the shrine of Harun Vilayat, which was also located on the south side of the Old Maydan.

78 See Abbas Daneshvari, 'A Preliminary Study of the Iconography of the Peacock in Medieval Islam', in *The Art of the Saljuqs in Iran and Anatolia: Proceedings of a Symposium Held in Edinburgh in 1982*, ed. Robert Hillenbrand (Costa Mesa: Mazda, 1994), 192–200.

79 Sipanta, *Tarikhcha-yi awqaf-i Isfahan*, 62.

80 Golombek, 'The Resilience of the Friday Mosque'.

81 Babayan, *Mystics, Monarchs and Messiahs*, 464.

82 See Rasul Ja'farian, *Qissa-khvanan dar tarikh-i Islam va Iran* (Qum: Intisharat-i Dalil, 1999), 104.

83 Imam Muhammad al-Ghazali, *Kimiya-yi sa'adat*, ed. Ahmad Aram (Tehran: Markazi, 1974), 404, 406. Cited and translated in Mahmoud Omidsalar, 'Storytellers in Classical Persian Texts', *The Journal of American Folklore* 97, 384 (1984): 204–12, at 206. The passage was part of a chapter on 'the iniquitous deeds prevalent among the people'.

84 Alastair Northedge, 'Early Islamic Urbanism', in *A Companion to Islamic Art and Architecture*, eds Finbarr Barry Flood and Gülru Necipoğlu (New Jersey: Wiley-Blackwell, 2017), 155–76, at 158.

85 Up to the present day, several of these mosques have retained this historical function and are traversed by ordinary people on a daily basis.

86 Muhammad Mahdi, *Nisf-i Jahan fi ta'rif al-Isfahan*, 61.

87 Interestingly, although the Shah Mosque originally featured only one monumental portal, it later acquired an ancillary gate. Completed in 1078 H (1667–68), according to the inscription, the new gate was built on the southwest side of the mosque, on the axis of the southwestern courtyard. See Hunarfar, *Ganjina*, 457. Another gate was added on the opposite courtyard in the nineteenth century when the residential cells were also constructed. With the addition of these gates, the Shah Mosque acquired something of the integrated character of the Old Friday Mosque: to reach the Maydan-i Naqsh-i Jahan from south, one could now pass through the courtyard of the mosque. It is not difficult to assume that, with the passage of time, had the new Safavid developments continued to prosper, renovations and additions would have further integrated the Shah Mosque into the social and spatial fabric of the city, diminishing its rigid formal character as a monument solely accessed from the sqaure.

88 McChesney, 'Waqf and Public Policy: The Waqfs of Shah 'Abbas', 170–73.

89 On Safavid coffeehouses, see Farshid Emami, 'Coffeehouses, Urban Spaces, and the Formation of a Public Sphere in Safavid Isfahan', *Muqarnas* 33 (2016): 177–220.

From the Kutubiyya to Tinmal: The Sacred Direction in Mu'minid Performance

Abbey Stockstill

The Masjid al-jami' al-Kutubiyya – the first major monument of the Mu'minid dynasty, the political iteration of the Almohad religious movement – stands tall as the defining landmark of Marrakesh, as much today as it did in the twelfth century. Located in the southwestern quarter of the medieval madina, the mosque was the centrepiece of Almohad Marrakesh, a monumental beacon to religious, scholarly, and public life. There is a solid monumentality to the mosque and its minaret, a strength that grounds the site in its foundation and grants it a permanence that echoes the dynasty's religious aspirations. Developed out of an eschatological Berber religious movement, Almohadism strove to reinvigorate North African Islam by adapting its tenets to local culture, appealing to local Sufi networks, and establishing its followers as the true champions of Islam.[1] As described by Amira Bennison,

> This context encouraged the Almohads to develop a style of urban architecture that was both militant and grand in scale, thus making visible their aspirations to defend the faith and return the population of the Islamic west to true monotheism after the perceived aberrations of Almoravid legalism and literalism and Fatimid Shi'ism.[2]

More significantly, such focus on the dynasty's North African and Berber origins would be continually reinforced through the early architectural efforts of the first Almohad caliph, 'Abd al-Mu'min (r.1147–63), in and around Marrakesh, as well as through the ceremonial practices of his successors, the Mu'minids (r.1147–1269). It is worth noting that 'Abd al-Mu'min's reign marks a pivotal moment in the transition of the Almohads from the unitarian religious movement (literally, al-muwahhidun) founded by Ibn Tumart (d.1130) to a political movement based on the hereditary succession of 'Abd al-Mu'min's descendants. Because the Mu'minid caliphs both refined and changed those tenets established by their spiritual founder, it is impractical and overly simplistic to group them together – hence the distinction between Ibn Tumart's belief system and the imperial apparatus of the Mu'minid era.

This essay explores the ways in which the religious experience of Almohadism is extended throughout the city at those sites that marked liminal interactions between the Mu'minids and the public – the Kutubiyya Mosque, the dynastic necropolis at Tinmal, and the public garden complex known as the Agdal – tangibly intertwining the dynasty with the religious leadership and salvation of the Almohad empire. In the Maghrebi context, such a connection is significant, marking the first time in which a dynasty without political or religious ties to the Islamic heartland established itself so thoroughly as the spiritual guide of the North African community. The Berber tribes that served as the base for early Almohad support – primarily from the Masmuda, but also from the Zanata and Sanhaja – granted the movement a distinctly local character that appealed to a populace historically treated as second-class due to their non-Arab heritage. The Atlas Mountains, the tribal home of the Masmuda and the location for the dynasty's *dar al-hijra* at Tinmal, would anchor this local character and Berber heritage to the landscape surrounding Marrakesh. As the city developed through a rapid effort of construction after the Almohad conquest in 1147, sites both religious and secular were co-opted in the development of a dynastic identity that repeatedly looked to the Atlas Mountains as the source of its legitimacy and right to rule. Though this tactic would prove both impractical and unsuccessful in other Mu'minid urban efforts – particularly on the Iberian Peninsula, where they faced Arab opposition and contended with a pre-existing urban framework – in Marrakesh they created a capital that would remain inextricably tied to their ethnic identity through the exploitation of the local landscape.

Founded in 1062 as a strategic campsite between the Sahara and the central Maghreb, Marrakesh was built in a flat, arid basin called the Haouz, which descends in a semi-circular fashion between the Atlas Mountains and the Atlantic Ocean.[3] Its founders, members of another dynasty of Berber origin, the Almoravids, had focused their development of the city around a lavish congregational mosque, of which only an ablution fountain, known as the Qubbat al-Barudiyyin, remains.[4] A fortified casbah for military options was constructed under Yusuf ibn Tashfin (*d.*1106), whose son 'Ali ibn Yusuf (*d.*1143) built a luxurious palace on the edge of the city. However, neither father nor son sought to build walls around the city until the imminent threat posed by Ibn Tumart, the famously ascetic spiritual founder of the Almohad movement, and his followers loomed. In 1126, 'Ali ibn Yusuf ordered the walls to be built, with particular attention paid to the southern front.[5] This effort, however, seems to have been too little, too late; after multiple attacks, the Almohads took the city in 1147.

What followed was a wholesale renovation of the city that was as much about removing reminders of the Almoravids as it was about creating an Almohad architectural idiom. The Almoravid mosque and palace were demolished, and their other monuments were similarly destroyed or whitewashed.[6] The conventional explanation for this destructive fervour has been couched in religious terms: the Almoravids, who subscribed to the mainstream Maliki school of Sunni Islam and paid nominal allegiance to the Abbasid Caliphate in Baghdad, were viewed as heretics by the Almohads. The former's architecture reflected their alleged spiritual decay through a preference for ornament, vegetal motifs, and domed mosques – Yasser Tabbaa has argued that this iconographic programme was part of the widespread Sunni revival in the eleventh century.[7] By replacing Almoravid monuments with their own, the Almohads revealed a triumphalist attitude toward their opponents' capital city, championing their own independent, local version of Islam, which was not subservient to a distant power.

Despite 'Abd al-Mu'min's dynastic ambitions, his role as the new Almohad caliph was in a perilous position. In 1153 and 1156 he faced open rebellion from Ibn Tumart's brothers, who were dissatisfied with 'Abd al-Mu'min's intention to declare his son Muhammad as his successor, thereby establishing dynastic precedent.[8] Ibn Tumart had famously chastised the Almoravid caliph 'Ali ibn Yusuf at court for pretending to the caliphate, which Ibn Tumart decreed was 'for God alone'; 'Abd al-Mu'min's pretension to the same office undoubtedly drew criticism from those who would have maintained Ibn Tumart's practice of awarding authority based on merit.[9] Historical sources from the period paint 'Abd al-Mu'min's succession as ordained by Ibn Tumart and sanctioned by the Council of Ten, Ibn Tumart's closest followers and councillors. However, as most of these sources were sponsored for or by the Mu'minid dynasty, their reliability on this particular matter is called into question.[10] 'Abd al-Mu'min was of the Zanata tribe, while the majority of Almohad support came from Ibn Tumart's tribe, the Masmuda, making the former's ascension to leadership both anomalous and contentious. Al-Baydhaq, Ibn Tumart's biographer, notes that the charismatic leader called the Almohads together and announced that he was departing the earth but had left instructions for the next three years, to be carried out under 'Abd al-Mu'min.[11] By comparison, the fourteenth-century writer Ibn Khaldun notes that the transition was much more fraught, with Ibn Tumart dying unexpectedly and the Council of Ten keeping his passing secret for three years while deciding how to proceed. According to Ibn Khaldun, the Masmudas' support could be obtained only by appealing to a prominent Masmuda shaykh, Abu Hafs 'Umar (d.1175).[12] 'Abd al-Mu'min would continue to be plagued by questions of legitimacy, to the point that he felt it necessary to undertake a ritual confirmation of alliances known as *tamyiz*. The process formalized alliances through a communal meal (*asmas*) and tribal council (*agrao*), and it also was used to cull those disloyal to the group and had been employed to great effect by Ibn Tumart.[13] 'Abd al-Mu'min performed another form of *tamyiz*, called the *i'tiraf* ('recognition' or 'acknowledgement'), in which the names of suspected dissidents were distributed among the Almohad territories; the accused were systematically arrested and executed.[14]

For 'Abd al-Mu'min, who struggled not only to maintain his legitimacy as Ibn Tumart's heir but also to establish the dynastic interests of his own family, the need to reinforce ties with the Almohad movement's ethnic, geographic, and spiritual origins was paramount. Though 'Abd al-Mu'min had politically secured his position amongst the Almohad elite, removing his rivals and establishing his confirmation by Ibn Tumart and the Council of Ten, his tenure, which was based on the cult of his personal charisma and success rather than on a hereditary claim, was inherently unstable. As he was responsible for the military and territorial success of the empire, he was reluctant to leave the survival of his family to chance and to watch tribal divisions destroy all that he had accomplished.[15] Instead, he appropriated symbols of legitimacy and authority that not only drew upon the dynastic heritage of the Islamic west but also, as shall be demonstrated below, developed the ethnic heritage of Almohadism into a religio-political ideology that utilized liminal urban spaces to ground that identity in the local landscape.

The Two Iterations of the Masjid al-jamiʿ al-Kutubiyya

One of ʿAbd al-Muʾminʾs first projects after taking control of the city was to erect a new congregational mosque to serve as the centrepiece of Almohadism. Built between 1147 and 1154, on the remains of the destroyed Almoravid palace (indeed, the northern exterior wall of the mosqueʾs current iteration is likely reused from this prior construction), the Kutubiyya follows the North African precedent for a single-storied hypostyle plan with a courtyard for ablutions axially positioned opposite the qibla wall.[16] Approximately 80 metres wide, east to west, and 60 metres long, north to south, the prayer hall features supportive piers organized in a T-shaped plan, with three wider aisles down the centre, toward the mihrab, and a transversal aisle along the qibla wall. This structural organization creates a remarkably symmetrical, visually directed space, lacking the broad length of regional precedents such as the mosque at Qayrawan. The east and west walls contained four entrances each – three opening directly into the mosque, and another into the courtyard – while the northern elevation offered another public entrance to the courtyard.[17] On the southern side of the elevation were two additional entrances, which were private and meant only for the Muʾminid caliphs and the imam; one was directly to the left of the mihrab, and another opened into the *maqsura*, the enclosure surrounding the mihrab and minbar along the transversal qibla aisle.

This is the extent of the information we have concerning the Kutubiyyaʾs original iteration, as a second adjoining version was added shortly after its initial construction. This second Kutubiyya, begun as early as 1154, was at least partially complete by 1158, when the first prayers were said there, and it is this iteration that remains extant today. The plan is almost exactly the same, extending from the qibla wall of the first, though the orientation of the second prayer hall is angled five degrees further toward the south, and the central aisles are slightly wider, granting the second Kutubiyya a slightly larger width. Additionally, the centremost aisle and the transverse aisle are enlarged slightly further, accentuating the T-shaped plan of the prayer hall. The result was an oddly angled construction, with two individual mosques separated by a thin wedge of space, each adjoining a corner of the minaret that stands between the two, the first at its southeast corner and the second at its northeast [Figure 1].

The explanation for such an odd expansion of the mosque is murky at best, for authors of the period merely comment on the second mosqueʾs existence, never its logic. In the anonymous twelfth-century text known as *The Book of Rational Insight* (*Kitab al-Istibsar*), the author notes the coexistence of the two structures, at least until the end of the twelfth century:

> And then the Caliph and imam [ʿAbd al-Muʾmin] constructed there a great congregational mosque, which he then enlarged with one similar to it, towards the qibla where the palace once was, and between them was raised the most grand minaret, of which there had been none like it [before] in Islam.[18]

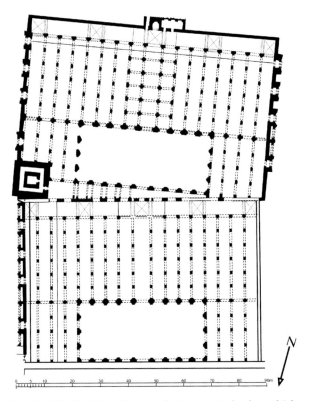

Figure 1: Ground plan of the Masjid al-Kutubiyya. Drawing after Meunié, *Recherches archéologiques a Marrakech.*

It is notable that the author appears more focused on the size of the complex, and on the achievement of the minaret, than on the motivations behind the expansion.

The odd arrangement of the two mosques has been a topic of much debate among scholars, especially considering the Maliki stipulation of having only one congregational mosque per madina.[19] Some, like archaeologist Jacques Meunié, theorize that the second iteration of the building was constructed to accommodate the rapid increase in the population of Marrakesh under 'Abd al-Mu'min.[20] This would not have been the first time a ruler in the Islamic west justified an expensive mosque expansion by citing pious concern for his constituents – in fact, the Spanish Umayyad caliph 'Abd al-Rahman claimed to have expanded the mosque in Cordoba for this very reason.[21] In Meunié's estimation, this second iteration of the mosque would have housed a number of Almohad military and court administrators, and simultaneously served to separate the caliph and his entourage from those who may have been critical of his reign. Jessica Streit has further supported this theory by demonstrating that such a separation would have proved necessary for 'Abd al-Mu'min as he struggled to establish legitimacy for the nascent Mu'minid dynasty over the merit-based leadership of the Almohad faithful.[22]

Another explanation focuses on the mosque's qibla orientation. In their 1925 study of Almohad architecture, Henri Basset and Henri Terrasse argued that this second mosque was constructed to correct the faulty qibla orientation of the original, a theory that was promoted by their colleagues George Marçais and Gaston Deverdun.[23] Yet such a claim is frustrated by the fact that the second building orients itself farther away from Mecca than the original. According to geographical and trigonometric calculations to determine the shortest distance to Mecca, the qibla direction in Marrakesh should follow a 91° azimuth. When construction on the first Kutubiyya began, it was oriented to 154° and was adjusted in the second structure to 159°.[24] Even accounting for a mathematical error, such a deviation begs an alternate explanation.

The Kutubiyya is by no means remarkable in its deviation from the norm. As Michael Bonine has demonstrated, Moroccan mosques vary widely in their interpretation of the qibla. In his survey of Moroccan qiblas, he notes that over the *longue durée* of Islamic architecture in the region, it is only under the Alawites, from the seventeenth century onward, that an effort was made to focus the qibla toward Mecca.[25] Almohad mosques, in contrast, maintain a qibla direction that falls in the upper 150°s, with the exception of the mosque at Salé, which was built on Almoravid foundations. This southerly orientation appears widespread in both the Maghreb and al-Andalus, and one possible explanation looks at the Spanish Umayyad precedent set in Cordoba, whose Great Mosque is also oriented due south. According to Nuha Khoury, the mosque's qibla is based on that of the Umayyad Mosque in Damascus, which served to directly 'reinforce a historical link between the mosque founded during the original conquest and the "new" mosque built after the reestablishment of the Umayyad caliphate of al-Andalus'.[26]

This orientation, and its persistence in the Islamic west, would be rationalized by Maliki scholars in the region, who decreed that an approximate directionality would suffice when the Ka'ba of Mecca was not in sight.[27] This may explain why the ninth-century Idrisid mosques in Fez, known as the Qarawiyyin Mosque and the Andalusian Mosque, also feature qiblas toward the south. Although the Spanish Umayyads had set a precedent for south-facing mosques at Cordoba, the logic for such a shift, which posits a directional reference to the Umayyad Mosque in Damascus, does not apply to later mosques in the region. While the Umayyads used their cultural and political connections with Damascus as a legitimizing tool for their Spanish caliphate, later dynastic mosques, particularly those in North Africa, were too geographically and culturally distant for this reference to carry much public weight. Despite these precedents, the Almohads needed to distance themselves from the interpretative measures taken by their rivals, which were seen as deviating from true knowledge – that is, as an awareness of the fundamental principles of Islam rather than any metaphysical concept.[28] Likewise, although 'Abd al-Mu'min and his successors would draw on the ritual and ceremony of the Spanish Umayyads, as will be discussed below, a direct architectural reference such as that posed by the qibla would have been inappropriate considering the radical reformism of Almohad doctrine.

Figure 2: Southern view from the top of the Kutubiyya minaret, with the Atlas Mountains in the distance. Photograph by the author.

In Marrakesh, the orientation of the Kutubiyya toward the south likely utilizes the astronomical method of establishing the qibla by Suhayl al-Wazn, or Canopus, a star that hovers over the horizon and thereby serves as a reliable directional tool.[29] This directs the viewer toward the Atlas Mountains, which appear to float above the city's southern horizon [Figure 2]. One cannot help but consider that, as the ancestral and spiritual home of the Almohad movement, the mountains would have had a special resonance for 'Abd al-Mu'min and his supporters. By orienting the Kutubiyya southward, and even more so in its second iteration, the Almohads created a visible link with the dynasty's religious heritage through the local landscape. Worshippers at the mosque would pray not toward Mecca but toward Tinmal, the mountain village where Ibn Tumart had gathered his early followers, been declared *mahdi*, and been buried.

The Mosque at Tinmal: The New *Dar al-hijra*

Located approximately 75 kilometres southeast of Marrakesh, Tinmal (also known as Tinmallal) became the mountain refuge of Ibn Tumart in the later years of his life – and after his death the city was organized around his veneration. Part necropolis, part holy site, the village witnessed the apotheosis of Ibn Tumart as he ascended to the role of the Mahdi, carrying the movement from its reformist nature into an eschatological mode. After a confrontation with the Almoravid emir 'Ali ibn Yusuf in 1120, the same meeting at which he admonished the emir for his caliphal ambition, Ibn Tumart fled potential retribution by escaping to the mountain village of Igliz. There, according to the majority of sources on the period, his followers proclaimed him the Mahdi in 1121, before the entire community relocated to Tinmal.[30] The exception to this account comes from al-Baydhaq (*d.*1164), a contemporary and companion of Ibn Tumart and an early chronicler of the dynasty, who states that Ibn Tumart's declaration as Mahdi actually took place in Tinmal.[31] It was here that Ibn Tumart developed the Council of Ten – his chosen followers, including 'Abd al-Mu'min – and received the *bay'a* (a form of allegiance ceremony) from the various Berber tribes who subscribed to his doctrine. From their new stronghold, well guarded by treacherous mountain passes that often were blocked by snow or falling rocks, Ibn Tumart and his followers would lead raids into Almoravid territory under the guise of divinely sanctioned jihad.[32] Ibn Tumart never saw his vision fully realized, having died in 1130 after a disastrous rout outside Marrakesh, the Battle of al-Buhayra, but his successor would defeat the Almoravids permanently.[33]

Having conquered and renovated Marrakesh, 'Abd al-Mu'min turned to Tinmal as a focus of his architectural and dynastic efforts. Ibn Tumart had been buried there following his death, and in 1153 'Abd al-Mu'min commissioned a new mosque to be built as a memorial to the founder of the Almohad movement. The mosque at Tinmal echoes the hypostyle typology of the first Kutubiyya, though on a smaller and more intimate scale, with only nine aisles instead of seventeen. Built during the period between the construction of the first and second Kutubiyya prayer halls, the Tinmal Mosque follows the qibla orientation of the latter, with an azimuth of 157°. The mere two-degree difference separating them is an acceptable variation considering the technological capabilities of the era and the difficulties posed by mountainous topology.[34] The most significant innovation at Tinmal was the construction of a minaret directly behind the mihrab, which rose above and enveloped it [Figures 3–4]. Thus, as Christian Ewert has noted, 'the call to prayer (from the tower) and the focus of its execution (the mihrab) are combined into an emphatic salient block'.[35] Jonathan Bloom has theorized that the Tinmal minaret, which never rose higher than a metre above the roof of the mosque, is indicative of spiritual and moral concerns about giving the call to prayer from an overly elevated place, a hypothesis that would appear untenable considering the magnitude of the minaret in Marrakesh, which was built at or around the same time.[36] However, as Bloom notes, this arrangement gives the structure a unity of form and symmetry, particularly when viewed from the valley that housed the village, positioned south from the mosque; thus, one views the qibla wall and minaret when approaching.[37]

From this vantage, a monumental minaret becomes extraneous, particularly in the unified geometrical conception of the Tinmal Mosque. Further, I suggest that this unique arrangement reflects Tinmal's status under the early Mu'minids – as a new pilgrimage site and a spiritual locus for the Almohads. Although the practice of venerating holy

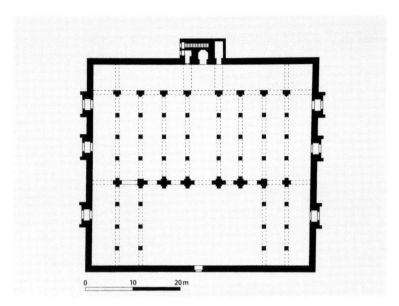

Figure 3: Plan of the Tinmal Mosque. Harvard Fine Arts Library, Digital Images & Slides Collection. Visual Information Access (VIA), http://www.via.lib.harvard.edu (accessed November 1, 2016).

Figure 4: South qibla wall of the Tinmal Mosque with minaret positioned directly in front of the mihrab. Photograph by the author.

men was widespread in the Maghreb, both the attention lavished upon Ibn Tumart and the institutional nature of the rituals surrounding the site suggest a particularly deep and powerful affinity with the spiritual founder. Notwithstanding Tinmal's remote location and the mosque's small size, the ornamental elements are remarkably lavish, especially considering the Almohad preference for graduated and specific ornamental focus. The lambrequin arches and stucco *muqarnas* vaulting, both concentrated within and before the mihrab, are of a similar quality to the same elements on the Kutubiyya, despite the much more intimate scale of the Tinmal Mosque [Figures 5 and 6]. The effect is a more intense, opulent scheme, even though the Tinmal Mosque utilizes the same local, readily available materials as the Kutubiyya.

The practices surrounding the site speak to its importance within the Almohad movement as well as Mu'minid dynastic authority. Two Qur'ans from the Mu'minid treasury, one that reportedly had belonged to the third 'rightly guided' Sunni caliph, 'Uthman, and another that had been Ibn Tumart's personal *mushaf*, were taken on an annual pilgrimage to Tinmal for a ritual recitation of the entire text.[38] These pilgrimages were highly publicized affairs, and although 'Abd al-Mu'min preferred a peripatetic court due to his military activity in al-Andalus and elsewhere in the Maghreb, he made a point of returning annually for this event, a practice that continued under his successors.[39]

Figures 5 and 6: Ornamental programmes around the mihrab at the Kutubiyya (left) and at Tinmal (right). Photographs by the author.

Additionally, 'Abd al-Mu'min, Abu Ya'qub Yusuf (*d*.1184), and Abu Yusuf Ya'qub al-Mansur (*d*.1199) would all be buried at Tinmal alongside Ibn Tumart, creating a dynastic necropolis at the holiest site for the Almohads.[40] The exact location of these tombs is unknown, with no marker or building to identify them for the visitor, an unusual absence considering the abundance of small shrines throughout the Maghreb from the early Islamic period onward. Whether this was intentional or merely the result of time and neglect is unclear, but archaeological evidence suggests that the tombs may have been located directly south of the mosque's qibla wall and in line with its mihrab.[41] This privileged positioning reinforces the notion of Mu'minid affiliation with Ibn Tumart – and takes it one step further, interweaving the role of the caliphate with that of the Mahdi through ritual visitation and veneration.

As the site of Ibn Tumart's hijra (emigration) and reception of the *bay'a*, Tinmal became a Maghrebi Medina for the Almohads and for 'Abd al-Mu'min's dynasty, the village playing into the narrative parallels mapping Ibn Tumart's life onto that of the Prophet Muhammad. And yet the rituals and patronage associated with the site would suggest an even more important role within the spiritual and social life of the twelfth-century Mu'minids. Ibn Tumart was the source of dynastic legitimacy not only for the dynasty's Almohad followers but also as the lynchpin that held together the complex and tenuous alliance of the Berber tribes on an unprecedented scale. Moreover, the decision to patronize Tinmal as part of a religio-political ideology can be directly traced to 'Abd al-Mu'min and his desire to, as Pascal Buresi has described, 'reject the Arab origins [of Islam] in a faraway eastern periphery' and instead favour the Maghreb as the new centre of the Islamic world.[42] A letter written by court secretary Abu 'Aqil 'Atiyya ibn 'Atiyya (*d*.1158), but circulated on behalf of the caliph after his return to Marrakesh from Tinmal in 1157, details the caliph's pilgrimage. The letter subsequently travelled throughout the Almohad empire at least twice during his reign. Though it describes 'Abd al-Mu'min's visit to the Mahdi's tomb to receive its baraka, or blessings, greater emphasis is placed on the number of tribes with which the caliph met along his journey, re-establishing alliances and hearing grievances.[43] Considering 'Abd al-Mu'min's difficulties in establishing hegemony during the early portion of his reign, and particularly the conflict with Ibn Tumart's brothers, publicly performing devotion to the movement's spiritual leader served an additional prosaic purpose in reinforcing pan-tribal cohesion. This practice of tribal negotiation and ritual visitation would become the hallmark of Mu'minid dynastic religio-political ideology.

Ceremonial and Performance in 'Abd al-Mu'min's Marrakesh

The twin sites of Tinmal and the Kutubiyya concentrated the efforts of 'Abd al-Mu'min's early caliphate to strengthen the tribal confederation established under Ibn Tumart through the unifying power of Almohadist Islam. The architectural patronage of the two mosques provided highly charged spaces in which the caliph and the elite could visibly reconnect

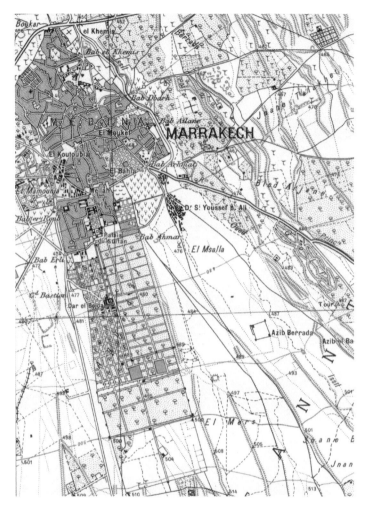

Figure 7: Detail from *Marrakech: Médina, Carte du Maroc au 50,000* (Rabat, 1951), showing the elevation of Marrakesh and the Agdal Garden toward the south.

with the movement that had placed them in power, a connection that was renewed with the performance of prayer and supplication. However, their locations, in the extreme landscapes of the Atlas Mountains and the Haouz basin, isolated the two mosques – and thus bore the potential to weaken their religio-political force. This risk was heightened when the directional focus of the Kutubiyya's dual prayer halls cues became entangled with Marrakesh's urban sprawl. Thus, the buildings alone were not sufficient to intertwine dynastic legitimacy with religious and ethnic authority, a problem that was addressed through the Mu'minid set of rituals and ceremony that extended the boundaries of spiritual engagement to those loci which served as sites of interaction between the public and the elite.

This pageant of ceremonial stems, both physically and aesthetically, from the Kutubiyya, the city's – and the dynasty's – most central and recognizable monument. Far from being the only urban building patronized by 'Abd al-Mu'min, the Kutubiyya was part of a large construction effort that transformed Marrakesh into a truly Almohad city. After any architectural reminder of Almoravid hegemony had been closed or demolished, efforts were made to establish the means by which the Mu'minid caliphs and the Almohad elite would interact with the public in their dynastic capital. Extending southward from the Kutubiyya, a number of foundations sponsored by 'Abd al-Mu'min served to enhance the prestige, legitimacy, and authority of his dynasty through mediated ceremonial. Moreover, these sites constructed a liminal space where the spiritual, the political, and the ethnic interplayed with one another in a highly public manner, grounding the caliph's dynastic ambitions in the urban space through religious ritual.

This extension of religious space began with the Mu'minid 'royal quarter', which started along the qibla wall of the Kutubiyya, where the entrance into the transverse aisle was through a covered passageway (sabat) that led directly to 'Abd al-Mu'min's new palace, allowing for both privacy and direct access for the Mu'minid caliphs.[44] When the caliph was present in the mosque, a wooden *maqsura* screen was raised out of the floor for added privacy, a feat of engineering that deserves attention. *Maqsuras* had been in common use throughout the Islamic world since the eighth century, and a lavish one had been installed at Cordoba as part of al-Hakim II's expansion of the Great Mosque, but the Kutubiyya's was the first of its kind. Hidden channels in the floor and grooves along the piers allowed the *maqsura* to be raised and lowered through a system of mechanical pulleys, establishing the visual effect of permanency with the practicality of the ephemeral. In other contexts, such as that of Cordoba or Damascus, the presence of a *maqsura* signified a separation of the ruler from the general public, as explained by the thirteenth-century lexicographer Ibn Manzur, who wrote that the root of the word, q-s-r (ق-ص-ر), means 'to restrict oneself' (literally 'to cut off').[45] However, in the case of the Kutubiyya *maqsura*, the temporary nature of the screen (thanks to its mechanical innovation) meant that it came to signify the presence of the caliph, rather than his separation from the public, as it was employed only when the caliph attended prayers.

The *maqsura* screen was part of a ritual emphasis on mediated visibility, the screen controlling how and when the caliph interacted with his subjects, yet simultaneously creating a sense of omniscient presence. This effect is echoed in the relationship between the palace quarter and the rest of the city. Though we do not know with archaeological accuracy the precise location of 'Abd al-Mu'min's palace, it was likely part of the walled casbah complex built up by his grandson, Abu Yusuf Ya'qub al-Mansur. The quarter was known as Tamarakusht, taking the feminine form of 'Marrakesh', and, according to the fourteenth-century Syrian historian al-'Umari (d.1349), it featured high walls and monumental gates with views over the city, taking advantage of the slight incline to the south as the Haouz basin rose into the Atlas.[46] Between the city and the enclosed royal quarter would have been a large open esplanade known as the *rahba*, accessed from Tamarakusht through a gate known as Bab al-Sada, the Gate of Lords. A long chain was strung across the gate, forcing entrants to dismount before entering – a practice that, as Amira Bennison has shown, recalls that of the Spanish Umayyads, who required all caliphal supplicants to dismount before entering Madinat al-Zahra' through the Bab al-Sudda. This practice also had been adapted in Idrisid Fez and Jabal Zarhun, where wooden beams blocked the streets leading to shrines 'in order to force riders to dismount in the presence of the sacred'.[47]

The *rahba* of Marrakesh served a variety of functions, the most significant of which focused on the Mu'minids' role as arbiters of ethnic disputes and religious debates. It was the site of the annual review of those troops stationed in Marrakesh, essentially the Mu'minids' standing army, known as the *jumu'*, as well as the ritual gathering of tribal representatives from the High Atlas, called the *'umum*.[48] Al-Marrakushi describes these two ceremonies in tandem, using the term *sanfan al-muwahhidin* ('the two classes of Almohads') when introducing them. It is tempting to view this rhetoric as describing the two sources of Almohad might and of the legitimacy of the Mu'minids, especially considering the way in which the ceremonies were ordered. In procession from the walled casbah, first came the family of Abu Hafs 'Umar al-Sanhaji, one of the original members of the Council of Ten and one of 'Abd al-Mu'min's early supporters, announcing the caliph and members of the Mu'minid family, who followed. They were in turn followed by the Council of Fifty, and afterward by the tribes; it is here that al-Marrakushi places the family of Ibn Tumart.[49] Notably, they are given pride of place amongst the tribal representatives but are placed under the rule of the Mu'minid dynasty. This may be due in part to the attempted revolt by Ibn Tumart's brothers, which could have led 'Abd al-Mu'min to distance them from positions of power.[50] However, symbolically at least, it was important for the Mu'minid dynasty to maintain a relationship with the family, albeit one with the power dynamics shifted heavily to one side, and at the same time to connect themselves to the legitimizing religious authority embodied by Ibn Tumart.

The emphasis placed on Ibn Tumart as the founder of the dynasty, and therefore as the source for legitimacy, is referred to again in the processions that took place between the *rahba* and the suburban gardens to the south of Marrakesh, known as the Agdal; Figure 6 shows that these gardens extended southward from the madina. The Agdal gardens were named after a Berber term meaning 'meadow enclosed by a stone wall', referring to the impression made by the verdant green landscape surrounded by high walls and framed by the rising Atlas Mountains.[51] The garden reached its zenith under Abu Ya'qub Yusuf, the second Mu'minid caliph, as the setting for a number of villa estates for the courtly elite. The garden itself was built under 'Abd al-Mu'min and appears to have been the site for military-religious processions into the *rahba*. During these parades, the caliph was preceded by two editions of the Qur'an, the same codices belonging to 'Uthman and Ibn Tumart that were routinely carried into the Atlas Mountains to Tinmal. Al-Marrakushi describes these parades through the Agdal as follows:

And this volume [of the Qur'an] we have mentioned was from the copies of 'Uthman – may God be satisfied with him – which came to [the Almohads] from the treasure stores of the Banu Umayya [Umayyads]. They carried it in front of them wherever they went upon a red she-camel [adorned] with precious trappings and a splendid brocade of great cost…Behind the camel came a mule similarly adorned carrying another copy [of the Qur'an] said to be written by Ibn Tumart, smaller than the Qur'an of 'Uthman and ornamented with silver.[52]

Bennison has discussed the significance of 'Uthman's codex in Mu'minid ceremonial as a symbol of caliphal legitimacy, drawing connections between 'Abd al-Mu'min's dynasty and the Spanish Umayyads.[53] However, it is important to consider the significance of Ibn Tumart's *mushaf* in these processions, which often coincided with military victories.

Upon initial inspection, it would appear that Ibn Tumart's *mushaf* is accorded a secondary place, following 'Uthman's, and their decorative materials would corroborate this claim. 'Uthman's codex is enclosed in a gold and silver case and famously adorned with jewels, including a large ruby in the shape of a horse's hoof.[54] By contrast, Ibn Tumart's is much simpler, covered only by gold-plated silver. Even their mode of transport seems to suggest this imbalance; Uthman's codex is accorded a red she-camel while Ibn Tumart's is placed on a mule. However, I would suggest that this arrangement instead could be symbolic of Almohad religious claims, particularly Ibn Tumart's status as the Mahdi, the prophesied redeemer of Islam who would rule before the Day of Judgment. As a reformist movement, Almohadism revolved around the character of the Mahdi, particularly his asceticism and his doctrinal focus on knowledge (*'ilm*) over opinion (*zann*).[55] The two Qur'ans were visual reminders of Ibn Tumart's criticisms of the Maliki school and their Almoravid patrons, whom, he believed, had strayed too far from the sources of true knowledge. They were at the same time mementoes of the source of his and his chosen successors' roles as redemptive spiritual guides. That his *mushaf* follows that of 'Uthman is in accordance with his role as a reformer and the Mahdi, the second coming of communal salvation. One could even compare the order in which the codices were processed with that of the *'umum* ceremony, in which the Mu'minid caliphs were 'announced' by the family of 'Umar al-Sanhaji. Similarly, though the 'Uthmanic codex is the Qur'anic standard, it is superseded by that of Ibn Tumart in his role as the Mahdi, figuratively emphasizing the 'second coming' of Islam and its holy text to the Maghreb.

Each of these ceremonies proceeded along the city's north-south axis, positioning the Mu'minid caliphs as continually emerging from the Atlas Mountains, despite their proximity to Marrakesh. The mediated visibility of the caliph emphasized this impression and cemented the new dynasty's connection to the authority of Ibn Tumart within the Almohad movement. Through the ceremonial precedent established under 'Abd al-Mu'min, not only was he confirmed as the rightful successor to Ibn Tumart, he also was able to transition the role of his dynasty from the spearhead of a popular reformist movement to the legitimate leadership of a broader community. This process would not remain successful throughout the tenure of the Mu'minid dynasty – indeed, by the time of 'Abd al-Mu'min's grandson, al-Ma'mun (*r.*1229–32), Ibn Tumart was actively expunged from all dynastic activity, and al-Ma'mun, in response to public criticism of the dynasty's spiritual leader, even denounced the

Mahdi as a false prophet from the minbar of the Kutubiyya.[56] For 'Abd al-Mu'min, however, this connection was crucial, and during his reign Marrakesh's development reflected this priority. Both the royal quarter and the garden complex were built as extensions to the south of the original city, along the axis of the mosque, *rahba*, and palace, and following a slight topological incline in that direction, which reflects a consciousness of the local landscape and its potential to reiterate the dynasty's roots and source of legitimacy. These spaces were activated through the ritual parades that explicitly placed the Mu'minid dynasty at the head of the ethno-religious community based in Marrakesh. This community was accessed through the communal space of the Kutubiyya, which directed spiritual activity through its south-facing qibla toward the dynasty's new *dar al-hijra* at Tinmal.

Conclusion

The nascent dynasty established by 'Abd al-Mu'min walked a thin line between religious leadership and political reality. The doctrine preached by Ibn Tumart easily could have alienated the broader population after the Almohad movement's initial successes, yet 'Abd al-Mu'min overcame this pitfall through the acquisition and re-contextualization of symbols associated with the Mahdi, which became emblems of the dynasty itself. These were then displayed in highly publicized yet mediated contexts, such as the parades led by the Qur'ans of 'Uthman and Ibn Tumart, and the *umum* that placed the family of Ibn Tumart under the patronage of the Mu'minids. Even the body of the Mahdi became a touchstone for dynastic piety, and the pilgrimage to his burial site, as well as the construction of a mosque in memoriam, speaks to its importance for dynastic identity. These events were staged through the dynamic orientation of 'Abd al-Mu'min's capital at Marrakesh, oriented with a south-facing axis that continually placed the Mu'minid caliphate as an intermediary between the general public and the source of religious and political authority. By doing so, 'Abd al-Mu'min integrated the Almohad movement into the socio-religious life of the city, creating a capital whose genius loci was inseparable from the dynasty.

The complex interplay among the religious, political, and ethnic dimensions of both the Almohad movement and the Mu'minid caliphate could not have occurred without the liminal space created through the development of urban and extra-urban spaces. The orientation of the Kutubiyya, echoed in the placement of the casbah and gardens, created a tangible link with Tinmal and resulted in a self-sufficient religio-political environment. The space was activated through regular and repeated acts of ceremonial performance, which pointed to the Mu'minid caliphs' responsibility for the community's religious guidance as well as to their own connections to the spiritual movement that put them in power. Marrakesh's sacred space was thus extended along its north–south axis, embodied by the royal quarter and the caliphate it housed. As long as a Mu'minid ruler reigned from Marrakesh, the ritual space of the city and its environs would confirm their authority. The dynasty's power resided in the liminal spiritual space it created, resulting in an urban structure that both supported and limited them – yet resonated deeply in the landscape and cultural memory of the Maghreb al-Aqsa.

Notes

1 Vincent Cornell's *Realm of the Saint* (Austin: University of Texas Press, 1998) provides an insightful overview of how Sufism functioned on a sociopolitical level in medieval Morocco.
2 Amira K. Bennison, 'Power and the City in the Islamic West from the Umayyads to the Almohads', in *Cities in the Premodern Islamic World*, eds Amira Bennison and Alison Gascoigne (New York: Routledge, 2007), 83–84.
3 Paul Pascon, *Le Haouz de Marrakech* (Rabat, 1977), 18–20.
4 See Jacques Meunié, *Recherches archéologiques a Marrakech* (Paris: Arts et métiers graphiques, 1952).
5 Gaston Deverdun, *Marrakech des origines a 1912* (Rabat: Éditions techniques nord-africaines, 1959–66; reprint, Casablanca: Éditions Frontispice, 2004), 108–9.
6 *Al-Hulal al-Mawshiyya fi dhikr al-Akhbar al-Marrakushiyya* (Tunis: Matba'at al-Taqaddum al-Islamiyya, 1979), 144.
7 Yasser Tabbaa, 'Andalusian Roots and Abbasid Homage in the Qubbat al-Barudiyyin in Marrakech', *Muqarnas* 25 (2008): 142.
8 Abu Bakr ibn 'Ali al-Sanhaji al-Baydhaq, *Akhbar al-Mahdi ibn Tumart wa-bidayat dawlat al-Muwahhidin* (Rabat: Dar al-Mansur lil-Tiba'ah wa-al-Wiraqah, 1971), 85; and Roger LeTourneau, 'Du movement almohade a la dynastie mu'minide: La révolte des frères d'Ibn Tumart de 1153 a 1156', *Mélanges d'histoire et d'archéologie de l'Occident musulman. Tom. II: Hommage à Georges Marçais*, ed. René Crozet (Algiers: Imprimerie Officielle, 1957), 112–13.
9 Vincent Cornell, 'Understanding is the Mother of Ability: Responsibility and Action in the Doctrine of Ibn Tumart', *Studia Islamica* 66 (1987): 83.
10 These court-sponsored sources include Ibn Sahib al-Sala's *Tarikh al-mann bil imama*, 'Abd al-Wahid al-Marrakushi's *al-Mu'jib fi talkhis akhbar al-Maghrib*, and the anonymous *Kitab al-Hulal al-mawshiyya*.
11 Évariste Lévi-Provençal, *Documents inédits d'histoire almohade* (Paris: P. Geuthner, 1928), 131 (French text), 81 (Arabic text).
12 Amira K. Bennison, 'The Almohads and the Qur'an of Uthman: The Legacy of the Umayyads of Cordoba in the Twelfth Century Maghrib', *Al-Masaq* 19.2 (2007), 143.
13 Allen J. Fromherz, *The Almohads: Rise of an Empire* (New York: I. B. Tauris, 2013), 96–99.
14 al-Baydhaq, *Akhbar al-Mahdi ibn Tumart*, 112.
15 Bennison, 'The Almohads and the Qur'an of Uthman', 144.
16 See Robert Hillenbrand, *Islamic Architecture: Form, Function, and Meaning* (New York: Columbia University Press, 1994), 85–89.
17 This earlier iteration of the Kutubiyya Mosque is no longer extant but has been excavated and published in Meunié, *Recherches archéologiques*.
18 *Kitab al-Istibsar fi aja'ib al-amsar*, ed. 'Abd al-Hamid and Sa'id Zaghlul (Casablanca: Dar al-Nashr al-Maghreb, 1985), 209 (Arabic text).
19 Akel Ismail Kahera, *Reading the Islamic City: Discursive Practices and Legal Judgment* (Lanham: Lexington Books, 2012), 59–60.
20 Meunié, *Recherches archéologiques*, 42.

21 See Nuha Khoury, 'The Meaning of the Great Mosque in the Tenth Century', *Muqarnas* 13 (1996): 83.

22 Jessica Streit, 'Monumental Austerity: The Meanings and Aesthetic Development of Almohad Friday Mosques' (Ph.D. diss., Cornell University, 2013), 86–87.

23 Henri Basset and Henri Terrasse, *Sanctuaires et forteresses almohades* (Paris: Maisonneuve & Larose, 2001), 201; Deverdun, *Marrakech*, 181; and Georges Marçais, *L'architecture musulmane d'occident: Tunisie, Algérie, Maroc, Espagne et Sicilie* (Paris: Arts et métiers graphiques, 1955), 205.

24 Michael E. Bonine, 'The Sacred Direction and City Structure: A Preliminary Analysis of the Islamic Cities of Morocco', *Muqarnas* 7 (1990): 52.

25 Bonine, 'Sacred Direction and City Structure', 32.

26 Khoury, 'The Meaning of the Great Mosque in the Tenth Century', 84.

27 Kahera, *Reading the Islamic City*, 7.

28 Cornell, 'Understanding is the Mother of Ability', 96.

29 Abbey Stockstill, 'A Tale of Two Mosques: Marrakesh's Masjid al-Jami' al-Kutubiyya', *Muqarnas* 35 (2018): 70–73.

30 'Ali ibn Abi Zar', *al-Anis al-Mutrib bi-Rawd al-Qirtas fi Akhbar Muluk al-Maghrib wa-Ta'rikh Madinat Fas* (Rabat: Imprimerie Royale, 1999), 226–27; and *Al-Hulal al-Mawshiyya*, 107. For more on Igliz, see Allen J. Fromherz, 'The Almohad Mecca: Locating Igli and the Cave of Ibn Tumart', *Al-Qantara* 26.1 (2005): 175–90.

31 Mercedes García-Arenal, *Messianism and Puritanical Reform: Mahdis of the Muslim West* (Leiden, Boston: Brill, 2006), 170.

32 Fromherz, *The Almohads: The Rise of an Islamic Empire*, 61–62.

33 Ronald Messier, *The Almoravids and the Meanings of Jihad* (Santa Barbara: Praeger, 2010), 151.

34 The azimuth of the mosque at Tinmal is measured at 157°. Bonine, 'Sacred Direction and City Structure', 54.

35 Christian Ewert, *The Mosque of Tinmal (Morocco) and Some New Aspects of Islamic Architectural Typology* (London: The British Academy, 1986), 122.

36 Jonathan Bloom, *The Minaret* (Edinburgh: Edinburgh University Press, 2013), 169.

37 Bloom, *The Minaret*, 170.

38 Ahmad ibn Muhammad al-Maqqari, *Nafh al-tibb min al-Andalus al-ratib* (Beirut: Dar Sadir, 1968), 1:611–15.

39 Maribel Fierro, 'Algunas reflexiones sobre el poder itinerante almohade', *e-Spania* (2009): 7, accessed February 18, 2016, doi: 10.4000/e-spania.18653.

40 'Abd al-Wahid al-Marrakushi, *al-Mu'jib fi talkhis akhbar al-Maghrib* (Cairo: al-Majlis al-A'la li'l-Shu'un al-Islamiyya, 1963), 334, 360.

41 Joudia Hassar-Benslimane, et al., 'Tinmal 1981: Fouilles de la mosque almohade', *Bulletin d'archéologie marocaine* 14 (1981–82): 311.

42 Pascal Burési, 'Les cultes rendus à la tombe du mahdî Ibn Tûmart à Tinmâl (XIIe–XIIIe S.)', *Comptes rendus des séances de l'Ácademie des inscriptions et Belles-Lettres* 152.1 (2008): 403.

43 Burési, 'Les cultes rendus à la tombe du mahdî Ibn Tûmart à Tinmâl', 392–93. Buresi points out that scholars have used the Almohad patronage of Tinmal as evidence of tension in the Maghreb between puritanical strains of Islam and the manifestation of popular religious

practice (particularly the veneration of saints), but such an interpretation here is both ahistorical and Orientalist in origin.

44 *Kitab al-Hulal li-muwashiyya fi dhikr al-akhbar al-Marrakushiyya* (Casablanca: Dar al-Rashad al-Haditha, 1979), 108.

45 Ibn Manzur, *Lisan al-ʿArab* (Beirut: Dar Sadir, 1955–56), 5:100.

46 Ibn Fadl Allah al-ʿUmari, *Masalik al-Absar fi Mamalik al-Amsar: l'Afrique moins l'Egypte*, ed. and trans. Maurice Gaudefroy-Demombynes (Paris: Geuthner, 1927), 181.

47 Bennison, 'Power and the City in the Islamic West,' 86.

48 Al-Marrakushi, *al-Muʾjib fi talkhis akhbar al-Maghrib*, 425.

49 Ibid., 426.

50 Pascal Buresi and Hicham El Aallaoui, *Governing the Empire: Provincial Administration in the Almohad Caliphate (1224–1269)* (Leiden, Boston: Brill, 2013), 56.

51 Mohammed El Faïz, 'The Garden Strategy of the Almohad Sultans and Their Successors (1157–1900)', in *Middle East Garden Traditions: Unity and Diversity*, ed. Michel Conan (Cambridge, MA: Harvard University Press, 2007), 95.

52 Al-Marrakushi, *al-Muʾjib fi talkhis akhbar al-Maghrib*, 326. This description is confirmed by Ibn Sahib al-Salaʾs contemporaneous account, *Tarikh al-mann bil imama* (Baghdad: Al-Jumhuriya al-ʿIraqiya, 1979), 467–68.

53 See Bennison, 'The Almohads and the Qurʾan of Uthman'.

54 Al-Maqqari, *Nafh al-tibb*, 1:611.

55 Cornell, 'Understanding is the Mother of Ability', 93.

56 Ibn Abi Zarʿ, *Rawd al-Qirtas*, 330.

Section III

Liminality and Negotiating Modernity

Perform Your Prayers in Mosques!: Changing Spatial and Political Relations in Nineteenth-Century Ottoman Istanbul

A. Hilâl Uğurlu

n article published on May 29, 1852, in the *Journal de Constantinople* reported a new environmental planning project for Istanbul's Tophane district. A range of shops would be demolished so that the main street could be widened and transformed into a square that ended at the flamboyant main door of the Nusretiye Mosque (1823–26). Tophane Fountain and certain other neighbouring fountains would be renovated, and trees would be planted between the boundaries of the Artillery Barracks and the widened main street, to make the Tophane district 'the most beautiful, pleasant and healthiest promenade' of the city. This reported endeavour was only a small aspect of a larger project that began in the 1840s, after the proclamation of the Gülhane Rescript (November 3, 1839), and it was considered a physical extension of Ottoman modernization.[1] Throughout the long nineteenth century, while the urban fabric of the capital was regularized and adjusted to the expectations and needs of the ongoing modernization efforts, novel building types, such as barracks, schools, and railway stations, and new social spaces, such as parks, theatres, and promenades, emerged.[2] Many existing building types and thus the daily routines shaped by them were also affected.

Although imperial mosques that embodied these existing building types were constructed according to a new architectural approach and mentality during the long nineteenth century, they are usually studied in a way that isolates them from their urban context. Earlier scholarship emphasized their royal pavilions, which dominate their frontal facades, their increasingly vertical proportions, the diminishing size of their prayer halls, and the growing adaptation of European decoration, rather than evaluating them with respect to their spatial relationship with the city and their social interaction with their users.[3]

The aim of this paper is to explore the ways in which institutional and urban modernization processes, as well as the transformation of architectural preferences for imperial mosques, affected the relationships among the mosque, the city, and its people. I will explore this theme in three parts. First, I will briefly introduce the early modern mosques of the Ottoman capital in order to arrive at a general understanding of the spatial and social transformations that the Ottoman imperial mosques underwent. Second, I will discuss the differences between the early modern and the nineteenth-century imperial mosques in context of their relations with the city and the public. Finally, I will deal with the changing character of nineteenth-century imperial mosques and the nature of the Friday processions, focusing on the second half of the Hamidian Era (1876–1909), when stately processions reached their peak in terms of importance, yet the number of venues decreased to one.

The Early Modern Imperial Mosque Courtyard as a Public Sphere

Following the Ottoman capture of Constantinople, their first physical intervention in the city was the conversion of Hagia Sophia, the religious and political centre of Eastern Christendom, into an imperial mosque. It became the symbol of the long-awaited conquest.[4] Shortly after declaring that Constantinople was the new seat of his throne, Mehmed II (r.1444–46, 1451–81) initiated a grand and ambitious urban programme that indicated the symbolic refoundation of the city.[5] By the end of his reign, aside from his grandly scaled monumental mosque complex, which defined the new socio-religious centre of Istanbul, there were around 200 mosques and masjids built throughout the city.[6]

In his book *Hadika't-ül Cevami* (Garden of Mosques), completed in 1781, Ayvansarayî Hafız Hüseyin Efendi (d.1787) lists 821 mosques of all sizes after recounting the grand imperial mosques of the city in detail.[7] In 300 years, the number of mosques and masjids in the city had quadrupled, and the number of monumental imperial mosques had increased to ten.[8] Each of these imperial mosques, carefully placed within Constantinople's walls, on sites that would leave their mark on the city's silhouette,[9] was the centre of large socio-religious complexes; together, they formed the social nuclei of the capital.[10]

Until the late nineteenth century, when regularizing the urban fabric and clearing around historical, symbolic buildings in order to emphasize their monumentality became one of the indicators of a 'modern' city, dense residential buildings filled the spaces between these large socio-religious centres.[11] Writing in the late eighteenth century, Ayvansarayî noted that Hagia Sophia, as well as the mosques of Mehmed II (1463–70), Bayezid II (1500–06), Selim I (1522), Şehzade Sultan Mehmed (1543–48), Süleymaniye (1548–59), and Sultan Ahmed (1609–17) had their own neighbourhoods (*mahalle*).[12] Others – such as the Yeni Cami (1663), Nur-u Osmaniye (1748–55), and Laleli (1760–63) mosques, which were not surrounded by neighbourhoods – were usually located in the heart of busy commercial districts.

The borders of these mosque complexes were not as defined as those of the mosques themselves were. Dependencies such as an imaret, madrasa, library, primary school, caravanserai, or group of shops would be sited in the immediate vicinity of the mosque, and alleys between them would connect to the existing street networks. However, the liminal spaces between imperial mosques and their dependencies were more defined. The outer and inner courtyards were the thresholds of the mosques. All early modern imperial mosques in Istanbul were positioned in the midst of a green open space, which was walled off. Through this outer courtyard one could enter the hard-floored inner courtyard, which was located at the northern facade of the mosque and typically surrounded by arcades [Figure 1].

Architectural evidence such as the elaborate ablutions fountains situated in the middle of inner courtyards (and sometimes in outer courtyards) refer to the self-purification aspect of preparation that was part of the original architectural programme. It may be assumed that these spaces were also planned as gradual transition zones that would draw the visitor away from the hustle and bustle of city life and help him or her enter a more spiritual mood in preparation for the prayers inside the mosque. Following the example of the Edirne Üç

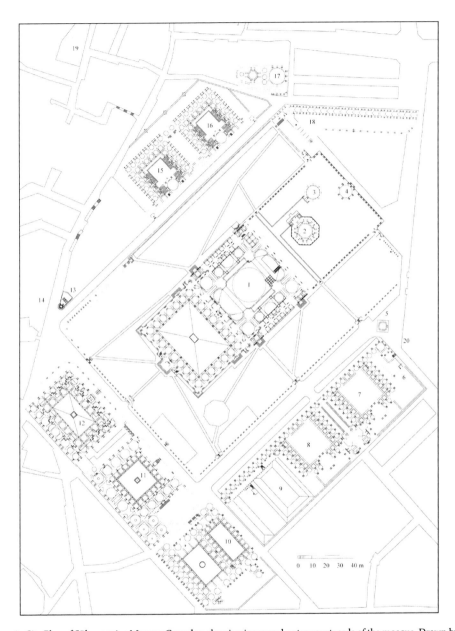

Figure 1: Site Plan of Süleymaniye Mosque Complex, showing inner and outer courtyards of the mosque. Drawn by Arben N. Arapi, Source: archnet.org. (1) mosque, (2) mausoleum of Süleyman, (3) mausoleum of Hürrem, (4) Koran recitation school, (5) public fountain, (6) elementary school, (7) first (*evvel*) madrasa, (8) second (*sani*) madrasa, (9) remains of medical school, (10) hospital, (11) hospice, (12) guesthouse, (13) Sinan's tomb with domed sabil and empty plot of his endowed school and residence, (14) the janissary agha's residence, (15) third (*salis*) madrasa, (16) fourth (*rabi*) madrasa, (17) bathhouse, (18) hadith college, (19) madrasa near the palace of Fatma Sultan and Siyavuş Pasha.

Şerefeli Mosque (1438–47), the first Ottoman imperial mosque with an inner courtyard, these areas were probably also meant to provide additional space for the congregation when the space inside the mosque itself was insufficient for communal prayers, such as Friday or Eid prayers.

On the other hand, many archival documents and other primary sources contain evidence indicating that mosque courtyards – and even mosques themselves – also became the settings for a variety of other events of daily life. In comparison to the mosques proper, where certain behavioural codes determined who could enter and in which manner, courtyards were much more accepting and embracing places. The common denominator for these open public spaces was urbanity rather than co-religiosity. These were the places where Muslim and non-Muslim Istanbulites could meet, gather, and express themselves in different ways, albeit most of the time under the control of the government. Sometimes this shared urbanity reveals itself in the notes of various events, carved on the metal rings of the column bases of the porticoes. They provide a broad array of records mostly connected to shared urban experiences, ranging from the dates of great fires that affected the city to notes concerning the departure of the Ottoman navy, from the dates of royal marriages to the restoration dates of imperial mosques.[13] At other times, the kinship of those who lived in the city would redound itself on the use of these spaces. For instance, during the 1807 rebellion, a military uprising which ended with the dethronement of Selim III (r.1789–1807), 400 janissary leaders gathered in the courtyard of Süleymaniye Mosque several times. They used it as one of their headquarters, where they made critical decisions about the course of the rebellion.[14] In contemporary times, squares and large parks meet a city's need for public space; in the pre-modern era, mosque courtyards fulfilled this need.[15] Obviously, these open public spaces were not used only when there was unrest but for all types of public social occasions. It is known that some attractions related to imperial celebrations took place in mosque courtyards. For instance, on December 30, 1808, during the imperial festivities for the birth of Fatma Sultan, the daughter of Mahmud II, a rope was hung on the minaret situated on the Kaşıkçı side of Bayezid Mosque, and an acrobat walked across it until he reached the minaret balcony.[16] Thousands of citizens who wanted to watch the show filled the Bayezid Mosque courtyard. Due to a lack of space, many people climbed up trees, to the point that some trees fell down due to the weight of the spectators. It is worth underlining that this courtyard was the Bayezid Mosque's outer courtyard, which was converted into one of the largest squares in Istanbul during the republican era.[17]

Because the Bayezid Mosque is located in the trade centre of Istanbul, various trade activities also took place in its outer courtyard. For example, butchers are known to have made sales there during the eighteenth century.[18] When archival documents are examined, it is clear that exhibitions and bazaars were present in the outer courtyards of all imperial mosques. These courtyards formed an intense commercial environment, over which the government attempted to keep firm control.[19] We can gather from orders to demolish unlicensed shops and booths in mosque courtyards that there were some unauthorized setups and sales in outer courtyards of mosques, and a struggle against them took place, but was not completely successful.[20] Commercial activities in outer courtyards sometimes also spread to the inner ones. For instance, up until the twentieth century, during the month of Ramadan, the inner courtyard arcades of many imperial mosques housed open bazaars called Ramadan Exhibitions.[21] Aside from their commercial facet, Ramadan Exhibitions, which brought together members of different social strata, also functioned as a medium through which regular people interacted with officials and, therefore, the state.[22]

Mosque courtyards also took on the role of urban shelters in the case of personal tragedies or natural disasters, mostly fires and earthquakes.[23] For almost all known fires, records indicate that Istanbulites found shelter in the inner courtyards of large mosques. These spaces took on this role in part because their building materials were more fireproof than wood and in part because they could hold large crowds and stand apart from otherwise dense urban spaces. Derviş Mustafa Efendi, in his book *Harik Risalesi*, which tells the story of two huge fires that ravaged Istanbul in 1782, describes people carrying the belongings they managed to save from the fire into the Sultan Ahmed Mosque, where they felt safe. In another big fire – referred to as the Harik-i Ekber (the greatest fire), which destroyed the Şehzadebaşı, Aksaray, and Laleli districts almost completely – those who saved their property took shelter in the Laleli Mosque and Şehzade Mosque courtyards as well as in the mosques' prayer halls. Unfortunately, however, this time the courtyard of the Laleli Mosque fell short in protecting the Istanbulites and their property. Due to the fire jumping into the inner courtyard and the mosque, around 600 people who took shelter there died. Mustafa Efendi writes that he could not forget the sight for months.[24] In books written by Ottoman historians, especially those like Selaniki, Evliya Çelebi, Şemdanizade, and Taylesanizade, who interested themselves in social life, such fire stories can be found regularly – sometimes with a happy ending, sometimes sad.[25]

In his book *Mür'it-tevarih*, the eighteenth-century historian Şemdanizade records another very interesting use of certain sultanic mosque courtyards.[26] This sometimes-snippy writer mentions men and women riding Ferris wheels, swings, and carousels placed in the courtyards of the Bayezid and Fatih mosques, among other locations.[27] Although the presence of such mixed-gender activities troubled this conservative writer, he does not seem to have been especially bothered that these activities took place in mosque courtyards rather than in other locations; he includes mosque courtyards in his list of places without putting any particular emphasis on them. If mosque courtyards had been attributed a specific sacredness, one might expect Şemdanizade to have objected explicitly to their use for mixed-gender entertainment. However, his apparent indifference suggests that their users understood mosque courtyards as broadly social spaces. These users varied according to the location of the complex as well as the functions surrounding it. For example, the primary regular visitors to the courtyards of imperial mosques that were surrounded by extensive madrasa complexes, such as the Mehmed II or Süleymaniye complexes, were the madrasa students, who most likely perceived these liminal spaces as spaces of their daily life. During the elections for student representatives, called *kemerbaşı*, on January 19, 1787, there arose a dispute that escalated into violent clashes between two student groups. In that incident, which took place in the courtyards of the Sultan Mehmed (Fatih) and Sultan Selim mosques, the main actors were the students of the many madrasas located in these very mosque complexes.[28]

The versatile use of mosque courtyards in daily life continued uninterrupted throughout the early modern era until the beginning of the twentieth century. As exemplified above, it was common to find trade, recreation, entertainment, political activities, and conflicts in those mosque courtyards – and sometimes even inside the mosques themselves. That they retained their primacy, especially in the eyes of the Istanbulites, until very late is usually ignored in studies of nineteenth-century imperial mosques.

The mosque plan with an inner courtyard – and, perhaps even more importantly, the tradition of building large mosque complexes within the city walls – came to be abandoned by the end of the eighteenth century. This architectural plan type, the last example of which is the Laleli Mosque, gave way to a single-domed, vertically elongated building type, the frontal facade of which would be covered by a large royal pavilion.[29] Possessing courtyards with less clearly delineated and more permeable boundaries, these mosques and their dependencies were not able to provide space for the urban activities that took place in the large, intramural imperial mosque complexes.

Reorganizing the Institutions, Redefining 'the City', Redesigning the Imperial Mosque

An imperial command (*hatt-ı hümayun*), part of a series of official correspondence found in the Ottoman state archives, regarding the current situation of France in 1804, states that 'the French administration was in the hands of the wretched (*esafil*) since there was no king [to rule] in France and therefore no friendship should be expected from them'. Additionally, it warns the Ottoman administration about the books concerning the 'republic' and 'freedom' that 'the wretched' published in various [local] languages, such as Greek, Armenian, and Turkish, and sent to Mora and other places within the Ottoman territories.[30] Only years after the outbreak of the French Revolution, the Ottoman rulers were forced to face nationalist ideologies that threatened the empire's territorial integrity, their basis of legitimacy, and the imperial ideology. Their first reaction to this existential challenge was an attempt to restore and reinforce the imperial system by modernizing the military as well as administrative, bureaucratic, and legal institutions.[31] These Western-inspired reforms, initial fragmented attempts of which can also be found earlier in the eighteenth century, were first introduced as a comprehensive programme, called the New Order (Nizam-ı Cedid), by Selim III (*r.*1789–1807) in 1792. Over the next fifteen years, with infrastructural requirements emerging from the military reforms, along with the rehabilitation and renovation of existing military facilities, five extensive new barrack complexes were built outside the walled city [Figure 2]. The greatest of them, Selimiye Barracks, belonged to the newly established modern central imperial army. The Selimiye Mosque, also in Üsküdar, was inaugurated on April 5, 1805, just a few years after the completion of this monumental barracks. The mosque was located on a hilltop overlooking the vast barracks building, the

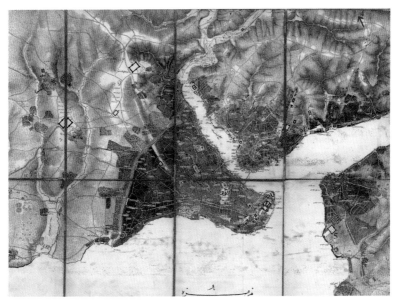

Figure 2: Barrack complexes commissioned by Selim III (*r.*1789–1807), plan of Istanbul by Helmuth von Moltke (1839). (1) Barracks for the bombardiers and miners corps *(Humbaracı ve Lağımcı Ocağı)* in Hasköy, (2) Barracks for the artillery and cannon carriers corps *(Topçu ve Top Arabacıları Ocağı)* in Tophane, (3) Barracks for the artillery and cannon carriers corps *(Topçu ve Top Arabacıları Ocağı)* in Taksim, (4) Levend Çiftliği, (5) Selimiye Barracks.

compound surrounding it, and the walled city. Selim III's clear preference for the location of his eponymous mosque underscored the importance he placed on the military reforms and also announced the personal connection between his new army and the city across the Bosphorus.

The Selimiye Mosque was located diagonally within a walled enclosure, on the northeast side of which a primary school, timekeeper's office, bathhouse, and fountains were aligned. When entering the courtyard, one would see the elongated northern facade of the mosque instead of the inner courtyard that all previously constructed imperial mosques possessed [Figure 3]. Its five-bay entrance portico led to the cubical prayer hall, which was smaller than most of the imperial mosques built in the walled city – and equivalent in size to royal women's mosques, such as the Ayazma Mosque, built in 1760–61 by Mustafa III, father of Selim III, in memory of his mother and brother.[32] On each side of the entrance portico were slender minarets and the two block-like lateral wings of the royal pavilion, which extended beyond the width of the prayer hall, the archetype of which could be found on the entrance facade of the Beylerbeyi Mosque (1778), built by Abdülhamid I in memory of his mother.

The imposing impact of the royal pavilion (*hünkar dairesi*) on the entrance facade of the mosque and the location of the royal tribune (*hünkar mahfili*) within the prayer hall were the continuation of an architectural experiment that began in the mid-eighteenth century.[33] It was also the first implementation of this spatial organization in an imperial mosque built for and by the sultan. In earlier classical mosques, the sultan's elevated tribune, a platform on

Figure 3: Site plan of the Üsküdar Selimiye Mosque. Courtesy of Avunduk Mimarlık.

slender columns, was situated in the southeast corner of the prayer hall. It was only accessed through a modest private royal entrance and a narrow staircase. This simple architectural solution gave way to an elaborate scheme in the seventeenth century, with the attachment of a royal pavilion to the southeast of the mosque from the exterior. The sultan would enter this royal pavilion through an elaborate gate and a wide ramp, rather than via the unpretentious entrance, and would directly reach his elevated platform inside the mosque from there.[34] In addition, the pavilions contained rooms in which he and his entourage could rest after prayer. These royal pavilions created an imperial focal point near the mosque and stressed the prominence of the sultan. Additionally, the tribunes placed the sultan above and in front of his subjects, underlining both his privileged position and his religiosity, which was a fundamental component of imperial legitimacy.[35] However, in Selimiye the royal pavilion was situated above the entrance on the northern wall of the prayer hall, and the royal tribune was now a part of this pavilion, which was connected to the prayer hall through an arched opening [Figure 4]. This new spatial organization shifted the sultan's place in the prayer hall from anterior to posterior but provided him a more spacious palatial setting in a more liminal zone between the mosque and the city. This alteration, which set the trend for later imperial mosques, also suggested an architectural and ideological change in which the visibility of the state was more central and dominant.

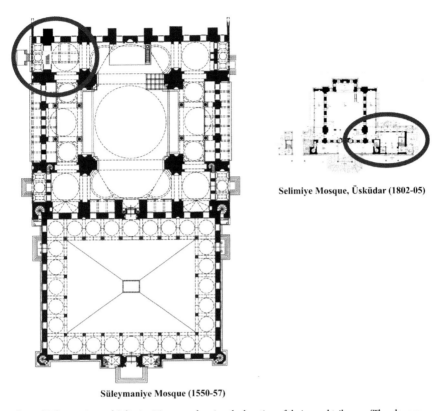

Selimiye Mosque, Üsküdar (1802-05)

Süleymaniye Mosque (1550-57)

Figure 4: Plans of Süleymaniye and Selimiye Mosques, showing the location of their royal tribunes. (The plans are proportional to each other) Left: Drawn by Arben N. Arapi, Source: archnet.org; Right: Courtesy of Avunduk Mimarlık.

The Selimiye Mosque's departure from architectural tradition was not limited to its location or its spatial organization but also included its status within the complex. Apart from its dependencies, it was also accompanied by numerous shops, a printing house, a bakery, various factories and workshops, and shoreline facilities for rowers and porters, all of which maintained fundamental spheres for urban life to flourish within the new military compound.[36] However, unprecedentedly, the mosque itself no longer constituted the focus of the complex. This was the most significant feature that distinguished the imperial mosques of the long nineteenth century from their predecessors. These mosques were mostly secondary buildings, shaped as satellites of military or palatial complexes. They no longer functioned as the chief determinants of daily life but took part in a social life shaped in accordance with the nature of the complex of which they were a part. Consequently, courtyards, which were the social spaces of classical imperial mosques, disappeared from the later mosques because the complexes of the late period already featured new social spaces that stemmed from their own raison d'être. For example, there were outdoor and indoor training areas in the barracks built in the late eighteenth and nineteenth centuries, where soldiers could congregate for various reasons. Therefore, the mosque did not need additional gathering spaces around it.

The barracks complexes built at the beginning of the long nineteenth century were located on the outskirts of the city as fully equipped urban centres. While the Selimiye barracks complex, as mentioned above, was built in the periphery of Üsküdar, occupying the grounds of the erstwhile Kavak Palace, the barracks for the Bombardiers and Miners Corps (Humbaracı ve Lağımcı Ocağı) were located in Hasköy, on the northern banks of the Golden Horn. Levend Çiftliği was situated further north, close to one of the main water supplies of the city. New barracks for the Cannon Carriers (Top Arabacıları) were located near the existing artillery barracks (Topçu Kışlaları) in Tophane, where the imperial cannon foundry (Tophane-i Amire) had been located for 300 years. Also, an additional barracks complex for the Artillery Corps (Topçu Ocağı) was built on the grounds of a mulberry orchard in Taksim, situated at the outer periphery of Pera [Figure 2]. In just a few decades, more were added to these barracks. However, this time most of them were situated in the valley behind the Beşiktaş waterfront palace, signalling major urban developments that would create a secondary centre for the capital.

In fact, the urban growth beyond the city walls, which occurred along the Golden Horn tributary but mostly along the suburban banks of the Bosphorus, had begun more than a century before.[37] However, there were scattered settlements both along the Golden Horn and to the north of the walled city of Galata.[38] In the second quarter of the nineteenth century, this growth became a full-scale urban transformation, which stemmed from the implementation of reforms based on Western models. When the Beşiktaş waterfront palace was rebuilt as the Dolmabahçe Palace by Sultan Abdülmecid I (r. 1839–61) and became the permanent residence of the court in 1856, subsequent imperial building activities mainly clustered behind it. The shoreline between Tophane and Dolmabahçe Palace, the road between Taksim and Şişli – which also defined an interface between the newly established neighbourhoods for Muslim and non-Muslim elites – and finally the street that connected Dolmabahçe Palace to Teşvikiye formed the sides of a large zone that functioned as a new centre. Large barracks buildings, military schools and hospitals, new neighbourhoods, and the facilities necessary for a modern palace were all located in that area.

During this time, Abdülmecid I and his two successors, Abdülaziz (1861–76) and Abdülhamid II (1876–1908), built (or decided to build) their mosques in and around this new centre, along the shores of Bosphorus. Besides practical reasons – such as the lack of space in the walled city, or the affordability of smaller mosques along the seashore – the main reason for this choice of location must have been the need for symbolic and visual Islamic predominance in creating the new 'modern' centre, which was situated close to the centuries-old non-Muslim centre of the capital. The proclamation of the Gülhane Rescript in 1839, as part of the modernization process, changed the balance and hierarchy between different confessional communities. Although the protection of the rights of all subjects, regardless of religious belief, was promised, the rulers needed to stress that the state's affiliation was with Islam.[39] Unease among Muslim subjects was a major concern.[40] The mosques that were built in the nineteenth century, with a novel architectural fashion and a new mentality, on the shores of the Bosphorus were thus creating the required dominant Islamic element in the silhouette of the new centre of the capital, similar to the silhouette of the walled city.

On an individual basis, they were built within or in very close proximity to the imperial palaces in which the sultans predominantly resided. Bezm-i Alem Valide Sultan Mosque was close to Dolmabahçe Palace; both the Küçük Mecidiye Mosque in Çırağan and the Büyük Mecidiye Mosque in Ortaköy hugged Çırağan Palace; the Aziziye Mosque was planned to be built behind the Dolmabahçe Mosque, at the place today known as Taşlık; finally, the Hamidiye Mosque and Yıldız Palace had a similar spatial relationship [Figure 5a-b]. They all were built by these sultans as small, semi-private mosques that belonged mainly to the palaces to which they were attached.

The interior spatial capacities of the later mosques were drastically smaller than their predecessors'. While a maximum of 400 people could fit for prayers in Yıldız Hamidiye Mosque, or 300 people in Büyük Mecidiye Mosque in Ortaköy, the capacity of Süleymaniye Mosque was 6000. Comparing the number of employees listed in the charitable foundations of Süleymaniye and Mecidiye Mosques in Çırağan makes it apparent that this dramatic spatial reduction also affected the number of people working in the imperial mosques [Figure 6]. The numbers of imams and preachers (*hatip* and *vaiz*) were similar, and the decrease in the number of muezzins could easily be explained by the decrease in the number of minarets from four to one. Likewise, the decrease in the number of employees working in support services could be related to the relatively limited requirements of a smaller space. However, the 213 people who were employed to recite certain prayers at specific times in the Süleymaniye Mosque were absent from the Mecidiye Mosque. Instead, a few of these recitations were made the duties of the first imam. Nine people (one *duagu şeyh* and eight *hatimhan*) were temporarily employed for special occasions. In addition to the differences between the relative centrality of their locations and their sizes, the scaling down of performances communicating the 'multi-sensorial messages of the divine' in the mosque signalled a change in the frequency and habits of users of the Mecidiye Mosque.[41] From the beginning of the nineteenth century, the increase in the number of official documents that warn Muslims to perform the five daily prayers in the mosques and request imams to inform judges (*kadı*) about people who did not attend mosques – and even order the punishment of people who did not attend prayers in mosques without a reasonable excuse – also indicate the changing praxes.[42] In one of the orders directed to the Chief Judge of Istanbul, the small size of congregations in the mosques and masjids of the capital was related directly to the Muslim Istanbulites' failure to perform the five daily prayers in these places.[43]

Seemingly, the imperial mosques of the nineteenth century were intended to serve the inhabitants of the neighbourhoods around them. For instance, the main purpose of the Yıldız Hamidiye Mosque's construction was stated in an archival document as 'to make the inhabitants of neighbourhoods close by the exalted imperial palace and the members of the army a partner of the virtues of the five times prayer' (*saray-ı mualla-yı tacidarileri*

Figure 5a–b: Photograph and site plan showing the spatial relationship of Bezm-i Alem Valide Sultan Mosque and Dolmabahçe Palace.

People responsible for reciting certain prayers at certain times (*Duaguyan*)	Number of people designated for the position in the *waqfiyya*	Number of people designated for the position in the *waqfiyya* of **Çırağan Mecidiye Mosque**
Cüzhan	120	0
Devirhan	10	First Imam
En'amcı	41	0
Yasinhan	1	First Imam
Tebarekehan	1	0
Ammehan	1	First Imam
Mühellil	20	0
Salavathan	10	0
Meddah	1	0
Muarrif	1	0
Musalli	6	0
Religious Officials		
Imam	2	2
Orator (*hatip*)	1	First Imam
Muezzin	24	3
Preacher (*vaiz*)	1	1
Maintanance support services		
Time keeper (*muvakkit*)	1	0
Qur'an reciter (*hafız-ı mushaf*)	2	0
Distributor and collector of Qur'an fascicles (*müteferrik-i ecza*)	4	0
Overseer (*noktacı*)	2	0
Door keeper (*bevvab*)	2	1
Care taker (*kayyum*)	10	0
Sweeper (*ferras*)	2	0
Garbage collector (*kennas*)	2	0
Protector of the mosque perimeter (*nazır'ül-cudran*)	1	0
Supervisor of the oil lamps and illumination (*sirâcî*)	8	0
Incence lighter (*buhurî*)	1	0
Person responsible for filling pitchers for ablutions (*ibrikçi*)	1	0
Gardener (*bağban*)	1	0
Gas lamp lighter and custodian of the imperial lodge (*gazcı ve mahfel-i daire hümayun bekçisi*)	0	1

Figure 6: Chart showing the number of employees listed in the charitable foundations of Süleymaniye and Çırağan Mecidiye Mosques. *Sources:* Kemal Edib Kürkçüoğlu ed., *Süleymaniye Vakfiyesi* (Ankara: Vakıflar Umum Müdürlüğü Nesriyati, 1962); Şefaattin Deniz, 'Sultan Abdülmecid Vakıflarından Çırağan Mecidiye Camii', *Vakıflar Dergisi* 43 (2015), 105–118.

civarındaki mahallat-ı islamiye ahalisiyle efrad-ı asakir-i nizamiye evkat-ı hamsede fezail-i cemaatten hissedar bilmek).[44] However, in contrast to the abundance of sources regarding various aspects of daily life in and around early modern mosques, there is hardly any evidence that this mosque was frequented by the 'desired' users or that it became a backdrop for any aspect of daily city life other than flamboyant Friday processions. When Friday ceremonies took place in these late Ottoman imperial mosques, the intended relationship that people would have had with the mosque was designed according to the perception from the outside. Seen from this perspective, the 'royal pavilions' (*hünkâr kasırları*), which overshadowed the mosques' prayer areas in terms of both scale and spatial organization, acquired a different meaning. It is certainly not surprising that, in a semi-private imperial mosque, the architectural aspect that represented the sultan himself was grander and more ostentatious. Another change in architectural design, the disappearance of the inner courtyard, is also meaningful in this regard. The inner courtyard became unacceptable by virtue of being an architectural element that would separate the royal pavilion, which symbolized the ruler, from the city and its people.

Friday Processions and 'The Mosque'

In the beginning of the eighteenth century, the Ottoman court was forced to return to the capital after 46 years of residence in Edirne following an upheaval in 1703, referred to as the Edirne Incident. The royal presence in Istanbul was critical to Istanbulites; thus, the court's visibility in the city became an essential tool in strengthening its legitimacy. New occasions for sacred ceremonies and secular festivals were instituted, and old ones were revived.[45] One of the key occasions on which the sultan could be seen and accessed by his subjects regularly was his procession to the Friday prayers in one of the city's mosques. These were not perceived as stately processions, as were the processions performed on religious holidays.

While eighteenth-century sources either do not mention the sultan's weekly visits to imperial mosques or give only the name of the mosque that was visited, nineteenth-century travellers' accounts provide detailed information on the Friday processions. For example, the geologist Hugh Edwin Strickland (*d.*1853), who visited Istanbul in 1836, recounts the visit of Sultan Mahmud II to a 'small mosque on the hill called Yeni-Djamie' for a Friday prayer. He writes, 'There was nothing very striking in the procession, which consisted of a few guards, pages, nobles and several of the Sultan's horses, in the midst of which Mahmoud himself appeared.'[46] He also seems not to have been impressed by the number of people who assembled to see the procession, which he reported was at most 100.

Another English traveller, Albert Smith, who spent a month in Istanbul in 1849, gives a detailed description of the Friday procession of Sultan Abdülmecid to the Beylerbeyi Mosque. He also expresses his disappointment: 'A dream of the Arabian Night had been somewhat harshly dispelled. I had seen a sultan and but for his fez, he might have passed for a simple foreign gentleman from Leicester Square.'[47]

Unlike the earlier, peripatetic Ottoman sultans of the eighteenth and nineteenth centuries, who seasonally moved between palaces and performed Friday prayers in different mosques every week, Abdülhamid II opted for a single centre of gravity, Yıldız Palace, where he resided in a semi-secluded fashion. This choice was a physical manifestation of Abdülhamid II's goal to consolidate and retain the power that had shifted toward the Sublime Porte (Bab-ı 'Ali) through the nineteenth century.[48] The Hamidiye Mosque, built within the boundaries of this palace by the end of 1885, acted as the palace's interface with the city.[49] In fact, it was transformed into 'the mosque' for that period. It was the sultan's predominant choice for all stately processions and the only place where his subjects encountered his physical presence. At a time when the central role of the caliphate was emphasized, these weekly ceremonies also helped construct the illusion of the caliph as a permanent and immobile centre.[50] I argue that making the Hamidiye Mosque the ultimate destination of these grandiose Friday processions and turning the masses from all over the city into essential participants, altered the physical boundaries of the mosque on a weekly basis, transforming the environs of the mosque into its courtyard and the city as a whole into a vast liminal space.

Georgina Adelaide Müller, the philologist Max Müller's wife, who watched one of the Friday ceremonies that took place in the Hamidiye Mosque in 1894, gives a detailed account of this procession. She notes that about 8000 soldiers were situated around the mosque. The carts that brought female dynasty members were waiting inside the courtyard, and the courtyard was filled with pashas, the sultan's aides-de-camp, and other state dignitaries in their elaborate uniforms. Going through this crowd, climbing the stairs that led to his private space in the royal pavilion, and returning to his palace using the same route was the sultan's only visible role in this procession. After the sultan took his place, pashas rushed inside the mosque using the main entrance, in order to join the prayer. Since the prayer hall could not accommodate all of the guests, prayer rugs were carried out to the courtyard for everyone to be able to participate.

Ambassadors and their companions, travellers and journalists who obtained permission to observe the ceremonies, and dignitaries who expected to be received by the sultan after the prayer, would watch the procession from embassy kiosks across from the Hamidiye Mosque, near the entrance to the palace.[51] Attending the Friday processions was mandatory for all the princes and dignitaries as well as selected high-ranking officers, and it was unacceptable for anyone to be absent without a valid excuse. Attendance and absences (along with reasons for absence), as well as ranks, official posts, classes, and the names of dignitaries and officers, were recorded in very detailed weekly charts. According to a chart prepared for the Friday procession that took place on March 20, 1908, 120 high-ranking officers were expected to attend, aside from the military corps.[52] This number changed from week to week, and the accounts were kept on a regular basis. There was also a section on these charts where opinions about each person were noted, which reveals the importance of Friday prayers as a tool of superintendence. This way both civilian dignitaries and military officers were constantly monitored by the central authority and had to declare their absolute obedience to the sultan periodically.

Another significant alteration to the Friday processions during the Hamidian Era was the regular and broad participation of numerous military regiments in the ceremony. A few days before every procession, various military groups would be summoned to attend the Friday ceremony. The pompous march of those regiments, accompanied by anthems, would start from their barracks, located in different corners of the capital. Using various routes, they would approach the Hamidiye Mosque in Yıldız, where they lined up and paid their tributes to their commander-in-chief. Among these military groups were regiments formed by soldiers from all over the empire, such as the Plevna regiment, the Albanian Imperial Guard Battalion known as Fesli Zuhaf, the Arab Imperial Guard Battalion known as Sarıklı Zuhaf, and the Ertuğrul Cavalry Guard Regiment, named after the eponymous father of Osman Gazi, the first sultan. The composite character of the regiments marching through the city every week would point to the grandeur of the empire as well as of the sultan himself.

Samuel Sullivan Cox, an American congressman who came to Istanbul in 1885 with a diplomatic mission, wrote in his memoirs:

> What a splendid attraction it is for the populace of Constantinople! What a fete day once every week! What a variety of the soldiers! What a changeable aspect the soldiers present from week to week! Today a regiment from Soudan, tomorrow a battalion from Albania. Each Friday there is a new greeting to new people of strange and distant parts of the World.[53]

The new concept of 'Ottoman Citizenry'[54] that the Abdülhamid administration proposed, to unite all Muslim elements – irrespective of ethnicity – under the only legitimate authority, the sultan himself, is reflected in this account. It also draws a picture in which the whole city becomes the stage for the Friday procession. A series of documents found in the Ottoman archives reveals which regiments attended which Friday processions and from which barracks they came.[55] According to these documents, from the 1890s onward, the groups attending the Friday processions came to be standardized: one battalion from the Ministry of War (Bab-ı Seraskeri), ten battalions from the vicinity of Yıldız, the fourth cavalry regiment from the Gümüşsuyu barracks and Şişli and Zincirli guardhouses, the Ertuğrul Cavalry regiment – some from Davudpaşa barracks and some from the vicinity of Yıldız Palace, the First Lancer Cavalry Regiment (*süvari mızraklı birinci alayı*) from Davudpaşa, a troop from the Beyoğlu Bombardiers Barracks, and the naval battalion from the imperial arsenal. Although the number of soldiers varied from week to week, the participation of these regiments became a regular feature of the ceremony [Figure 7].

The march of these large groups of soldiers along various routes through the city every Friday probably created a new routine in the daily life of Istanbulites. Fausto Zonaro (*d*.1929), the court painter of Sultan Abdülhamid II, portrayed a very lively scene from this routine in one of his paintings, in which he depicted the Ertuğrul Cavalry regiment passing through the Galata Bridge on the march from their barracks in Davudpaşa to Yıldız [Figure 8]. In his memoirs, he also described his first encounter with the Ertuğrul Cavalry, on a Friday morning in the spring of 1894. He first portrays the soundscape by recounting the 'rather familiar march approaching from a distance', the 'March of the Ertuğrul Regiment', and 'the rhythmic sounds of the trained horse's shoes'. Then, he continues,

Figure 7: Abdülhamid II going to the Hamidiye Mosque for a Friday Prayer, surrounded by soldiers.

Figure 8: Fausto Zonaro, 'The Imperial Regiment of the Ertugrul on the Galata Bridge'. Courtesy of the National Palaces Painting Museum, Istanbul.

I stand leaning against the railing on the left side of the Bridge, and there, in front of the scene of distant mosques appears a stream of red pennons and the white silhouettes of the horses can be distinguished. I wait.

The regiment approaches in strict lines, their footsteps in tune with the music. It is an extraordinary spectacle. I watch this official parade with great interest. First the music, then the Commander Pasha, the officers, followed by the Regimental Banner and snow-white horses arranged in lines with their stiff-backed, sparkling cavalrymen in their green uniforms, and in a dazzling light, the red pennants rising up to the fiery sunfilled sky.[56]

A very detailed attendance chart, from approximately six years after Zonaro's first encounter with the Ertuğrul regiment, informs us that 388 cavalries and 61 soldiers from the court band unit (*mızıka bölüğü*) marched from the Davudpaşa Barracks to the Yıldız Hamidiye Mosque on August 17, 1900, for the procession [Figure 9].[57]

To understand the dynamism that Friday processions created throughout the city, one should imagine a scene in which approximately 500 soldiers, at least 80 per cent of them on their horses, leave their barracks in Davudpaşa. Along the way, they meet up with another regiment of 500 coming from their barracks in Rami, located, like Davudpaşa, in the outer peripheries of the city. Entering the city from Edirnekapı as a group of 1000 soldiers, most of them on their horses, they march along the road near Fatih Mosque and join another regiment (*1. fırka 1. tabur*) coming from the Ministry of War (Bab-ı Seraskeri), comprising at least 100 soldiers on foot. Those 1100 soldiers, most on horseback, would march together in great splendour through the narrow roads of the walled city. After they crossed the Galata Bridge, they would go to Beşiktaş. Meanwhile, another military group would take the Kasımpaşa–Şişhane–Cadde-i Kebir (today İstiklal Caddesi)–Maçka–Beşiktaş route, and, after joining the previously mentioned group, they would parade up the steep hill toward the Hamidiye Mosque [Figure 10].[58]

The music played, the noise and the dusty smell of the horses filled the air, the uniforms and banners of the regiments created a dense visual picture as they marched, one after another, through the city. And then, a still, deep silence, followed by organized chanting of 'long live the Sultan' (*padişahım çok yaşa*) at the Hamidiye Mosque. These sensory experiences allowed people who lived in different parts of the city to temporarily move into a liminal state of mind, between their daily routines and the extravagant procession that sought to trigger the feeling of belonging to a grand empire by being part of such a vast procession as a proud citizen. Although it had a limited inner space, the Hamidiye Mosque, as the centre stage of this weekly performance, used its own vicinity, namely the Yıldız Valley, as an outer courtyard, thus redefining its own boundaries [Figure 11]. The absolute silence around the mosque also created yet another threshold between the mosque and the rest of the city.

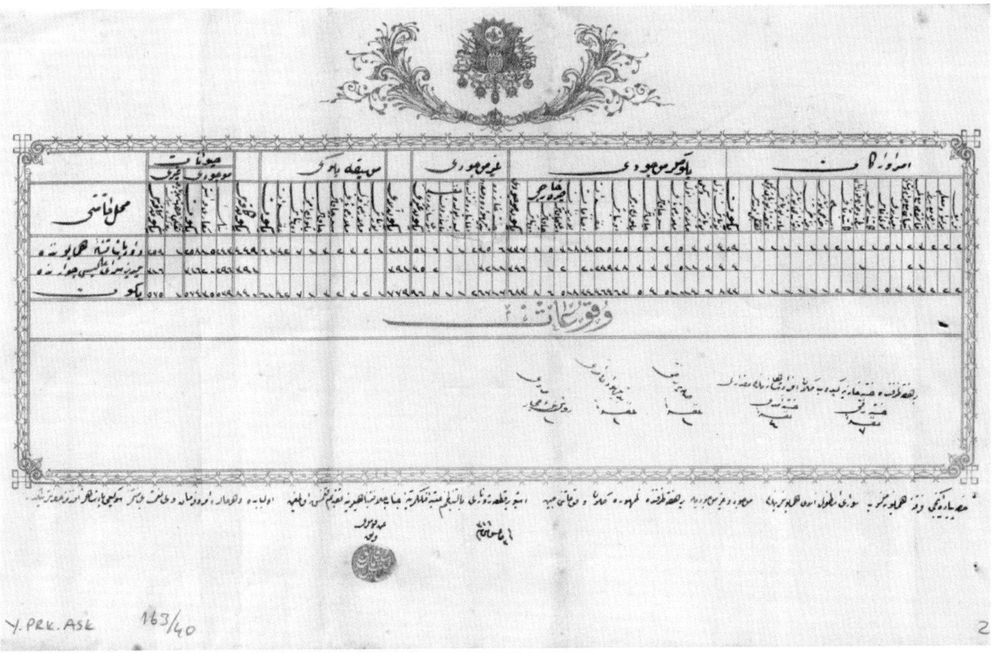

mahall-i ikameti	hayvanat – gayri – yekun-ı kaffesi	hayvanat – gayri – tüfenkçi-i hazret-i şehriyari bölüğünde	hayvanat – mevcudi – yekun	hayvanat – mevcudi – merkubi ve ester	hayvanat – mevcudi – binek	yekun-ı kaffesi	musika bölüğü – yekun	musika bölüğü – neferat	musika bölüğü – onbaşı	musika bölüğü – bölük emini	musika bölüğü – çavuş	musika bölüğü – ser çavuş	musika bölüğü – mülazım-ı sani	musika bölüğü – mülazım-ı evvel	musika bölüğü – yüzbaşı	yekun-ı alay
davudpaşa kışla-i hümayununda	259	1	258	15	243	449	61	42	7	1	3	2	3	2	1	388
yıldız sarayı aliyyesi civarında	316		316	20	296	391										391
yekun	575	1	574	35	539	840	61	42	7	1	3	2	3	2	1	779

mahall-i ikameti	gayr-ı mevcudu – yekun-ı gayri	gayr-ı mevcudu – neferen – alay-ı sairede	gayr-ı mevcudu – neferen – na-mezun	gayr-ı mevcudu – neferen – Liverpol'da	gayr-ı mevcudu – Almanya'da, Fransa'da	gayr-ı mevcudu – tebdil-i havada ve sılada	gayr-ı mevcudu – hastahanede	yekun-ı mevcudu – yekun-ı mevcudu	yekun-ı mevcudu – sıra harici – onbaşı	yekun-ı mevcudu – sıra harici – çavuş	yekun-ı mevcudu – sıra harici – alay çavuşu	yekun-ı mevcudu – borozan	yekun-ı mevcudu – esnafat	yekun-ı mevcudu – Neferat	yekun-ı mevcudu – onbaşı	yekun-ı mevcudu – bölük emini	yekun-ı mevcudu – çavuş	yekun-ı mevcudu – ser çavuş	yekun-ı mevcudu – mülazım-ı sani	yekun-ı mevcudu – mülazım-ı evvel	yekun-ı mevcudu – yüzbaşı vekili	yekun-ı mevcudu – yüzbaşı-yı evvel
davudpaşa kışla-i hümayununda	51	6	1	1	2	35	6	337	8	5	3	18	14	215	25	2	1	2	5	3	3	4
yıldız sarayı aliyyesi civarında	45	2				32	11	346		1	2		20	249	38	3	3	3	5	11	3	4
yekun	96	8	1	1	2	67	17	683	8	6	5	18	24	464	63	5	4	5	10	14	6	8

mahall-i ikameti	merâ ve erkân – yekun	merâ ve erkân	tüfenkçi ustası	sancakdar yüzbaşı vekili	yaver yüzbaşı	esvabcı yüzbaşı	eczacı	eczacı yüzbaşı	imam	katib-i sani	baytar ve cerrah kol ağası	katib-i alay	kolağası	emin-i alay	binbaşı ma'a cerrah ve misafir	kaimakam ma'a tabib	miralay ma'a baytar	mirliva ve muallim	ferik
davudpaşa kışla-i hümayununda	29		1	1	1	1	1	1	2	1	2	1	5	1	2	3	2	2	2
yıldız sarayı aliyyesi civarında	4										1				2	1			
yekun	33		1	1	1	1	1	1	2	1	3	1	5	1	4	4	2	2	2

vukuat

firari
macar
1

tebdil-i havadan amedi
neferen
1

sılaya refti
neferen
1

bir hafta zarfında hastahaneye gidub gelen efrad-ı şahanenin mikdarı
hasta-i amedi neferen 4
hasta-i refti neferen 7

hassa piyade ikinci fırka-i hümayuna mensub süvari anadolu alay-ı hümayunlarının mevcud ve gayr-ı mevcuduyla bir hafta zarfında zuhura gelen vukuatını mübeyyin işbu bir kıta jurnali bi't-tanzim atabe-i felek mertebe-i cenab-ı Hilafet-penahilerine takdim kılınmış olmağın ol babda ve herhalde emr u ferman veliyy-i nimet-i bi-minnetimiz sevgili padişahımız efendimiz hazretlerinindir.
an-kulları: ferik süleyman faik b. halil   fi 3 agustos sene [1]316

Figure 9: Document showing the detailed attendance chart to the Friday Procession in 17.08.1900, Ottoman Archives Y.PRK.ASK 163-40/2.

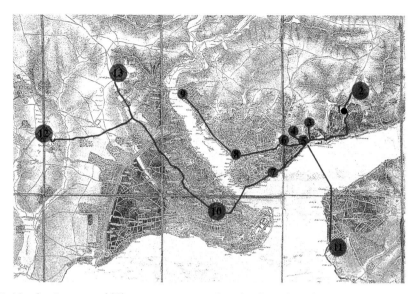

Figure 10: Map showing routes of different regiments going from their barracks to the Hamidiye Mosque. *Drawn by the author.* Plan of Istanbul by Helmuth von Moltke (1839). (1) Hamidiye Mosque in Yıldız, (2) Ertuğrul and Orhaniye Barracks behind the Yıldız Palace, (3) Maçka Barracks, (4) Mecidiye Artillery Barracks (*Taşkışla*), (5) Gümüşsuyu Barracks, (6) Barracks for the artillery and cannon carriers corps (*Topçu ve Top Arabacıları Ocağı*) in Taksim, (7) Barracks for the artillery and cannon carriers corps (*Topçu ve Top Arabacıları Ocağı*) in Tophane, (8) Imperial arsenal, (9) Barracks for the bombardiers and miners corps (*Humbaracı ve Lağımcı Ocağı*) in Hasköy, (10) Ministry of War near Bayezid Square, (11) Selimiye Barracks in Üsküdar, (12) Davudpaşa Barracks, (13) Rami Barracks.

Figure 11: Photograph showing a part of the Yıldız valley during a Friday procession.

Conclusion

The imperial mosques of Istanbul were not only monumental buildings that symbolized imperial power and authority but also spaces that were socially produced by the people of Istanbul. This paper illustrated the changing relationship between the imperial mosques of Istanbul and the city during the long nineteenth century, from a bottom-up perspective, by exploring how spatial experiences and practices in and around these mosques changed over time.

As stated in the first section of this paper, in the early modern era the imperial mosques were all located inside the city walls of Istanbul and were enclosed by organically formed residential or commercial areas. Although the boundaries of the liminal spaces between the mosques and the city were defined by high walls surrounding the mosques, their functions were not. With the diverse functions that took place within them, these liminal spaces, namely the inner and outer courtyards of imperial mosques, formed the nuclei of social life.

Like the city itself, imperial mosques were adapted to the changing needs of the state, especially during the long nineteenth century, when the administrative and socioeconomic structure of the empire was transformed. These new imperial mosques were located outside of the walled city, mostly within newly established barracks or palatial complexes. They were no longer the focus of the complexes of which they were parts, and although they were physically more connected to their environments, with their almost non-existent boundaries and light, porous walls, the social life around them was not as lively as that of their predecessors. While the early modern imperial mosques retained their primacy in the life of the city until the last days of the empire, the later imperial mosques were mostly perceived by their users as scenes of spectacle.

Acknowledgements

I would like to acknowledge the support of the Research Center for Anatolian Civilizations (ANAMED) at Koç University, the Istanbul Research Institute, SALT and The Barakat Trust during various stages of my research. I would also like to thank Sibel Bozdoğan, Elvan Cobb, Ezgi Dikici, Cemal Kafadar, Hakan Karateke, K. Mehmet Kentel, Meredith Moss Quinn, Akın Sefer, Melis Taner, Deniz Türker, and Suzan Yalman for their invaluable insights and constructive criticism.

Notes

1   For detailed information on the regularization of the capital's urban fabric during the nineteenth century, see Zeynep Çelik, *The Remaking of Istanbul* (Berkeley and Los Angeles: University of California Press, 1986), 49–82.

2   Çelik, *Remaking of Istanbul*; and Yonca Köksal, 'Urban Space and Nationalism: Changing Local Networks in the Nineteenth Century Ottoman Empire', in *Social and Historical Studies on Greece and Turkey*, eds Çağlar Keyder and Thalia Dragonas (New York: I. B. Tauris, 2010), 35–52.

3   Doğan Kuban, *Türk Barok Mimarisi Hakkında Bir Deneme* (Istanbul: İTÜ Mimarlık Fakültesi, 1954); Godfrey Goodwin, *A History of Ottoman Architecture* (London: Thames and Hudson, 1971); Ayda Arel, *Onsekizinci Yüzyıl Istanbul Mimarisinde Batılılaşma Süreci* (Istanbul: İTÜ Mimarlık Fakültesi Baskı Atölyesi, 1975); Aptullah Kuran, 'The Evolution of the Sultan's Pavilion in Ottoman Imperial Mosques', *Islamic Art* 4 (1990–91): 281–300; Betül Bakır, *Mimaride Rönesans ve Barok: Osmanlı Başkenti Istanbul'da Etkileri* (Ankara: Nobel Yayın Dağıtım, 2003); and Gözde Çelik, 'Sultan Abdülmecid'in Istanbul'da Yaptırdığı Camiler', in *Nakş-ı Istanbul – Ortaköy Büyük Mecidiye Camii*, ed. Ahmet Uçar (Istanbul: Gürsoy Grup, 2015), 121–53.

4   Çiğdem Kafescioğlu, *Constantinopolis/Istanbul: Cultural Encounter, Imperial Vision and the Construction of the Ottoman Capital* (Pennsylvania: Pennsylvania State University Press, 2007), 18–22.

5   For a general overview of building activities in Istanbul after 1453, see Halil İnalcık, 'Istanbul: An Islamic City', *Journal of Islamic Studies* 1 (1990): 1–23; Kafescioğlu, *Constantinopolis/ Istanbul*; and Gülru Necipoğlu, 'From Byzantine Constantinople to Ottoman Kostantiniyye: Creation of a Cosmopolitan Capital and Visual Culture under Sultan Mehmed II', in *From Byzantion to Istanbul: 8000 Years of a Capital* (Istanbul: Kitap Yayınevi, 2010), 263–76.

6   In *Fatih Devri*, Ayverdi lists 192 mosques in Istanbul. In *Istanbul Vakıfları Tahrir Defteri*, he and Barkan list 190 mosques in addition to 17 converted churches. See Ekrem Hakkı Ayverdi, *Fatih Devri Mimarisi*, vol. 3 (Istanbul: İstanbul Fetih Cemiyeti Neşriyatı, 1953), 538–41, Ömer Lütfi Barkan and Ekrem Hakkı Ayverdi, *İstanbul Vakıfları Tahrir Defteri: 953* (1546) *târîhli*, (Istanbul: Baha Matbaası, 1970), 11.

7   Ayvansarayi Hafız Hüseyin Efendi, Ali Satı Efendi, and Süleyman Besim Efendi, *Hadikatü'l-Cevami (İstanbul Camileri ve Diğer Dini-Sivil Mimari Yapılar)*, vols. 1–2, ed. Ahmed Nezih Galitekin (Istanbul: İşaret Yayınları, 2001).

8   These ten mosques were Hagia Sophia, the Mosques of Mehmed II, Bayezid II, Selim I, and Şehzade Sultan Mehmed, as well as Süleymaniye, Sultan Ahmed, Valide Sultan (in Eminönü), [Nur-u] Osmaniye, and Laleli Mosques.

9   For detailed information on the location selection criteria for the classical imperial mosques of Istanbul, see Gülru Necipoğlu, *The Age of Sinan: Architectural Culture in the Ottoman Empire* (London: Reaktion Books, 2007), 117.

10 The Friday mosques that were built by the women of the dynasty were smaller in size, less grandiose, and lacked some of the architectural features that were considered imperial prerogatives, such as marble-paved inner courtyards or multiple minarets with several galleries. Most of them were surrounded by dependencies such as madrasas, public baths, imarets, or caravanserais, creating a rich sociocultural environment around them. They would either be located intra muros where certain social functions were deficient or needed, such as in the case of Haseki Complex in Avratpazarı, or in the townships of Üsküdar, Eyüp, and Galata. See Necipoğlu, *The Age of Sinan*; Lucienne Thys-Şenocak, *Ottoman Women Builders: The Architectural Patronage of Hadice Turhan Sultan: Women and Gender in the Early*

Modern World (Aldershot: Ashgate, 2006); Marianne Boqvist, 'Ottoman Women Builders: The Architectural Patronage of Hadice Turhan Sultan, Women and Gender in the Early Modern World', *Journal of Early Modern History* 12.5 (2008): 452–54; and Muzaffer Özgüleş, *The Women Who Built the Ottoman World: Female Patronage and the Architectural Legacy of Gulnus Sultan* (London: I. B. Tauris, 2017). Although the term 'imperial mosque' (*cevami-i selatin*) refers both to the Friday mosques built by and for the sultans and to those built by and/or for the women of the imperial household, in this chapter I will use the term rather restrictively, to refer to the former. For the significations of the imperial mosques and a general synopsis, see Howard Crane, 'The Ottoman Sultan's Mosques: Icons of Imperial Legitimacy', in *The Ottoman City and Its Parts: Urban Structure and Social Order*, eds Irene A. Bierman, Rifa'at A. Abou-El-Haj, and Donald Preziosi (New Rochelle, NY: Aristide D. Caratzas, 1991), 173–243.

11 Çelik, *Remaking of Istanbul*, 49–81.

12 Ayvansarayi Hafız Hüseyin Efendi, Ali Satı Efendi, and Süleyman Besim Efendi, *Hadika't-ül Cevami*, 44, 50, 53, 56, 57, 58. (There is contradicting information on the neighbourhood of the Selim I Mosque in two different copies of *Hadikat'ül Cevami*, 56n7.)

13 Remzi Duran, *Selatin Camilerindeki Avlu Sütunlarının Madeni Bileziklerine Hakkedilmiş Yazılar Üzerine, D.E.Ü. İlahiyat Fakültesi Dergisi*, vol. 11 (İzmir, 1998), 135–40. See also, Nazif Arıman, *İstanbul'un Bilezik Yazıları* (Istanbul: Kültür A.Ş., 2018).

14 Aysel Yıldız, *Crisis and Rebellion in the Ottoman Empire: The Downfall of a Sultan in the Age of Revolution* (London and New York: I. B. Tauris, 2016), 32.

15 The political demonstrations at Tahrir Square, Cairo, in 2011, Occupy Wall Street protests at Zuccotti Park near New York City's Wall Street financial district in 2011–12, and Gezi Protests in Gezi Parkı, Istanbul, in 2013 are some of the examples that come to mind regarding the use of squares and large city parks in contemporary times.

16 Kemal Beydilli, ed., *Osmanlı Döneminde İmamlar ve Bir İmamın Günlüğü* (Istanbul: TATAV Yayınları, 2001), 115.

17 On the transformation of Bayezid Mosque's outer courtyard to Bayezid Square, see Neşe Gürallar, *Emergence of Modern Public Space from a Traditional Mosque Courtyard* (Saarbrücken, Istanbul: Verlag Dr. Müller, 2009); and Turgut Akbaş, *Osmanlı İstanbul'unda Bâyezid Meydani ve Tarihi Çevresi* (MA thesis, İÜ, Istanbul, 2011).

18 Ottoman Archives (Republic of Turkey Prime Ministry Ottoman Archives) C.BLD. 89-4413, (1185) *İstanbul'da Bayezid Camii avlusunda bir kasap dükkanı gediği mahlul olup, müstahakkına İstanbul kasabbaşısı ve kethüdalar sekbanbaşı Yusuf Ağa'ya inha etmekle ol vechile tevcihi.*

19 On trade activities in the inner and outer courtyards of mosques, see documents from the Ottoman Archives Y.A.HUS.163-131, BEO 220-16439, BEO 215-16079, BEO 296-22189.

20 On demolitions of unlicensed buildings in the outer courtyards of mosques, see Ottoman Archives IMVL 485-21974.

21 For more information on Ramadan Exhibitions, see Abdülaziz Bey, *Osmanlı Adet Merasim ve Tabirleri Toplum Hayatı* (Istanbul: Tarih Vakfı Yurt Yayınları, 1995), 251–53; '*Beyazıt Camii ve Külliyesi*' in TDVİA, vol. 6, 47; and Ebru Boyar and Kate Fleet, *A Social History of Ottoman Istanbul* (Cambridge: Cambridge University Press, 2010), 152.

22 I would like to thank Prof. Mehmet Kalpaklı for bringing the case of Zati (*d.*1546), the renowned sixteenth-century poet, to my attention as an earlier example of people perceiving mosque courtyards as places where they could interact with the state. After being disfavoured by the court, Zati began writing amulets and working as a fortune-teller (*remmal*) at the inner courtyard of the Bayezid Mosque, with the hope of presenting his new work to the state elite and winning back the favour of the court. For more information on the poet Zati, see Sooyong Kim, 'Minding the Shop: Zati and the Making of Ottoman Poetry in the First Half of the Sixteenth Century' (PhD diss., University of Chicago, 2005).

23 Mosque inner courtyards, apart from their function of protecting the populace during disasters, also exhibit a much more clichéd protection function. Even today, newborn babies who lack parental care are frequently left in mosque courtyards with the hope that they will be adopted by someone who can care for them. In the early modern era, imperial mosques were considered prime places to abandon babies because people thought that they would grow up near wealthy people connected to the palace. Should the baby be a girl, the probability that the child would be supported by the government until she married was relatively high. See Ottoman Archives A..}MKT.MVL 79-61, 1272.

24 Derviş Efendi-Zade Derviş Mustafa, *1196–1782 Yangınları, Harik Risalesi*, ed. Hüsamettin Aksu (Istanbul: İletişim Yayınları, 1994), 40.

25 The pools built in the outer courtyards of the Beyazıd, Laleli, Süleymaniye, and Nuruosmaniye Mosques in the late eighteenth century were also added to the list of precautions taken against the Istanbul fires. Though the water that accumulated within these pools was supposed to be used against fires within the city, it can be speculated that people who took shelter in the mosque and its courtyard used it to protect themselves and the building. See Ottoman Archives HAT 239-13342.

26 This is also mentioned by other writers from earlier and later periods. See Ertuğrul Oral, 'Tarih-i Gılmani' (PhD diss., Marmara University, Istanbul, 2000), 9; and *Abdülaziz Bey Osmanlı Adet Merasim ve Tabirleri Toplum Hayatı (Âdet ve Merâsim-ı Kadime, Tabirat ve Muamelât-ı Kavmiye-i Osmaniye)*, eds Kazım Arısan and Duygu Arısan Günay (Istanbul: Tarih Vakfı Yurt Yayınları, 1995), 268.

27 Fındıklılı Şemdanizade Süleyman Efendi, *Mür'i't-Tevarih*, vol.1, ed. Münir Aktepe (Istanbul: Istanbul Üniversitesi Edebiyat Fakültesi, 1978), 3.

28 Taylesanizade Hafız Abdullah Efendi, *İstanbul'un Uzun Dört Yılı (1785–1789)*, ed. Feridun Emecen (Istanbul: TATAV, 2003), 184–85.

29 In his book *The Panorama of the History (Mür'it Tevarih)*, Şemdanizade Süleyman Efendi uses a conscious and descriptive vocabulary when depicting buildings. His choice of the word '*mualla*', which can either mean 'glorious' or 'elevated/high', when describing imperial mosques such as the Nuru Osmaniye, Ayazma, Laleli, and Zeyneb Sultan Mosques, may point to Şemdanizade's – and, consequently, Istanbulites' – awareness of the elongating vertical proportions of mosques in that era, compared to the classical proportions.

30 Ottoman Archives HAT 139-5763.

31 Elif Andaç, 'Transnational Ideologies and State Building: The Ottoman Empire in Transition', *Political Power and Social Theory* 20 (2009): 133–66. For a general overview of the New Order (*Nizam-ı Cedid*) Reforms and their aftermath, see Virginia Aksan, *Ottoman Wars*

1700–1870: An Empire Besieged (Harlow: Longman/Pearson, 2007), 180–206; Frederick F. Anscombe, *State, Faith, and Nation in Ottoman and Post-Ottoman Lands* (New York: Cambridge University Press, 2014), 33–60; Carter V. Findley, *Bureaucratic Reform in the Ottoman Empire: The Sublime Porte, 1789–1922* (Princeton: Princeton University Press, 1980); Aysel Yıldız, *Crisis and Rebellion in the Ottoman Empire: The Downfall of a Sultan in the Age of Revolution* (London and New York: I. B. Tauris, 2016); and Ali Yaycıoğlu, *Partners of the Empire: The Crisis of the Ottoman Order in the Age of Revolutions* (Stanford, CA: Stanford University Press, 2016).

32 Üsküdar, one of the three boroughs of Ottoman Istanbul (*bilad-ı selase*), housed many imperial mosque complexes built by and for the women of the Ottoman dynasty, the nearest example of which was Ayazma Mosque, built in 1760–61 by Mustafa III, father of Selim III, in memory of his mother and brother, Şehzade Süleyman. However, the Selimiye Mosque marked the first time that an Ottoman sultan built an eponymous mosque there.

33 For a general synopsis of the eighteenth-century imperial mosques, see Ünver Rüstem, *Ottoman Baroque: The Architectural Refashioning of Eighteenth-Century Istanbul* (Princeton and Oxford: Princeton University Press, 2019).

34 According to Çiğdem Kafescioğlu, the spatial organization of the new mosque of Mehmed II, especially its royal pavilion, was novel among the architecture of Ottoman congregational mosques, marking a radical change in the Ottoman style of rulership. See Kafescioğlu, *Constantinopolis/Istanbul*, 79. For detailed information on the development of royal tribunes and pavilions in the early modern era, see Abdüllah Kuran, 'The Evolution of the Sultan's Pavilion in Ottoman Imperial Mosques', *Islamic Art* 4 (1991): 281–300.

35 Hakan T. Karateke, 'Legitimizing the Ottoman Sultanate: A Framework for Historical Analysis', in *Legitimizing the Order: The Ottoman Rhetoric of State Power*, eds Hakan T. Karateke and Maurus Reinkowski (Leiden, Boston: Brill, 2005), 13–54.

36 Gözde Ramazanoğlu, 'Osmanlı Yenileşme Hareketleri İçerisinde Selimiye Kışlası ve Yerleşim Alanı' (PhD diss., Yıldız Teknik Üniversitesi, 2003); and Rüstem, *Ottoman Baroque*.

37 For cultural and urban transformations in Istanbul throughout the eighteenth century, see Tülay Artan, 'Architecture as a Theatre of Life: Profile of the Eighteenth-Century Bosporus' (PhD diss., MIT, 1989); and Shirine Hamadeh, *The City's Pleasures: Istanbul in the Eighteenth Century* (Seattle: University of Washington Press, 2007).

38 See Eremya Çelebi Kömürcüyan, *Istanbul tarihi: XVII. asırda Istanbul*, trans. Hrand D. Andreasyan, ed. Kevork Pamukciyan (Cağaloğlu, Istanbul: Eren, 1988); P. İncicyan, *Onsekizinci Asırda Istanbul* (Istanbul: Istanbul Fetih Cemiyeti Yayınları, 1976); and Sarraf Sarkis Hovhannesyan, *Payitaht Istanbul'un tarihçesi* (Istanbul: Tarih Vakdı Yurt Yayınları, 1996).

39 http://www.oxfordislamicstudies.com/article/opr/t125/e753, accessed November 26, 2017.

40 Ahmet Cevdet Paşa, *Tezakir (1–12)*, ed. Cavid Baysun (Ankara: TTK, 1991), 68–72.

41 See Nina Ergin, 'A Multi-Sensorial Message of the Divine and the Personal: Qur'anic Inscriptions and Recitation in Sixteenth-Century Ottoman Mosques', in *Calligraphy in Islamic Architecture: Space, Form, and Function*, eds Mohammad Gharipour and Irvin C. Schick (Edinburgh: Edinburgh University Press, 2013), 105–18; and Nina Ergin, 'The Fragrance of the Divine: Ottoman Incense Burners and Their Context', *Art Bulletin* 96.1 (2014): 70–97.

42 For examples of these documents, see Ottoman Archives A.}MKT. 86-85, A.}MKT.NZD. 21-75, A.}MKT.NZD. 297-57, A.}MKT.UM.. 118-63, A.}MKT.UM.. 118-65, A.}MKT.UM..

119-18, A.}MKT.UM.. 119-75, A.}MKT.UM.. 120-51, A.}MKT.UM.. 121-24, A.}MKT.UM..
122-47, A.}MKT.UM.. 122-50, A.}MKT.UM.. 122-67, A.}MKT.UM.. 123-11, A.}MKT.UM..
124-14. A significant number of these type of documents are dated to 1852–53. The signs
of this increase can also be traced in the accounts of Ahmed Lütfi Efendi (1816–1907)
for the year 1853: Advice for performing the prayers; Muslim people are warned by an
announcement which elucidates that [the people that are] reluctant to attend the five prayers
– which is the basis of the people of Islam and the pillar of the true religion – regularly will
be subjected to an admonition (*tenbih-i salat; ehl-i İslam'ın esas ve imad-ı din-i mübini olan
salavat-ı hamsenin cema'atle müdavemetde tekasül edenler haklarında ta'zirat-ı şer'iyye icra
olunacağı efrad-ı müslimeye i'lan ile tenbih olundu*).

43 Firman registers of Istanbul court (no. 213), p. 102 (21.6.1847): all faithful Muslims are
obliged to perform the five daily prayers, the most protected symbol of Islam, with the
congregation regularly. Despite the warnings issued from time to time in this regard, some
people – although they do not face any obstacles – idle away time, which causes the esteemed
mosques and masjids to be empty (*şe'a'ir-i islamiyyenin en takvası olan salat-ı hamse-i
mefruzayı cemaatle edaya müdavemet etmek kaffe-i mü'minin-i muvahhidine lazime-i
zimmet olup bu babda aralık aralık tenbihat-ı mukteziye icra olunmakta ise de bazı kesan
bir gune mevanim ve maslahatı olmadığı halde öteye beruye beyhude vakit geçirerek ka'in
cevami' ve mesacid-i şerifenin cema'atten hali kalmasını mucib olup*). For the transliteration
and analysis of the whole register, see Ahmet Eryüksel, 'İstanbul Kadılığı 213 No.lu Ferman
Defterine Göre 1831–1863 Senelerinde Sosyal ve İktisadi Hayata Dair Kararlar' (MA thesis,
Istanbul University, 1990).

44 Ottoman Archives Y.PRK.AZJ. 9–99.

45 Hamadeh, *City's Pleasures*, 51.

46 Hugh Edwin Strickland, *Memoirs of Hugh Edwin Strickland*, ed. William Jardine (London:
John Van Voorst, Paternoster Row, 1858), 102.

47 Albert Smith, *A Month in Constantinople* (London: D. Bogue, 1850), 102–06.

48 From the early nineteenth century on, princes were allowed to attend Friday ceremonies
in the mosques of their choosing. Despite the relative simplicity of the Friday processions
compared to those that took place on religious holidays, this critical change must have
affected the visibility of the imperial family in the city. During the Hamidian Era, Abdülhamid
II specifically chose members of the high-ranking elite and sent them to certain imperial
mosques, such as Hagia Sophia, Sultan Ahmed, or Süleymaniye, to attend Friday prayers.
As representatives of the sultan, these individuals should also have played an intermediary
role in transmitting the vibes of authority and power that accumulated in Yıldız.

49 A contract was arranged for the construction in the first months of 1883 (Ottoman Archives
Y.PRK.BSK.6-83), and a ground-breaking ceremony took place on October 28 of the same
year (Ottoman Archives Y.PRK.AZJ. 9-99). On the inscription panel, the construction
date of the mosque is recorded as 1885. For more information about the building process
and the architecture of Yıldız Hamidiye Mosque, see Selman Can, *Yıldız Camii'nin İnşası
ve Mimarına İlişkin Yeni Bilgiler*, 'Nurhan Atasoy'a Armağan', ed. Ahmet Akcan (Istanbul:
Lale Yayıncılık, 2014), 59–67; Ahmet Ersoy, 'Aykırı Binanın Saklı Kalfası: Hamidiye Camisi
ve Nikolaos Tzelepis (Celebis)', *Batılılaşan İstanbul'un Rum Mimarları*, (Istanbul: Tavaslı

Yayıncılık , 2010), 104–17; Selçuk Batur, 'Yıldız Camii', *DBİA* vol. 7 (1994): 514; and Selman Can, 'Yıldız Camii', *DVİA,* vol. 43 (2013): 540–41.

50 For an example of a very similar use of ceremonies as a tool for stressing the vital role of the caliphate, see Paula Sanders, *Ritual, Politics, and the City in Fatimid Cairo* (Albany: State University of New York Press, 1994).

51 Theophile Gautier, who visited Istanbul in the early 1850s, records that he watched the Eid procession of Sultan Abdülmecid I from within an old building with many windows just near the Hagia Irene. It is known that such temporary structures were built so that non-Muslims could watch significant religious ceremonies from the early nineteenth century on. These can be perceived as predecessors to the embassy kiosk that became permanent during the second half of the Hamidian Era. See Théophile Gautier, *Constantinople* (Paris: Michel Levy Freres, 1856), 243–44.

52 Ottoman Archives Y.PRK.ASK. 254-89.

53 Samuel Sullivan Cox, *Diversions of a Diplomat in Turkey* (New York: C. L. Webster & Company, 1893), 34–35.

54 Selim Deringil, 'The Invention of Tradition as Public Image in the Late Ottoman Empire, 1808 to 1908', *Comparative Study of Society and History*, 35.1 (January, 1993): 3–29.

55 Ottoman Archives Y.PRK.ASK. 13-42; 38-95; 23-29; 31-55; 33-16; 38-95; 41-7; 41-79; 50-70; 68-83; 76-41; 98-96; 104-80; 106-73; 110-49; 159-22; 162-50; 163-40; 163-100; 178-53; 180-8; 184-46; 199-61; 207-58; 208-33; 208-89; 211-15; 213-1; 217-36; 224-120; 225-12; 225-140; 226-55; 228-11; 230-100; 231-42; 234-89; 240-21; 243-60; 244-8; 247-29; 247-101; 248-96; 251-1; 252-81; 253-63; 254-13; 254-89; 162-21; Y.PRK.SGE. 5-102; Y.PRK.TŞF. 5-71; 6-53; 7-30; 8-9; 7-34; 7-41; 7-51; 7-55; 7-58; 8-25; 8-44; Y.PRK.ZB. 32-32; Y.PRK.BŞK. 69-30; Y.PRK.MYD. 26-22; Y.PRK.HH. 37-14; Y.PRK.MYD. 26-105; Y.MTV. 20-98; 73-46.

56 Fausto Zonaro, *Twenty Years under the Reign of Abdülhamid: The Memoirs and Works of Fausto Zonaro,* eds Erol Makzume and Cesare Mario (Istanbul: G Yayın grubu, 2011), 97.

57 Additionally, it includes meticulous information on the excuses of ninety-six soldiers of that regiment who were not able to attend the procession: seventeen were in hospital, sixty-seven were on duty in other places, two were in Germany and France with various missions, two were penalized, and eight were on duty in other regiments. See Ottoman Archives Y.PRK. ASK. 163-40.

58 Hakan Karateke, *Padişahım Çok Yaşa: Osmanlı Devletinin Son Yüz Yılında Merasimler,* (Istanbul: Kitap Yayınevi, 2004), 108.

Urban Morphology and Sacred Space: The Mashhad Shrine during the Late Qajar and Pahlavi Periods

May Farhat

In 1971, the French architect and urban planner Michel Écochard was invited by the Iranian government to make recommendations for the regeneration of the surroundings of the shrine of Imam Reza in the Shi'i holy city of Mashhad.[1] Flying over the city and 'walking for ten days through the crowds, by shops, bazaars, alleyways, caravanserais, madrasas, and from top of minarets',[2] he observed that the shrine complex, marked by towering gold, blue, and turquoise domes, was the 'raison d'être' of the city [Figure 1]. Its purpose was to welcome the pilgrims who came from all over Iran and Central Asia, generating in the process intense commercial and artisanal activity in its proximity. The neighbourhoods surrounding the shrine complex had a high concentration of hotels to accommodate the mostly low-income visitors. The series of recommendations Écochard proposed, which targeted the rehabilitation of commercial and artisanal spaces, was not followed.[3] In 1975, the governor of Khurasan and

Figure 1: Aerial view of Mashhad, 1971. Archives Écochard.

Figure 2: Aerial view of Mashhad, 1977. Archives Écochard.

deputy custodian of the Mashhad shrine, Abdul-Azim Valian, in a highly controversial gesture, ordered the indiscriminate destruction of Mashhad's bazaars along a radius of 320 metres from the shrine's golden dome [Figure 2].[4] The shrine, liberated from centuries-old urban clutter, stood across a vast circular green void, visible to all.

This is a study of the Mashhad shrine and the modernizing transformations that redefined its urban space in the context of the emergence of a centralized nation-state under the Pahlavi shahs (1925–79). Set against the shahs' aggressive drive toward change and modernization, it focuses on the impact of state-sponsored urban renewal projects on the city of Mashhad, and the changing nature of the shrine at its centre. In particular, it spotlights the development and transformation of two public spaces that mediated between the imam's sacred domains and the city, the co-called Bala-Khiyaban and Pain-Khiyaban *basts*, which framed the entrance to the shrine's courtyard from the west and the east, respectively. Refurbished during the late Qajar period, these two open spaces were extensions of the medieval city's main rectilinear boulevard (*khiyaban*), created by Shah Abbas in the early seventeenth century, which carved out west–east access to the shrine, linking one city gate to another. Each was a *bast*, meaning 'sanctuary', and demarcated the sacred spaces of the shrine, which provided refuge to people seeking the protection of the imam from injustice or persecution. Non-Muslims were categorically barred from access, and animals that ventured inside became the imam's property. A permeable boundary, composed of iron chains and wood barriers, demarcated a negotiating space, where the judicial authority of Mashhad's clerical establishment could be appealed to, and possibly a reprieve obtained, against the political authority of Mashhad's governor. The abolishment of this custom (*bast-nishin*) during the reign of Reza Shah, the opening of the shrine to non-Muslims, the massive urban transformations that reshaped the city of Mashhad in the 1930s, and the tabula rasa approach to urban renewal used in 1975 to demolish Mashhad's historic bazaars illustrate the contest over boundaries between sacred space and the public sphere that, via modern authoritarian political power, shaped Mashhad's contemporary sacred centre.

Mashhad in the Late Qajar Period

Unlike Tehran, the Qajar capital, which was refashioned during the reign of Nasir al-Din Shah (r.1848–96), Mashhad maintained its medieval structure well into the early twentieth century.[5] Mashhad – a short form for *mashhad al-Rida* (place of martyrdom of Imam Rida) – developed around the tomb of the eighth Shi'i imam, Ali al-Rida (d.818, also known as Imam Reza), who died in eastern Khurasan during the reign of the Abbasid caliph al-Ma'mun (d.833) and who was buried in a small village, next to the tomb of al-Ma'mun's father, Harun al-Rashid (d.809).[6] Embodying the charisma of the prophetic line, Mashhad emerged as a site of visitation during the late tenth century and assumed increasing importance in the religious landscape of eastern Khurasan thereafter. In the post-Mongol period, enshrined saints emerged as "iconic sources of sovereignty"[7] in the Persianate sphere, and the Mashhad shrine attracted the patronage of the Turkic rulers of Iran and Central Asia, with the Timurids outfitting the shrine with a spectacular Friday mosque in 1418. Safavid patronage, particularly that of Shah Abbas (r.1588–1629), transformed Mashhad into the preeminent Shi'i pilgrimage centre in Iran and into a stage for the performance of Safavid sovereignty and religious legitimacy.[8] During Nadir Shah Afshar's short reign (r.1736–47), it flourished as a capital city and important commercial centre. In 1802, with its recapture by Fath Ali Shah Qajar from Nadir Shah Afshar's last descendants, it became an important outpost in the Qajar domains.

Mashhad was referred to as this 'most holy land' (*arz-i aqdas*) in Qajar sources,[9] and its popularity as a Shi'i pilgrimage city did not decrease during the nineteenth century, despite the hardships associated with long-distance travel, the insecurity of the roads, and occasional famines and epidemic flare-ups.[10] A mutually beneficial relationship linked the Qajar shahs with Mashhad's religious establishment. The Shi'i clerics extended their political support to the shahs, who in turn secured a measure of political stability and military protection for the shrine city.[11] Members of the royal family who were appointed to the governorship of the city established a provincial court in the city's citadel (*arg*) and maintained control over the notoriously unruly tribes of Khurasan. The shrine's custodians (*mutawalli bashi*) were political appointees, chosen from among the extended Qajar family and prominent administrators. In many instances after 1845, the positions of governor-general and custodian of the holy shrine were held by the same appointee, building a close relationship between the Qajar shahs and Mashhad's clerical establishment. Following Safavid precedent, the Qajars lavished gifts on the shrine, financed its expansion and embellishment, and performed highly publicized pilgrimages.[12] Members of the Qajar court established significant endowments that contributed to the welfare of pilgrims and the upkeep of the shrine.[13]

The first scientifically drawn plan of the city, prepared by topographers who were part of Russian Orientalist Nicolas de Khanikoff's scientific mission to Mashhad in 1858,[14] shows an irregularly shaped city, enclosed by a wall of unbaked brick and punctuated by five gates. It stretched from west to east along one broad avenue, the Khiyaban, constructed by Shah Abbas in 1611, which functioned as a monumental public hub. Travellers' accounts describe it as filled with a dense crowd of different nationalities and classes and lined with caravanserais and miscellaneous stores.[15] A canal ran through the middle, lined by trees on either side and spanned by footbridges. The citadel, located to the southwest, was a large rectangle, with four towers in the corners. Built by Malik Mahmud Sistani between 1722 and 1726, it was significantly enlarged by the Qajars. The governor's palace, the audience hall (*diwankhane*), and other administrative units were organized around inner courtyards and extensive gardens.[16] An ample open space, Maydan-i Arg (Citadel Square), was used for military parades on official occasions, and for public executions. By 1890, the two imperial powers that dominated Qajar political life, Britain and Russia, had established consulates in Mashhad. The British Consulate, an important compound, was located on Citadel Square. In her description of that neighbourhood, Ella Sykes, sister of Britain's Consul General of Khurasan, Percy Sykes (in Mashhad from 1905 to 1913), captures the dual centres of authority, temporal and sacred, of the holy city:

> This quarter is well-planted with trees, which give it a green look in spring and summer, and it may be called the *material force* of the Holy City for here are the Governor in his citadel, ill-clad soldiers, and some dozen cannons. The magnificent group of buildings constituting the Mosque and Shrine may be looked upon as the *spiritual force* of Meshed, the very heart, and soul of the city.[17]

Mashhad was an introverted city; its houses as well as its religious and commercial structures were built around interior courtyards. Khanikoff left a vivid portrait of the pilgrimage town, where religious piety, commercial activity, and pleasure contributed to the economy.[18] To the weary pilgrim, who had travelled through arid and harsh landscapes, Mashhad offered 'a populous city, in the middle of vast markets and caravanserais, filled with objects of necessity and luxury'. A large class of clergy, dervishes, and elegy reciters (*marsiye khan*), he wrote, 'vibrate the strings of his soul by means of warm words and images' and 'a large population of young and beautiful women' presents him with the possibility to contract out a temporary marriage (*sigheh*), 'an easy means to forget that he is far from home'.[19]

The holy quarter (Haram) formed the main urban core of the city, with the major bazaars radiating from the centre toward the city gates.[20] The six residential neighbourhoods (*mahallah*) were organized around the holy quarter concentrically.[21] Population estimates ranged between 60,000–80,000 residents,[22] a mix of those native to the area and migrants from various part of Iran, Afghanistan, and Central Asia. A small community of Europeans (mostly Russian and British citizens affiliated with their consulates and Belgian officials employed by the Iranian treasury) resided in the holy city by the late nineteenth century.

A population of pilgrims coursed continuously along the city's Khiyaban and congregated around the central shrine area. Each neighbourhood had its own graveyard. The most important was the Qatlgah cemetery, a massive space which extended to the northwest of the shrine, where bodies dispatched from various parts of the Muslim empire found their last resting place. Guardhouses (*qaravul-khane*) doted the urban landscape, and a police force watched over the daily lives of Mashhadis, and meted out punishments for criminal activities that took place on the outskirts of the sacred city, its streets, bazaars, workshops, and coffeehouses.[23] To European visitors, Mashhad had a miserable appearance and offered little attraction aside from the magnificent ensemble of buildings at its centre.[24] This holy quarter, however, was strictly forbidden to non-Muslims.

The Holy Quarter, or *Bast*

The sacred quarter at the heart of Mashhad comprised the cluster of religious, educational, administrative, charitable, and commercial structures that had accumulated around the imam's tomb since the tenth century.[25] A unique map of the Mashhad Haram (*naqshe-ye haram-e mutahhar razavi*), drawn in 1924 by the engineer Ali Asghar Khan, preserves the layout of the Mashhad *bast* prior to the urban upheavals of the Pahlavi period [Figure 3].[26] All

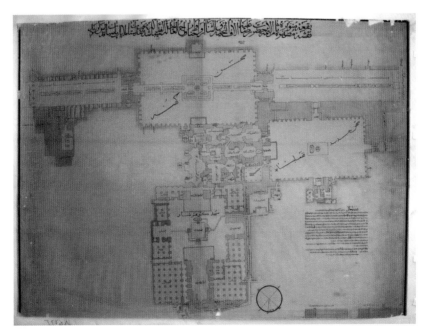

Figure 3: Map of the Razavi sacred Haram, 1343/1924, by Ali Asghar Khan Muhandes. Astan-i Quds-i Razavi. Archives of the Central Library, document no. 62258.

the important spaces are carefully labelled. The body of the imam, buried in a square mausoleum (sacred garden/*rawze-ye muqaddase*), constituted the sacred vortex around which all spaces were organized. A series of beautifully adorned mosques, tombs, and ceremonial halls (dating from the Ghaznavid to the Qajar period) surrounded the tomb chamber on four sides, forming the shrine's inner sanctum. Strategically located windows (in Dar al-Siyyada, and the Old Court) allowed pilgrims to gaze at the imam's tomb from a distance. The map carefully identifies the tomb of Shah Tahmasp (*soffe-ye shah tahmasbi*), the only Safavid shah to be buried in Mashhad, and numerous Qajar dignitaries who had the exclusive privilege of being interred within this area, a reminder that the Haram was a sacred burial ground.

Gawharshad's monumental mosque created a nucleus to the south of the mausoleum, its sides lined with shops that were part of the mosque's endowment. Bazaar-i Bozorg (surprisingly not shown on this map),[27] a covered market located on the mosque's southwestern side, was the most important market inside the *bast* and extended from the mosque toward the city. The seventeenth-century Safavid cluster created a new locus to the northeast of the tomb chamber, composed of the Old Court (*sahn-i kuhna*) and the Khiyaban that extends from the northwest to the Bala-Khiyaban Gate, and from the southeast to the Pain-Khiyaban Gate. The Iwan of Ali Shir Nava'i (*d.*1501) provided the main access to the mausoleum. Two imposing Safavid madrasas, the Madrasa of Mirza Ja'far (1649) and the Madrasa of Khayrat Khan (1647), were built to the northeast of the shrine.

The Old Court gave access to many bazaars (such as the Stonecutters and Cloth-sellers bazaars), and to covered passageways (*dalan*) of the silversmiths, goldsmiths, and summer shoes sellers. The nineteenth-century Qajar New Court (*sahn-i now*), added in 1817–18, during the reign of Fath Ali Shah, to the southeast of the tomb chamber created new access to the tomb chamber. Two ceremonial halls (Dar al-Diyafe/Hall of Hospitality and Dar al-Sa'ade/Hall of Happiness) were built along with the new courtyard. A coffeehouse (*qahveh-khane*) connected with Dar al-Diyafe, and must have functioned, as its name indicates, as a venue for hosting important visitors.

The spaces extending from the Old Court's eastern and western iwans, formed, respectively, the 'Pain-Khiyaban Sanctuary' (*bast-i pain khiyaban*) and the 'Bala-Khiyaban Sanctuary' (*bast-i bala khiyaban*). Lined with shops and bazaars, and with boundary markers on either side blocking access to animals, vehicles, and non-Muslims, these were the most coveted commercial spaces of Mashhad. The interstitial spaces between the three large courts and the two *basts* were occupied by madrasas, caravanserais, bazaars, private residences, and many of the shrine's departments, such as the kitchen of the shrine's servitors (*ashpaskhane-yi khudam*), the pilgrims' refectory (*karkhane-yi mubarak*), the pharmacy (*sherbet khaneh*), and the hospital (*dar al-shifa*).[28] A lively flow of activities, religious and profane, animated the spaces of the shrine at all times of the day. At night, a considerable outlay of lamps and candles illuminated the shrine's spaces, although they were replaced by electrical lights in 1893.[29]

The Mashhad *Bast* or the Shrine as Refuge

Entering Mashhad from the western gate (Bala-Khiyaban), the holy quarter began about two-thirds of the length of the Khiyaban. European travellers, riding down the avenue, arrived in front of a brick arch that blocked their access to the shrine quarter. Guards directed them into the side alleys that circumvented the holy quarter, and they sometimes made great detours to reach their assigned quarters.[30] Over the course of the nineteenth century, many Europeans attempted to enter the *bast* in disguise, to see what lay beneath Mashhad's golden dome.[31] In an unusual episode narrated by Edward B. Eastwick, the European-educated *mutawalli* Mirza Sayyid Ja'far, Mushir al-Dawla Tabrizi (*d.*1863),[32] took the initiative to lead Eastwick through the *bast* into the Old Court. The Qajar official, a known reformer, was testing the power of the shrine's clerics. He seems to have provoked their anger, for they wrote to Tehran in protest. Eastwick claims to have left Mashhad under threat to his life.[33]

Khanikoff described the holy quarter as squarish in plan, about 400–500 metres per side, and enclosed by '*palisades*'. Boundary markers – brick walls, wood barriers, and iron chains – were used to demarcate the shrine's sacred territory. A 'state within a state', the holy quarter had its own administration, headed by the shrine custodian and composed of an extensive staff,[34] a police force, tribunals, and a prison. The term *bast* is best translated as protected territory or sanctuary; individuals avoiding arrest, or seeking redress from injustice, could seek asylum (*bast neshini*) within its premises.[35] In this sacred realm, the Shi'i imam, believed to be alive in his tomb, extended his protection to all those seeking justice. Government forces were not allowed to enter the shrine and arrest them.

The practice of seeking sanctuary in sacred spaces dates to antiquity, with the Ka'ba in Mecca providing the first prototype in the Islamic period.[36] In Iran, Timur (1336–1405) reportedly granted the status of a sanctuary (*bast*) for the tomb of Shaykh Safi al-Din (1252–1334) in Ardabil in 1404. The practice became very popular under the Safavids and extended to religious and non-religious spaces, such as shrines, royal stables, the threshold of royal palaces (i.e., 'Ali Qapu in Isfahan), and public squares.[37] Rules regulating the practice of *bast* at the Mashhad shrine were recorded in *Tumar-i 'Alishah*, the eighteenth-century waqf recension ordered by 'Adil Shah (*d.*1749), the nephew of Nadir Shah, the first surviving record of the administrative guidelines for the shrine and its endowments.[38] It was the shrine custodian's responsibility to ensure that the *bast*'s wooden fences were firm, and that the iron chains were fastened. Protection was extended to whomever sought the protection and the intercession of the saint. The role of the shrine's assistant administrator (*ishiq-aghasi-bashi*)[39] was to see that petitions were appropriately handled and that asylum-seekers were protected from harassment by government officials. An exception was made for murderers, who, following an old law (*dastur-i qadim*), were imprisoned in the shrine's courtyard and were given bread and water each day. They remained detained until they agreed to leave the *bast* of their own accord and to surrender to the governor.[40]

Attempts under the Qajar shahs to abolish this practice, or to restrict the right to take sanctuary and thus limit its abuse by criminals, murderers, and opportunists, were unsuccessful.[41] By the end of the nineteenth century, the practice of taking sanctuary in shrines, and in non-religious spaces, such as telegraph houses and the extraterritorial spaces of the British and Russian legations, became a formidable tool of resistance for Shiʿi clerics and the urban population as they challenged the arbitrary rule of the Qajar monarchy and its corrupt practices during the Tobacco Protest (1890–92) and the Constitutional Revolution (1906–11). In Mashhad, these events played out differently.[42] The religious classes and the shrine administration favoured stability and preserving the status quo. The high-ranking clerics (*mujtahids*) formed a conservative and non-politicized group. They were financially independent thanks to control of the shrine's large endowments and did not feel compelled to respond to popular demands. In October 1891, when a crowd gathered at the shrine and the main bazaar (in Pain Khiyaban) to protest the tobacco concession granted by Nasir al-Din Shah to the British, they refused to respond.[43] Following the election of the first National Assembly (Majlis), the leading *mujtahid*, described as 'reactionary to the core', declared that he would not submit to the Majlis, pledging his assistance to the shah.[44]

In the tumultuous years that followed the Constitutional Revolution and the 1921 political coup that put Reza Khan in power, the shrine and its administration were caught in the jockeying for power that erupted between the various pro- and anti-constitution parties in reaction to the deterioration of Qajar authority.[45] The situation was further complicated by the heavy-handed interference of Britain and Russia. The Anglo-Russian agreement of 1907 divided Iran into two spheres of influence, with Khurasan and Mashhad falling within the Russian zone. In 1911, Russian Cossack troops occupied northern Iran, and by 1912 they were heavily invested in Mashhad. An alliance between supporters of the exiled shah, the anti-constitutional party, and the Russian Consul provoked a series of confrontations. Yusuf Khan Herati, a shadowy character working for the Russians, and Sayyid Muhammad Yazdi Talib al-Haqq, an anti-constitutionalist preacher, had taken refuge (*bast*) in the shrine and in Gawharshad Mosque in February 1912. They asked for the return of the exiled shah and the abrogation of the Constitution. The general breakdown of order gave the Russians a pretext for taking control of the city. On March 30, 1912, to universal outrage, they ordered the bombardment of the shrine, causing significant damage to its buildings and killing a large number of people. Russian soldiers on horseback stormed the sacred precinct, breaking the shrine's inviolability.[46] British consular reports between April and July 1912 show that negotiations over the reinstitution of the *bast*'s boundaries and over restricting Russian access were underway between the Russians and the Iranian government. On July 27, 1912, Percy Molesworth Sykes reported 'the *bast* has been restored to its original limits with the exception of a covered bazaar. If the Persian government are wise, they will limit it themselves, but it is unlikely.'[47] It is not clear whether Sykes was in favour of abolishing the shrine's sanctuary status, but his scepticism reflects the Iranian government's reluctance to challenge the entrenched privileges of Mashhad's clerics.

The Modernization of the Mashhad Shrine under Reza Shah

The military coup of 1921 put Reza Khan, a Cossack colonel, in power, leading to his meteoric rise from war minister to prime minister to shah in 1925.[48] Reza Shah ushered in an era of radical transformation aimed at state-building through secular reform and modernization.[49] Reforms to the judicial system, the introduction of legal codes based on European models, and the development of a secular system of national primary and secondary schools seriously curtailed the prerogatives of Shi'i *ulama* and contributed to their disengagement from the Pahlavi regime. Further anti-clerical measures were taken, such as banning the traditional Shi'i commemoration of 'Ashura, the performance of Ta'ziya, and traditional storytellers (*rawzakhans*).[50] Architecture and urban planning projects became essential tools for shaping a modern Iranian identity.[51] The emergent nationalist ideology shifted the focus from Islamic forms of legitimation and Shi'i symbols toward Iran's pre-Islamic history and the revival of the majesty of ancient Iran.[52] In Khurasan, it translated into the planning and building of the tomb of the poet Firdowsi in Tus, located a few kilometres from Mashhad, under the aegis of the Society of National Heritage, a group of elite politicians who were driving Reza Shah's reform agenda.[53] Firdowsi's tomb, along with memorials planned for Iranian heroes, created alternative national pilgrimage sites to the Shi'i shrines that monopolized the devotions of Iranians.[54]

In Mashhad, Reza Shah firmly assumed control over the shrine through a series of reforms that recast the organization of Astan-i Quds and sought to modernize it. A new organizational

Figure 4: View of Mashhad's Bala Khiyaban bast, Phalavi Period (1923–41). Astan-i Quds-i Razavi Photo Archives.

261

structure (*nizamnameh*) was promulgated, naming the shah as overseer of the shrine and his appointed representative, the *na'ib al-tawliya*, as deputy custodian.[55] Chairs and tables were introduced into offices, and new accounting procedures were adopted to replace *siyaq* numerals.[56] Following planning principles developed in Tehran and applied uniformly in all Iranian cities, a network of large avenues cutting through the historic urban fabric of Mashhad was planned [Figure 4].[57] Revenue from the shrine's extensive endowments was diverted for the construction of roads, the construction and maintenance of a large hospital (Imam Reza Hospital, 1934), improvements to the town's water supply, and support for education.[58] The citadel, symbol of the deposed Qajars, was dismantled and replaced by new governmental buildings, which formed the new centre of the modern town.[59] New zones for urbanization toward the west and south were opened beyond the medieval walls, which were systematically razed. Astan-i Quds played an essential role in this expansion by converting the endowed agricultural lands located outside the medieval walls into residential allotments.[60]

The *Falake*

In 1928, Reza Shah ordered the construction of a 30-metre-wide peripheral avenue (*falake*) around the shrine, clearing away the madrasas, houses, hostels, bathhouses, and shops that had proliferated in the area. The northern and southern parts of the *falake* were speedily constructed between 1930 and 1931, under the supervision of deputy custodian Asadi and the German-trained Iranian architect Karim Taherzadeh Behzad.[61] D. M. Donaldson, missionary of the American Presbyterian Church in Mashhad, wrote with approval that 'round about the entire Shrine district a boulevard is being built to afford a convenient and necessary detour for traffic'. The southern half of the boulevard cut through a section that was congested with 'inferior buildings such as old hostels and bathhouses that have been a real menace to the health of the city'. Even more 'marvellous', the northern part of the boulevard forced the clearing of Qatlgah cemetery, which was turned into a garden (*bagh-i rizvan*).[62] Khiyaban-i Tabarsi, named after a twelfth-century Shi'i scholar buried in Mashhad, cut through the old cemetery of Qatlgah, toward the old neighbourhood of Nauqan (1930–34). The opening of Khiyaban-i Tehran, toward the south, was planned to frame the view of Imam Reza's golden dome between the shrine's two minarets. Two-story buildings, with extroverted facades, were rapidly built along the new avenues. Stores, banks, travel agencies, and hostels catering to pilgrims lined the circular road.[63]

The *falake* and the avenues radiating from it introduced a new spatial order to the holy town. A space, public and secular, ruptured the organic connection between the shrine and the city. Although large gates marked the entrance to the two main *basts* of the shrine, the encroachment of Reza Shah's authority over the sacred space is evident in a series of letters in the shrine's archives. The letters present inquiries from the army command of the eastern division (*lashkar-i sharq*) concerning army recruits escaping the compulsory conscription imposed by Reza Shah, and from police officers concerning common criminals known to have sought refuge in the

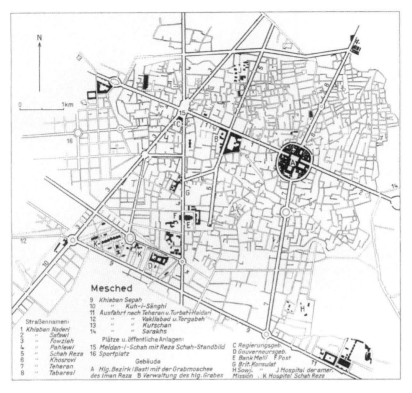

Figure 5: Plan of Modern Mashhad. After Kurt Scharlau, 'Moderne Umgestaltungen im Grundriss iranischeer Stadte', *Erdkunde* 15 (September 1961): 185.

shrine in 1928. In all cases, the response from shrine officials states that orders were given to apprehend these individuals and turn them over to the authorities.[64]

Although Reza Shah's anti-clerical policy was opening mosques in other Iranian cities to non-Muslims, European visitors hesitated to venture inside the Mashhad shrine. British policy did not encourage non-Muslim British subjects to avail themselves of the possibility of visiting the Mashhad shrine.[65] In 1930, Fred Richards stood by one the *bast*'s gates, barred from entry [Figure 5].[66] Having arrived at Mashhad by air, he described the radical changes that were transforming the city. Observing Iranians wearing European-style clothing and Pahlavi hats – imposed following the Uniform Dress Act of 1928 – Richards lamented the loss of the colourful diversity of dress and head covers. Three years later, Robert Byron commented on the motley crowd of Turkmens, Kazaks, Afghans, Tajiks, and Hazaras mixing with the 'dingy crowd of pseudo-European Persians'.[67] Unable to enter the shrine, Byron observed it on his second visit to Mashhad through field glasses from rooftops across the *falake*.[68] Given the deputy custodian Asadi's reluctance to secure his protection, Byron entered the holy precinct in disguise on his third visit in May 1934.

1935: *Kashf-i hijab* and the Gawharshad Mosque Incident

One year after marking the millennium of Ferdowsi and inaugurating his tomb in Tus to great fanfare, resistance to Reza Shah's reforms erupted in Mashhad, provoked by the unveiling policy (*kashf-i hijab*).[69] In July 1935, on the anniversary of the shelling of the shrine by the Russians, a mullah by the name of Shaykh Mohammad Taqi Bohlul (*c.*1900–2005) mounted the minbar of the mosque of Gawharshad, spoke against the unveiling of women, asked for a repeal of the Uniform Dress Act of 1928, and demanded the lowering of taxes. A confrontation and scuffle soon erupted between the police who rushed to the shrine and the gathered crowd. Military troops blocked the sanctuary and opened fire, killing several people. They soon retreated and waited for orders from Tehran. Over the following days, villagers began coming into town, and the bazaar closed.

Orders came from Tehran to use force, even if the shrine was levelled to the ground.[70] An army detachment stormed the shrine, and soldiers stationed on the roofs around the old court opened fire on the crowd, killing an untold number of people. Many more were arrested. The bodies of the dead were rapidly cleared away and buried in ditches that had been prepared in advance. In the aftermath of the bloody repression, the deputy custodian, Asadi, was held responsible for the violent eruption, summarily tried, and executed on December 12, 1935.[71] His property was seized, and his relatives were dismissed from government service. To Mashhad's British consul, it was evident that it was 'desired to represent that the outbreak was deliberately instigated and was not, as was certainly the case, the popular movement to voice disapproval of H.I.M the Shah's efforts to "modernize"'.[72]

This event marked a severe rupture between Mashhad's clerical establishment and Reza Shah. Many left their jobs at the shrine; others were sent into exile.[73] Despite the unpopularity of *kashf-i hijab* in Mashhad, officials could not oppose it. Many occasions were staged during which officials were asked to bring their wives. On one occasion, the birthday of Imam Reza in February 1936, fully armed military troops marched into the shrine to prepare for the arrival of officials with their unveiled wives.[74] In a gesture that must have offended Mashhad's religious class further, a police escort was given to Europeans wishing to enter the tomb of Imam Reza. Arriving a few months after the riots, Baroness Ravensdale, Lord Curzon's daughter, was taken by surprise when the governor expressed his willingness to arrange for her to visit the shrine complex. Covered with a chador, she slowly made her way through the courtyards into the tomb of the imam:

> I was concealed in a chaddar, and though I expect that no devout pilgrims ever look up at the unbelievable tiles in the different domes, and adjacent chambers, I meant to see as much as my frightened eyes could take in. But indelibly stamped on my mind for always will be the agonized look of about eight mullahs, kneeling by the walls, reading their Korans. They saw our pitiable little group filling through, their looks were not of murder, or hatred but of pain, as if we had done some injury to their innermost soul that could not

be repaired, combined with the look of cowed and beaten men. One of the Englishmen knowing Persian heard many times murmured 'foreigners', 'infidels'.[75]

A year later, the American art historian Arthur Upham Pope (1881–1969), who was engaged in documenting the art and architecture of Iran, was granted 'constant access' to Imam Reza's tomb chamber. Already in 1934, the team had photographed the Mosque of Gawharshad as well as precious objects and manuscripts in the shrine's collection.[76] This time, his crew entered the tomb chamber to film the crowd of pilgrims. Pope, aware that he was trespassing, gushingly wrote:

> We abashed intruders from the prosaic West just a bit flustered try to keep cool, get our cameras and surveying instruments into action, seeking in the midst of the beauty and passion of the Orient to get on with our unemotional scientific task of making a record that would enable all to share in these moving experiences.[77]

The Pahlavi Court

In 1937, the project to create a new court (Sahn-i Pahlavi, or Sahn-i Muse), which would incorporate a new museum and library, was initiated. Several commercial and educational structures were cleared to the southwest of the Qajar court,[78] and the tomb of Shaykh Bahai (d.1621), the celebrated Safavid theologian, was relocated to create a new court. The foundation stone, engraved with a text stating that Reza Shah Pahlavi ordered the building of the museum and library, was laid in a special ceremony on December 5, 1937.[79] The museum, funded by the shrine's endowments, was designed by French architect André Godard

Figure 6: Pahlavi Court/Sahn-e Muze. Astan-i Quds-i Razavi Photo Archives.

(1881–1965), who since 1928 had been directing Iran's General Service of Archaeology. In 1934 he had designed Tehran's Archaeology Museum (Iran-Bastan), which opened in 1939, and other provincial museums conceived to showcase Iran's cultural heritage.[80] The selection and organization of the displayed objects were undertaken by Mahdi Bahrami, the director of the Archaeology Museum, in consultation with prominent European and American art historians, such as Arthur Pope, Ernest Kühnel, and Friedrich Sarre.[81]

The construction of the museum was delayed due to the Allied occupation of Iran in 1941 and the abdication of Reza Shah, who died in exile in 1944. It was finally inaugurated eight years later, in December 1945, by Muhammad Reza Shah. Unlike the two other courts, planned along axes leading to the imam's tomb chamber, the Pahlavi court opened onto the *falake*, its outer edge marked by a visually permeable iron grill. Planted parterres and large reflective pools transformed the court into an ornamental garden [Figure 6]. The inclusion of a new ceremonial hall (*talar-i tashrifat*) in the museum building to host all official visits outside of the Haram proper illustrates the shah's decision to refashion the shrine into a cultural institution and to minimize the religious visitation ritual centred on the imam's tomb.

High Modernism: The Razing of the Periphery of Mashhad's Shrine

Following his accession, Muhammad Reza Shah did not at first assume an openly antagonistic posture toward Iran's clerical class. Claiming a spiritual connection with the imams, he believed that they protected him during an assassination attempt in 1953.[82] During his reign, annual scheduled inspection tours took him each May to Mashhad, where he solemnly performed a prayer at Imam Reza's tomb.[83] Highly symbolic objects, such as the silver and gold grill around the tomb of the imam (1955–57), a magnificent gold door, and precious candelabra for the mausoleum, were gifted to the shrine by him and Queen Farah Diba.[84] This gesture expressed piety and did not conflict with the shah's desire to push forward with the state's modernist transformative programme, nor with his determination to curtail clerical power.

By the early 1960s, Mashhad had expanded toward the west and south, with planned upscale neighbourhoods, recreational parks, and a new university.[85] A significant increase in population had taken place due to migration from rural areas.[86] Two very different cities were visible: the old town recognizable by its narrow alleys and the newly developed areas laid out in a grid pattern with open spaces and bigger houses.[87] This urban morphological difference reflected a socioeconomic duality. The old town, concentrated around the Haram, had a high density, with the population showing a lower standard of literacy and education compared to the new neighbourhoods, which were inhabited by the emerging middle classes of professionals, government employees, landowners, and merchants. Migrants from rural areas moved in as wealthier families left. Neighbourhoods to the east (Pain-khiyaban) and north (Nauqan) of the shrine were severely degraded, inhabited by an impoverished population of low-income families and pilgrims. A higher concentration of retail shops and services connected to the religious economy of the city had developed around the shrine, pushing away wholesale trading and industries requiring cheaper land to the peripheries of the city.

With an ever-increasing number of pilgrims exerting pressure on the infrastructure of the holy city, plans to regenerate the surroundings of the shrine were underway from the early 1960s and were advertised in newspapers.[88] The plan, developed under the aegis of the Ministry of Development and Housing, promised to transform the city and to 'revalorize its mausoleums within this year'. The new plan consisted of 'fundamental reconstructions around the mausoleums … formed of several public places and enriched by new housing buildings, as well as "a 15,00 square-meter public park"'. In 1967, a plan of urban renewal developed by the architect and planner Dariush Borbor (b.1934) gained the approval of the shah.[89] His design was based on an extensive survey undertaken by a team of experts who surveyed the neighbourhoods immediately surrounding the shrine complex. Borbor's design philosophy aimed at recreating the 'relative isolation' of the shrine under the Qajars through a series of rings that acted as buffer zones between the shrine and the city. It called for the removal of all non-religious structures directly adjacent to the mausoleum and for the creation of an outer green belt reserved for pedestrian traffic. On that belt's outer periphery, a series of buildings was planned in modern architectural forms on four levels, to accommodate warehouses, public parking, commercial areas, offices for social welfare, and public utilities. The implementation was to be carried out in phases, to allow for the relocation of existing businesses.[90] When completed, this project would turn Mashhad into one of the most interesting Islamic religious and pilgrimage centre in Iran.[91]

The justification for clearing the bazaars was presented in newspapers as a 'huge slum clearance project'.[92] Little value was given to the historic fabric, compared to the rising real-estate market value of the land around the shrine. Strong objections were made to the project by the aforementioned Michel Écochard as well as Kamran Diba, a leading Iranian architect who at the time was developing a modern architecture that was responsive to its regional and social contexts.[93] He describes in his memoirs a meeting with Asadullah Alam, the court minister, along with architects Muhsin Furoughi and Ali Sadeq, as well as Abdul-Azim Valian,[94] during which he strongly opposed the project and refused to sign on to it.

According to Ataridi, Muhammad Reza Shah's appointment of Abdul-Azim Valian as governor-general of Khurasan and deputy custodian of the shrine was predicated on his implementation of the urban renewal plan for Mashhad.[95] Valian proceeded swiftly to execute the project. The demolition campaign was undertaken in two phases. A radius of 320 metres from the golden dome defined the area to be cleared.[96] In one year, buildings located in the area defined by the new radius and the outer edge of the *falake* were indiscriminately destroyed, irrespective of historical worth and architectural merit and without regard to the effect on various local interests.[97] The second phase targeted buildings within the inner *falake*. Buildings from the Timurid, Safavid, and Qajar core that served a religious purpose exclusively and possessed high aesthetic and formal value were preserved. All commercial, residential, and service structures were removed, transforming the heterogeneous ensemble of interconnected courts and buildings into a 'museified' monument [Figure 7].[98] A facade revetment, using traditional brick and mosaic decoration, was planned to create a unified exterior.

This radical surgery created an expansive, clutter-free – and memory-free – space around the shrine that was alien to the inner-looking architecture of the shrine complex. The older museum and library were pulled down, and a new museum-library building, also designed by Dariush Borbor, was built into the corner of Sahn-e Pahlavi (1977–1982).[99] In 1976, Bazaar-i Reza, a large-scale linear commercial building, was planned; it opened in 1977 to house the displaced merchants. Airy and organized, Bazaar-i Reza heralded the era of commercial shopping malls, markers of modernity. These events registered briefly in modern historiography. The obliteration of the social space of bazaaris – an urban class that remained traditional in its outlook and supportive of Shi'i *ulama* – was interpreted as one of the repressive measures taken by Muhammad Reza Pahlavi against the Shi'i clerical establishment.[100] The shah often expressed antagonism toward the bazaars, which he perceived as 'outdated', 'fanatical', and 'badly-ventilated'.[101] For him, the replacement of the bazaars by modern structures was an inevitable outcome of modernization and progress. In an interview conducted a decade later, and in response to criticism of the destruction scheme, Abdul-Azim Valian, living in exile in the United States, justified the destruction as an attempt to purify the area from male solicitors who harassed female pilgrims in search of 'temporary marriage', and from smugglers and opium smokers who had taken up residence. Furthermore, he added that financial compensation was paid to all the displaced.[102] An agreement emerged among the main actors – the shah, the governor-general, and the urban planner – that the removal of these 'corrupted', 'socially diseased', and 'outdated' spaces was essential for the urban renewal of the holy city and for recasting the shrine complex into a modern, ordered, and legible space that would appeal to the more affluent and westernized religious tourists flocking to the regenerated shrine.

Figure 7: Mashhad Shrine after 1975 demolitions. Astan-i Quds-i Razavi Photo Archives.

Conclusion

The Islamic Revolution of 1979 put a halt to the project of Mashhad's regeneration. Immediately after assuming power, Imam Khomeini granted the custodianship of the shrine to Ayatollah Vaez-Tabasi, an influential cleric who remained in control of Astan-i Quds-i Razavi until his death in March 2016.[103] It is, however, undeniable that the Pahlavi period shaped the successful transition of the Mashhad shrine into the twentieth century and prepared it for the challenges of the contemporary world. This new phase in its history falls beyond the scope of this chapter. Suffice it to say that an underpass diverted vehicular traffic underneath the shrine complex, transforming it into an isolated pedestrian island. The large open space was replaced by a series of expansive courts to accommodate the ever-increasing number of pilgrims (15 million annually, to a projection of between 23 and 31 million a year in 2021). The building of a great central library, new museums, an Islamic university, a research institute, and a publishing house further expanded the role of the shrine as a cultural powerhouse. Four *basts* now channel pilgrims into the courts, named after four prominent Shi'i scholars, functioning as spaces to control access to the shrine. A general guide to the shrine complex defines *bast* as the 'space outside the courts, that terminates into an avenue (*khiyaban*)'.[104] There, pilgrims stop to learn the etiquette of visitation (advertised on large billboards) and to collect themselves before entering the Haram. The historical memory of *basts* as sanctuaries, or spaces of resistance, seems irrelevant now, as popular resistance has moved into the public squares and streets of the contemporary city. Beyond the shrine's sacred space, the absence of protective public policies to preserve the historical fabric of Mashhad is causing the destruction of old neighbourhoods under the pressure of real-estate speculation and investment in grand development projects.[105] The history and memory of old Mashhad is rapidly disappearing in the new globalized world, causing a profound sense of loss, disquiet, and anomie among Mashhad's inhabitants.[106]

Notes

1   Michel Écochard, 'Remarques sur l'évolution récente de la ville de Mashad', *Revue des études islamiques* 53 (1985): 7–20.
2   Écochard, 'Remarques', 9.
3   Écochard, 'Remarques', 16–17.
4   Aziz Allah 'Ataridi, *Tarikh-i astan-i quds-i razavi*, vol. 2 (Mashhad : Astan-i Quds-i Razavi, 1371/1992), 638–47.
5   The most important source on Qajar Mashhad is Muhammad Hasan Khan I'timad al-Saltana, *Matla' al-shams. Tarikh-i ard-i aqdas va mashhad-i muqaddas*, ed. Taymur Burhan Limudihi (Tehran, Intisharat-i Yasavuli Farhangsara, 1362/1983–84).
6   For a general history of Mashhad, see Aziz Allah 'Ataridi, *Tarikh-i astan-i quds-i razavi*.

7   A. Azfar Moin, 'The Politics of Saint Shrines in the Persianate Empire', in eds Abbas Amanat and Assef Ashraf, *The Persianate World: Rethinking a Shared Sphere* (London, 2019), 105.

8   May Farhat, 'Islamic Piety and Dynastic Legitimacy: The Case of the Shrine of Ali b. Musa al-Rida in Mashhad (10th–17th Century)' (PhD diss., Harvard University, 2002); and May Farhat, 'Safavid Piety and Dynastic Legitimacy: Mashhad under the Early Safavid Shahs', *Iranian Studies* 47 (2013): 201–15.

9   Muhammad Hasan Khan I'timad al-Saltana, *Matla' al-shams*; and Assef Ashraf, 'From Khan to Shah: State, Society, and Forming the Ties that Made Qajar Iran' (PhD diss., Yale University, 2016), 267–77.

10 For Mashhad's importance as a Shi'i pilgrimage destination, see Ulrich Marzolph, 'From Mecca to Mashhad: The Narrative of an Illustrated Shiite Pilgrimage Scroll from the Qajar Period', *Muqarnas* 31 (2014): 207–42.

11 Ashraf, 'From Khan to Shah', 111, 307.

12 Nasir al-Din Shah performed two highly publicized pilgrimages to the shrine, in 1867 and 1882.

13 Tomoko Morikawa and Christoph Werner, eds, *Vestiges of the Razavi Shrine. Athar al-Razaviya: A Catalogue of Endowments and Deeds to the Shrine of Imam Riza in Mashhad* (Tokyo: The Toyo Bunko, 2017).

14 Two topographers, Jarinof and Petrof, accompanied Khanikoff during his travels in Iran. See Nicolas de Khanikoff, *Mémoire sur la partie méridionale de l'Asie Centrale* (Paris: Imprimerie de L. Martinet, 1861), 69. The map was first published in Mohammad Mehryan et al., *The Visual Documents of Iranian Cities in the Qajar Period* (in Persian) (Tehran: The Cultural Heritage Organization and Shahid Beheshti University Joint Publication, 1999), 143.

15 Descriptions of Mashhad's Khiyaban abound in European travel literature. See George N. Curzon, *Persia and the Persian Question*, vol. 1 (London: Longmans, Green, and Co., 1892), 153. The length of the Khiyaban was about three kilometres.

16 St. John Lovett and Euan Smith, *Eastern Persia: An Account of the Journeys of the Persian Boundary Commission 1870-71-72*. Vol. 1 (London: The Macmillan and Co., 1876), 359–61.

17 She was the sister of Sir Percy Molesworth Sykes (1867–1945), Britain's Consul General for Khurasan in Mashhad between 1905 and 1913. Ella C. Sykes, *Persia and Its People* (New York: The Macmillan Company, 1910), 91. Original emphasis.

18 M. N. de Khanikoff, 'Meched, La ville saint, et son territoire. Extraits d'un voyage dans le Khorassan (1858)', in *Le Tour de Monde, Nouveau Journal des Voyage* no. 096 (Paris: Hachette, 1861), 272–88; and Khanikoff, *Mémoire sur la partie méridionale de l'Asie centrale*, 95–111.

19 Khanikoff, *Mémoire sur la partie méridionale de l'Asie Centrale*, 97.

20 Masoud Kheirabadi, *Iranian Cities: Formation and Development* (Austin: University of Texas Press, 1991), 71–73. The bazaars leading to Idgah, Sarab, and Nauqan were the city's primary commercial arteries. Charles Edward Yate, *Khurasan and Sistan* (Edinburgh and London: William Blackwood and Sons, 1900), 328.

21 For a description of Mashhad during this period, see 'Gazetteer of Persia. Vol. I', British Library: India Office Records and Private Papers, IOR/L/MIL/17/15/2/1, in *Qatar Digital Library*, https://www.qdl.qa/archive/81055/vdc_100025472703.0x000001; and Morteza

Nouraei, 'Mashhad between 1890 and 1914: A Socio-Historical Study' (PhD diss., University of Manchester, 2000), 28–42.

22 A census was conducted in the later Qajar period by Zayn al-Abidin Mirza Qajar.

23 For an interesting study of crime in late Qajar Mashhad, see Farzin Vejdani, 'Illicit Acts and Sacred Space: Everyday Crime in the Shrine City of Mashhad', *Journal of Persianate Studies* 7 (2014): 22–54.

24 Charles Metcalfe MacGregor, *Narrative of a Journey through the Province of Khurasan and by the N.W. Frontier of Afghanistan in 1875*, vol. 1 (London: W. M. Allen and Co., 1879), 283.

25 Establishing the legal boundaries of the Mashhad *bast* requires further research in the archives of Astan-i Quds-i Razavi. According to the study published by the consulting firm SCET in 1974, Astan-i Quds owned very few properties inside the old city, besides the sanctuary itself. All of its endowed properties were in the peripheral zone of the old town, which was initially rural land and became urbanized subsequently. Astaneh Ghods Razavi, *Les biens fonciers urbains de l'Astaneh Ghods: Ville de Mashhad, Annexe 1* (Tehran: SCETIRAN Ingénieurs Conseils, 1974), 1–2.

26 Shadi Ghafurian, 'Tahlili kuhnetarin naqsheha-ye abniye haram-e mutahhar razavi', *Astan-e Hunar* 22 (Autumn-Winter 1396/2017), 6–17.

27 Possibly, by 1924, this bazaar was not considered part of the *bast*.

28 See Christoph Werner, 'Sozial Aspect von Stiftungen zugunsten des Schreins von Imam Riza in Mashhad, 1527–1897', in eds Astrid Meier, Johannes Phalitzsch, and Lucian Reingfands, *Islamisches Stiftungen zwischen Juristischer Norm und sozialer Praxis* (Berlin: Akademia Verlag, 2009), 167–89. For the Mashhad's *dar al-shifa*, see Hormoz Ebrahimnejad, *Medicine, Public Health and the Qajar State* (Leiden, Boston: Brill, 2004), 69.

29 For the importance of illumination in Mashhad, see Christoph Werner, *Vaqf en Iran: Aspects culturels, religieux et sociaux* (Paris: Studia Iranica, Cahiers 65, 2015), 93–113.

30 Curzon, *Persia and the Persian Question*, 153.

31 See Fatema Soudavar Farmanfarmaian, 'James Baillie Fraser in Mashhad, or the Pilgrimage of a Nineteenth-Century Scotsman to the Shrine of the Imam Rida', *Iran* 34 (1996): 101–15; and Arminius Vambery, *Mes aventures et mes voyages dans l'Asie Centrale* (Tours: Alfred Mame et Fils, 1886), 363–69.

32 See Ghulam Riza Jalali, ed., *Mashahir madfun dar haram-i razavi*, vol. 2 (Mashhad: Astan-i Quds-i Razavi, 1387/2008), 241–46.

33 Edward B. Eastwick, *Journal of a Diplomat's Three Years' Residence in Persia*, vol. 2 (London: Smith, Elder, and Co., 1889), 224–28.

34 Yate, *Sistan and Khurasan*, 344–45.

35 Roger Mervyn Savory, 'Bast', in *Encyclopaedia of Islam, Second Edition*, eds Peri Bearman, Thierry Bianquis, Clifford Edmund Bosworth, et al., http://dx.doi.org.ezproxy.usek.edu.lb/10.1163/1573-3912_islam_SIM_1270; J. Calmard, 'Bast', in *Encyclopedia Iranica*, ed. Ehsan Yarshater (London: Routledge and Kegan Paul, 1989), vol. III, fasc. 8, 856–58, and Peyman Eshaghi, 'Quietness beyond Political Power: Politics of Taking Sanctuary (Bast Neshini) in the Shi'ite Shrines of Iran', *Iranian Studies* 49 (2016): 493–514.

36 Calmard, 'Bast'.

37 Savory, 'Bast'.

38 The *tumar* is dated Ramadan, 1160/September 1747. See Muhammad Habibi, 'Bast va bast-neshini dar haram-e imam reza', *Dafter-i Asnad* 2–3: 231–32.

39 The *ishiq-aghasi-bashi* refers to the principal court official in charge of protocol and palace administration under the Safavids. Presumably, he assisted the shrine's custodian in his tasks.

40 The British Consul General Yate, who resided in Mashhad in 1894, witnessed the execution of a murderer – who had sought refuge in the shrine – on the square in front of the citadel. Yate, *Sistan and Khurasan*, 334–35.

41 Eshaghi, 'Quietness beyond Political Power', 500–5.

42 Morteza Nouraei, 'Mashhad between 1890 and 1914: A Socio-Historical Study', (PhD diss., University of Manchester, 2000), 253–83.

43 Nouraei, 'Mashhad between 1890 and 1914', 225–26.

44 Stephanie Cronin, *Soldiers, Shahs and Subalterns in Iran: Opposition, Protest and Revolts, 1921–1941* (Basingstoke; New York: Palgrave Macmillan, 2010), 52.

45 See Nouraei, 'Mashhad between 1890 and 1914'; and Stephanie Cronin, 'An Experiment in Military Modernization: Constitutionalism, Political Reform and the Iranian Gendarmerie, 1910–20', *Middle Eastern Studies* 32 (1996): 106–38.

46 For a recent account, see Rudi Matthee, 'Infidel Aggression: The Russian Assault on the Holy Shrine of Imam Reza, Mashhad, 1912', in *Russians in Iran: Diplomacy and Power in the Qajar Era and Beyond*, eds Rudi Matthee and Elena Andreeva (London: I. B. Tauris, 2018), 136–72.

47 File 52/1912 Pt 1 'Persia Diaries' [301] (436/900), British Library: India Office Records and Private Papers, IOR/L/PS/10/209, in *Qatar Digital Library*, https://www.qdl.qa/archive/81055/vdc_100029742539.0x000025.

48 Cronin, *Shahs, Soldiers and Subalterns in Iran*, 16.

49 See Ervand Abrahamian, *Iran between Two Revolutions* (Princeton: Princeton University Press, 1982), 135–65.

50 Ta'ziya is a passion play commemorating the martyrdom of Husayn, third Shi'i imam, grandson of Prophet Muhammad, and son of 'Ali and Fatima, on the tenth of Muharram, 680 CE.

51 Talinn Grigor, *Building Iran: Modernism, Architecture, and National Heritage under the Pahlavi Monarchs* (New York: Periscope Publishing, 2009).

52 Christian Funke, 'Embodying the State: Iranian Banknotes During the Pahlavi Era', *International Bank Note Society Journal* 52 (2013): 10–14.

53 Grigor, *Building Iran*; and Afshin Marashi, *Nationalizing Iran: Culture, Power and the State, 1870–1940* (Seattle: University of Washington Press, 2008).

54 Grigor, *Building Iran*.

55 Zahra Ghulamhusaynpur, 'Nizamnameh asasi astan-i quds dar sal 1305 khorshidi', *Payan-e Baharestan* 2 (1387), 463. The first *na'ib al-tawliyya* was Muhammad Vali Khan Asadi (d. 1935).

56 Ghulamhusaynpur, 'Nizamnameh asasi astan-i quds', 460.

57 K. Scharlau, 'Moderne Umgestaltungen im Grundriss iranischeer Stadte', *Erdkunde* 15 (September 1961): 184–88; and Eckart Ehlers and Willem Floor, 'Urban Change in Iran, 1920–1941', *Iranian Studies* 26 (1993): 251–75.

58 Laurence Lockhart, *Persian Cities* (London: Luzac, 1960), 39–40.

59 These included the office of the governor-general, the national bank (*bank-e milli*), the army headquarters, and the post office. David F. Darwent, 'Urban Growth in Relation to Socio-Economic Development and Westernization: A Case Study of the City of Mashhad' (PhD diss., Durham University), 292.

60 Astaneh Ghods Razavi, *Les biens fonciers urbains de l'Astaneh Ghods: Ville de Mashhad, Annexe 1, 2*.

61 'Ali Akhavan Mahdavi, 'Falake-yi hazrat-i mashhad', *Mishkat* 126 (Bahar, 1394/2015): 111.

62 Dwight M. Donaldson, *The Shiite Religion: A History of Islam in Iraq and Persia* (London: Luzac and Company, 1933), 178–79.

63 Mahdavi, 'Falake-ye hazrat-i mashhad', 113.

64 Habibi, 'Bast va bast-neshini', 235–43.

65 Grigor, *Building Iran*, 33.

66 Fred Richards, A *Persian Journey Being an Etcher's Impressions of the Middle East* (London: Jonathan Cape, 1931), 190–93.

67 Robert Byron, *Road to Oxiana* (London: Vintage Books, 2010), 93.

68 Byron, *Road to Oxiana*, 153.

69 See Houchang Esfandiar Chehabi, 'Staging the Emperor's New Clothes: Dress Codes and Nation-Building under Reza Shah', *Iranian Studies* 26 (1993): 216–17; Houchang Esfandiar Chehabi, 'The Banning of the Veil and Its Consequences', in Cronin, *Soldiers, Shahs, and Subalterns in Iran*, 32–34; and Michael M. J. Fischer, *Iran: From Religious Dispute to Revolution* (Cambridge, MA and London: Harvard University Press, 1980), 98–99.

70 Donald N. Wilber, *Riza Shah Pahlavi: The Resurrection and Reconstruction of Iran, 1878–1944* (Hicksville, NY: Exposition Press, 1975), 166.

71 On Muhammad Vali Asadi, see Jalali, *Mashahir madfun dar haram-i razavi*, 2:25–29.

72 'Persia Dairies', 382r.

73 Wilber, *Riza Shah Pahlavi*, 167.

74 'Persia Dairies', 365r.

75 Baroness Ravensdale, 'Persia in 1935', *Geographical Journal* 88.3 (1936): 224–25.

76 Arthur Upham Pope, 'The Photographic Survey of Persian Islamic Architecture', *Bulletin of the American Institute for Persian Art and Archaeology* 3.7 (1934): 31–32.

77 Keelan Overton, 'Filming, Photographing and Purveying in "The New Iran": The Legacy of Stephan H. Nyman, c.1937–42', in Arthur Upham Pope and A New Survey of Persian Art, ed. Yuka Kadoi (Leiden: Brill, 2016), 326–70.

78 Madrasa Sa'd al-Din, built during the reign of Shah Sulayman Safavi.

79 Ali Mu'taman, *Rahnama-yi va tawsif-i vilayatmadar-i razavi* (Tehran: Chapkhanah-i Bank Milli, 1348/1969), 200.

80 Sarah Piram, 'S'approprier un modèle français en Iran? L'architecte André Godard (188–1965) et la conception des musées iraniens', *Les Cahiers de l'École du Louvre* [En ligne], 11 | 2017, published October 26, 2017, accessed April 22, 2018, http://journals.openedition.org/cel/825.

81 Sayyid Habib Allah Samadi, *Rahnama-ye muze-ye astan-e quds* (Mashhad: Astan-i Quds-i Razavi, 1334/1955), 7.

82 Muhammad Reza Shah, *Mission for My Country* (London: Hutchinson and Co., 1961), 54–58.

83 See Muhammad Ihtisham Keyvanian, *Shams al-Shumus ya Tarikh-i astan-i qods* (Mashhad: Astan-i Quds-i Razavi, 1355/1977), for numerous photographs documenting the visits of Muhammad Reza Shah to the shrine.

84 The royal family performed a yearly ten-day trip to Mashhad in May. See Andrew Scott Cooper, *The Fall of Heaven: The Pahlavis and the Final Days of Imperial Iran* (New York: Henry Holt and Company, 2016), 182. For Mashhad during the Pahlavi period, see Astan-i Quds-i Razavi, *Diruz va amruz* (Mashhad: Astan-e Quds-i Razavi, 1977), 118–33.

85 Darwent, 'Urban Growth in Relation to Socio-Economic Development and Westernization'.

86 William Bayne Fisher, 'Physical Geography', in *Cambridge History of Iran*, ed. W. B. Fisher (Cambridge: Cambridge University Press, 1968), 1:72. See also Alireza Rezvani, 'Physical Evolution Course in Cities: Case-Study: Mashhad-Iran' (PhD diss., Technical University of Dortmund, 2012), 112.

87 Darwent, 'Urban Growth in Relation to Socio-Economic Development', 97.

88 Talinn Grigor, 'Cultivating Modernities: The Society for National Heritage, Political Propaganda, and Public Architecture in Twentieth-Century Iran' (PhD diss., Massachusetts Institute of Technology, 2005), 452.

89 Dariush Borbor, 'Nowsazi atraf-i haram-i motahar hazrat-i riza', *Hunar va mi'mari* 20 (January–March 1974), 30–39.

90 Borbor, 'Nowsazi atraf-i haram-i motahar hazrat-i riza', 37–38.

91 Prabhat Chand, 'Shrine to Escape Mashhad Bulldozer', *Tehran Journal* (December 13, 1967): 5.

92 *Tehran Journal*, 1967, '20th Century Claims Old Mashhad', November 12, 1967, 4.

93 Kamran Diba was related to the queen, Farah Diba, who lobbied for the preservation of the bazaars and was shocked when she learned of their destruction. See Cooper, *The Fall of Heaven*, 210.

94 Kamran Diba, *Baghi miyan do khiyaban: Chehar hazar o yak ruz az zendigi Kamran diba (in conversation with Riza Danishvar)* (Paris: Alborz Edition, 2010), 145.

95 Ataridi, *Tarikh-i astan-i auds-iaRazavi*, 2:639.

96 Thirty hectares, more than three times the size of Isfahan's Maydan.

97 *Encyclopedia Iranica*, s.v. 'Astan-e Qods-e Razavi', vol. II, Fasc. 8, 826–37.

98 Interestingly, a study of the Mashhad shrine, commissioned by Queen Farah Diba from the Asia Institute of Pahlavi University in Shiraz, presents it as a cultural artefact from the past, not as a thriving pilgrimage centre for an active Shi'i religious practice. It focuses exclusively on the historical buildings that were preserved. Bijan Sa'adat, *The Holy Shrine of Imam Reza: Mashhad,* 4 vols. (Shiraz: Asia Institute, Pahlavi University, 1976).

99 Anthony Krafft, *Architecture Contemporaine/Contemporary Architecture*, vol. 5 (Paris, Lausanne: Bibliotheque des arts, 1983–84), 225–28.

100 Amir Said Arjomand, 'Traditionalism in Twentieth-Century Iran', in *From Nationalism to Revolutionary Iran*, ed. Said Amir Arjomand (London: The Macmillan Press Ltd, 1984), 224.

101 Ervand Abrahamian, *A History of Modern Iran* (Cambridge: Cambridge University Press, 2008), 151.

102 Interview with Abdul-Azim Valian by Manouchehr Bibiyan in August 4, 1985, published in Manouchehr Bibiyan, *Secrets of the Iranian Revolution: Jaam-e-Jam Television Open Forum*, [United States]: Xlibris Corporation, 2010.

103 Astan-i Quds-i Razavi, *Iqlab-i Islami va astan-i qods-i razavi* (Mashhad: Astan-i Quds-i Razavi, 1364).

104 Bozorg 'Alamzadeh, *Rahnama-ye harim-i razavi* (Mashhad: Astan-i Quds-i Razavi, 1994), 63–65.

105 For similar developments in other Islamic holy cities, see Robert Saliba, 'Sites of Worship: From Makkah to Karbala; Reconciling Pilgrimage, Speculation, and Infrastructure', in *Urban Design in the Arab World: Reconceptualizing Boundaries*, ed. Robert Saliba (London, New York: Routledge, 2018). For Mashhad, see Samar Saremi, 'Mashhad City Center: Oscillation Between Planned and Unplanned' (paper presented at the Iran Heritage Society conference 'Urban Planning and Civic Design in Modern Iran', London, November 18, 2017).

106 The movie *Nisyan* addressed this situation. (I have only been able to see the promotional material for the movie.)

Towards a New Typology of Modern and Contemporary Mosque in Europe, Including Russia and Turkey

Nebahat Avcıoğlu

R eligious architecture occupies a special place in the European modernist repertoire. Since the early twentieth century, their state-of-the-art technology and formal ingenuity make them seem like the most up-to-date trials of the movement. This status is attested by the cover illustration of Kenneth Frampton's celebrated *Modern Architecture: A Critical History* (first published in 1980), which depicts Notre-Dame du Phare, a church and religious centre, designed in 1931 (unrealized) by the Swiss-Italian modernist architect Alberto Sartoris [Figure 1]. While Sartoris's project, with its modular assembly, flat roof, polychrome walls, translucent cladding, and weight-defying columns, discloses a

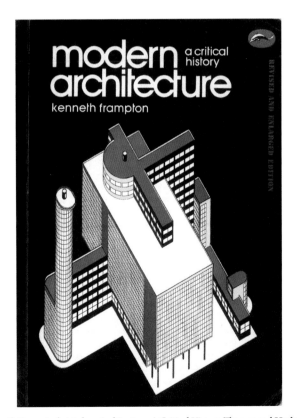

Figure 1: Cover of Kenneth Frampton's *Modern Architecture: A Critical History*, Thames and Hudson, 1985, second edition.

modern aesthetic idiom, the absence of any traditional religious iconography also establishes its contribution to modernity's secular cultural intentions. What warrants Frampton's iconic use of a church as the opening image to his critical analysis of modern architecture is the tension between sacred and secular, past and present, traditional and modern, as well as between vernacular and technologic, tensions that are most palpable in modern religious edifices. Yet rather than engaging directly with these buildings as a separate group, Frampton subsumes them under the general categories of universalism, romantic nationalism, monumental vernacular, and critical regionalism, all of which are typically discussed as glaring paradoxes of modernism. In his *Modern Movements in Architecture* (first published in 1973), Charles Jencks also reads places of worship as a way of articulating the modern project and focuses on a broader selection of examples, such as Frederick Gibberd's Liverpool Cathedral (1960–67), Walter Gropius's Baghdad Mosque (1958), Le Corbusier's Ronchamp Chapel (1950s), and Alvar Aalto's Imatra Church (1957–59). What both books make obvious is that some of the most significant proponents of the movement have either made their careers as ecclesiastical architects or indulged in playing with sacred symbolism. They also demonstrate, given the alleged irrational connotations of religion and its potential to challenge modern values, how these architects often drew on non-European features for their aesthetic sensibility. In Frampton's words:

> the intention behind these procedures of deconstruction and re-synthesis … [was] first, to revitalize certain *devalued* Occidental forms (i.e., sacred architecture) through an Oriental re-casting of their essential nature; and second to indicate the secularization of the institutions represented by these forms. This is arguably a more appropriate way to render a church in a secular age, where traditional ecclesiastic iconography always risks degeneration into kitsch.[1]

Although far from explaining the gravitas of sacred architecture for practitioners, this view depicts, rather interestingly, the modern church as the product of a stylized East, a source of tradition/religion, meeting an equally stereotypical West as defender of reason/secularism. I contend that understanding the modern mosque in Europe within this context becomes a matter of understanding this modernist outlook, that is, the anxiety expressed in the idea of religion generally (rather than Islam specifically) and the tempering of hyper-secularism with Oriental forms. It is not difficult to see the problematic tension in this formula when dealing with an Islamic building, for how can a mosque, an Eastern edifice with Islamic features, undergo so profound a redefinition (that is, rejecting the saturation of its shape by its function, and vice versa) without degenerating into kitsch, to use a modernist vocabulary?

This ideological conundrum has indeed been a challenge for practitioners ever since the mosque appeared on the European stage at the end of the nineteenth century and 'reappeared' after the establishment of the secular Republic of Turkey (1923), following the collapse of the Ottoman Empire and the demise of the Caliphate (1924). Yet architecture is never sheer implementation of values, ideas, or power systems; nor is modernism a mere prescription, as critics have shown.[2] Consequently, the modern mosque has never been merely about critiquing modernism – it is also a question of imperialism, postcolonialism, secular republicanism, Islamophobia, and identity politics, and here it clearly parts company with the history of the modern church. Placed within these sociopolitical debates that extend beyond architecture and faith, liminality, understood as a transition toward the other, again separates the mosque from the modern church. Although the mosque features a number of transfers, transitions, and interstices characteristic of all contemporary religious architecture, such as the obvious functional threshold of a passage from secular to sacred space, or the transition between the classical and modern, local and global, or national and post-national agendas, the mosque in Europe embodies yet another feature of liminality: otherness. In defining the transitional modalities necessitated by the introduction of the mosque in Europe and the role that architecture played in smoothing this transition toward the other (east to west or west to east), it is helpful to think in terms of the typology of the modern mosque.

In this context, four key architectural phases may be identified, which are more or less chronological and represent different forms of liminality: the marginal, the ideal, the in-between, and the unbound. Each category, moreover, corresponds to hotly debated architectural practices of orientalism, nationalism, post-modernism, and globalization. First, the *orientalist mosques*, whose purpose was to display and promote tolerance as an imperial building block. They drew their styles directly from the arts of Islam, and the stylistic variations only came to reflect the different European colonial presences in the region. Second, the *nationalist mosques*, where secularism was pursued as a modern condition, particularly under Kemalism in Turkey and the socialist regimes of Eastern Europe, and where architects tried to reform Islam in their exploration of modern architectural principles. Third, the *diasporic mosques*, where historicism is promoted as a legitimate means of claiming agency on the part of Muslim immigrants who in the 1980s began to constitute a political category in their host countries, and where architects reacted against the homogenizing tendencies of the modern movement by investing in postmodernism with a partial return to traditional forms, use of archetypes, and common visual tropes. Fourth, and finally, the *emancipated mosques*, where both clients' and architects' political stance adhere to the discourse of multiculturalism and globalization, and where secularist or ecumenical desire becomes commensurate with a will to creativity. Emancipated here refers to Jacques Rancière's politics of aesthetics, which rests on the dissensus surrounding the meaningfulness of signs. According to him 'there are no more privileged forms than there are privileged departure points. Everywhere there are points of departure, crossing points and knots that allow us to learn something new provided we recuse, first, radical distance, second, distribution of roles, and third, frontiers between territories.'[3] The detailed analysis of these categories will contribute to an appreciation of the adaptable, dynamic nature of the modern and contemporary mosque and, given their strong political substance, will also lead to a more accurate historical sense of its trials and tribulation.[4]

The Orientalist Tradition

This category of mosques belongs to the period of European imperialism, when Great Britain, France, and Russia ruled over a large number of Muslim subjects and competed with each other for mastery of the East.[5] Consequently, mosques were erected as imperial feats, showcasing European presence in the Islamic lands as well as Muslim loyalty to their new overlords. One contemporary observer wrote that the Great Mosque of Paris (1922–26) [Figure 2] was built 'because France is a great Mussulman power ... [and] when you are a "great Mussulman power" you have to prove your claims to the title'.[6] The foundation stone of the Cathedral Mosque of St. Petersburg [Figure 3a and b] in Russia was laid in 1910, to commemorate the 25th anniversary of the reign of Abd al-Ahad, the co-opted emir of Bukhara, whose political legitimacy depended on the patronage of Tsar Nicholas II. It was opened in 1913, before completion, to coincide with the tercentenary celebrations of the Romanov dynasty, to which Muslims demonstrated their loyalty by praying for the tsar rather than for the caliph, the sultan in Istanbul.[7] In 1911, the London Mosque Committee

Figure 2: Great Mosque of Paris, 1926, Maurice Tranchant de Lunel, Robert Fournez, Maurice Mantout and Charles Heubès. Photograph by the author.

Figure 3a–b: St. Petersburg Mosque, St. Petersburg, 1910–1921, Nikolai Vasiliev. Photograph by Ergun Cagatay.

suggested that an 'enquiry might be made from the Russian Embassy as to the exact area of the mosque at St. Petersburg' before embarking on a specific site in London.[8] According to the Committee '[i]t is felt that London should not fall behind St. Petersburg, where a large mosque was opened two years ago by the Tsar himself. And there are only 15,000,000 Mahometans in Russia, against 100,000,000 in the British Empire.'[9]

These mosques also constituted one aspect of an imperial policy of tolerance, aimed at portraying 'Islam as a democratic religion'.[10] The first imam of the Shah Jahan Mosque (1889) in Woking, 25 miles southwest of London, Khwaja Kamal-ud-Din, belonged to a brand new Islamic movement known as the Ahmadiyya with its headquarters in Lahore. It was considered heretical by the Sunni orthodox.[11] The Ahmadiyyas' visibility in England grounded the British authority in its defence of religious freedom in India and beyond, and the movement came to distinguish itself by 'leadership in intellectual modernism (liberalism) in Islam, especially of English-reading Islam'.[12] Russians, as Robert Crews has argued, also 'devised a policy of toleration to make faiths such as Islam the basic building blocks of empire' and, accordingly, patronised many mosques in the newly conquered Muslim territories.[13] In France, because of the 1905 law separating church and state, they distanced themselves from the discourse of tolerance and turned to preservation of Islamic culture as 'part of official protectorate policy'.[14]

Orientalism in architecture conjured up European discourses of power and knowledge as architects searched for Islamic authenticity in a non-Muslim context and mined its essence, one that distinguished it from European forms. The St. Petersburg Mosque differed dramatically in size and style from unassuming, state-sponsored, provincial 'model mosques' promoted by Catherine the Great, which were simple structures with minarets, in decorative terms, resembling contemporary church architecture.[15] It was directly inspired by the Gur-i Amir Complex in Samarkand, which was built by Timur (1400–04), a monarch who gave meaning to the phrase 'architecture of power'. In assembling from the original, which lay in ruins, so impressive a structure – with a ribbed double-skin dome, towering *pishtaq*, (tall portal) and awesome *muqarnas* (honeycomb vaulting) – Nikolai Vasiliev, the winner of an architectural competition that attracted 49 entries, must have been familiar with the archaeological and restoration work carried out by the emir in both Bukhara and Samarkand.[16] In tsarist Russia, religion was important to imperial rule, and every individual was required to belong to a confessional group.[17] Yet Islam clearly mattered more than other religions, meriting the erection of what remains Europe's largest metropolitan mosque, with a 39-metre-high dome and two minarets of 49 metres.

The Shah Jahan Mosque was a more modest project [Figure 4], promoted by the Orientalist Gottlieb Wilhelm Leitner, who had been the principal of Punjab College in Lahore.[18] Designed by William Isaac Chambers as a freestanding square building measuring sixteen by sixteen feet, it was covered with a bulbous dome. Its facade, flanked by two pavilions,

Figure 4: Shah Jahan Mosque, Woking, UK, 1889, William Isaac Chambers. Photograph by the author.

visibly incorporated features from Mughal architecture, including a *pishtaq* decorated with a carved cartouche framing the gate, ogee arches, crenellation, and *chatri*-topped plinths (domed kiosk). The vegetal scrolls in the spandrels, the incised band of stars around the dome, and the carved leaves at the capital and the base of the decorative globes altogether alluded to the famous Badshaahi Mosque in Lahore and to the Taj Mahal in Agra. The Woking mosque became the 'prototype' for later Ahmadiyya commissions, such as the Fazl Mosque in London and the Berlin Mosque, both opened in 1926.

The Great Mosque of Paris, which was then called Le Centre Islamique de Paris, was explicitly articulated around the notion of arts and crafts. It was designed by the artist Maurice Tranchant de Lunel, inspector general of the Beaux-Arts in Morocco, who took his aesthetic cues from architectural idioms across the Maghrib, including the famous Alhambra in Spain. The mosque was exquisitely built by a group of Parisian architects with the help of North African craftsmen.[19] Unlike the Shah Jahan and St. Petersburg mosques, the Paris complex included, in addition to the prayer hall and a minaret of 33 metres, a courtyard with a fountain, a reception hall, a library, offices, formal gardens, a hammam (public bath), and a restaurant, as well as a house for the imam, all located around the periphery of the building site, with the intention of hiding the actual mosque from view. The general approach – as for other imperial mosques – was historicist, but the symmetrical plan, with a prayer hall rotated at 45 degrees, showed all the tenets of the Art Deco movement. Built in reinforced concrete and richly decorated with Islamic geometrical patterns, it was admired for successfully uniting art, craft, and technology. One observer who was not persuaded by its religious import likened it to the display pavilions erected for the Exposition Internationale des Arts Décoratifs et Industriels Modernes (International Exposition of Modern Decorative and Industrial Arts) of 1925 in Paris, where, unsurprisingly, Tranchant de Lunel also oversaw the Moroccan section.[20]

In each of these three mosque-building enterprises, European empires maintained a policy of neutrality, which also became an aspect of nationalism – though structured around the notion of secularism rather than of tolerance. But this neutrality was not so much a question of religious liberties as of economic interests. The mosque at Woking was financed by Leitner himself and Shah Jahan, Begum of Bhopal, whom the British had restored to power in India and after whom the mosque is named.[21] The St. Petersburg Mosque was built with funds supplied entirely by the co-opted emir and the Tatar minority of the city. Although the land for the Paris complex, unlike the others, was given by the French government following intense negotiations, which began as early as 1893, most of the funds for it came from overseas.[22] State neutrality, in effect, gave rise to patchy foreign contributions that, paradoxically, also impeded the buildings' progress, as the funds had to be cobbled together from donations that took time to gather and often came with strings attached.

The building of the mosque in metropolitan London is a case in point. Officials believed that it 'would serve British interests and enhance British prestige' but could not secure the necessary funds until after the Second World War.[23] In 1939, Lord Lloyd, president of the British Council, former governor of Bombay, and high commissioner to Egypt, began actively lobbying for a mosque in London with the support of Hasan Nashat Pasha, the

Egyptian ambassador. They were in fact following earlier attempts, which date to the very beginning of the century, but diplomatic issues, budget deficits, and disputes within Islam, as well as over architectural styles, halted plans until the late 1960s. According to the *Architects Magazine* published in 1904, 'a well known Egyptian Pasha' requested from the architect Robert Williams sketched plans for a mosque that could be submitted to the sultan in Istanbul, who was still the caliph, for his approval.[24] It is clear from the description that the design was to resemble the Ottoman-style mosque of Muhammad Ali in Cairo (1828–48). It was to measure 46 x 37 metres and feature a 'graceful' minaret of 60 metres, slightly smaller than its model. When this project came to naught in 1926, the highly regarded architect Alfred Brumwell Thomas was hired by the newly created London Nizamiah Mosque Trust Fund to propose an Islamic centre with a mosque.[25] Having provided large sums of money, the Nizam of Hyderabad stipulated that the mosque should be 'grand' with a dome like that of the Taj Mahal as well as a minaret, befitting a monarch declared by the British as the leader of all Indian Muslims, and even 'a potential claimant to the khalifat'.[26] Once again, however, the project was abandoned due to lack of funds when another newly crowned king, Ibn Sa'ud, the second contributor, withdrew his support because of the mosque's association with the Ahmadiyya sect.[27] This also resulted in the architect suing the Trust for unpaid bills.[28] Shortly after that the umbrella organization split; the Nizamiah Mosque Trust separating from the Egyptian led London Mosque Fund.

Objective Secularism

After World War II, gradual decolonization marked the shift toward a secularist doctrine of modernism, purged of any imperialist allusion to tolerance. Secularism also became a potent intensifier of the Turkish Republic's cultural endeavours. The Central London Mosque in Regent's Park (1977) [Figure 5] and the Kocatepe Mosque in Ankara (1987), [Figure 6] the new capital of Turkey, are the most telling examples of this transformation. Both projects were announced in 1944 and realized more than 30 turbulent years later. In London, the Mosque Committee led by Hassan Nashat Pasha and Lord Lloyd, who later became Secretary of State for the Colonies, commissioned the Egyptian architect General Ramzy Omar to prepare designs for the mosque.[29] Omar's imported traditional plans were found unsuitable by the London County Council and the Fine Arts Commission for London; instead they proposed a new international competition hosted in 1969. Of 50 submissions, most of them from Muslim architects, Sir Frederick Gibberd's modernist rendering of an Ottoman mosque with a central cupola and a pencil minaret was selected and construction of the building began in 1974. The mosque was primarily funded by Persian Gulf petro-monarchies, and its interiors benefited from additional Muslim contributions. The modern interpretation of Ottoman features delineated the building quite differently from the neighbouring structures. Yet the more secularist issue was signalled when Functionalists declared its iconic architecture 'frivolous', especially disapproving the presence of a redundant minaret.[30]

Figure 5: The Central London Mosque, London, 1969–77, Sir Frederick Gibberd. Photograph by the author.

Figure 6: Kocatepe Mosque, Ankara, 1967–1987, Hüsrev Tayla, Fatih Uluengin. Photograph by the author.

In Ankara, the state-sponsored new mosque project fuelled the already-turbulent relationship between religion and the young republic. The search for a suitable design turned into an ideological battle between progressives (secularists) and conservatives during a period of political crisis, which climaxed with the 1960 military coup.[31] Beginning in 1947, several competitions were launched that produced no winner. Then, in 1957, a highly modernist project by Vedat Dalokay and Nejat Tekelioğlu was awarded the first prize. However, the government regarded the building in progress as 'irreligious', even profane, resembling a dance club or a bar, and orchestrated an anti-Dalokay campaign that ultimately thwarted the project.[32] Finally, in 1967, when the conservatives pleaded for a building more rooted in the Ottoman tradition, a new architectural competition was launched, calling for a classical design. A neo-Ottoman project by Hüsrev Tayla and Fatih Uluengin was chosen to compensate, as it were, for Turkey's growing secularism.[33]

While Gibberd's design placed greater emphasis on the undifferentiated specificity of the dome and minaret, Dalokay's drew attention to them by emphasizing not the overwhelming (physical and cultural) weight of a monumental dome but the man-made spirit of a vernacular tentlike shell and the plasticity of stark minaret-like poles. Gibberd's compromising approach thus stressed the symbolic form (that is, the traditionalism of religion), whereas Dalokay's emphasized the content (that is, the secularization of religion). Dalokay's mosque was on par with landmark modernist religious buildings and yet unadulterated with the exoticism and romanticism of the masters. For instance, in 1957, when Gropius was asked to build a new university campus grouped around a central mosque in Baghdad, his sensitivity to difference became particularly heightened, giving way to exoticism.[34] He designed the mosque as a circular structure enclosing a rectangular prayer hall, covered by a playful bulbous dome that touches the ground at three points inside a reflecting pool. The light-emanating transparent walls further infused the building with atmosphere and sensuality. The central tenet behind the work, according to Gropius, was a call for drama, and a desire to make it the most memorable object of the campus' 'silhouette'.[35] Although it remained unrealized, Gropius's design nevertheless established a new trend in mosque architecture in Europe. The two earliest examples of this interesting twist – both founded by the Ahmadiyyas – are the Nusrat Jenan Mosque in Hvidovre, near Copenhagen, erected in 1967 by the engineer John Zachariassen, and the Freimann Mosque in Munich.

Dalokay's project had a much wider influence formally and ideally: above all, he demonstrated to his compatriots that designing mosques in the modern age need not be a sign of backwardness. Indeed, after the 1960s many architects in Turkey, followed in his footsteps, either by imitating his design or by giving their mosques an emphatically modern character.[36] For instance, the runner-up to Gibberd's London Mosque, designed by Turkish architects Levent Aksüt and Yaşar Marulyalı, was more than a nod in Dalokay's direction.[37] Others, such as the Etimesgut Armed Forces Mosque (1964), the Kınalı Island Mosque (1964–65), the TEK Mosque (1986–88), and the Turkish Grand National Assembly Mosque (1989), though formally different, were no less radical, with their flat roofs, irregular facades, deformed towers, and distorted floor plans.[38]

Of all these works, perhaps the most radical is the Grand National Assembly Mosque in Ankara, designed by Behruz and Can Çinici [Figure 7].[39] Using a functionalist approach, the architects created a structure with a rectangular prayer hall that is embedded in the hillside. It is covered with a ziggurat, which echoes the stepping walls of the landscaped garden and the cascading transparent mihrab niche that protrudes from the exposed wall where the hill ends and the reflecting pool begins. Irrespective of the architects' claim that the mosque includes allusions to the Prophet's house, which is considered to be the first mosque, one would be hard pressed to find any concrete references other than in pure abstraction, such as the corner poplar tree standing for a minaret. A mosque attached to Parliament was already at odds with the republican cult of secularism, and the drastic design is clearly intended to make religion its complement. Behruz Çinici described the project as a symbolic reinterpretation of Islam, writing: 'the fact that Islam has not gone through reformation is the reason for the continuing prevalence of the domed and centralized square plan in mosque architecture'.[40] Turkish architects of this era indeed aimed at revolutionizing mosque architecture by refusing dominant visual iconographies and projecting a secular content unto its form.

Mosques designed in the European continent in the late 1970s and erected in the 1980s also tried to emancipate themselves from centuries-old dictates of imperialist representation, be it Ottoman or European. Zlatko Ugljen's Sherefudin Mosque in Visoko, Bosnia and

Figure 7: Grand National Assembly Mosque, Ankara, Turkey, 1987, Behruz and Can Çinici. Photograph by the author.

Herzegovina, and the Mosque and Cultural Centre of Rome by Sami Mousawi and Paolo Portoghesi attach great importance to the question of modernity.[41] The Sherefudin Mosque was commissioned and funded by the local community to replace a demolished Ottoman mosque on the same site. Boldly sculptural in overall expression, the new mosque objectifies not the past but architecture itself: it is an homage to Le Corbusier's Ronchamp Chapel, which has acquired the iconic status among modern sacred buildings for architects. Built on a sloping terrain, the prayer hall is reached by two entry points: through a ramp winding down around an existing cemetery and a staircase descending onto an internal patio with ablution fountains. Sparsely decorated on the interior, it also breaks with conventions: the curvilinear ceiling culminates not above the mihrab or in the middle of the hall but on the side; the light is unevenly admitted through three funnel openings in the roof. Yet, Ugljen also provides a good illustration of how one may still retain the past as a design concept, as is evident in one of the drawings, in which one sees a classical Ottoman mosque emerging from beneath the geometric forms nestled within one another.[42] Overall, the mosque is concerned with the status of modern architecture in Muslim societies rather than religion in a secular society, which had been the case for Turkish architects of the same period.

With the Cultural Centre of Rome [Figure 8], attention shifts toward a formal synthesis between tradition and modernity as well as East and West (or Christianity and Islam), as it was built in a non-Muslim country. It was designed by the UK-based Iraqi architect Sami

Figure 8: The Cultural Centre of Rome, Italy, 1989, Sami Mousavi and Paulo Porteghesi and Vittorio Gigliotti. Photograph by Aldo Ippoliti ©Aga Khan Award for Architecture.

Mousavi together with one of the early proponents of postmodernism, Paolo Portoghesi, who made his postmodern debut at the Venice Biennale of 1980 with a project entitled 'The Presence of the Past'.[43] They were invited to collaborate after being declared joint winners of an international competition held in 1975. Their design unites the very similar, yet non-identical, features of Islamic and Roman traditions, such as domes, courtyards/piazzas, and *riwaqs*/arcades. The square prayer hall with a central dome is a reference to both the Ottoman mosque and the Pantheon. Yet the hypostyle plan, with ribbed columns joined at concentric circles, denotes a set of geometrical conventions more specific to Islamic architecture, found, for instance, in the Great Mosque of Cordoba (784–987). The courtyard, by contrast, has more of a Roman feeling, with the double-story walkway and open arcades with a flat roof. The overall design advocates juxtapositions of 'universally valid' Islamic and Roman forms, which, in Portoghesi's words, are 'inalienable and stamped in the minds of everyone through the common experience of historical space'.[44] But the final outcome falls short of its postmodern ambitions of historical memory and contextualization as it lapses into historicism within the modernist conceit of universalism and symbolism.[45] When it was shortlisted for the Seventh Aga Khan Award Cycle in 1998, the jury – made up of avowed postmodernists like Fredric Jameson, Charles Jencks, Zaha Hadid, and Peter Eisenman, among others – found it unconvincing, if not a modernist epigone.[46]

Regaining the Past: Postmodernism or Diasporic Desire

Having reached its modernist potential, was the mosque now capable of reinventing itself in the language of the postmodern? If modernity facilitated a decisive link between formalism and secularism, then postmodernity encouraged hybridity, humour, plurality, and heterogeneity without hierarchizing particular times or places. It celebrated the end of great teleological narratives underlying national, religious, or cultural meanings. This outlook had direct consequences both on the Muslim migrants' and the host countries' perceptions of the mosque and gave way to three kinds of formulations: the conversion mosques, multipurpose cultural centres, and neo-Orientalism.

The mosques that were converted from old, unused spaces make the connotation of *hybrid* particularly explicit. This practice was in place even before the term became a postmodern catchphrase. For instance, Green Lane Masjid in Birmingham was converted from a public library as early as 1970. In the early 1980s, several disparate buildings, such as the Oslo Nour Mosque, which was a stately home built in the late nineteenth century, and the Fatih Mosque in Amsterdam [Figure 9a and b], originally a Jesuit church erected in 1921, were reconsecrated for Muslim use. The first mosque in Dublin (1984) was also a recycled church, built in 1860 [Figure 10]. Because Islam does not dictate a particular shape for mosques, the reappropriation of existing spaces is, in effect, in keeping with Muslim tradition. Much more significant is the relative architectural condition of these buildings. What they have in common is the monumentality inherent in their size and style (neo-

Figure 9a–b: Fatih Mosque, Amsterdam, View towards the mihrab. Originally a Jesuit church erected *c.*1921. Converted in 1981. Photographs by Zehra Gülbahar.

Figure 10: Dublin Mosque, converted in 1984, Dublin, Ireland. Photograph by Barry Flood.

Gothic, neo-Romanesque, neo-Classical), which imparts a certain sense of autonomy and power. Yet it may be argued that they lack the authority and identity politics so central to postmodern practice, for hybridity is here presented as assimilation, something to which Muslims are expected to aspire. Low visibility, moderation, and conformity became the very embodiment of the assimilation for which the European host nations were looking in their immigrants, and the reused buildings, charmingly picturesque, inadvertently underlined integration.

If the converted mosque was too sweeping with identities and roots, the 1990s saw another kind of Islamic institution: the multipurpose cultural centre, which rose to prominence from social necessity to showcase the new generation of prosperous and well-integrated European Muslim citizens. Often located outside urban hubs, these centres have a corporate flavour, featuring parking lots, exhibition halls, and sports facilities. Visually, they make only partial use of standardized iconographies of Islamic architecture on their exteriors, while their interiors burst with traditional references. Examples such as the Madrid Islamic Cultural Centre and Mosque (1992), the Evry Islamic Cultural Centre near Paris (1995), and the Dublin Islamic Cultural Centre (1993) give us a good idea of the scope of design variations found in these institutions.

The Evry complex [Figure 11a and b] was among a number of religious buildings, including a pagoda, cathedral, and synagogue, projected for the new satellite town, built in the 1960s near Paris. Designed by Marc Henry-Baudot as the second-largest mosque in France, it is surprisingly modest in appearance. Though clearly indebted to La Grande Mosquée de Paris in its frontally located, tall, square minaret, it has none of the bold surface carvings and wood adornments facing the street. The centre was planned as an introverted group of buildings, with slit windows and flat roofs enclosed within walls, which make it virtually indistinguishable from a shopping mall. The street access opens into a small garden, which faces a doorway that is more ornate and colourful. The entrance hall is embellished

Figure 11a–b: Evry Islamic Centre, Evry, France, 1995, Marc Henry-Baudot. Photographs by Marc Henry-Baudot, ©Aga Khan Award for Architecture.

with a glass dome, which is only partially visible from the street level, and the prayer hall is covered with a flat ceiling supported by columns with plaster stalactite capitals. The interior, as if to compensate for the bare nature of the exterior, is overwhelmingly decorated with polychrome mosaic and arabesque motifs.

The Madrid Islamic Cultural Centre was the result of an international competition held in 1980, which attracted 455 entries.[47] The winning design by a team of Polish architects, which was finally completed in 1992, is equally withdrawn from its surroundings. Nevertheless, the solidity of the forbidding walls succeeds in capturing public attention. The polished white stone walls, the red roof tiles, and the filigree openings, embedded in pointed and horseshoe-shaped reliefs, give the design a modern vernacular touch. Inside, the regional reference is that of the Great Mosque of Cordoba, the timeless Islamic reference. The Dublin Islamic Centre [Figure 12], on the other hand, is the epitome of the International Style, in which only technique, material, and modular form seem to have any relevance, though all of these characteristics are subtly inflected with the Ottoman idiom. Built on the outskirts of the city by the local firm of Michael Collins, it has a welcoming entrance: a shiny marble portico and stainless steel railings over a monumental staircase that rises to a courtyard before the prayer hall covered by a dome, which is, in fact, a modern quotation of Sinan's

Figure 12: Islamic Cultural Centre, Dublin, Michael Collins Architects. Photograph by Kevin Dunne @Aga Khan Award for Architecture.

Sokullu Mehmed Pasha Mosque (1571) in Istanbul. Inside, the spaces are divided evenly, and the lightweight skeleton steel frame is left exposed over the smooth, undecorated surfaces. The airy feeling of the complex departs from the inwardly focused suburban projects, with their inner prayer halls serving as spiritual hideaways.

Arguably less compromising than the converted mosque, the Islamic cultural centre nevertheless draws attention to Muslims' moderation and sociability rather than to Islam's visibility. By contrast, it is with neo-Orientalist mosques that an entirely new form of political coding has emerged in recent decades. In adopting a greater number of ethnic and national iconographies, these buildings aim to speak of European pluralism and not only of Muslim assimilation.[48] This approach is particularly significant because European assimilationist ideologies – imposing urban regulations and building bylaws, time and financial constraints, and such overt discrimination as the legal banning of the construction of minarets in Switzerland, which came into effect in November 2009 – often precluded the articulation of traditional Islamic features. Consequently, battles over minority identities are now waged around the very inclusion of minarets and their heights as well as domes,[49] which, arguably, is a historical low in the appreciation of mosque architecture. The Westermoskee in Amsterdam, opened in 2015, having been commissioned more than a decade before by the Turkish-German Islamic organization Milli Görüş (National Vision) in conjunction with the city council, is a case in point [Figure 13]. The local Dutch community continues to protest the mosque, adducing its emphatically traditional style as an excuse for its unacceptability. With its octagonal support system, central cupola, half-domes, portico, and pencil-shaped minaret it pays homage to the

Figure 13: Westermoskee, Amsterdam, Netherlands, 2010, Breitman and Breitman. Photograph by Breitman and Breitman.

canonical Ottoman type: Hagia Sophia, Istanbul (built as a church in 532–37 and converted to a mosque in 1453). But it is, in fact, designed as part of a rehabilitation of the 1930s neighbourhood in the spirit of the Neo-Rationalists.[50] It stands in the middle of an irregular piazza, surrounded by 118 units of housing and shops that were generated by the same project. The continuous use of red brick decorated with white stripes – drawn from local buildings – creates a vernacular atmosphere despite the Ottoman character of the mosque. This approach challenges Orientalist aesthetics as it reverses the imperial prerogative of making Islamic architecture a showcase. It turns the mosque into an urban project whereby typology (sacred building), rather than style, expresses the hierarchical status of the building. Although the project, in its traditionalism, seems to recall the early imperialist mosques of Paris and St. Petersburg, the overwhelming emphasis on local context sets it apart from them.

The notion of authenticity, so fetishized by imperialism, offers the capacity for detachment in order to promote a diasporic transcultural stance. The Cologne Mosque in Germany (2010), designed by the local architect Paul Böhm, reflects this shift in its mix of modern and traditional idioms [Figure 14]. The project resulted from an open architectural competition initiated by the Diyanet İşleri Türk İslam Birliği (DITIB), funded by Turkish government, which stipulated that the final design should include two minarets and 'possibly a dome'.[51] Although the monumental scale of the building, which features two pencil-thin

Figure 14: The Cologne Mosque, Cologne, Germany, 2010, Paul Böhm. Photograph by Dipti Khera.

minarets, looks back to the Ottoman 'Golden Age', it prioritizes transparency. There are no forbidding walls, and the courtyard, which features a fountain, becomes a public square. The prayer hall, set within a hemispherical concrete skin, is airy and literally opens up to be viewed between the incised gaps of the vertical windows. In this way the 'alien' aspect of its character is not so much camouflaged, as in the Westermoskee, which shares common masonry with neighbouring buildings, but rather reworked into a visual gesture of harmonious coexistence. Yet the cultivation of neo-Orientalism by Muslim communities seeking an explicit means of promoting pluralism has prompted an antagonistic response from those Europeans who refuse to see these mosques as anything other than integration-defying 'homesick' or 'hideout' places. Many contemporary architects and architectural critics also believe that any form of Orientalism is a delusion, a false consciousness about identity, as it tries to assume an otherness to which second- and third-generation Muslim citizens do not necessarily relate.[52] Consequently, architects have begun to make the most of these challenges by bringing their designs in new directions.

Aesthetic Regime: Collaboration and Transgression

The Strasbourg Mosque competition provides an example through which one can assess several of these recent developments. In 2000, the city of Strasbourg, the official seat of the European Parliament, launched an international competition calling for the city's first purpose built mosque. The competition was managed by the Muslim Institute of Europe and Muslim Association of Strasbourg (Conseil de Coordination des Associations Islamiques de Strasbourg), and enthusiastically approved by the then socialist mayor Catherine Trautmann, a member of the European Parliament.[53] Among the five short-listed proposals, which included one from the late Zaha Hadid, renowned for her bold and fluid abstract forms, and one from Mario Botta, best known for his flawless brick-clad Louis Khan-like ecclesiastical structures, the jury of community representatives and city officials selected the design by Paolo Portoghesi, the architect of the Rome Islamic Cultural Centre [Figure 15]. Hadid's proposal, the Elevated Mosque [Figure 16a and b], which takes its name from its seemingly floating prayer hall, is formally striking and idiosyncratic in every way. Rejecting any outright temporal and cultural references, it demonstrates a frank fascination with the aesthetics of new technology and fractal space as it creates a convulsion in the landscape before dematerializing at the edges. Reminiscent of her secular projects, the flowing lines – according to Hadid, inspired by Arabic calligraphy – create a surface rhythm and enhance the symbolic capacity of the building, though not convincingly enough to win the competition.[54]

Portoghesi, on the other hand, adapted traditional Islamic forms to produce a structure that is clearly inspired by the Dome of the Rock, reaching further back in time than the Ottoman or the Cordoba Mosque. The prayer hall is essentially a cube sitting on a raised platform, yet the eight external structural posts supporting the roof give it the impression of being an octagon. The curvilinear posts resemble the sails of a boat (or a shark's fin),

Figure 15: The Strasbourg Mosque, Strasbourg, France 2000–2010, Paolo Portoghesi. Photograph by Yumna Masarwa.

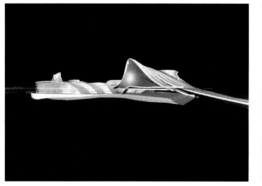

Figure 16a–b: Elevated Mosque, project commissioned by City of Strasbourg, 2000, Zaha Hadid. @ Zaha Hadid.

which may have been a symbolic reference to the building's location near the water. The spiral minaret, though unapproved by the Strasbourg municipal administration and left unrealized, was also a distant quotation from the Samarra-type mosques, built about a century and a half after the Dome of the Rock. It is not uncommon to find archetypes in Portoghesi's work, as he argues that architecture is but 'an instrument for the production and transmission of communicative models'.[55] The selection of his design reminds us that the public authorities continue to endorse the historicist readability of mosques rather than highly individual and assertive aesthetics for them.

The Strasbourg competition nevertheless gave great momentum to creative designs thanks to the participation of Hadid and other renowned architects. Thus, an ever-increasing number of projects is now inflected with the political potential of daring formalism. In the London Abbey Mills Islamic Centre project by Mangera Yvars Architects, winners of an international competition held in 2005, we once again find an atypical concept. Described as a mega-mosque with multifunctional facilities because of its extraordinary capacity for 70,000 worshippers, it is conceived as part of an urban development and regeneration project that draws the architect's attention to the complex's inclusive nature rather than to the exclusiveness of the prayer hall. By employing curvilinear forms, confluent spaces, sound, and light as design criteria, as well as an ecological programme, the architects interpreted the complex as an ideal city, organically linked to its context. The underlying Islamic concept of their vision was offered by the famous hadith 'The whole Earth is a mosque'. The high-tech latticed roof structure and cladding, stretching over multifunctional spaces and public walkways, form an abstract silhouette in the landscape, which is as tradition-defying as Hadid's audacious 'calligraphy' in reinforced concrete. The resemblances between the two projects are not pure coincidence: Ali Mangera worked under Hadid's direction before establishing his own practice.

Both designs enflamed debates between Muslims and non-Muslims. Some find them exalting, some disregard them as mere digital fantasies unable to captivate the imagination or capture the aura of a sacred space, and still others see a subversive edge in their narratives of surface and fluidity. And although both remain unrealized, contemporary mosque designs seem to have digested both the artefactual nature of traditional buildings and aesthetic ideologies of the modern, as well as postmodern contextualism, wit, and irony.

Today there is almost no consensus as to what a mosque should look like or where it can be built, as the newly invented gated-community mosque in Turkey demonstrates. Upscale gated residential compounds are not new to Turkey, but finding religious structures within them is a recent development. The Refiye Soyak Mosque by Mutlu Çilingiroğlu, erected in 2004 [Figure 17], and Adnan Kazmaoğlu's Yeşil Vadi Mosque, finished in 2009 [Figure 18], both in the outskirts of Istanbul, are exemplary for their bold appearance.[56] Their presence may indicate a desire to fill the 'spiritual void' of postmodern suburban settlements, but, architecturally, they do not seek integration with their surroundings nor do they employ regional vernacular idioms. Instead, they feature a deliberately modern approach, with geometrical purity, modular panels, white walls, and simple iconic features. Refiye Soyak, built in the middle of a parking lot, and Yeşil Vadi, over a conference hall, are hermetic small structures, strategically located at the entrances to the complexes in which they are sited; one enjoys a prolonged view of them while driving into and out of the communities. The traditionalism suggested by the presence of a mosque in this case is an allusion to the 'local', a by-product of the global, distinguishable in the sprawling highways.

What is interesting about these mosques, however, is not so much that their presence restrains globalization but the generally unorthodox thinking behind them. This last aspect is perhaps best demonstrated in reverse, as it were: the global in the local, by the

Figure 17: Refiye Soyak Mosque, Istanbul, 2004, Mutlu Çilingiroğlu. Photograph courtesy of the architect.

Figure 18: Yeşil Vadi Mosque, 2009, Adnan Kazmaoğlu. Photograph by the author.

much-discussed Şakirin Mosque (2009) in Üsküdar, Istanbul, by Hüsrev Tayla, the architect of the controversial Kocatepe Mosque in Ankara, and Zeynep Fadıllıoğlu, a high-society interior designer [Figure 19]. Although it is not a gated community mosque, it is nevertheless a 'semi-public' monument dedicated to a wealthy Turkish/Arab family, for which both architect and decorator were given almost complete freedom. Stylistically, it revisits Vedat Dalokay's original design for the Kocatepe Mosque: a reinterpretation of an Ottoman centrally planned mosque with a courtyard surrounded by arcades in 'brutalist' mode, which is clearly part of Tayla's ongoing dialogue with Dalokay. The anachronism of its structure is balanced by a highly contemporary aesthetic, which reflects Fadıllıoğlu's confidence and international success. The decoration was inspired by traditional techniques of metal casting, glasswork, carpentry, and calligraphy, yet it is rendered impeccably 'fashionable' by the use of transparent cladding, exaggerated proportions, vibrant colours, and multiple references to Islamic arts and crafts (calligraphy, tiles, glass, cut-marble, etc.). The national and international media exploited the contrast between the grey metallic skin of the exterior and the exuberant and daring detailing of the interior; the gender differences between architect and decorator were presented as the main reason for the achievement. CNN Europe claimed that 'this was a mosque with a woman's touch'.[57] And yet the glamour in this context also plays a political role: it mediates a different view of Islam, one that is modern and global, even feminist.

A similarly energetic attitude to detailing also occurs in recent mosques in Bosnia and Herzegovina, albeit in quite different ways. The White Mosque complex by Husejn Dropic, opened in 2005 in Brcko, adapts the modernist principles of efficiency and function with

Figure 19: Şakirin Mosque, Üsküdar, Istanbul, 2007, Hüsrev Tayla and Zeynep Fadıllıoğlu. Photograph by the author.

streamlined shapes and non-decorative surfaces, which testifies to the influence of Zlatko Ugljen, with whom Dropic has collaborated on different projects since 1999.[58] Yet the round shape of the land gives birth to a dynamic plan, and the simplicity of the building's form clearly suggests dedication to technique. The perfection of the circle seems to be deliberately contrasted with the irregular shapes and sizes of the spaces within. There are three entrances, none of which is identified as primary; the square prayer hall is located off-centre, breaking out of the circle on one corner. It is linked by corridors and open spaces to the other facilities, housed in a separate block that adheres to the contours of the bounding wall. The minaret emerging between the blocks gives the illusion of being in the centre of the circle. The illusionism is also evident in the structural elements: the roof of the prayer hall is a 'boat' turned upside down, executed in laminated wood fitted with thermo-reflecting glass. The pergola, the purpose of which is to cast shadows, is a totally transparent glass structure supported by exposed rafters. And the capitals of the columns serve as sun breaks. When the building is lit, each element gives the impression of floating above the others. Symbolically, the disjunction, contrast, and illusion suggest the trauma of recent history, as Bosnian Muslims return to their towns after being expelled in 1992.

Post-communist and post-conflict republics have given priority to building mosques that try to negate the oppressive rhetoric of the nationalism of previous eras. The Vatan Memorial [Figure 20] by Kurbanmagomed Kerimov, completed in 2004 in Dagestan, Russian Federation, where Islam's presence is becoming increasingly palpable, offers another good example.[59] Commissioned to commemorate an eighteenth-century military victory,

Figure 20: Vatan Memorial Mosque, Dagestan, Russian Federation, 2004, Kurbanmagomed Kerimov. Photograph courtesy of the architect @Aga Khan Award for Architecture.

Figure 21: Sancaklar Mosque, Büyükçekmece, Istanbul, 2014, Emre Arolat. Photograph by the author.

the memorial unites two historically and ideologically distinct building types through the visual syntax of a medieval fort: the museum and the mosque, one seeking political consensus and the other religious persuasion. The use throughout the entire complex of local material – natural stone quarried on site – integrates the two buildings, while different functions are distinguished by formal attributes: domes are reserved for the mosque, and height for the museum. In terms of layout, they are mirror images of each other: square with rooms attached and similar in size, the prayer hall measuring 5.4 x 5.4 m and the exhibition hall 4.5 x 4.5 m. The dialogical strategy employed by the architect unsettles the status of each institution and creates a hybrid monument, curbing their separate orthodox potentials. Only the terraced landscape enhances the grandeur, solidity, and durability of the memorial, which rises in what look like stalagmites. Behind this idea of emerging from the ground seems to lay a preoccupation with the 'local', also suggested by the name Vatan, meaning motherland, which reminds us of vernacularism's (as well as religion's) continuing vital role in globalization.[60]

In a very different way, the dialectic between the local (territory) and the universal (global modernism) is also evident in Emre Arolat's Sancaklar Mosque (2014), named after its sponsor and built on the roadside of a still largely rural suburb of Istanbul on the Sea of Marmara [Figure 21]. However, while in Dagestan the local plays an important role in remembering the past and rights of Muslims, in Turkey the goal has been to dislodge religion from the abstraction of politics.[61] The Sancaklar Mosque embodies resistance to the nationalist Muslim identity ushered in by Turkey's Islamist movement.[62] Its modern vernacularism (to be understood as a specificity of the site) is a reaction to the officious patterns of standardized mosques propagated by the government since 2002, which are often built with ominous visibility, without any regard for material, topography, history or environment, and instrumentalized as a basis of Turkey's economic influence globally. Stylistically they insist on the Ottoman type, especially those designed by the sixteenth-century architect Sinan, which has now become a global Turkish brand. The paradox is

303

that neo-Ottomanism (or neo-Orientalism), for the Muslim diaspora of the 1990s, was a way to manage European pluralism in cultural terms, but under Turkish official patronage it now carries strong ethnic overtones as 'Turkish Islamic architecture' that Muslims from other backgrounds cannot or will not relate to. President Erdoğan has also alienated his own citizens by proactively preventing deviation from the Ottoman style as if he were the master architect.[63] The recently inaugurated hulk of a state mosque with six minarets, comprising a 63,000 worshipper capacity prayer hall and a large courtyard, built atop Çamlıca, the highest hill on the Asian side of Istanbul, has stirred intense debates in the media for its copycat style, decadence, and destruction of precious greenery crucial for the choking metropolis as well as for disfiguring the city's silhouette [Figure 22]. The president, in an answer to his critics, said: 'You pitiful souls, these [mosques] are seals, the stamp [of Turkish Islam]!'[64] What he meant was that this is the official style and the doors to creativity are closed.

Arolat's mosque is an 'iconoclastic' monument that defies such political dictates.[65] It rejects historicism-turned-absolutism in favour of a hermetically sealed yet open-ended religious architecture. The mosque renounces visibility. It faces away from the recently built bombastic gated housing estates and a shopping mall called Toskana (which already seems abandoned and on the verge of decline, as is often the case with malls in remote gated estates). By contrast, the mosque, mostly built with natural stones, lies hidden on the hill, integrated with the surrounding landscape and overlooking the gently undulating fields. Rectangular shapes and blocks of walls, visible above ground, frame the site and direct people towards the underground prayer hall. The worshippers approach the mosque obliquely by a series of steps and ramps rather than by direct confrontation of a gate or high portal.

Figure 22: Çamlıca Mosque, Istanbul, 2012, Hayriye Gül Tolu and Bahar Mızrak. Photograph by the author.

The mosque's regard for topography is both a pragmatic and a spiritual principle in this design. The ground and the roof almost become one, creating an ever-proliferating metonymic chain of natural effects and artifice, public and private, here and beyond. Nature also slips into the interior programme in the form of a cave, which reinforces the moral and ethical principles expounded in Islam, i.e., reflection upon time, piety, and modesty, etc. Interestingly, while good deeds, such as prayer, must be hidden from public view, Arolat makes the invisible (death), visible, by placing the semi-covered funerary courtyard at the entrance by the roadside. The muted stone slabs reserved for coffins, arranged in threes, endow the courtyard with dignity. This is a mosque that begins with the end of life and descends into 'its primitive beginnings in the cavern'.[66]

Arolat's modern rendering of a mosque has nothing to do with the secularist movement of the previous generation of Turkish architects. Yet, his architecture sits very well within the modern paradigm – from Frank Lloyd Wright's organic modernism to Tadao Ando's minimalism – in terms of the intense formalism, fluidity of spaces, flat roof, play of light and shade, and technology. The disavowal of historicism is not so much a secularist objective or a clean break with the past as it is a deeply modern exaltation of the mythic qualities of nature. As Vincent Scully argues 'the attainment of the sacred was one of the well hidden agendas of canonical modern architecture' of all types.[67] Indeed Arolat's secular and sacred buildings resemble each other. This typological compatibility makes his mosque even more radical within the Turkish context, considering the fact that Vedat Dalokay's Kocatepe scheme and more recently Nevzat Sayın's Malatya project were ousted for allegedly looking like a nightclub or a factory (i.e., not a 'mosque'). Arolat's design succeeds in avoiding the rigid identifications systematically attached to both the secular or sacred buildings by affirming Modernism's enchantment with nature, landscape, and the environment, as well as plasticity and new technology.

The interior of the mosque also encapsulates the same concerns for meditation and reverence for the mysteries of nature. It rejects the worldly ostentation of neo-Ottoman architecture. The angular walls, exposed concrete, rough stone, terraced floor, and rippling roof induce drama [Figure 23]. The light-flooded white concrete qibla wall is the focal point for devotion, where an even brighter small niche indicates the mihrab, flanked by the minbar, which is interpreted as built-in curved steps leading to a dark opening. The contrast between the two invokes imaginative musings, and so does the single quotation from the Qur'an ('Believers, remember God often')[68] inscribed in exquisite Thuluth script like a tantalizing apparition inside a cavern.

If Arolat seems not to have entirely done away with the minaret, which is visible to the passerby from the main road, it is because strictly speaking, it may not be a minaret. It grows, as if organically, out of the qibla wall below just above the minbar, which is a very unusual placement for a minaret, suggesting that they in fact belong together. The minbar, which could be very simple or elaborate, symbolizes the presence of the Prophet in a mosque. The reference to the Prophet is a thread that runs throughout the whole design. Uğur Tanyeli provides a persuasive explanation for the metaphor of the cave with respect to the Sunni cult of the Prophet:

Figure 23: Sancaklar Mosque, Büyükçekmece, Istanbul, 2014, Emre Arolat. Photograph by the author.

In form and atmosphere … [the prayer hall] resemble[s] a cave, an allusion that has wider symbolic significance. The divine revelations that would later form the Quran first reached Muhammad in the year 610 in a cave on Mount Hira, near Mecca. For the faithful, this utterly plain and confined space enhances the spiritual bond with their prophet. Everyone who worships here experiences an existence within a timeless space devoid of worldly references.[69]

Therefore, it is possible to suggest that Arolat conceived the minaret not as a pervasive symbol of Islam (certainly not a symbol of Ottoman Islam since he rejects the pencil-shaped minaret) but as an externally visible sign of the prophet's presence in the Sancaklar Mosque. However, such a reading and the sanctity of the space very much depend on the conviction that there is nothing ontological about Islamic architecture. Indeed, Arolat had to argue his client out of conventional ideas in order to achieve this project. As he writes:

After a long pause we resumed our conversation. He was aware of the views that I had previously expressed on the subject: about how hard it was to design a new mosque in Turkey, how such an undertaking was a battle that was in any case impossible to win, how much I despaired of the simplistic conservatism that typically defined conventional expectations of mosque architecture. He said he had been especially moved by my assertion that there was in fact no formal description anywhere of what an Islamic house of worship ought to be: neither in the Qur'an itself, nor in any other text that deserved to be taken seriously. After this brief – and to me utterly astonishing – exposition, he declared that he had come to me to have 'some other kind' of mosque built.[70]

Thus, the emancipated mosque is not only a physical manifestation of modernist abstraction but also a conviction in the quality of human subjectivity in matters of fate. In conclusion, then, this brief account of mosque architecture across time and space from Britain to Turkey shows that it is shaped by the notions of imperialism, assimilation, reinterpretation, transgression, and reconciliation. If imperialist mosques expressed the political values of tolerance and the nationalist ones those of democracy, the contemporary mosque must be said to express both the cultural and aesthetic values of emancipation from the dogmas of secularism, economic, climatic, regional, and even gender restrictions. While modernism insisted on the universal and the secular with architects turning to purity of forms, it also looked back to the history of Islamic architecture and its essentializing iconography. Political transformations brought a mandate and a breakthrough in religious architecture, diversifying design, and symbolism. Postmodernism insisted on the inseparability of forms from lived experiences and drew our attention to issues of formal memory, multiculturalism, and the politics of images. These changes have altered architects' relationship to places of worship; they no longer search for a secularist subtext, nor are they accused of being retrograde. Today, they focus on aesthetics as a polemical vehicle to question the radicalism of religion in contemporary life. Thus, once again we witness a premium artistic value put on designing and constructing religious monuments. And such an aesthetic regime, in a way, returns mosque architecture back to its heterogeneous origins.

Notes

1 Kenneth Frampton, *Modern Architecture: A Critical History* (London: Thames and Hudson, 1985), 314.

2 The literature on this topic is too vast to be listed here, but see, most recently, Timothy Mitchell, ed., *Questions of Modernity* (Minneapolis: University of Minnesota Press, 2000); and Modjtaba Sadria, ed., *Multiple Modernities in Muslim Societies* (Geneva: Aga Khan Award for Architecture, 2009).

3 Jacques Rancière, *Le Spectateur émancipé* (Paris: La Fabrique, 2008), 23–24.

4 On contemporary European mosques, see, for example, Ihsan Fethi, 'The Mosque Today', in *Architecture in Continuity*, ed. Sherban Cantacuzino (New York: Aperture, 1985), 59–62; Hasan-Uddin Kahn, 'An Overview of Contemporary Mosques', in *The Mosque*, ed. Martin Frishman and Hasan-Uddin Khan (1994; London: Thames and Hudson, 2002), 247–68; Ismaïl Serageldin and James Steele, ed., *Architecture of the Contemporary Mosque* (London: Academy Editions, 1996); Renata Holod and Hasan-Uddin Khan, ed., *The Mosque and the*

Modern World: Architects, Patrons and Designs since the 1950s (London: Thames & Hudson, 1997); and Ergün Erkoçu and Cihan Buğdacı, eds, *The Mosque: Political, Architectural and Social Transformations* (Netherlands: Nai Publishers, 2009). See also Karla Cavarra Britton, ed., *Constructing the Ineffable: Contemporary Sacred Architecture* (New Haven: Yale University Press, 2010) and Nebahat Avcıoğlu, 'The Mosque and the European City' in *Islam and Public Controversy in Europe*, ed. Nilüfer Göle, (Farnham: Ashgate, 2014), 57–68.

5   Nebahat Avcıoğlu, 'Form-as-Identity: The Mosque in the West', with response by Nasser Rabbat, *Cultural Analysis* 6 (February 2008): 91–112, http://socrates.berkeley.edu/~caforum/.

6   Ernest Dimnet, 'The Paris Mosque', *Saturday Review of Politics, Literature, Science and Art* 142.3697 (1926): 250. Dimnet's article was motivated by criticism of the French government for making concessions for Islam but not for Catholicism.

7   Jeremy Bransten, 'The World's Northernmost Mosque', *Russian Life* 46.1 (2003): 28.

8   Proceedings of the Mosque Committee, *Camden Fifth Series* 38 (2011): 82.

9   'A Mosque for London', *The Manchester Guardian,* April 10, 1911, 5.

10 'A London Mosque Egyptian Ambassador's Statement', *The Times* 48528, February 1, 1940, 5.

11 Abdul-Latif Tibawi, 'The History of the London Central Mosque and the Islamic Cultural Center, 1910–1980', *Die Welt des Islam* 21 (1983): 1–4, 194.

12 Tibawi, 'The History of the London Central Mosque'. In 1930, Woking mosque denied association with the sect and broke ties with it when it declared adherence to Sunni Islam.

13 Robert D. Crews, *For Prophet and Tsar: Islam and Empire in Russia and Central Asia* (Cambridge: Harvard University Press, 2006), 2.

14 Roger Benjamin, *Orientalist Aesthetics: Art, Colonialism, and French North Africa* (Berkeley: University of California Press, 2003), 210.

15 Robert Crews, 'Empire and the Confessional State: Islam and Religious Politics in Nineteenth-Century Russia', *The American Historical Review* 108.1 (February 2003): 50–83, especially figures 6 and 7.

16 Milan Kasanin and M. V. Kotvich, 'Oriental Studies in Petrograd between 1918 and 1922', *Bulletin of the School of Oriental Studies* 3.4 (1925): 643–57.

17 Crews, *For Prophet and Tsar*, 2–8.

18 Tibawi, 'The History of the London Central Mosque', 194; and Mark Crinson, 'The Mosque and the Metropolis', in *Orientalism's Interlocutors: Painting, Architecture, Photography*, ed. Jill Beaulieu and Mary Roberts (Durham: Duke University Press, 2002), 81–85.

19 Moustafa Bayoumi, 'Shadows and Light: Colonial Modernity and the Grande Mosquée of Paris', *Yale Journal of Criticism* 13.2 (2000): 267–92.

20 Dimnet, 'The Paris Mosque', 251.

21 Crinson, 'The Mosque and the Metropolis', 82.

22 Marie-Laure Crosnier Leconte and Mercedes Volait, *L'Egypte d'un Architecte: Ambroise Baudry (1838–1906)* (Paris: Somogy Editions d'Art, 1998), 126–30.

23 'A London Mosque', *Journal of the Society of Architects* 4.47 (September 1904): 213.

24 Ibid.

25 Tibawi, 'The History of the London Central Mosque', 196.

26 For the discussion of the Nizam as a potential claimant to the kalifat see Margrit Pernau-Reifeld, 'Reaping the Whirlwind: Nizam and the Khalifat Movement', *Economic and Political Weekly*, 34.38 (1999): 2745–51.

27 Abdur Rahim Dard, 'Prince Feisal and the London Mosque', *Saturday Review of Politics, Literature, Science and Art* 142.3704 (1926): 468.

28 Tibawi, 'The History of the London Central Mosque', 197.

29 Ibid.; Crinson, 'The Mosque and the Metropolis', 86–90; James Steele, 'Mosque and Islamic Cultural Center Regent's Park, London', in Serageldin and Steele, *Architecture of the Contemporary Mosque*, 165–67.

30 Crinson, 'The Mosque and the Metropolis', 88.

31 Gökhan Ersan, 'Secularism, Islamism, Emblemata: The Visual Discourse of Progress in Turkey', *Design Issues: MIT* 23.2 (2007): 66–83.

32 Ersan, 'Secularism, Islamism, Emblemata', 72.

33 Ibid., 73. See also Jale Erzen and Aydan Balamir, 'Contemporary Mosque Architecture in Turkey', in Serageldin and Steele, *Architecture of the Contemporary Mosque*, 108–11.

34 Mina Marefat, 'From Bauhaus to Baghdad: The Politics of Building the Total University', *Taarii Newsletter* 3.2 (Fall 2008): 2–12.

35 Marefat, 'From Bauhaus to Baghdad', 8.

36 Kemal Kutgün Eyüpgiller, '20th century Mosque Architecture in Turkey', *EJOS* 9.6 (2006): 1–37.

37 For images, see http://arkiv.arkitera.com/p2050-londra-islam-kultur-merkezi-cami-yarisma-projesi.html#myslidemenu.

38 Erzen and Balamir, 'Contemporary Mosque Architecture in Turkey', 100–18.

39 Mohammad Al-Asad, 'The Mosque of the Turkish Grand National Assembly in Ankara: Breaking with Tradition', *Muqarnas* 16 (1999): 155–68.

40 In Turkish: 'Dinde bir devrimin geçirilmemesi, caminin kare tabanlı, merkezi ve yuvarlak kubbeli olarak sürmesinin nedenidir'. Behruz Çinici, 'Mimarizm: Mimarlık ve Tasarım Yayın Platformu', http://www.mimarizm.com/KentinTozu/Makale.aspx?id=404&sid=387.

41 Sherban Cantacuzino, 'Sherefudin's White Mosque', in Cantacuzino, *Architecture in Continuity*; James Steele, 'The New Mosque and Islamic Cultural Center in Rome', in Serageldin and Steele, *Architecture of the Contemporary Mosque*, 151–53; and Ashraf Salama, 'Tolerance and Peaceful Fusion of Cultures', *Faith and Form Magazine* 37.2 (2004).

42 For images and details of the project, see http://archnet.org/system/publications/contents/290/original/FLS0294.pdf?1384747394.

43 Peter Davey, 'Post Modern in Venice', *Architectural Review* (1980): 132–34.

44 Paolo Portoghesi, *Postmodern, the Architecture of the Post-Industrial* (New York: Rizzoli, 1983), 42.

45 Charles Jencks, *The Language of Postmodern Architecture*, 6th ed. (New York: Rizzoli, 1991), 13.

46 Cynthia C. Davidson, ed., *Legacies for the Future: Contemporary Architecture in Islamic Societies: The Aga Khan Award for Architecture*, (London: Thames and Hudson, 1998).

47 Fethi, 'The Mosque Today', 59–62.

48 For the complex entanglement of European and diasporic identity claims, see Avcıoğlu, 'Form-as-Identity'.

49 Ibid.

50 For architectural drawings, see http://www.breitman-breitman.com/amsterdam.htm# Brandevoort.

51 'Muslims Should Not Try to Hide', Interview between Paul Böhm and Thilo Guschas, trans. John Bergeron, *Qantara.de 2006,* http://wirednewyork.com/forum/showthread. php?t=18998.

52 Erkoçu and Buğdacı, *The Mosque,* especially 8–12.

53 'Strasbourg attend sa mosquée', *Le Journal des Arts,* 139 (2001).

54 http://www.vam.ac.uk/collections/architecture/architecture_features/alternating_currents/ contemporary/mosque/index.html. The link between Hadid's futuristic designs and Arabic calligraphy was made for the first time by Kenneth Frampton in 1983. The connection generated both excitement for the Iraqi-born architect and her work, though the comparison does not reflect authenticity, rather it suggests inherent Orientalism. See Kenneth Frampton, 'A Kufic Suprematist: The World Culture of Zaha Hadid', in *Planetary Architecture Two/Zaha Hadid,* ed. Zaha Hadid (London: Architectural Association, 1983), n.pag.

55 Portoghesi, *Postmodern, the Architecture of the Post-Industrial,* 11.

56 'Refiye Soyak Camii', ARKIV, http://arkiv.arkitera.com; and 'Yeşil Vadi'ye "Atilgan" gibi cami", http://www.arkiteracom.com.

57 Ivan Watson, 'Women take lead in building mosque in Turkey', CNN.com Europe, July 16, 2009, http://edition.cnn.com/2009/WORLD/europe/07/13/turkey.mosque.women/.

58 For details, see 'White Mosque', ArcNet, https://archnet.org/sites/176.

59 For details, see 'Vatan Memorial', ArcNet, https://archnet.org/sites/6300.

60 Maiken Umbach and Bernd Hüppauf, eds, *Vernacular Modernism: Heimat, Globalization, and the Built Environment* (Stanford: Stanford University Press, 2005).

61 Uğur Tanyeli, 'Profession of Faith: Mosque in Sancaklar, Turkey by Emre Arolat Architects', https://www.architectural-review.com/today/profession-of-faith-mosque-in-sancaklar- turkey-by-emre-arolat-architects/8666472.article.

62 Emre Arolat, 'Parallel readings in contemporary Mosque Architecture and Bait ur rouf' in *Architecture and Plurality,* ed. Mohsen Mostafawi (Zurich: Lars Muller Publishers, 2016), 116–21.

63 In Turkish: 'Ey zavallılar, bunlar mühürdür mühür!' http://www.arkitera.com/haber/17533/ nevzat-sayin-tasarimi-camiye-revizyon-mu-geliyor; Cüneyt Özdemir, 'Mimar Erdoğan'a cami beğendirmek!', accessed September 16, 2019, http://www.radikal.com.tr/yazarlar/ cuneyt-ozdemir/mimar-erdogana-cami-begendirmek-1178079/.

64 https://www.independentturkish.com/node/27441/haber/6-yıldır-tartışmaların-odağında- olan-proje-çamlıca-camii.

65 Tanyeli, 'Profession of Faith'.

66 Vincent Scully, 'The Earth, The Temple, And Today', in *Constructing the Ineffable: Contemporary Sacred Architecture,* (New Haven, Connecticut: Yale University Press, 2010), 27.

67 Scully, 'The Earth', 27.

68   For the English translation of 33:41, see *The Qur'an: English Translation with Parallel Arabic Text*, trans. M. Abdel-Haleem (Oxford: Oxford University Press, 2010), 269.

69   Scully, 'The Earth, The Temple, And Today', 27.

70   Arolat, 'Parallel readings in contemporary Mosque Architecture and Bait ur rouf'.

Author Biographies

Nebahat Avcıoğlu is the author of *Turquerie and the Politics of Representation, 1737–1876* (2011), winner of the prestigious Millard Meiss publication award. She co-edited *Globalising Cultures: Art and Mobility in the Eighteenth Century* with Finbarr Barry Flood (2011). Currently, she is finishing a book on *The Modern and Contemporary Mosque: A Cross-Cultural Analysis*. She also has authored a number of articles, among which are 'Istanbul: The Palimpsest City in Search of its Architext', *RES* (2008), 'Form-as-Identity: The Mosque in the West', *Cultural Analysis* (2008), 'The Mosque and the City in Europe,' in *Islam and Public Controversy in Europe* (2014), '*Jeux de miroir*: Architecture of Istanbul and Cairo from Empire to Modernism' (with Mercedes Volait), in *A Companion to Islamic Art and Architecture* (2017), and 'Immigrant Narratives: The Ottoman Sultan Portraits in Elisabeth Leitner's Family Photo Album of 1869–1873', *Muqarnas* (2018).

Susana Calvo Capilla is Associate Professor at the Department of History of Art, University Complutense of Madrid. Member of several research projects and currently Principal Investigator with Juan Carlos Ruiz Souza in a project entitled 'Al-Andalus, art, science and contexts in an open Mediterranean. From the West to Egypt and Syria' (RTI2018-093880-B-I00) (a continuation of the previous project HAR2013-45578-R), funded by the Spanish State Plan for Scientific and Technical Research and Innovation. Her publications focus on the visual culture of al-Andalus and Islamic religious architecture, specially on the analysis of the decorative and epigraphic programmes. She is author of *Mezquitas de al-Andalus* (2014); "Reuse of Classical Antiquity in the Palace of Madinat al-Zahra' and Its Role in the Construction of Caliphal Legitimacy" (*Muqarnas*, 2014); 'Los espacios de conocimiento en el Islam: Mezquitas, Casas de la Sabiduría y Madrasas' (2017); 'Peregrination and Ceremonial in the Almohad Mosque of Tinmal' (2020); and editor of *Las artes en Al-Andalus y Egipto. Contextos e intercambios* (2017).

Mehreen Chida-Razvi is an independent scholar and former research associate in the Department of History of Art & Archaeology at SOAS, University of London. She is a specialist on the art and architecture of Mughal South Asia and regularly teaches courses and lectures on Islamic and Indo-Islamic art at universities and museums in London and Oxford. Additionally, she works for The Khalili Collections as the in-house editor for their volumes on Islamic Art, and is an Assistant Editor for the *International Journal of Islamic Architecture*. In 2019 she guest-edited a special issue of *South Asian Studies*, titled 'Resituating Mughal Architecture in the Persianate World: New Investigations and Analyses', in which her article 'From Function to Form: *Chini-khana* in Safavid and Mughal Architecture' appeared. Her other publications include chapters in various edited volumes: 'Patronage as Power, Power in Appropriation: Constructing Jahangir's Mausoleum' (2019); 'A Sultan before the Padshah? Questioning the identification of the turbaned figure in *Jahangir Preferring a Sufi Shaykh to Kings*' (2016); and 'Where Is "The Greatest city in the East"?: The Mughal City of Lahore in European Travel Accounts between 1556 and 1648' (2015). She has shared her expertise with wider audiences through her participation and consultation for documentaries on the Taj Mahal, programming on BBC World Service Radio and BBC2, and as an expert lecturer on cultural tours.

Farshid Emami is Assistant Professor of art and architecture of the Islamic world at Rice University. He received his PhD in history of art and architecture from Harvard University in 2017. His primary field of specialization is architecture, urbanism and art in the early modern period with a focus on Safavid Iran. His recent publications include: 'Coffeehouses, Urban Spaces, and the Formation of a Public Sphere in Safavid Isfahan' (*Muqarnas*, 2016) and 'Royal Assemblies and Imperial Libraries: Polygonal Pavilions and their Functions in Mughal and Safavid Architecture', (*South Asian Studies*, 2019). He is currently completing a book manuscript that offers a new interpretation of architecture and urbanism in seventeenth-century Isfahan through the analytical lens of urban experience.

May Farhat received her PhD in Islamic art and architecture from Harvard University in 2002. She taught Islamic art history for many years at the American University of Beirut, and presently teaches architectural history at the University of the Holy Spirit in Kaslik (USEK), Lebanon. She is the author of many articles, such as, 'In Praise of Hybridity: The al-Umari Mosque of Beirut,' for *Articles of Faith: Visual Cultures in the Byzantine and Islamic Worlds. Essays in Honor of Erica Cruikshank Dodd*, eds. Eva Boubala, Lesley Jessop, and Marcus Milwright (Brill, forthcoming); 'Shi'i Piety and Dynastic Legitimacy: Mashhad under the Early Safavids,' *Iranian Studies* 47, 2 (2014); and 'A Mediterraneanist's Collection: Henri Pharaon's "Treasure House of Arab Art,"' *Ars Orientalis* 42 (2012).

Fadi Ragheb is an Assistant Professor, Teaching Stream, at the Department of Near and Middle Eastern Civilizations at the University of Toronto, Canada. He is a Joseph-Armand Bombardier Canada Scholar, an Avie Bennett Scholar, and a recipient of federal and provincial scholarships in Canada. He completed his undergraduate studies at McGill University and his graduate studies at the University of Toronto. His fields of specialization include medieval Islamic history, medieval pilgrimage, the history of the central Islamic lands during the Age of the Crusades, and Qur'anic studies. He teaches courses on Arabic and Islamic history, and is currently writing a longer study on Islamic pilgrimage to Jerusalem during the Mamluk and Ottoman period.

Abbey Stockstill received her BA in near Eastern languages and civilizations from the University of Pennsylvania, and her PhD in history of art and architecture from Harvard University. Her most recent work focuses on the intersection of architecture, landscape, urbanism and identity in the medieval Mediterranean, particularly in the region of the Islamic West known as the Maghrib (comprising present-day Morocco, Algeria and Tunisia). This research has been supported by a number of international institutions including the Oxford Research Centre for the Humanities (TORCH), Dumbarton Oaks Research Library and Collections, and the École Nationale d'Architecture du Maroc. She is currently working on a book manuscript that examines the development of Marrakesh in the twelfth century as a dynastic capital that speaks to both its regional precedents and its local heritage.

A. Hilâl Uğurlu is an Associate Professor of architectural history at MEF University, Istanbul. She completed her PhD dissertation entitled *Selim III's Istanbul: Building Activities in the Light of Political and Military Transformations* in 2012, in which she endeavoured to describe the relationship between the physical and socio-political structure of the Ottoman capital at that time. Thanks to her project on nineteenth-century imperial mosques of Ottoman Istanbul and their changing spatial relations with the city, she was granted fellowships from ANAMED, SALT Research and Istanbul Research Institute. She also received a Barakat Trust Post-Doctoral Fellowship at the Khalili Research Centre, Oxford University (2017–18), and Barakat Trust Major Awards (2018–19) with her project: 'A Reformist Sultan in the Age of Revolutions: Politics, Art and Architectural Patronage of Selim III (r. 1789–1807).' She is currently working on a project that analyzes the interventions of nineteenth-century Ottoman sultans in sacred places and objects in the context of their political agendas.

Suzan Yalman received her PhD in 2011 from the Department of History of Art and Architecture at Harvard University and is currently an Assistant Professor in the Department of Archaeology and History of Art at Koç University, Istanbul. Her research interests include memory, perceptions of the past and antiquarianism in medieval Islamic art; mirrors-for-princes; patronage in medieval Islamic architecture; medieval Islamic cities and urban networks; pilgrimage and shared sacred spaces; intersections between mysticism and visual culture. Recently, she has co-edited two volumes for Koç University's Research Center for Anatolian Civilizations (ANAMED); *Spolia Reincarnated: Afterlives of Objects, Materials, and Spaces in Anatolia from Antiquity to the Ottoman Era* with Dr. Ivana Jevtić (2018) and *Sacred Spaces and Urban Networks* with Dr. A. Hilâl Uğurlu (2019).

Index

Almoravid(s), 32, 199, 200–2, 204, 206, 213
alms, 27–28, 83
American, 238, 262, 265–66
Amphilochius, Saint, 127, 141, 143, 146
Amritsar, 60
Amsterdam
  Fatih Mosque, 291
  Westermoskee, 295
Anatolia (Asia Minor), 7, 93, 131, 143–44,
  146–47, 168
al-Andalus, 23–24, 26, 30, 34, 35, 41, 204, 208
Ando, Tadao, 305
André Thévet, 4
Ani, 131, 133
Ankara, 286, 288, 289, 301
  Etimesgut Armed Forces Mosque, 288
  Grand National Assembly Mosque, 288
  Kocatepe Mosque, 286, 301, 305
Arab, 23, 32, 39, 137, 200, 209, 236, 238, 301
Arabic, 3, 82, 137, 142, 164, 166, 171, 173,
  176, 297
arcades, 4, 185, 224, 227, 291, 301
arch(es), 30, 208, 285
Archangel Gabriel, 87, 100
archeology, 23, 38, 128, 131, 203, 209, 211,
  266, 284
Ardabil
  Jannatsara, 170
  tomb of Shaykh Safi al-Din, 170, 259
Armenian, 131, 142, 164, 228
Arolat, Emre, 303
Artuqid, 146
Asad, Talal, 12
Ashab al-Kahf, 144
ashlar(s), 35–36, 38, 41
Asia, 304
  Central Asia, 179, 184, 253, 255–56
  South Asia, 53, 55, 68
  West Asia, 176
Asutay-Effenberger, Neslihan, 128, 141
'Ataridi, Aziz Allah, 267
Atlas Mountains, 9, 200, 205, 210, 212–3
Augustine, Saint, 147

Aurangzeb 'Alamgir (emperor), 53–54, 56,
  58–63, 67, 69
Ayatollah Vaez-Tabasi, 269
Ayaz (atabeg), 136, 138, 140, 145–6
Ayvansarayî Hafız Hüseyin Efendi, 224
Ayyubid, 80, 89–93, 144, 147
Azerbaijan, 175
al-Azraqi (author), 96, 98–100

B

bab, 27–28, 87, 94–95, 180, 137, 212, 238, 240
Babayan, Kathryn, 184
Baghdad, 3, 4, 200, 280, 288
  Baghdad Mosque, 280
Baha al-Din Valad, 141
Bahadur Shah (emperor), 60
Bahrami, Mahdi, 266
balcony, 40, 163, 168, 226
baradari, 62–64
Baron Charles Hugel, 61
Baroness Ravensdale, 264
barrack(s), 9, 61, 223, 228, 231–32, 238, 243
Basset, Henri, 204
bast (sanctuary), 171, 182, 254, 257, 258, 259,
  260, 262, 263, 269
bathhouse(s), 35, 90, 229, 262, 285
bay'a, 24, 100, 206, 209
Al-Baydhaq, 201, 206
bazaar(s), 159, 186, 226, 227, 253–58, 260,
  264, 267–68
Belgian, 256
Bennison, Amira, 199, 212, 213
Berber, 199, 200, 206, 209, 212
biblical, 77, 79, 81–82, 143, 147
Bierman, Irene, 138
Bihishti (poet), 176
Birmingham, Green Lane Masjid, 291
Black Sea, 146
Bloom, Jonathan, 206
Böhm, Paul, 296
Bonine, Michael, 204
Borbor, Dariush, 267–68
Bosnia, 12–13, 289, 301–2

I

i'tikaf, 164, 167
Iberian Peninsula, 200
Ibn 'Abi 'Amir al-Mansur (vizier), 24,
    28–30, 35
Ibn 'Arabi, 77
Ibn 'Idhari, 26, 35
Ibn al-Abbar, 34
Ibn al-Firkah, 80
Ibn al-Jawzi, 80
Ibn al-Maghazili, 175
Ibn al-Murajja, 79
Ibn Bashkuwal, 28
Ibn Battuta, 77, 98–100
Ibn Bibi, 139–40, 143, 145
Ibn Habib, 33
Ibn Hafsun, 30
Ibn Jubayr, 98
Ibn Khaldun, 201
Ibn Manzur, 211
Ibn Masarra, 29, 30
Ibn Rida, 34
Ibn Rushd, 34
Ibn Sa'ud (king), 286
Ibn Taymiyyah, 101
Ibn Tumart (mahdi), 199–200, 205–6, 208–9,
    212–14
iconography, 180, 280, 307
Idrisid, 204, 212
Igliz, 206
ihram, 7, 9, 83–84, 96–98
Ilkhanid, 179
Imam, twelfth, 4, 8, 162, 164, 175
imaret, 224
Imatra, Imatra Church, 280
imperialism, 11, 281–82, 286, 289, 296, 307
India(n), 77, 283, 285–86
inscription(s), 9, 23–24, 26–30, 32, 41, 91,
    128, 131, 133, 135–42, 145–46, 162,
    164, 166–67, 171, 173, 175–76, 178,
    180, 183, 186
Iran, 11, 137, 168, 173, 179, 184, 253, 255–56,
    259–61, 265–67

Constitutional Revolution, 260
    Islamic Revolution, 269
Iranian, 253, 256, 260–63, 267
Iraq, 35, 175
Isfahan, 4, 8, 9, 137–38, 159, 162, 164, 167–76,
    179, 180, 184–87, 259
    Ali Qapu, 163–64, 168, 170–72, 174, 179,
        182, 187, 259
    Harun Vilayat shrine, 168, 180
    Maydan-i Naqsh-i Jahan, 159, 162–64, 173,
        179–80, 182–84, 186–87
    Old Maydan, 159, 167–68, 173, 180, 182,
        186
    Old Mosque, 159, 167, 173, 176, 182,
        184–86
    palace complex, 163
    Qaysariyya, 163–64, 173–74
    Shah Mosque, 159, 162–64, 173–76,
        178–80, 182, 184, 186–87
    Shaykh Lutfallah Mosque, 8, 162–64,
        167–68, 170–73, 176, 179, 187
    Tawhidkhana, 170–1, 182
    Zayanda River, 159
Iskandar Beg Munshi, 173–74
Islamabad, Faisal Mosque (1986), 53
Islamophobia, 281
isra', 77, 79, 82, 87
isra'iliyyat, 79, 82, 84
Istanbul, 4, 6, 9–10, 145, 148, 224, 226–27,
    229, 233, 236, 238, 243, 282, 286,
    295–96, 299, 301, 303, 304. *See also*
    Constantinople
Bosphorus, 229, 232
contemporary mosques of, 288, 301, 303, 306
districts of, 223, 227–28, 232–33, 236, 238,
    240, 301
early modern mosques of, 5, 224, 226–28,
    229, 233, 236, 240, 295
military complexes of, 9, 223, 228, 231–32,
    238, 240
nineteenth-century mosques of, 9–10, 223,
    228–31 233, 237–38, 240
palace complexes of, 232, 233, 236, 237, 238